ALGOL 68

ALGOL 68

a first and second course

ANDREW D. McGETTRICK

Department of Computer Science
University of Strathclyde
Glasgow, Scotland

CAMBRIDGE UNIVERSITY PRESS

CAMBRIDGE

LONDON · NEW YORK · MELBOURNE

Published by the Syndics of the Cambridge University Press
The Pitt Building, Trumpington Street, Cambridge CB2 1RP
Bentley House, 200 Euston Road, London NW1 2DB
32 East 57th Street, New York, NY 10022, USA
296 Beaconsfield Parade, Middle Park, Melbourne 3206, Australia

First published 1978

Printed in Great Britain at the University Press, Cambridge

Library of Congress cataloguing in publication data
McGettrick, Andrew D.   1944-
ALGOL 68: a first and second course
(Cambridge computer science texts; 8)
Includes index
1. ALGOL (Computer program language) I. Title
II. Series
QA76.73.A24M3   001.6'424   77-1104
ISBN 0 521 21412 2 hard covers
ISBN 0 521 29143 7 paperback

CONTENTS

10295

To my wife, Sheila

PREFACE

This book originated from lectures first given at the University of Strathclyde in 1973–4 to first year undergraduates, many of whom had no previous knowledge of programming. Many of the students were not taking computer science as their main subject but merely as a subsidiary subject. They therefore served as a suitable audience on whom to inflict lectures attempting to teach ALGOL 68 as a first programming language.

The book itself is concerned with the revised version of ALGOL 68 (see Acta Informatica, vol. 5, Fasc 1–3, 1975, pp. 1–236). It consists of nine chapters. I believe that, for a first course on programming, the material contained in chapters 1–5 is suitable; this forms an ALGOL-60-type-subset. The more advanced features of ALGOL 68 are contained in the later chapters and these provide suitable material for a second course. The individual chapters (chapters 6–9) are for the most part self-contained. Appendix A summarises in a convenient way the ALGOL 68 standard environment. Appendix B summarises the syntax of ALGOL 68 by means of a syntax chart due originally to J. M. Watt, J. E. L. Peck and M. Sintzoff.

Throughout the book there are exercises and problems to accompany the chapters. The exercises are intended to test whether the student has a sufficient understanding of the theory in the preceding chapter; sample solutions to these can be found at the end of the book. The problems on the other hand are intended to be programmed and for these no solutions are provided. It is hoped that via both the exercises and problems the student can develop an interest in other branches of computer science. It would also be invaluable if students can be trained not just to answer each question but for every question to ask themselves two other similar questions and answer these.

I should like to take this opportunity of thanking various people for helping me in the preparation of this book. My debt to the authors of the Revised ALGOL 68 Report is obvious. I must also thank J. M. Watt, J. E. L. Peck and M. Sintzoff for their permission to use their syntax chart.

During the writing of the book I had many valuable discussions on ALGOL 68 especially with Dr. R. B. Hunter but also with Dr. R. Kingslake and other colleagues at Strathclyde. My thanks are due to several people who commented on different parts of the earlier draft of the manuscript. Mr. Ian Walker of the Computer Laboratory, Cambridge University, read the entire manuscript and his comments and our subsequent discussions were most valuable. Other people deserving thanks include Dr. C. Hawksley of the Computer Science Department, Keele University, and Dr. R. Needham of the Computer Laboratory, Cambridge. The typing of the manuscript, and other forms of secretarial work, were performed most willingly and ably by my mother Mrs. M. McGettrick and also by Mrs. M. MacDougall, Miss M. Barron and Miss A. Wisley. On a more personal level I must thank my wife Sheila for her constant support and encouragement throughout the entire period of writing the book.

Finally I am greatly indebted to the Syndics of Cambridge University Press for publishing this book.

Glasgow, April 1976.   A. D. McG.

1

INTRODUCTION TO ALGOL 68

1.1. Preliminaries

The preface to volume one of D. E. Knuth's seven-volume set of books on 'The Art of Computer Programming' begins:

'The process of preparing programs for a digital computer is especially attractive because it not only can be economically and scientifically rewarding, it can also be an aesthetic experience much like composing poetry or music. This book is the first of a seven-volume set of books that has been designed to train the reader in the various skills which go into a programmer's craft.'

From this quotation it follows that in an introductory text such as this it will not be possible to cover all aspects of programming.

The word *program* – and *programming* is just the art of writing programs – is rather difficult to define. Roughly speaking, a program is a set of instructions which have usually to be performed or executed by a computer. The instructions which computers actually execute are very simple. They will vary from one make of computer to another but usually include such primitive operations as adding and sub-tracting two numbers, moving information from one part of the machine to another or reading and printing information. These primitives are called *machine-code instructions*: a large computer may possess as many as 100 or 200 and sometimes more. The set of such instructions for a particular computer together with the method of expressing them forms what is called a *programming language*. Since these instructions are very primitive, such a language is called a *low-level* programming language. It is possible to write programs to solve complicated problems using only machine-code instructions but this can prove a very frustrating introduction to the computer.

Fortunately another class of programming languages has been developed. These so-called *high-level languages* allow the use of a mathematical sort of notation. In a high-level language it might be possible to write

$$a + b \times (c + d)$$

1

and the computer will evaluate this assuming that a, b, c and d had at an earlier part of the program been given some values. If, for instance, a had not been given a value the program would be at fault. The sort of instructions one can write in high-level languages are still restricted and it is necessary to learn the different kinds of instructions that are available and the effect these have. The process of carrying out the various instructions in a program will be referred to as the *elaboration* or *execution* of the program.

High-level languages (like natural languages such as English) possess a *syntax* and when writing programs it is necessary to adhere to this syntax. Thus if in writing the above expression a bracket had been omitted then a syntax error would (probably) have been flagged. Syntax errors tend to be caused by such mistakes as omitting brackets, including too many brackets, omitting semi-colons, full-stops, quotation marks and operators. When presenting the computer with a program, therefore, it is preferable that the program should contain no syntax errors, wrong spellings, etc.

The computer will do only as it is asked. It will not deduce the intentions of the careless programmer. If an instruction requests that two numbers be added and the programmer intended that they should have been subtracted, the computer will add them. To counteract this it is advisable to prove if possible that the program does what was intended and to carry out a reasonable number of checks to give confidence in the results.

Earlier it was remarked that the computer executes machine-code instructions. How does it deal with instructions presented in a high-level language? It cannot execute these directly and therefore some form of translation must take place. For each high-level language that a particular computer can handle there is available a (usually fairly large) program called a *compiler* which will take a program written in that language and translate it into machine-code instructions which are then executed by the computer. If the program in the high-level language contains syntax errors (or some other kinds of errors) the compiler should inform the writer of the program of his errors.

The most widely used high-level languages include FORTRAN, COBOL, ALGOL 60, PL/1 and ALGOL 68.

FORTRAN was originally designed *c.* 1955–6 to simplify the writing of programs for numerical calculations. It is one of the most commonly used high-level languages. However, it lacks many modern facilities and is quite unsuitable as a tool for present-day programming.

ALGOL 60, as the name suggests, was designed in 1960 and some

2

amendments were later added *c*. 1962. Like FORTRAN, ALGOL 60 was designed for numerical calculation. It had a great impact on Computer Science in general.

COBOL is a language whose use is confined almost entirely to the business world. It is used for writing programs to perform tasks such as producing payrolls, factory stock control, etc.

PL/1 and ALGOL 68 are more modern languages and have much wider application than the earlier languages. PL/1 was developed by IBM *c*. 1965 and the original specification of ALGOL 68 appeared in 1968. The revised version of ALGOL 68 appeared in 1974.

The aim of this book is to introduce programming and ALGOL 68. The two topics will be considerably interwoven since the more ALGOL 68 one knows the more sophisticated the programs one can write. ALGOL 68 will therefore have a dual role. It will be used as a high-level language in which to write programs and it will itself be an object of study.

1.2. Remarks on symbolism

In mathematics frequent use is made of symbols to denote constants or variables of different kinds.

(i) The expressions $2\pi r$ and πr^2 give, respectively, the circumference and area of a circle whose radius is r. In these expressions 2 and π represent constants and r is a variable whose value can be any non-negative real number.

(ii) In the expressions $ax + by + c$ and $ax^2 + bx + c$ one might regard a, b and c as real constants and x and y as variables whose values range over the set of real numbers.

(iii) Each of *sin*, *cos* and *tan* is a function which is constant in the same sort of way as, for instance, π is constant. On the other hand a sentence starting "Let f be a function . . . " will often indicate that f is a variable whose value can be any function with the stated property. This may be a unique function but there may be more than one function with that property.

Other examples should come readily to mind.

A similar symbolism is used in ALGOL 68. Constants such as *pi*, 14 and *sin* will be used and variables can be introduced. But there are some important differences and it is necessary to be very clear about the values associated with ALGOL 68 constants and variables. Some of these differences arise from the way in which variables are represented in the computer. In order to understand this an extremely simple-minded explanation follows.

The main store of a computer consists of many *locations* (usually called *words* or *bytes*). The exact number varies from computer to computer but the number is usually expressed in units of K where $1K = 1024 = 2^{10}$. The storage capacity of a modern computer lies between about $4K$ and $1024K$ bytes. These locations are capable of holding different kinds of information e.g. integers, real numbers, characters, etc. and this information can be altered. The locations themselves are accessed by means of *addresses*. The address of a particular location is often thought of as a unique integer in the range 0 to (n-1) where there are n locations in the machine.

When the compiler is translating an ALGOL 68 program into machine-code it will represent a variable by means of an address. Altering the value of a variable amounts to altering the contents of the location with that address. It is extremely important to distinguish between the address of a location and the contents of that location.

1.3. Introduction to ALGOL 68

Some simple examples of ALGOL 68 programs now follow. The examples are trivial but they serve to illustrate certain points. They should not be taken as models of perfect programs. Example 1.3b, for instance, attempts to find the circumference of a circle. It will certainly accomplish this but some instructions should be included to ensure that the radius is not a negative number. Such improvements, together with others of a different nature, could be made but their introduction would cause extra complications which are better avoided for the moment.

Example 1.3a. Write a program to calculate the circumference of a circle whose radius is $e = 2.7182818284$.

> **begin real** $e = 2.7182818284$; **real** *circum*;
> $circum := 2 \times pi \times e$;
> *print* (("*circumference of a circle of radius e is*", *circum*))
> **end**

Clearly this program is extremely limited since it will calculate the circumference of only one particular circle. A more useful program would calculate the circumference of an arbitrary circle (see example 1.3b). A certain generality is desirable in a program.

In order to understand the effect of the various steps in the program above consider successive parts separately.

(i) The (initial) **begin** denotes the start of the program.

(ii) **real** $e = 2.7182818284$ allows e to denote the constant value 2.7182818284. **real** indicates that e represents a real number. The

4

equals sign is crucial in this section of the program.

(iii) The next action to be executed is that following the semi-colon. For this reason the semi-colon is often referred to as the *go-on symbol*. No mention will be made of the remaining semi-colons in this program. Each semi-colon indicates that the next action to be executed follows that particular semi-colon.

(iv) **real** *circum* causes space to be reserved for a variable and this variable is to be identified as *circum*. The variable takes values which are real numbers.

(v) *circum* := $2 \times pi \times e$ The expression on the right hand side of the *becomes symbol*, i.e. := , is evaluated. The symbol × denotes multiplication and must be stated explicitly; thus *2pie* would be illegal. Note that *e* has already been defined and its value thereby known. *pi*, however, is automatically known to the ALGOL 68 compiler. There is no need to define its value.

The effect of the statement is that the value obtained from the evaluation of $2 \times pi \times e$ is given or assigned to the variable *circum*.

(vi) *print* (("*circumference of a circle of radius e is*", *circum*)) The characters between " and " are printed. These are followed by the current value of the variable *circum*. Thus two objects are printed, a string of characters and the current value of a real variable. In the print statement above these two objects are separated by a comma and surrounded by brackets. If a single object, say *circum*, had to be printed then *print* (*circum*) would have been adequate. The output produced by this print statement might look like

$$\textit{circumference of a circle of radius e is } + 1.7079 \ldots _{10} + 1$$

where the dots denote the remaining figures after the decimal point and $_{10} + 1$ indicates that $1.7079 \ldots$ is to be multiplied by 10^1 thus producing $17.079 \ldots$ ($_{10} + 4$ would similarly indicate multiplication by 10^4).

(vii) **end** denotes the end of the program and matches the initial **begin**. Note that there is no go-on symbol between the print statement and the **end**.

Example 1.3b. Write a program to calculate the circumference and area of a circle of arbitrary radius. (The radius is assumed to be non-negative but again no check is included.)

```
begin real r, circum, area;
      read (r);
      circum := 2 × pi × r; area := pi × r × r;
      print (("circumference and area of a circle of radius ", r,
      " are", newline, circum," and", area))
end
```

This program strongly resembles the earlier program. If it is supplied with the number 3.5 it will calculate the circumference and area of a circle of radius 3.5 and print the appropriate result. In fact, given any number it will calculate the circumference and area of a circle of that radius and print appropriate results.

In general the information supplied to a program in this way is called the *data* for that program. (Strictly speaking a single item of information should be called a datum.)

Five sections of this program require some explanation.

(i) **real** *r, circum, area* causes space to be reserved for three variables which are to be identified as *r, circum* and *area*. As in the previous example these variables can only take values which are real numbers.

(ii) *read* (*r*) causes a real number (since *r* is a real variable) to be read from the data.

(iii) *circum* := $2 \times pi \times r$ as before causes the expression on the right hand side of the becomes symbol to be evaluated. Unlike the previous case, however, *r* is now a variable. It is the current value of this variable which is used in the evaluation. The result of the evaluation of the right hand side is assigned to the variable *circum*.

(iv) *area* := $pi \times r \times r$ As in (iii) above the expression is evaluated and assigned to *area*.

(v) *print* (("*circumference and area of a circle of radius*", *r*, " *are*", *newline, circum*," *and*", *area*)):

In this print statement seven items are separated by commas and surrounded by brackets. The output might appear as

> *circumference and area of a circle of radius* $+ 2.718 \ldots$ *are*
> $+ 1.7079 \ldots_{10} + 1$ *and* $+ 2.3208 \ldots_{10} + 1$

The appearance of *newline* in the print statement causes the printer to take a new line.

Example 1.3c. Write a program to evaluate $n(n + 1)(2n + 1)$ for an arbitrary integer *n*.

```
begin int n, result;
      read (n);
      result := n × (n + 1) × (2 × n + 1);
      print (("value of n(n + 1) (2n + 1) when n is", n," is",
            result))
end
```

The only section of this program that should require clarification is

> **int** *n, result*

This introduces two variables whose values can be only integers.

These first examples of programs illustrate certain features of programming and of ALGOL 68. From the programming point of view the programs are extremely simple. Yet there is a certain structure that runs through each program. This structure can be represented as:
1. set up (what shall be for the moment called) mnemonics for constants and introduce variables, if any;
2. read information;
3. perform calculations;
4. print results.

Note that in example 1.3a no information had to be read and hence stage (1) is absent.

In order to check that a program is faultless, it is necessary to check that there are no mis-spellings, typing errors, etc. and that each of the four stages in the structure does as was intended. Many simple programs can be written using a similar structure. The remarks about checking correctness of programs still apply.

One can think of these programs as sequences of instructions in ALGOL 68. Using these, objects can be manipulated within the computer. In examples 1.3a, b real numbers were manipulated, the manipulation taking the form of reading information, multiplication, etc. In example 1.3c integers were manipulated.

From an ALGOL 68 point of view many ideas have been introduced and many questions should naturally arise. For instance,
(a) what sort of mnemonics can be used to identify constants and variables?
(b) what operators, mathematical or otherwise, are available?
(c) apart from variables taking only real values or only integer values, what other kinds of variables are there?
(d) what precisely does **real** *circum*, *r* mean?

1.4. Preparing programs for the computer

When a program has to be run on a computer it will have to be prepared in some suitable manner. The program and any accompanying data will usually have to be typed on a device such as a card-punch. One line of program is typed on each card. Unfortunately, however, these and similar devices do not permit the printing in bold type of words such as **begin**. Indeed, often small letters are also unavailable.

To overcome these difficulties certain conventions have to be used. These vary from one computer to another. It is therefore necessary for the programmer to learn about the local conventions and adhere to them. Typically **begin** might appear in one of the forms

.BEGIN.   'BEGIN'   'BEGIN   BEGIN

A modern computer system will usually demand that the programmer surrounds his program with a certain amount of 'red tape'. It might insist for example that the programmer indicates in some suitable fashion

  (i) that he is authorised to use the computer; he might have to quote a number he has been allocated and/or a password

 (ii) the start and end of the job to be submitted to the computer

(iii) which programming language he is using

(iv) the start and end of his program and the start and end of his data, if any.

Some of these conventions are imposed so that errors do not have catastrophic effects.

For simple programs these are usually adequate. In more complicated cases the programmer might be asked to state other requirements such as the length of time he expects his program to take, the amount of paper required for his results, etc. Again there will be local conventions for stating such requirements.

To demonstrate the kind of rewriting that has to take place the program of example 1.3b may be altered as follows:

```
JOB ADMCGETTRICK, :CADU10
ALGOL 68
*PROGRAM
'BEGIN' 'REAL' R,CIRCUM,AREA;
        READ(R);
        CIRCUM := 2*PI*R; AREA := PI* R*R;
        PRINT(("CIRCUMFERENCE AND AREA OF
            A CIRCLE OF RADIUS", R, " ARE",
            NEWLINE, CIRCUM," AND",
            AREA))
'END'
*FINISH
*DATA
 2.718
*END
ENDJOB
****
```

There are fifteen lines in total. *PROGRAM and *FINISH delimit the ALGOL 68 program. *DATA and *END delimit the data for the program. CADU10 is the identification to be quoted to gain access to the computer. The line containing ALGOL 68 invokes the relevant compiler.

Note finally the conventions used. **begin** appears as 'BEGIN' and capitals are used in place of small letters. Moreover the multiplication sign has been replaced by an asterisk.

2

BASIC CONCEPTS

In this chapter some of the basic ideas of ALGOL 68 will be examined. These will be introduced by considering in detail the kind of objects that can be manipulated within ALGOL 68 programs, how these objects can be represented by the programmer and what form their manipulation can take.

2.1. Modes

It is convenient to group the set of objects that can be manipulated in ALGOL 68 into certain mutually exclusive subsets. The word for such a subset is *mode*. These subsets include integers, real numbers and single characters. Objects of these subsets are said to have mode **int**, **real** and **char** respectively. Using the terminology of chapter 1 the objects of mode **int** are just the integer constants, the objects of mode **real** are the real constants, and so on.

In more general terms one always associates with an object a mode indicating the set to which that object belongs. And, of course, one always associates a value with an object. Thus in example 1.3a the mode **real** is associated with e and the value is 2.7182818284.

2.2. Denotations

Constants are written explicitly in programs by means of denotations. Integers are represented by integer denotations, reals by real denotations, etc.

2.2.1. Integer denotations

Integer denotations take the form of a sequence of decimal digits, i.e. 0, 1, ... , 9. Note that no commas or decimal points can appear.

Example 2.2.1a. Integer denotations.
  (i) Each of

| 000 | 43 | 456 | 0 |

is an acceptable integer denotation.

(ii) The following are not integer denotations:

    1,234 since a comma is not allowed;

    $+1$ since a plus sign is not part of an integer denotation;

    1 234 since spaces are not allowed.

To be precise, one cannot expect any sequence of decimal digits to be acceptable to a computer. Computers do possess physical limitations and only integers of a certain magnitude will be acceptable. The allowable range will depend on the particular computer being used. For example, the ICL 1900 computers will hold integers of magnitude less than approximately 2^{23} – note that $2^{23} = 8388608$.

2.2.2. Real denotations

Real denotations take one of two forms:

(1) a string of decimal digits with a single decimal point appearing at the beginning of the string or between any two digits;

(2) the form xey where x is either of the form (1) above or is an integer denotation, y is an integer denotation possibly preceded by a sign (i.e. $+$ or $-$), and e denotes the 'times-ten-to-the-power' symbol. Thus xey represents $x10^y$. Some computers will allow e to be replaced by $_{10}$ or $\backslash$. However the e form will be used here.

Example 2.2.2a. Real denotations.

(i) Real denotations of the form (1) above include:

    .5   0.5   2.0   .001

(ii) Real denotations of the form (2) include:

    $2.3e1$ $2e0$ $2e+0$ $2e-0$

(iii) Each of the following is not a legal real denotation:

    5.   since the decimal point may not appear last;

    $2e3.0$ since e must be followed by an integer denotation, possibly preceded by a sign;

    5   since this is an integer denotation;

    $e6$ since e must be preceded by either an integer denotation or a numeral of the form (1);

  $-5e-3$ since the initial minus is not part of a denotation.

As with integers only a certain subset of the set of real numbers can be manipulated. For the ICL 1900 range of computers real numbers are usually restricted to those whose magnitude is in the range 5×10^{-76} to 5×10^{76} together with zero.

In programming, real numbers should be used with considerable care. Computers hold real numbers to only a limited accuracy (in the ICL 1900 series this is about 10 decimal digits). Consequently only approximate answers can be expected.

2.2.3. Character denotations

Character denotations, like other denotations, provide a means of writing single character constants in programs. As yet no example of their use has been given. But typically one might wish to count the number of X's appearing in a piece of text and consequently somewhere in the program a character denotation for the letter X should appear.

With one exception character denotations take the form of the required character enclosed within quotes.

Example 2.2.3a. Character denotations.
The following are all acceptable character denotations:

$$"X" \qquad "a" \qquad "1" \qquad "." \qquad " "$$

The last of these is a character denotation for a space. Each of these has mode **char** and the value associated with them is just the character itself.

The exception to the above rule is the character denotation for the quotes symbol itself. This is written as $""""$, i.e. four consecutive quotes.

At each particular computer installation the set of characters that can be used will be limited.

2.2.4. Boolean denotations

Boolean denotations take one of two possible forms: **true** and **false**. These are logical constants and have a mode **bool** associated with them. Their use will become apparent at a later stage.

2.3. Identity and variable declarations

In example 1.3a a section of the program read

> **real** $e = 2.7182818284$

This is an example of a declaration and serves to introduce e. e becomes associated with a specific value (namely 2.7182818284) and a specific mode (namely **real**). In general identity declarations such as the above serve to introduce identifiers – in the above example e is an identifier – and to associate with this identifier a specific value of a specific mode. More precisely a value is said to be *ascribed* to an identifier.

12

Identifiers take the form of a letter followed by an arbitrary string, possibly null, of letters and/or digits.

Example 2.3a. Identifiers.
(i) Each of the following is a legal identifier:

circum   *r*   *ibm*   *a1*   *log2*   *begin*

(ii) The following are illegal as identifiers:
2a   since this begins with a digit;
a − 1 since the minus sign is not allowed;
a.2   since the point is forbidden;
a[2]   since square brackets are forbidden.

Example 2.3b. Identity declarations.
(i) **real** *e* = 2.7182818284, *log2* = 0.618
introduces two identifiers, namely *e* and *log2*. The value 2.7182818284 of mode **real** is ascribed to *e* and 0.618 also of mode **real** is ascribed to *log2*.
(ii) **real** *e* = 2.7182818284, *log2* = 0.618, **int** *ten* = 10, *g* = 32
introduces four identifiers. Real values are ascribed to both *e* and *log2* and integer values are ascribed to *ten* and *g*.

Consider now the following piece of program taken from example 1.3a:

real *circum*

It was pointed out that this introduces a variable to hold the result of some calculation. As such this is called a *variable declaration*. A real variable such as *circum* has mode **ref real** (**ref** being an abbreviation for reference). Integer variables, character variables, etc. have mode **ref int**, **ref char**, etc. respectively. There is an identity declaration which is equivalent to, i.e. has the same effect as, this variable declaration. It is instructive to consider this since it highlights the precise effect of a variable declaration.

If one wishes to make use of a variable then effectively one wants to make available space to hold the current value of the variable and introduce an identifier by which this space, and hence the value of the variable, can be accessed.

In ALGOL 68 space must be obtained (or made available) by invoking a *generator*. Two types of generators exist, local generators and global generators. For the present only local generators will be discussed.

Local generators can be called into action by **loc**. The effect of

loc real for example is to create space (by reserving a location) for an object of mode **real** and to return as result the address or name of the location within the computer. (Here *name* is used in a technical sense: there is a subtle distinction between a name and the identifier used to access that name.) The result is an object of mode **ref real** since this is the name or address by which the contents of the location can be accessed.

Consider now the identity declaration

   ref real *circum* = **loc real**

Using only earlier knowledge of identity declarations this introduces an identifier *circum* and ascribes to it an object of mode **ref real**. The object is just the result of elaborating the right hand side of the declaration. In this case it is the address or name of the location made available by the action of the local generator **loc real**. The effect of this identity declaration is therefore to introduce a variable *circum* which takes only real values. Fortunately (to save writing, typing, etc.) it follows that the identity declaration

   ref real *circum* = **loc real**

has the same effect as the variable declaration

   real *circum*

However, the identity declaration does describe more fully the precise effect of the variable declaration. In particular it shows that the mode associated with *circum* by either of the declarations is **ref real** and not **real**. The other point to note is that variable declarations cause space to be made available.

The declaration

   real *r*, *circum*

is equivalent to

   real *r*, **real** *circum*

and this in turn is equivalent to

   ref real *r* = **loc real**, **ref real** *circum* = **loc real**

Note that a local generator has been invoked twice. This is essential since the original declaration asks for the introduction of two variables. The mode associated with both *r* and *circum* is **ref real**.

Example 2.3c. Equivalent declarations.
   (i) **real** $x = 2.34$

14

is itself an identity declaration. In this case no generator is involved. The value 2.34 is ascribed to x and this value is of mode **real**.

(ii) **int** n,m

is equivalent to

ref int $n = $ **loc int, ref int** $m = $ **loc int**

In writing programs it is permissible to use either variable declarations or their identity declaration equivalents. However variable declarations are usually used since they are more convenient and less verbose. The identity declaration is a fundamental concept in ALGOL 68 and it will appear again several times. Its use is not confined to the introduction of constants and variables of the kind already discussed.

There are some points regarding identity declarations which require clarification. For example, must identity declarations appear immediately after the initial **begin**? Must a program always contain a declaration of some kind? Can variables be given values when they are declared? Another question, whose answer will be left until a later section, is: after space is produced by invoking local generators, how long does it remain available?

The answers given below will be, to a certain extent, incomplete. They assume only simple programs, i.e. programs of a complexity similar to that portrayed in examples 1.3a–c. More complete answers will be given later.

In principle a program need not contain any declarations whatsoever. Thus

begin *print* (*"This is a trivial program"*) **end**

is an acceptable, though useless, ALGOL 68 program. If declarations are to be used, and most programs will require declarations, then they must appear before the identifiers thereby declared are used. This is a perfectly natural restriction. One would not expect, for example, to assign a value to a variable and afterwards declare the variable. The space to hold the value should be there prior to any attempt to access the value. It follows that it would be pointless – and indeed it would result in an error – to have a declaration at the end of a program, for the identifier so declared could not be used.

Another point regarding declarations is that the same identifier cannot legally be declared twice within the one program – again assuming only simple programs of the kind already encountered.

Example 2.3d. Erroneous declarations I.

(i) **int** n, **real** m, **char** n

is erroneous since n appears twice.

(ii) The statement $read(n)$ in the program

      begin $read\ (n)$; **int** n; $print\ (n)$ **end**

would be illegal since n is used before being declared.

The question of initialisation of variables will be answered by means of illustrative examples. Suppose it is required to introduce a real variable called *sum* and give it the initial value 0.5. This can be achieved by means of the variable declaration

      real *sum* $:= 0.5$

or by means of the equivalent identity declaration

      ref real *sum* $=$ **loc real** $:= 0.5$

To consider a more complicated example suppose that two real variables *sum* and *product* have to be declared and initialised to, respectively, 0.5 and 2.5. This can be achieved by

      real *sum* $:= 0.5$, *product* $:= 2.5$

or by equivalent identity declarations.

Suppose finally that three integer variables n, m and p have to be declared. n has to be initialised to 2, p has to be initialised to 32 and m has not to be initialised. This can be achieved by

      int $n := 2, m, p := 32$

It is important to note the difference between the two declarations

      real *sum* $:= 0.5$ and **real** *sum* $= 0.5$

In terms of symbols there is only a colon distinguishing one declaration from the other. Yet the effects are quite different. The first is a variable declaration and the second an identity declaration. Of course, there would be less similarity between these declarations if they had both been written as identity declarations since then the local generator would have appeared explicitly in the first declaration.

Example 2.3e. Initialisation.

The declaration

      char *firstchar* $:=\ "A"$, *lastchar* $:=\ "Z"$, *currentchar*

introduces three character variables. The variables *firstchar* and *lastchar* are initialized to $"A"$ and $"Z"$ respectively and *currentchar* is not initialised.

A single declaration such as

int $n := 2, m, p := 32$

introduces a set of identifiers. As a consequence a common mode is associated with these identifiers. In the above example the common mode is **ref int**. In the declaration

real $e = 2.718, log2 = 0.618$

the common mode is **real**. If an attempt is made to introduce in a single declaration identifiers associated with different modes then errors would occur. The desired effect can be obtained by separating declarations from each other by semi-colons or commas. The significance of the semi-colon or comma will be left until later. In the meantime a semi-colon is the safer alternative.

Example 2.3f. Erroneous declarations II.
The declaration

real $x := 2.7, e = 2.7182818284$

is erroneous. The intention seems to be that x should be of mode **ref real** and e of mode **real**. The desired effect would be obtained by either

real $x := 2.7,$ **real** $e = 2.7182818284$

or

real $x := 2.7;$ **real** $e = 2.7182818284$

As regards the use of declarations in programs, note that a certain amount of freedom is allowed in the choice of identifiers. Sensible use should be made of this facility. Whenever possible one should use identifiers which reflect the role played by the corresponding value in a program. This can help considerably the task of writing and reading programs.

2.4. The basic arithmetic operators

In this section the exact meaning of these operators, which include addition, subtraction, multiplication, etc., will be examined. But apart from this it will be necessary to consider the meanings to be attached to formulae, i.e. expressions. For example $a + b \times c$ can be interpreted in at least two ways. It could mean add a to b and multiply the result by c or it could mean add a to the product of b and c. These two interpretations, or implied bracketings, can be expressed symbolically as $(a + b) \times c$ and $a + (b \times c)$ respectively. In normal circumstances it will happen that the second implied bracketing is understood. But the rules which govern this decision must be clearly specified.

2.4.1. Addition, subtraction and multiplication
Addition, subtraction and multiplication are defined for all pairs of objects of mode **real** and **int**. The mode of the result is **int** if both operands are of mode **int** and is **real** if either or each of the operands is of mode **real**. Since they have two operands these are called *dyadic* operators.

Example 2.4.1a. Addition, subtraction and multiplication.
  (i) $2 + 3$ gives the value 5 of mode **int**.
 (ii) 2.7×3 gives 8.1 of mode **real**.
(iii) $3.7 - 2.7$ gives 1.0 of mode **real**.

It is possible for the result of one of these operations to be too large in magnitude to be held in a machine location. This produces an error condition called *overflow*. Similar problems arise with other arithmetic operations – especially if the machine is asked to divide by zero!

In many implementations the asterisk, *, is used to denote multiplication to avoid confusing the symbol $\times$ with the letter x.

2.4.2. Division
Two types of division exist in ALGOL 68. In both cases division by zero is meaningless. The first is called *ordinary division* and is denoted by $/$. Ordinary division can be performed between two objects of mode **int** or **real** and the result is always of mode **real**.

Example 2.4.2a. Ordinary division.
  (i) $4/2$ gives 2.0, of mode **real**.
 (ii) If a and b are declared as in

   int $a = 4, b = 7$

then a/b gives a result of mode **real**.

The second form of division is called *integer division*. This operator is usually denoted by either $\div$, % or **over**. It is defined only for operands of mode **int** and gives a result of mode **int**. Of course, when two

18

integers a and b are divided as in $a \div b$ then a will not in general be a multiple of b. The result of using this operator is obtained by evaluating the correct mathematical result of the division a/b and then forgetting about the decimal point and all the digits after it.

Example 2.4.2b. Integer division.
(i) $2.3 \div 4$ is illegal and should give a syntax error since $\div$ is defined only between two integers.
(ii) $4 \div 2$ gives 2, of mode **int**.
(iii) $5 \div 3$ gives 1, of mode **int**.
(iv) Consider $n \div 3$ and $n \div m$ where n and m denote, respectively, the constant integer values -5 and -3. The results produced are, respectively, -1 and 1, both of mode **int**.

Closely associated with integer division is an operator for finding the remainder when one integer is divided by another. This new operator, the *modulo* operator, can be represented in various ways, e.g.

> **mod** $\div \times$ $\div *$ $\% \times$ $\% *$

This book uses the first two of these representations. Note that some of these representations result from the fact that $*$ and $\%$ are alternative representations of $\times$ and $\div$ respectively. (See also example 2.5a (iii).)
The result yielded by m **mod** n can be expressed precisely as follows. Suppose n is nonzero and q and r are integers such that

$$m = (n \times q) + r$$

where $0 \leqq r < |n|$. Then m **mod** n yields the value r. If n is zero an error will result.

Example 2.4.2c. On using **mod**.
(i) 0 **mod** 4 gives 0 of mode **int**.
(ii) $5 \div \times 3$ gives 2 since $\div \times$ can be used in place of **mod**.
(iii) If m and n denote 5 and -3 respectively then m **mod** n yields 2.

2.4.3. Exponentiation
The last of the basic dyadic operators is the exponential operator. This is used for raising numbers to an integral power. The operator can be denoted by

> $\uparrow$ $**$ **up**

The representation $\uparrow$ is favoured here.

There are essentially two cases to consider. Take $m \uparrow n$ where m and n are both of mode **int**. The result produced is just that obtained by repeatedly multiplying m by itself n times, i.e.

$$m \times m \times \ldots \times m \qquad\qquad (n \text{ terms})$$

The result is of mode **int**. The result of $\uparrow$ is not defined, and therefore it should not be used, when n is negative. If n is zero the value 1 is always obtained regardless of the value of m. In particular $0 \uparrow 0$ produces 1.

Consider now $x \uparrow n$ where x is of mode **real** and n is of mode **int**. In this case the result is of mode **real** and n may be positive, negative or zero. Note that negative powers are now allowed. Again the result of any real number, even 0.0, raised to the power 0 is 1.0 and of mode **real**.

Example 2.4.3a. Exponentiation.

(i) $2 \uparrow 3$ produces a result 8 of mode **int**.

(ii) $2 \uparrow 0.5$ is illegal since a number can be raised only to an integral power.

(iii) Consider $10 \uparrow 2$ and $10e2$. There are two important respects in which these differ. The first produces a result of mode **int**, the second is of mode **real**. Furthermore the first involves the computer in performing some calculation, namely the multiplication of 10 by itself, and the second does not since it is a real denotation.

2.4.4. Monadic operators

The operators $+$ and $-$ can appear as monadic operators. Consider, for example, $-y + 4$. The initial minus has one operand, namely y, and is therefore said to be monadic. The operand can be of mode **int** or mode **real** and the result is of that same mode. Similarly for monadic plus.

The particular example given above again illustrates the need for some method of interpreting formulae. It must be made clear that the initial minus sign does apply to y and not to $y + 4$. These rules will be considered in the next section.

As a final remark on monadic operators note that -4 and -3.14159 are expressions, not denotations. The initial minus has as operands 4 and 3.14159 respectively.

2.5. Operator priority and bracketing

Each operator has associated with it a positive integer called its *priority*. This positive integer lies in the range 1 to 10 inclusive.

20

Table 2.1 gives the priorities of the basic arithmetic operators (note that the monadic operators have priority 10; in fact all monadic operators will have this priority).

<small>TABLE 2.1.</small>

Operator	Representations	Priority
monadic plus	$+$	10
monadic minus	$-$	10
exponentiation	$\uparrow$, **, **up**	8
multiplication	$\times$, *	7
ordinary division	/	7
integer division	$\div$, %, **over**	7
modulo	**mod**, $\div \times$, % $\times$, $\div$ *, %*	7
dyadic plus	$+$	6
dyadic minus	$-$	6

The priority of operators is used in interpreting the meaning to be associated with formulae. In the expression

$$a + b \times c$$

the $+$ is dyadic plus and as such has priority 6. The multiplication operator $\times$ has priority 7. Since the priority of $\times$ is greater than the priority of $+$, the operator $\times$ binds more tightly than $+$. Thus the implied bracketing is

$$a + (b \times c)$$

i.e. b has to be multiplied by c and the result added to a.

In the more complicated formula

$$a + b \times c \uparrow n$$

$+$ has priority 6, $\times$ has priority 7 and $\uparrow$ has priority 8. Since higher priority operators bind more tightly than lower priority operators the implied bracketing is

$$a + (b \times (c \uparrow n))$$

i.e. $c \uparrow n$ is evaluated, the result is multiplied by b and this result is added to a.

These examples imply that the higher the priority of the operator the tighter it binds. This is the general rule, but it is not quite complete. Consider, for example,

$$a \uparrow b \uparrow c$$
$$a/b \times c$$

and
$$a + b - c + d$$

The rule as it stands will not give any information about these expressions since in each example taken separately all the operators have the same priority. To cover these cases the rule has to be extended. When several dyadic operators have the same priority the operators bind in the order in which they are encountered in reading from left to right.

Consider $a \uparrow b \uparrow c$. In moving from left to right the first operator is $\uparrow$ (in $a \uparrow b$). Thus $a \uparrow b$ has to be evaluated. The result is then raised to the power c. The implied bracketing is therefore $(a \uparrow b) \uparrow c$. The other two expressions can be interpreted in a similar manner.

Example 2.5a. Implied bracketing.

(i) $a/b/c$ and $(a \times c)/b$ are equivalent (ignoring the possibility of overflow)

(ii) $-2 \uparrow 2$ has an implied bracketing $(-2) \uparrow 2$; the result is therefore different from the result of evaluating $0 - 2 \uparrow 2$.

(iii) If p and q are both of mode **int** consider $p - p \div q \times q$. If it is positive this gives the same result as p **mod** q. Note that the equivalence of these two expressions provides a reason for $\div \times$, etc., being used instead of **mod**.

In these examples only dyadic operators of equal priority were considered. The situation can arise where several monadic operators can appear together. Consider $- - 4.3$. In this case the operators bind in the reverse order, i.e. from right to left. The above is evaluated as $-(-4.3)$.

The rules for interpreting expressions containing several operators are:

higher priority operators bind more tightly than lower priority operators;

dyadic operators of equal priority bind in order from left to right;

monadic operators (of equal priority) bind from right to left.

Having stated these rules it should now be pointed out that brackets themselves can always be used to override the priority of any operator. In $(a + b) \times c$ the addition is performed before multiplication. Extra brackets may also be included to improve readability.

Does the possibility of allowing operators to appear side by side result in confusion between monadic and dyadic operators? Consider the rather artificial example

$$a + - - - 2\uparrow - - 3 + 4$$

There is only one reasonable interpretation of such an expression the operators $+$ and $\uparrow$ are dyadic and all the minus operators are monadic. In general all operators immediately following identifiers and denotations are dyadic, the remaining operators are monadic. (This rule has to be modified slightly if brackets are used in an expression. The modification is straightforward.)

While on the topic of interpreting sequences of operators note that $\div \times$ represents a single operator (the modulo operator). Only certain such combinations of operators have this privilege and ALGOL 68 is carefully designed to ensure that no possible ambiguity can result from their use.

The use of brackets is a convenient way of introducing questions about order of evaluation. Consider

$$(a + b) \times (c + d)$$

$a + b$ and $c + d$ have to be multiplied. This, however, necessitates the prior evaluation of $a + b$ and $c + d$. But in what order does this evaluation take place? Is $a + b$ evaluated before $c + d$ or $c + d$ evaluated before $a + b$?

ALGOL 68 answers this and similar questions by saying that the operands of dyadic operators are *elaborated collaterally*, i.e. the programmer should not assume anything about the relative order of evaluation of the operands. In the above example $a + b$ may be evaluated before or after $c + d$ or their evaluations may overlap in time.

Consider the more complex example

$$a + (b + c) \times d \uparrow (n + m)$$

The operands of $\times$, i.e. $(b + c)$ and $d \uparrow (n + m)$ are elaborated collaterally. Similarly, the operands of $\uparrow$ are elaborated collaterally. Thus in particular one cannot assume anything about the relative order of evaluation of $b + c$ and $n + m$.

2.6. Comparison and boolean operators

The arithmetical comparison operators are listed in table 2.2 together with their priority and possible representations. All these operators are dyadic and therefore have two operands of mode **int** or **real**, in any combination. The meaning associated with each operator is the usual mathematical meaning. These operators therefore give a result which is either **true** or **false**, i.e. the result is always of mode **bool**.

23

TABLE 2.2.

Comparison operator	Representations	Priority
less than	$<$, **lt**	5
less than or equal to	$\leqq$, $<=$, **le**	5
equal	$=$, **eq**	4
not equal	$\neq$, $/=$, **ne**	4
greater than or equal to	$\geqq$, $>=$, **ge**	5
greater than	$>$, **gt**	5

Care should be exercised in using these operators since real numbers are held to a limited accuracy. Consequently using the equals operator to test the equality of two real numbers, for example, is liable to lead to unexpected results.

The comparison operators are defined also between objects of mode **char**. Thus expressions such as

$$"A" < "Z" \text{ or } ch1 = ch2$$

where $ch1$ and $ch2$ are of mode **char**, are meaningful. These operators compare the position of the various characters in the character set of the computer. *Character set* is used here to include not only letters and digits but also such characters as %, \$, $+$, $-$, etc. The precise character set and the order in which the various characters occur in it will depend on the particular computer installation and the particular compiler being used.

Example 2.6a. Comparison operators.
Assume the following declarations

real $x = 2.7$, $y = 3.6$, $z = 4.7$

(i) $x < y$ gives the result **true** of mode **bool**.
(ii) $x < y < z$ is illegal. The implied bracketing is

$$(x < y) < z$$

and the second $<$ has therefore one operand, i.e. the result obtained from evaluation of $(x < y)$, of mode **bool** and the other of mode **real**. But $<$ is not defined for such a combination of operands.
(iii) $"B" \neq "C"$ gives the result **true**, of mode **bool**.

The boolean operators – their operands are of mode **bool** – are listed in table 2.3. The priorities indicate that **not** is a monadic operator and the other boolean operators are dyadic. The definitions of the five operators are as follows.

TABLE 2.3.

Boolean operator	Representations	Priority
not	¬, ~, **not**	10
and	∧, **and**	3
or	∨, **or**	2
equals	=, **eq**	4
not equals	≠, /=, **ne**	4

not gives a result **true** if the operand is **false** and a result **false** if the operand is **true**.

and gives a result **true** if and only if both operands are **true**. Otherwise the result is **false**.

or gives a result **false** if and only if both operands are **false**. Otherwise the result is **true**.

= gives a result **true** if both operands are **true** or both operands are **false**. The result is **false** otherwise.

≠ gives a result **false** if both operands are **true** or both operands are **false**. The result is **true** otherwise.

Example 2.6b. Comparison operators and boolean operators. Consider the declarations

$$\textbf{int } a = 4, b = 5, c = 6, \textbf{real } x = 4.7, y = 5.7, z = 6.7$$

The expression

$$\textbf{not } (x + y < z) \textbf{ and } a + b = c$$

is meaningful. From the priority of the operators the implied bracketing is

$$(\textbf{not } ((x + y) > z)) \textbf{ and } ((a + b) = c)$$

2.7. Coercions – dereferencing and widening

In the expression $2 \times pi \times e$ taken from the program in example 1.3a the multiplication operates between objects of mode **int** and **real** or **real** and **real**. Multiplication has been defined in these cases.

In the program in example 1.3b the expression $2 \times pi \times r$ appears. The implied bracketing is $(2 \times pi) \times r$. Consider the second multiplication symbol. The result obtained from evaluating $2 \times pi$ is of mode **real**. But r is of mode **ref real**. Thus it appears that a request has been made to perform multiplication between an object of mode **real** and an object of mode **ref real**. But the multiplication operator is not defined in this case. Similar difficulties occur in the program in example 1.3c.

25

Although there are these problems with operators the intention is clear and it is desirable that the ALGOL 68 compiler should implement this intention. In mathematics, expressions such as these are often used. It is important to realise, however, that in the expression (taking one of the above for illustration) $2 \times pi \times r$ where r is of mode **ref real**, it is intended that the second multiplication operator should multiply together objects of mode **real**, not an object of mode **real** and an object of mode **ref real**. In more usual mathematical jargon the intention is not to multiply together a real number and a variable but it is to multiply a real number and the value of the variable. In this example therefore it is not the **ref real** r that has to be used in the calculation but it is the real number referred to by r.

The compiler can deduce that the object r used in this formula is of mode **ref real** and the required object is of mode **real** or mode **int** (since multiplication is defined only for objects of these modes). Therefore a mode change has to take place. These (automatic) mode changes, or *coercions* as they are called, are fundamental in ALGOL 68 and will arise frequently.

In example 1.3a the expression $2 \times pi \times e$ appeared and in example 1.3b the expression $2 \times pi \times r$ appeared. Considered only as a sequence of characters they are identical apart from a simple renaming (and, for instance, in example 1.3a the identifier r could have been used instead of e). In other words, ignoring the modes there is no essential difference between one expression and the other. But in the second expression a coercion is necessary and in the first expression no coercion is required. Consequently the mode changes that take place must depend to some extent on the original modes of the constituent objects and on the modes that must result from the coercions. These are called, respectively, the *a priori mode* and the *a posteriori mode*.

Example 2.7a. The a priori mode and a posteriori mode.

(i) In the expression $2 \times pi \times r$ (from example 1.3b) the a priori mode of r is **ref real** and the a posteriori mode of r is **real**.

(ii) In the expression $n \times (n + 1) \times (2 \times n + 1)$ in example 1.3c the a priori mode of each occurrence of n is **ref int** its a posteriori mode is **int**.

The coercions that can be applied to a particular occurrence of an object will depend partly on the position of that occurrence of the object within the program. More precisely, it will depend on what is called the *syntactic position* of that occurrence of the object. The various syntactic positions will become clearer as more concepts and constructions are introduced. But in passing two important syntactic positions have already been encountered: an operand in a formula, and the right hand side of an identity or variable declaration (i.e. the right hand side of the equals or becomes symbol).

Example 2.7b. On syntactic positions.

(i) In the expression -2.7, 2.7 is an operand since the minus sign is the monadic minus and therefore an operator.

(ii) In the identity declaration

ref real $x =$ **loc real**

loc real is on the right hand side of the identity declaration.

To simplify matters syntactic positions are grouped into five main classes. These are called *strong, firm, meek, weak* and *soft* positions. It will materialise that in a soft syntactic position only a very limited subset of the set of coercions can be applied. In a strong syntactic position any of the allowable coercions can be applied. The weak, meek and firm positions lie between these two extremes. A larger set of coercions can be applied as the syntactic position varies from soft through to strong in the order specified above. Indeed the very words 'soft', . . . , 'strong' convey this idea of being able to accept increasing amounts of coercion. Formally, they describe the *strength* of a syntactic position.

To be more explicit the operand in a formula always occupies a firm position. The right hand side of the equals or becomes symbol in declarations are strong positions.

Even in a strong position it is not possible to move, using only coercions, from an object of mode **real** to an object of mode **int**. Nor is it possible to change from an object of mode **int** to an object of mode **char**. Consequently the power of coercions is limited.

It should be stressed that coercions are *automatic* mode changes. They take place without the programmer having to ask explicitly that the mode changes be performed. Later it will appear that there are special operators allowing the possibility of, for example, a mode change from **real** to **int**. As stated above this cannot be performed by coercions.

The coercions that take place depend on the a priori mode, the a posteriori mode and the strength of the syntactic position.

In order to introduce the coercions that can be applied in different syntactic positions it will be convenient to look at certain basic coercions. There are six of these but for the moment only two will be considered: *dereferencing* and *widening*.

To give some examples, dereferencing takes place in going from an object of mode **ref real** to an object of mode **real** or from an object of mode **ref int** to an object of mode **int**. In general dereferencing takes an object of mode **ref x** (where **x** is some arbitrary mode) to an object of mode **x**. The initial **ref** is removed – hence the term 'dereferencing'. In more usual jargon, instead of using a variable in a part of a program, dereferencing allows the use of the value of the variable.

Dereferencing can be applied in all meek, firm and strong positions. In particular, therefore, dereferencing can be applied to the operands in a formula. This is just what is necessary to resolve the difficulty in the expressions considered at the start of this section.

Example 2.7c. Dereferencing.
Consider the program in example 1.3b. In the formula $2 \times pi \times r$ r occupies a firm position and is dereferenced.

To introduce widening, consider the identity declaration

real $x = 1$

Examples such as this have not yet been used. The right hand side of this identity declaration is an integer denotation, not a real denotation. Yet it should be quite clear what the intention is. In cases such as this a real number is expected. If an integer is found it is converted to the equivalent real number. This conversion is an example of the process known as *widening*. (This seems an appropriate term to describe a process which maps each element of a set into a corresponding element of a larger set.)

Widening is allowed only in strong positions. To allow widening in firm positions would lead to ambiguity. Consider $1 + 2$. This gives a result of 3 of mode **int**. If widening were allowed in firm positions both the 1 and 2 could be widened to mode **real**. Addition between real numbers would give a result of mode **real**. The mode of the result would therefore be ill-defined. Consequently widening is not allowed in firm positions.

Example 2.7d. Widening.

real $x := 4, y := 7, z := 2.7$

Here the 4 and the 7 are both widened from mode **int** to mode **real**. Widening can take place since these occur in strong positions, namely the right hand side of the becomes symbol in a variable declaration.

28

The examples given above employ only a single basic coercion for each necessary mode change. In fact the basic coercions can be applied repeatedly, if necessary, in order to make the transition from an object of one mode to an object of another mode. Of course, the allowed coercions are restricted to those permitted by the particular syntactic position.

Example 2.7e. Dereferencing and widening.
Consider the identity declaration

    real $x = n$

where n is an object of mode **ref int**. An object of mode **real** is expected on the right hand side. Since this position is a strong position an object of mode **real** can be delivered by first dereferencing n to give an object of mode **int** and then widening the result to give an object of mode **real**. Widening will never coerce from **ref int** to **ref real**.

2.8. Assignations (or assignment statements)

Assignations (or 'assignment statements' as they are often called in other languages) have already been encountered in the earlier examples in section 1.3.

Example 2.8a. Examples of assignations.
   (i) *circum* $:= 2 \times pi \times e$ (see example 1.3a)
   (ii) *result* $:= n \times (n + 1) \times (2 \times n + 1)$ (see example 1.3c)

A simple assignation assigning a value to the variable x has the form

    $x := expression$

The effect of an assignation is that the expression on the right hand side of the becomes symbol is evaluated and the result given to the variable x. For the assignation to be legal it is necessary that some requirements involving modes are satisfied. In particular the left hand side should be a variable and therefore possess a mode such as **ref int**, **ref real**, etc. It would thus be illegal (and undesirable) to place an object of mode **real** on the left hand side of an assignation.

Suppose the left hand side (or the *destination* as it is also called) of an assignation delivers a result of mode **ref x** (here **x** may be **real**, **int**, etc.). Then the right hand side (or the *source*) must deliver an object of a posteriori mode **x**. Thus **x** is the mode after any coercions have been applied. The source of an assignation is a strong syntactic position. Consequently both dereferencing and widening can be applied if necessary to the result obtained by evaluating the right hand side of the assignation. The destination of an assignation is a soft syntactic position and none of the coercions so far mentioned can be applied.

Example 2.8b. Coercions and assignations.
Suppose that y has mode **ref real** and n and m have mode **ref int**. Consider the assignation

$$y := n \div m$$

n and m are operands in the expression $n \div m$ and each occupies a firm position. Consequently they can be dereferenced and the integer division can be performed on the resulting integral values. The result of the expression has mode **int** and this is then widened to give a result of a posteriori mode **real** as required. This is permitted since the expression $n \div m$ occupies a strong syntactic position.

Example 2.8c. Illegal assignations.
In the context of the declarations

int n, **real** y, **char** a

and assuming where necessary that the variables have values, each of the following is an illegal assignation for the reason given.

(i) $n := y$ since there is no coercion to change an object of a priori mode **real** or **ref real** to an object of a posteriori mode **int**.

(ii) $n := 4/2$ since $4/2$ produces a real result.

(iii) $n := a$ since there is no coercion for changing character variables to integers.

(iv) $a := n$ since no coercion changes integer variables to characters.

Apart from widening there is no coercion that will take an object from one of the four primitive modes (i.e. **bool**, **char**, **int** and **real**) to another such mode. Widening can be applied only in a strong position and, restricting the remarks to coercions between the primitive modes **int**, **real**, **bool** and **char**, will convert only an object of mode **int** to an object of mode **real**.

The usefulness of assignations can be increased by extending the concept. One extension arises from associating a value with an assignation. Consider (where z has mode **ref real**)

$$z := n + m$$

and assume all considerations of mode, etc., are satisfied. One can associate with the assignation a value and therefore a mode, the mode of the value. The value is just the object on the left hand side of $:=$, i.e. z of mode **ref real**.

Having stated that an assignation delivers a value this value can now be used in expressions. Thus it is possible to write assignations such as

$$y := 6 \times (z := n + m) + 4$$

This has the same effect as the pair of assignations

$$z := n + m; y := 6 \times z + 4$$

Note the coercions occurring in the more complex assignation. Assume that z and y have mode **ref real** and n and m have mode **ref int**. Certainly n and m are dereferenced. The inner assignation is performed and the result, i.e. z, is dereferenced. The remaining calculations take place and no further coercions are required.

There are several reasons for using longer assignations such as $y := 6 \times (z := n + m) + 4$ rather than the two separate assignations described above: the single assignation is liable to be more efficiently executed by the computer; sensible use of this facility helps in making programs easier to read and understand.

It is often convenient to use assignations to assign the same value to a number of variables. For instance

$$x := y := 2.7$$

where x and y have mode **ref real** assigns 2.7 to both the variable x and the variable y. There is a certain bracketing implicit in this assignation, namely

$$x := (y := 2.7)$$

The effect of this is as follows: the inner bracket is evaluated, giving the result y; this is dereferenced and the result assigned to x. Note that the implied bracketing is not what one would expect of a dyadic operator.

If w is also of mode **ref real**, the assignation

$$x := y := z := w := 0$$

sets the values of the four variables x, y, z and w to zero. The implied bracketing is $x := (y := (z := (w := 0)))$. Again dereferencing takes place several times but widening takes place only once.

Example 2.8d. Further assignations.
Suppose the following declarations have occurred

>**real** y,z,w, **int** n,m,p

Suppose also that, where necessary, the variables have values. Examples of legal assignations are:

>$w := n + m \times (y := 4 \times (z := 3))$
>$w := (p := n := m \div 4) \times 4 + 3 \times (z := pi \times 7)$
>$w := y := n := 4$

It is convenient to look back at certain assignations that were introduced earlier in another context. The initialisation of a variable involves an assignation. The variable declaration

>**real** $x := 4.7$

has an equivalent identity declaration

>**ref real** $x = $ **loc real** $:= 4.7$

The implied bracketing here is

>**ref real** $x = ($**loc real** $:= 4.7)$

Thus there is an assignation on the right hand side of the equals symbol. The value of the assignation is just an object of mode **ref real**. After the execution of the identity declaration this object can then be accessed by the identifier x.

Certain pitfalls may arise from misuse of the facilities already introduced. Consider

>**begin real** $x,y := 4.5$;
> $x := y + (y := 7.2)$;
>   *print* (x)
>**end**

The effect of the assignation $x := y + (y := 7.2)$ is undefined and such assignations should not appear in programs. Remember that operands are elaborated collaterally and by definition therefore one cannot assume anything about their order of evaluation. Thus the source of the above assignation could be evaluated as either $4.5 + 7.2$ or as $7.2 + 7.2$ depending on when the assignation $y := 7.2$ takes place.

Example 2.8e. Formulae whose effects are undefined.
The effect of each of the following formulae (which are assumed to be otherwise correct) is undefined:

>$(y := z := 4) \uparrow 2 + 3 \times z$

$$m + p \div n + (m := p - 4)$$
$$- b/(a2 := 2 \times a) + sq\ disc/a2$$

2.9. Standard operators

The operators to be considered here fall into three classes:
  (i) arithmetical assignment operators;
  (ii) operators performing mode changes;
  (iii) other operators.
For each new operator the following have to be discussed: whether the operator is monadic or dyadic, the mode(s) of the operand(s), the priority if the operator is dyadic, and the effect of the operator.

2.9.1. Arithmetical assignment operators

The arithmetical assignment operators have no counterparts in normal mathematical usage. To illustrate consider the 'plus-and-becomes' operator **plusab** (which can also be written as $+:=$). If m is of mode **ref int** and n is of mode **int** then

m **plusab** n or $m + := n$

has the same effect as the assignation $m := m + n$. The result delivered is even of mode **ref int**.

   In general, expressions such as

x **plusab** y or $x + := y$

can be written. x can be of mode **ref int** or **ref real** and y can be any expression delivering a result of mode **int** or **real**. The restrictions placed on the modes of x and y are just those necessary to make the assignation

$x := x + y$

legal. The plus-and-becomes operator has priority 1, the lowest possible priority.

   Apart from **plusab** there are five other arithmetical assignment operators. The complete set of operators together with their possible representations, meanings, etc. is given in table 2.4. The final two columns give the allowable modes of the left hand and right hand operands respectively. The allowable combinations of modes are given on separate rows of table 2.4. The mode restrictions are those that must be enforced in order to make the corresponding assignations legal.

   It should be remembered that these new operators may, in the usual

TABLE 2.4. Arithmetical assignment operators.

Operator op	Representations of **op**	Priority	Meaning of x **op** y	Mode of x	Mode of y
plus-and-becomes	**plusab**, $+ :=$	1	$x := x + y$	**ref real** **ref int**	**real** or **int** **int**
minus-and-becomes	**minusab**, $- :=$	1	$x := x - y$	**ref real** **ref int**	**real** or **int** **int**
times-and-becomes	**timesab**, $\times :=, {}^* :=$	1	$x := x \times y$	**ref real** **ref int**	**real** or **int** **int**
divide-and-becomes	**divab**, $/ :=$	1	$x := x/y$	**ref real**	**real** or **int**
over-and-becomes	**overab**, $\div :=, \%:=$	1	$x := x \div y$	**ref int**	**int**
mod-and-becomes	**modab**, $\div \times :=, \% \times :=,$ $\div {}^* :=, \% {}^* :=$	1	$x := x \bmod y$	**ref int**	**int**

way, have operands that undergo coercion. If both m and n are of mode **ref int** then an expression containing

m **modab** n

will result in n being dereferenced.

Example 2.9.1a. Arithmetical assignment operators.
Consider the declaration

int m, $n := 4$, **real** x

(i) n **plusab** 1 has the effect of assigning 5 to n.
(ii) $m + := x$ is illegal since the result of adding an integer and a real number is a real and this cannot be assigned to m.
(iii) m **divab** n is illegal for m/n produces a result of mode **real**.

2.9.2. Operators performing mode changes
The operators to be introduced are, not surprisingly, all monadic. They act on an object of one mode and produce as result an object of another mode. Being monadic their priority will automatically be 10. The representation and the effect of each operator is given below:

round converts a real number to the nearest integer; when the fractional part is .5 the effect of the operator is implementation dependent (converts **real** to **int**).

entier gives the largest integer less than or equal to the real number (converts **real** to **int**).

abs applied to an object of mode **bool** gives the value 1 if the operand is **true** and 0 if it is **false** (converts **bool** to **int**).

34

abs applied to an object of mode **char** gives an integer code for this character; each character has a unique code (converts **char** to **int**).

repr applied to a suitable integer gives as result the character whose code is that integer (converts **int** to **char**). Note that not every integer is the code of some character; hence the use of 'suitable'.

odd applied to an integer gives the result **true** if the integer is an odd number and **false** otherwise (converts **int** to **bool** and performs the inverse of **abs** when applied to booleans).

Example 2.9.2a. Operators causing mode changes.

(i) **round** 5.6 gives 6.

(ii) **round** 4 is illegal since 4 is of mode **int** and being an operand occupies a firm syntactic position; it cannot therefore be widened to **real**.

(iii) If *rad* is of mode **int**,

$$\textbf{round} \ (rad \times 360/(2 \times pi))$$

converts *rad* radians to degrees, the answer being correct to the nearest integer.

(iv) **entier** − 5.5 gives − 6; note the presence of the two monadic operators, **entier** and minus.

(v) **repr abs** *"A"* gives *"A"*.

2.9.3. Other operators

It is convenient to gather here the definitions of other monadic operators which are frequently used:

abs applied to object of mode **int** or **real** gives the absolute value of that object (negative signs are removed); if the operand is of mode **int** the result is of mode **int** and if the operand is of mode **real** the result is of mode **real**.

sign applied to objects of mode **int** or **real** always delivers a result of mode **int**; if the operand is positive the result is + 1, if negative the result is − 1 and if zero the result is 0.

Example 2.9.3a. Miscellaneous operators.

(i) **abs** − 4 gives 4 of mode **int**.

(ii) **odd abs entier** − 6.5 gives **true**.

2.10. Layout, comments and pragmatic remarks

Consider first the significance of spaces, new lines and new pages within programs. These are generally referred to as *typographical display features*. For the most part they are ignored but there are two exceptions to this.

Firstly, spaces used within quotes are significant. For example " " is the character denotation for a space. New lines and new pages should not appear within quotes.

Secondly, typographical display features should not occur within symbols but can occur between symbols. Of course, this remark is relevant only if a symbol consists of more than one character. Examples of such symbols include the words **begin, end, int, abs**, etc. together with $\div \times, \div \times :=$, etc. In general, when a combination of letters has to be treated as an indivisible word, operator or mode, etc. the individual characters cannot be separated by typographical display features. These remarks do not apply however to identifiers but they do apply to all denotations already encountered. Thus spaces etc. can appear within identifiers and they are effectively ignored.

Spaces, new lines and new pages are not the only items which, subject to the earlier provisions, are ignored. One can introduce what are usually called 'comments' by enclosing text within special pairs of symbols. The allowable pairs of symbols are

¢	and	¢ (¢ is the cent, as opposed to dollar, symbol)
#	and	#
comment	and	**comment**
co	and	**co**

(Note that commentary cannot be enclosed within, say, ¢ and #.) Commentary usually takes the form of some kind of explanatory text which helps the reader in understanding the program. These comments can appear in those parts of a program at which spaces and new lines are ignored except that they cannot be used to separate parts of an identifier.

Pragmatic remarks are enclosed within special pairs of symbols **pragmat** and **pragmat** or **pr** and **pr**. It is awkward to describe their effect since their form will vary from one version of ALGOL 68 to another. But they are intended to pass special information to the compiler. This information might take the form of requests to supply the mode of identifiers and the position of their declaration, a listing of this part of the program, special checks in the compiled program, e.g. to test for division by zero, etc. Pragmatic remarks and comments can appear in similar positions in programs.

It is convenient to make here a remark that can affect considerably the layout and readability of a program. The symbols **begin** and **end** can be replaced respectively by (and). However, an error results from replacing **begin** by (and leaving **end** unaltered. It is necessary therefore to be consistent. If **begin** appears there must be a matching **end** and if (appears there must be a matching).

Sensible use should be made of the facilities for controlling layout and including commentary. Meaningful identifiers, sensible comments, and the judicious use of spaces and new lines make it easier for programmers to read and to understand each other's programs, although the precise constitution of good layout depends on individual taste.

2.11. Simple transput

Transput is the term used in ALGOL 68 for the passing of information between a program and other parts of the computer such as line printers, card readers and even discs, drums, magnetic tapes or other programs. In particular, therefore, transput is concerned with all forms of input and output. Only relatively simple transput is considered here.

In general a program may communicate with many different sets of input and of output. In ALGOL 68 this communication is by means of *files*. The use of the word *file* is, of course, significant. A file, where the word is used in a programming sense, resembles the more common idea of a file. In particular it 'holds' information. (The precise meaning of the word 'hold' as used here will be described in chapter 9. For the present the usual meaning of the word suffices.) The information can be held for short periods of time or for long periods of time, e.g. several months. Moreover files can be created and deleted and one or several people can be granted access to a particular file. It will be seen later that files can have varying properties and by appropriately choosing these properties a programmer can restrict the kind of access to his files.

To take some specific examples an input file allows the programmer only to read from the file. The data associated with the simple programs of section 1.3 for instance would be held in an input file. One would not normally dream of writing to such files and indeed it would not be permitted. Input files are therefore said to have read-only access. Output files similarly allow only the writing of information and have write-only access.

In this introduction to transput it will be assumed that programs require at most one input file and one output file. The input file used will be referred to by *standin*, and the output file by *standout* (standard input and standard output, respectively).

The finer points of control in transput are obtained by using objects called *formats*. It will be sufficient for the moment to consider only the control that can be exercised without resorting to formats. This form of transput is therefore referred to as *formatless transput*.

Formatless input is achieved using the read statement and formatless output is achieved using the print statement. Both *read* and *print* are examples of objects called *routines*. Both can be thought of as abbreviations for pieces of program which perform specific tasks, in this case the reading of information from *standin* and the writing of information to *standout*.

2.11.1. The read statement

Each occurrence of *read* can be followed by brackets which enclose a variable or an ordered list of variables. For example,

$$read((a, b, c, d))$$

is a read statement containing an ordered list of the variables a, b, c and d, the ordered list appearing as (a,b,c,d). The variable or list of variables is called the *actual parameter* or *data list* of that particular read statement.

The effect of a read statement such as

$$read((a, b, c, d))$$

is, at least for present purposes, the same as the four read statements

$$read(a); read(b); read(c); read(d)$$

It is convenient therefore to consider only read statements of the form $read(a)$ where a is a single variable or, more precisely, a single object. The effect of more complex read statements can then be defined in terms of the simpler statements.

The effect of $read(x)$ will now be considered. There are several cases to be discussed. These arise from the different possible modes of x.

(i) Suppose x has mode **ref int**. The input is devoured until the first non-blank character is encountered. New lines are taken if necessary. The integer is then read and assigned to the variable x. It will be terminated by a non-digit character or by a new line, whichever comes first. If some faulty character happens to appear the consequence is undefined. The following would be acceptable examples of integers appearing as data (the different examples are separated by commas):

$$+123, + 123, - 123, -123, \quad 123$$

Thus the sign is optional and blanks before and after the sign are optional. Blanks may not appear within the string of digits. (Note that these are not integer denotations.)

(ii) Suppose x has mode **ref real**. The input is scanned until the first non-blank character is reached. New lines are taken if necessary. The real number is read and assigned to the variable x. The form that a real number occurring in data may take can be described as follows. It can:

(a) be of the form described in (i) above, i.e. where x has mode **ref int**;
(b) take the same form as a real denotation;
(c) take form (b) preceded by a $+$ or $-$;
(d) be of the form (b) or (c) where each $+$, $-$ and $e(\backslash\text{or}_{10})$ may be followed or preceded by blanks.

(iii) Suppose x has mode **ref bool**. The input is scanned until the first non-blank character is reached. New lines are taken as required. The first non-blank character must be either the *flip* symbol (which denotes **true**) or the *flop* symbol (which denotes **false**). These two symbols are implementation dependent. The character is read and the appropriate value assigned to x.

(iv) Suppose x has mode **ref char**. If the reading position is at the end of a line, a new line is taken. The first character is read and assigned to x.

(v) *read* (*space*) causes the next character in the data to be skipped.

(vi) *read* (*new line*) has the effect of skipping all data between the current position and the start of the next new line.

(vii) *read* (*backspace*) moves the current data position back one character and thus allows the character just read to be re-read. However this cannot be used to jump backwards past the start of the current line.

Example 2.11.1a. The read statement.
(i) If x, y and z each have mode **ref real** the effect of

$$read\,((x,y,\ space,\ z))$$

is the same as the effect of

$$read(x);\ read(y);\ read(space);\ read(z)$$

(ii) Suppose *standin* contains

7/3/1975

If *day*, *month*, *year* and n are all of mode **ref int** the read statement

$$read\,((day,space,month,space,year,backspace,backspace,n))$$

has the effect of giving to *day, month, year* and *n* the values 7, 3, 1975 and 75 respectively.

2.11.2. The print or write statement

In earlier examples print statements were introduced and their effect partially described. It was not mentioned, however, that an alternative to *print* is *write*. So the statements

print (("*The result is*", *res*)) and *write* (("*The result is*", *res*))

have the same effect.

The print or write statement has, in common with the read statement, actual parameters or data lists. These consist of either a single item to be printed or a list of items. The list must appear as a sequence of objects separated by commas and enclosed in brackets. For the present, the effect of applying a print statement to a list of objects is the same as that of applying *print* to each of the objects separately, in the appropriate order. Consequently it is necessary to consider the effect of printing only a single item. The effect of more complex print statements can then be described in terms of the simpler cases.

Among the objects that a print or write statement will expect to handle are objects of mode **int**, **real**, **char** and **bool**. Included also are strings of characters enclosed by quotes. An actual parameter of a print statement should be regarded as occupying a firm syntactic position and consequently dereferencing but not widening is allowed. Thus a statement such as *print* (*n*) where *n* is of mode **ref int** will result in *n* being dereferenced and the value of the variable being printed.

The print or write statement can have expressions as actual parameters. The following are therefore meaningful, assuming they appear in a context in which there are suitable declarations,

print (*a* + *b*)
write (**entier** (4.6 + (*x* := 3.7 + *z* + (*y* := 7))))

In each case the expression appearing as the actual parameter is evaluated and the result printed.

Consider *print* (*x*) where *x* delivers an object of mode **int**. If the integer does not appear at the start of a line it is preceded by a space. The number of character positions then allocated to the integer itself does not depend on the size or sign of the number. Consequently just as much room as would be required by the largest positive integer and its sign is allocated. An integer is printed at the rightmost end of its allocated space with leading zeros suppressed and imme-

40

diately preceded by its sign.

Example 2.11.2a. Printing an integer.
Consider a machine allowing integers n in the range

$$-8388608 \leq n \leq 8388607$$

Using ⌐ to denote a space, a request to print the integer 1234567 not at the start of a line results in the printing of the characters

⌐ + 1234567

Similarly *print*(1) would cause the characters

⌐ ⌐ ⌐ ⌐ ⌐ ⌐ ⌐ + 1

to be printed.

If there is not enough room on the current line to hold all the characters (including the initial space) a new line is automatically taken. The integer is then printed on the new line but now without the preceding space.

Consider *print*(x) where x delivers an object of mode **real**. As with integers the real number is preceded by a space if it does not appear at the start of a line. The number of character positions then allocated to the real number itself depends on two quantities. First there is the number of decimal digits of accuracy to which a real number is held in the computer. Let this be N. The second quantity depends on the size of the real numbers the machine can hold. Suppose that the largest real number requires an exponent occupying M decimal digits, not taking the sign into account. Then a real number is printed as follows: one position for the initial sign $(+ \text{ or } -)$; one position before the decimal point; the decimal point itself; $N-1$ places after the decimal point; the times-ten-to-the-power symbol$_{10}$; one position for the sign of the exponent; and M places for the magnitude of the exponent. The exponent part is always an integer and is treated as such. Thus it is printed to the right of its allocated space. Again if there is not enough room on the current line for all these characters a new line is automatically taken and the initial space ignored.

Example 2.11.2b. Printing a real number.
In a machine holding real numbers of magnitude less than 10^{77} to an accuracy of 11 decimal digits
   (i) the result of printing *pi*, not at the start of a line, would be

⌐ + 3.1415926538$_{10}$ ⌐ + 0

where $\llcorner$ denotes a space.

(ii) the result of printing -450.5 would be

$$- 4.5050000000_{10} \llcorner + 2$$

provided the number appears at the start of a line.

The remaining cases are much simpler and are listed below.

If x is of mode **bool**, *print*(x) causes either the *flip* or the *flop* symbol to be printed. These symbols correspond to **true** and **false** respectively and might typically be just the characters "T" and "F". Note that no initial space is printed but if necessary a new line is taken before printing occurs.

The statement *print*(x) where x is of mode **char** causes the printing of that character possibly preceded by the taking of a new line. Again there is no initial space.

If a string of characters, enclosed within quotes, has to be printed the individual characters are merely printed. Again there is no initial space but new lines will be taken whenever required.

The statements *print* (*newline*) and *print* (*newpage*) cause a new line and a new page to be taken respectively. The statement *print* (*blank*) is equivalent to *print* (" "). Indeed one can assume in general that the compiler knows about *blank* in the same way as it knows about *pi*. It treats *blank* as if it were " " and it is therefore of mode **char**.

No mention has yet been made of *print* (*space*) and *print* (*backspace*). In a sense these do what one would expect; but note that *backspace* cannot be used to retreat beyond the start of the current line. A thorough understanding of their effect, and indeed the effect of *print* (*newline*) and *print* (*newpage*), requires some further investigation.

Consider what is happening as output takes place. Printing gradually moves the current printing position along lines and down pages, ignoring for the moment the use of *backspace*. At any time there will be a most advanced position which the printer has reached. This is called the *logical end of file*, the file in this case being the standard output *standout*. Use of *backspace* causes the printing position to become different from the logical end of file. The effect of using *space*, *newline* and *newpage* can now be described precisely.

When the current printing position is the same as the logical end of file use of *space*, *newline* and *newpage* causes blanks to be inserted and the logical end of file moved accordingly.

When the printing position is not the same as the logical end of file the effect of *space*, *newline* and *newpage* is to cause the characters between the current printing position and the logical end of file to remain unaltered and thereafter spaces appear as before.

Example 2.11.2c. *space* and *blank*.

Note the difference in the effects of *print* (("a", *backspace*, *space*)) and *print* (("a", *backspace*, *blank*)). In the first case the letter *a* is still present in *standout* and in the second case it has been replaced by a blank.

2.11.3. The conversion routines

Used alone the print or write procedures print integers and real numbers in a very crude manner. To have greater control over the way in which numbers are printed is highly desirable. The three standard routines *whole*, *fixed* and *float* go some way towards giving the required flexibility. Each can be used to print a number, either an integer or a real. The number is not preceded by a space and the various characters are printed one after the other, a new line being taken when there is no room left on the current line for a particular character.

The routine *whole* prints numbers as if they were integers (and this removes, in a manner to be prescribed, the decimal point, the fractional part, the times-ten-to-the-power symbol and the exponent). Routine *fixed* prints numbers as if they were decimals. In certain circumstances *fixed* behaves like *whole* but usually will supply a decimal point together with a certain number of digits before the point and a certain number after the point. Routine *float* will usually print numbers in the form given by *fixed* but with a times-ten-to-the-power symbol and an exponent added.

Roughly speaking, these three routines allow the programmer to specify the exact length of the space to be allocated to the number, the number of places before and after the decimal point and in the exponent part. Moreover it is possible to indicate whether or not a sign is required either for the number itself or for its exponent part. (Of course, for negative numbers and negative exponents a sign will always be required but in other cases there is the choice of inserting " + " or omitting it.)

It sometimes happens that the programmer is unaware of the size of the number he expects. The routine *whole* offers the possibility of printing an integer in just as much room as the number requires; similar possibilities are available when using *fixed* and *float*.

The mechanisms for indicating the total number of character positions to be allocated to the number to be printed and for indicating whether a sign is required are closely linked. To illustrate this, consider the width parameter which is common to each of the three routines. This indicates the total number of character positions to be allocated to the number including any signs, decimal points, times-ten-to-the-power symbols and digits that may be present. There are three cases to consider:

if the width parameter is positive the sign of the number is always produced; for printing purposes zero is regarded as positive and therefore preceded by a plus sign;

suppose the width parameter is negative: the sign of the number is printed only if the number is negative; for positive or zero numbers the sign is omitted, it just does not appear (note that it is not replaced by a blank); the magnitude of the width then indicates the number of spaces allocated for printing and this includes any sign that might be present;

if the width is zero the number is allocated just as much space as it needs; positive numbers and zero are not preceded by a sign.

The standard routine *whole* is used in statements such as

   print (whole (exp, width))

where *exp* denotes any expression delivering a result of mode **int** or **real** and *width* denotes any expression delivering an integer. This integer is the width parameter described in the previous paragraph.

Several points should be noted. If *exp* delivers a real then that real is rounded to the nearest integer and the result, if it is suitable, is printed. If by this means or otherwise the integer (with sign, if any, attached) is too long to fit into the space demanded by *width* then there appears on the output a sequence of error characters occupying the entire field that should contain the number.

Example 2.11.3a. Using *whole*.
If $\llcorner$ denotes a space and $"*"$ the error character, the result of
  (i) *print (whole (76, 4))*   would be $\llcorner + 76$
 (ii) *print (whole (76, − 4))*   would be $\llcorner \llcorner 76$
(iii) *print (whole (− 76, − 4))*   would be $\llcorner - 76$
 (iv) *print (whole (1234, + 4))*   would be $****$
  (v) *print ((whole (− 76, 0), "x↑ ", whole (4, 0)))* would be $- 76x↑ 4$
 (vi) *print (whole (pi, 3))*   would be $\llcorner + 3$

The standard routine *fixed* can be used in statements such as

   print (fixed (x, width, after))

Both *width* and *after* can be any expressions delivering results of mode **int** and *x* can be any expression delivering a result of mode **real** or mode **int**.

44

The parameter *width* has its usual significance and *after* indicates the number of decimal digits that should follow the decimal point. The number delivered by *x* is printed correct to *after* places following the decimal point. Of course, if *after* is too large the final digits may be of little value since real numbers are not held accurately. *after* should never be negative; if it is zero the point is not printed–the routine then behaves like *whole*. If the width parameter is zero the number is printed in as much space as it requires subject to the restriction that there should be *after* decimal digits following the decimal point. Some examples should clarify these rules.

Example 2.11.3b. Using *fixed* I.
If ⌐ denotes a space then the result of

(i) *print* (*fixed* (*pi*, 6, 3))	would be	+ 3 . 1 4 2
(ii) *print* (*fixed* (*pi*, − 6, 3))	would be	⌐ 3 . 1 4 2
(iii) *print* (*fixed* (*pi*, − 6, 0))	would be	⌐ ⌐ ⌐ ⌐ ⌐ 3
(iv) *print* (*fixed* (123, − 6, 2))	would be	1 2 3 . 0 0
(v) *print* (*fixed* (*pi*, 0,4))	would be	3 . 1 4 1 6

When using *fixed* the error character plays a slightly different role from that played in using *whole*. If the number does not fit the specification demanded then it is altered slightly and another attempt is made at printing. To be more specific, if

$$print\ (fixed\ (x, width, after))$$

does not produce a result then

$$print\ (fixed\ (x, width, after - 1))$$

is tried. If this fails the statement

$$print\ (fixed\ (x, width, after - 2))$$

is tried, and so on until the parameter *after* − *n* becomes negative. Then failure results and the error character appears.

Example 2.11.3c. Using *fixed* II.
If the error character is "*" then

(i) *print* (*fixed* (128.148, 4, 2)) produces + 128: for the specification demand fails as does that demanded by *print* (*fixed* (128.148, 4, 1)). However, *print* (*fixed* (128.148, 4, 0)) will result in the printing of + 128

(ii) *print* (*fixed* (128.148, 3, 2)) results in *** being produced; even *print* (*fixed* (128.148, 3, 0)) will not produce an integer since the "+" sign is sought.

The standard routine *float* can be used in statements such as

$$print\ (float\ (x, width, after, exp))$$

As usual, x can be any expression delivering the integer or real number to be printed, *width* indicates the size of the field in which the number has to appear, and *after* indicates the number of decimal places following the decimal point; $after = 0$ implies the decimal point is omitted. The extra parameter *exp* indicates the size of the field in which the exponent is to appear. Moreover if $exp \geq 0$ then a sign will always appear and if $exp < 0$ the sign appears only if the exponent is negative. Note that when $exp = 0$ a sign appears before the exponent even if it is positive.

But with *float* a complication arises. Consider the request

$$print\ (float\ (12.3456, 12, 4, 2))$$

Does the result appear as ($\llcorner$ denoting space)

$$\llcorner\llcorner + 1 . 2345_{10} + 3$$
or
$$\llcorner + 1\ 2 . 3450_{10} + 2$$
or
$$+ 1\ 2\ 3 . 4500_{10} + 1$$

or in some other form? Note that all represent the number to be printed and all satisfy the specification demanded by the parameters of *float*. In fact the third alternative is produced, the reason being that as much accuracy as possible is desirable and so as many significant digits as possible are supplied before the decimal point, though for a negative width an initial $+$ is replaced by blank.

Example 2.11.3d. Using *float* I.

    (i) *print* (*float* (123.4567, 12, 5, 2))   produces $+ 12.34567_{10} + 1$

    (ii) *print* (*float* (123.4567, $-$ 10, 5, $-$ 1))   produces $\llcorner 1.23457_{10} 2$

Consider now what happens if the number cannot be fitted to the specification demanded by

$$float\ (x, width, after, exp)$$

The routine does not immediately admit defeat but, like *fixed*, it attempts to let the programmer know the value to be printed by trying to adjust the specification so as to allow the number to be printed using this new specification. Only in extreme cases does it admit defeat and produce a sequence of error characters.

    The routine assumes on failure that the exponent part has not been allowed enough room and consequently *exp* is increased by 1 (or decreased by 1 if *exp* is negative) and one decimal place after the decimal point is, if possible, sacrificed. If failure still results the *after* parameter is, if possible, decreased by 1 and the *exp* parameter increased by 1 (or decreased by 1 in the negative case). If *after* reaches zero it is held there and the exponent part increased. This process is continued until either some number is printed or the routine has to admit defeat. The latter occurs only when as a result of the size and sign demanded by the exponent part no digits can appear before the exponent if the number has to fit the specified width. This implies that a number cannot be printed with only an exponent part.

Using a width parameter of zero with *float* leads to an undefined result. The reason for this lies in associating a sensible meaning with the implied intention of printing a floating-point number in just as much room as is needed.

Using an *exp* parameter of zero also leads to a perhaps unexpected result. In fact, using zero here is equivalent to using an *exp* parameter of $+1$. The reason again lies in associating a sensible meaning with this. For instance, should *print* (*float* (12.3,8,1,0)) produce $123.4_{10}-1$ or $\_\ \_\ 12.3_{10}0$ or indeed something other than these?

Example 2.11.3e. Using *float* II.
If x is of mode **real** and has the value 4.567×10^{60} then if $''*''$ is the error character

  (i) *print* (*float* $(x,-5,1,-1)$) produces $\_5_{10}60$
  (ii) *print* (*float* $(x,-6,2,0)$)   produces $\_5_{10}+60$
  (iii) *print* (*float* $(x,-3,0,0)$)   produces ***

Exercises for chapter 2

1. Which of the following are integer denotations?
   (i) 1   (ii) 6, 324
   (iii) 000   (iv) $3+4$
   (v) -1 (vi) 2e4
   (vii) 1.0   (viii) $+1$

2. What results are produced by the program

   begin *print* ((6, 324)) **end**   ?

   Does this suggest a reason for the fact that commas are forbidden in integer denotations?

3. Which of the following are real denotations? Give reasons for your answers.

(i) 5.   (ii) .4

(iii) π (iv) *pi*

(v) *e*23   (vi) 6.0*e* − 0

(vii) 4*e*4   (viii) *e*

(ix) 40   (x) 6*e* − 4.0

4. Is ″″*A*″″ a character denotation?

5. In ALGOL 68 the multiplication sign must be inserted explicitly. By considering the program below indicate why, if multiplication were not explicit, ambiguity would result.

> **begin real** *a*, *b*, *ab*; *read* ((*a*, *b*, *ab*));
>   *a* := *ab*; *print* (*a*)
> **end**

6. What modes are associated with the identifiers as a result of the declarations:

    (i) **real** *x*, *y*, *z*   (ii) **char** *a* = ″*A*″

   (iii) **real** *x* = 2.7   (iv) **real** *x* := 2.7

    (v) **real** *x*, *y* := 3.7, **int** *z* = 4, **bool** *t* ?

7. Give an identity declaration which is equivalent to

    (i) **real** *x* := 2.7

   (ii) **real** *x* = 2.7

   (iii) **char** *a* := ″*A*″, *b*

   (iv) **bool** *t* = **true**, *f* = **false**

8. In each case state whether or not the program is legal. Give reasons for your answers.

    (i) **begin** *print* (6); **real** *x*; *read* (*x*); *print* (*x*) **end**

   (ii) **begin real** *e* = 2.7; *print* (6); **real** *e*; *read* (*e*); *print* (*e*) **end**

   (iii) **begin real** *e* = 2.7; *print* (*e*); *read* (*e*); *print* (*e*) **end**

9. Indicate the implied bracketing in the following expressions.

    (i) $a \times b/c$ (ii) $a + b \uparrow n$

   (iii) $a \times b \times c + a \uparrow b \uparrow$ $c + a/b/c$ (iv) $- a \uparrow b \uparrow c + d$

    (v) $- c \times - d \uparrow e$ (vi) $a - - + b - - - c$

10. Given the declarations

> **int** $a = 12, b = 3, c = 4$

state the (a priori) modes and values of

    (i) $a/c/b$ (ii) $a/b \times c$

   (iii) $- b \uparrow c$ (iv) $81 - b \uparrow c$

    (v) $b \div c$ (vi) $- b \uparrow 2 \div c$

11. Given the declarations

> **int** $m := - 11, n := 7, p := 3$

what would be the values referred to be each of m, n and p after the following (do not consider the cumulative effect, only the effect of each formula considered separately)?

(i) $m + := n \ \mathbf{modab} \ p$

(ii) $m \times := p + := n$

(iii) $m + := (n \div \times := p)$

12. Assuming a strong syntactic position, how would one perform mode changes between objects of the following modes (state any restrictions, where necessary)?

(i) from **bool** to **real**

(ii) from **char** to **real**

(iii) from **real** to **char**

(iv) from **int** to **real**

(v) from **bool** to **char**

13. Assume the declaration

   int $n := 5$

Which of the following are illegal or undefined?

(i) $n + := n + := n$ (ii) $n + := (n + := n)$

(iii) $(n + := n) + n$ (iv) $n + n + := n$

In the formulae which are legal, what happens to the integer value referred to by n?

14. Given the declarations

   int $m, n,$ **real** x, y

which of the following are legal? Where appropriate indicate the necessary coercions.

(i) $(m \ \mathbf{modab} \ n) + := 2$ (ii) **round** x

(iii) **round** n (iv) **odd** $m + := 1$

(v) $x := \mathbf{entier} \ x$ (vi) **round entier** $- x$

(vii) $y + := \mathbf{entier} \ x$ (viii) **entier** $x + := y$

(ix) $m + := 2 + := 4$ (x) $x + := (n + := 2)$

15. What is the implied bracketing in the expression

   $x + 4 < y + z = a/b < 2 \ \mathbf{or} \ a < b \ \mathbf{and} \ x < y$?

16. In some of the examples given below coercions are applied to fulfil the mode conditions. In other cases coercions cannot be applied. Indicate the category to which each example belongs. Where coercions can be applied give the details. The a priori modes are determined by the declarations

   int $m, n,$ **real** x, y

(i) $m := n \times (n + 1)/2$
(ii) $m := n + m \uparrow 2$
(iii) $x := n + m \uparrow 2$
(iv) $m := (x := n) \uparrow 2 + 4$
(v) $x := y := n := 2$
(vi) $x := n := y := 2$

17. Assume m and n are of mode **int**. Write a boolean expression which delivers the value **true** only if m is a divisor of n (assume $m \neq 0$).

18. State the a priori mode, a posteriori mode and strength of the syntactic position of n and x in each of the following constructions. Assume the declarations

    int n, **real** x, y

    (i) $y := n + x$
    (ii) **real** $y = n$
    (iii) $x := -n$
    (iv) $x := (y := x) \uparrow n$

19. Some of the following assignations are meaningless in the sense that their result is undefined. Indicate such assignations giving reasons for your answer. Assume x and y are real variables.

    (i) $y := (x := 4) \uparrow 2 + x$
    (ii) $x := x + 10$
    (iii) $y := (x := 4) \uparrow 2 + (x := 6) \uparrow 3$

20. A particular assignation may contain several other (smaller) assignations. Is it true to say that an assignation is not meaningless in the sense described by the previous example provided that both
    (i) no variable appears as the destination in more than one assignation;
    (ii) a variable appearing as destination does not appear elsewhere in the formula other than in the source of the assignation of which it is the destination?

21. What does the following piece of program do to the integer which is supplied as data?

    begin int s, r, m; $read(m)$;
        $r := m + := m$; $s := r + r$; $m := s + := s + r$;
        $print(m)$
    end

22. Is

> **int** $a := b := 0$

an acceptable declaration of both a and b ?

23. Is the following argument acceptable? Give reasons for your answer.

'The declaration

> **char** $opbr = ''('', clbr = '')''$

introduces two identifiers *opbr* and *clbr*. After these declarations *opbr* and *clbr* can be used wherever (and) are used respectively. Hence one can now write statements such as

> *print opbr opbr "result is", pi clbr clbr*'

Programming problems for chapter 2

Miscellaneous

1. Write a program to read three real numbers and print their sum.

2. If r denotes the radius of a sphere the surface area and volume of that sphere are given by $4\pi r^2$ and $\frac{4}{3}\pi r^3$ respectively. Write a program to read r and print out the surface area and the volume of the sphere with this radius.

3. Write a program which accepts data of the form

$$2x + 3y = 5 \qquad 7x + 10y = 17$$

and prints out the solution of these simultaneous equations. Assume if necessary that the equations do have a unique solution.

Symbolic integration and differentiation

4. Write a program to integrate with respect to the first variable expressions of the form $x \uparrow n$ where n is integral and $n > 0$ or $n \leq -2$.

5. Integrate and differentiate by program expressions of the form

> $x \uparrow (a/b)$

making such assumptions as
 (i) a and b are integers and $b \geq 1$
 (ii) $a \neq 0$ and a/b is a fraction in its simplest form.

Storage media and communications

For the purpose of comparison with printed matter in books assume that, on average, there are 5 characters to a printed word, 12 words to a line, and 45 lines to a page.

6. A disc has these characteristics:

    number of cylinders = 404;

    number of tracks per cylinder = 19;

    maximum data capacity per track = 13030 characters;

    character transfer rate = 806000 characters per second.

    Write a program which uses suitable data and calculates:

    (i) the capacity of the entire disc;

    (ii) the number of 200-page books whose information can be held on the disc; and

    (iii) the number of pages of information that can be transferred per second.

7. A magnetic tape unit makes use of reels of tape with the following characteristics:

    length of tape is 2400 feet;

    number of characters per inch of tape is 1511;

    when reading or writing the tape moves at a speed of 112.5 inches per second.

    Write programs to calculate:

    (i) the number of 200-page books whose information can be held on such a reel of tape;

    (ii) the number of characters that can be written to the tape in a second;

    (iii) the total time taken to read the entire tape;

    (iv) the time taken to write to the tape as much information as would be held in a single 200-page book.

    Note: in practice the tape is stopped and started at areas where there is no data. These are called inter-block gaps. Ignore this and calculate the theoretical capacity.

8. In modern high-speed computers the average time taken to execute individual machine code instructions is often measured in nanoseconds (1 nanosecond = 10^{-9} second). To gain some feeling for the nanosecond write a program to calculate in inches the distance travelled by light in one nanosecond. The speed of light is approximately 186 000 miles per second.

3
CLAUSES

If one considers a parallel between learning a foreign language such as French or German and learning ALGOL 68 then chapter 2 would correspond to learning vocabulary and the use of verbs. Chapter 3 corresponds to the formation of sentences and paragraphs.

By the end of this chapter it should be possible to write fairly sophisticated programs and to make much more use of the power of the computer.

3.1. Environments

One can think of programs being executed in a particular environment. In that environment certain information is known and the meaning of certain identifiers is understood. This includes information about *pi* including its value and its mode, the procedures *read*, *whole*, etc., the meaning of operators such as $+$, $-$, $+:=$, **round**, etc. including their priorities. This basic information is called the *standard environment*.

Besides information of the above nature there is available in the standard environment information of a different kind. When studying integer denotations, etc., it was remarked that only integers or reals of a certain magnitude, and in the case of reals only a certain limited degree of accuracy, could be handled by any particular implementation. Information about these magnitudes is contained in the standard environment in the form of constant identity declarations.

For integers the predeclared identifier *max int* is of mode **int** and gives the largest integer that can be manipulated.

Real numbers require two identifiers to take care of both the magnitude and degree of accuracy to which reals are held. The identifier *max real* gives the largest real number and is of mode **real**. The identifier *small real*, also of mode **real**, is the smallest positive real number such that when added to 1 the computer can tell that

$$1 + small\ real > 1$$

and when subtracted from 1 the computer can tell that

$$1 - small\ real < 1$$

Thus if real numbers are held to about 11 decimal places of accuracy then *small real* would be approximately 10^{-11}.

When studying characters it was pointed out that **abs** will produce an integer from a character. The predeclared identifier *max abs char* will give the largest integral equivalent of any of the characters. Thus if an implementation allows 64 characters and **abs** converts these to integers between 0 and 63 included then *max abs char* will have the value 63. The mode associated with this identifier is **int**.

Closely related to these identifiers is another set of identifiers which are introduced primarily for transput. These give the number of character positions required for the default printing of an integer or real.

The identifier *int width* gives the number of character positions required for the printing of the largest integer, *max int*, excluding both the sign and any initial spaces.

The identifier *real width* of mode **int** is the smallest positive integral value such that the printing, using *print*, correct to (*real width* − 1) places after the decimal point of 1 and 1 + *small real* result in the production of different strings of characters. (Note that there is a single figure before the decimal point and this accounts for the subtraction of 1 from *real width*.)

The identifier *exp width*, also of mode **int**, gives the number of character positions required for the printing of the exponent part of the largest real number. The sign and the times-ten-to-the-power-symbol are excluded.

This brief discussion should give some feeling for the idea of an environment and the kind of information contained therein. But one should not think of an environment as being something which is fixed. The declarations in a program serve to augment the standard environment. If there is the declaration

real $e = 2.718$

at the start of a program then the remaining actions demanded by the program are executed within an environment which is the standard environment augmented with the information that the identifier e is of mode **real** and has ascribed to it the value 2.718.

By introducing declarations the programmer is therefore able to alter the environment in which his instructions are executed. He can add to the environment information about constants and variables. Later it will be seen that he can also add his own operators, procedures and even his own modes provided that he keeps to certain rules.

3.2. Unitary clauses

Unitary clauses, or 'units' as they are also called, are constructions of a certain kind. As the name suggests they are rather fundamental and indeed form the basis for the building of more complex constructions.

Single statements, ignoring declarations, are examples of unitary clauses. Thus referring back to example 1.3a

$$circum := 2 \times pi \times e$$

is a unit. The print statement contained in that example is a unit.

Constructions appearing in other positions are also units. For example, the parameter in a print statement, the source of an assignation, the right hand side of the becomes symbol in a variable or identity declaration and the right hand side of the equals symbol in an identity declaration are all units.

From this description the reader may quite correctly have deduced that a particular construction such as, say,

$$x := a + b$$

assuming suitable declarations of x, a and b, becomes a unit not through any merit of its own but by means of the position it occupies within a program. If it appeared in a program looking like

$$\ldots ; x := a + b; \ldots$$

then it would indeed be a unit since it is a simple statement and simple statements are units. However if it appeared in

$$\ldots ; y := x := a + b \times 4; \ldots$$

it would not be classified as a unit since $x := a + b$ does not occupy any of the positions mentioned earlier.

This discussion of unitary clauses can now be twisted another way and this will give some insight into the way in which more sophisticated programs can be written. If one is told that in a particular construction a unit can appear in a particular position then one can place any unitary clause there. In some cases modes may come into the picture. If n is of mode **ref int** and n appeared as the destination in an assignation then the source of that assignation would have to be a unit delivering a result of (a posteriori) mode **int**. But any unit with this property would be acceptable as the source. In the rest of this study of ALGOL 68, if a particular construct is classified as a unit then such constructs can appear in any of the positions in which units are allowed, mode conditions permitting.

It may help the reader to note at this stage that there is a close connection between clauses as used in the English language and clauses as used in programming languages.

Usually one associates with all units a particular mode and a particular value. With units appearing in assignations, declarations, etc. the mode and value are obvious. But other examples of units do not deliver a value in the usual way. Included in this category are the read and print statements. In such cases it is customary to say that the mode associated with these is **void**, and there is only one value of mode **void**. It can now be stated that all units have associated with them a particular value of a particular (a priori) mode.

Example 3.2a. Unitary clauses.

(i) Assuming suitable declarations, each of the following could be units

$$6 \times (c + d), y := x := 2, read\ (r)$$

(ii) Consider the declarations
real $x = unit\ 1$;
real $y := unit\ 2$;
ref real $z = $ **loc real** $:= unit\ 3$

Here $unit\ 1$, $unit\ 2$ and $unit\ 3$ are all unitary clauses. Note also that

loc real $:= unit\ 3$

is a unitary clause since it appears to the right of an equals symbol in an identity declaration.

3.3. Serial clauses

If the **begin** and **end** are removed from each program in examples 1.3a to 1.3c the resulting constructions are all examples of serial clauses. More formally, a serial clause is built from declarations and unitary clauses. These phrases – the declarations and units are each examples of phrases – are separated from each other by means of the go-on-symbol, i.e. the semi-colon. It will be seen later that there are restrictions on the relative positions of declarations and units.

Drawing a parallel with the approach adopted for unitary clauses, a sequence of declarations and units becomes a serial clause by dint of its position within a program. But in all cases, wherever a serial clause is allowed to appear, one can put any construction containing declarations and unitary clauses provided restrictions such as the relative position of declarations and units are satisfied (see later in this section).

To illustrate the concepts of serial clause and unitary clause consider example 1.3a. Removing the **begin** and **end** leaves a serial clause. This serial clause is built from

real $e = 2.7182818284$	which is a declaration;
real *circum*	also a declaration;
circum $:= 2 \times pi \times e$	which is a unit with a value *circum* of a priori mode **ref real**;

print (("*circumference* . . .", *circum*)) a unit of mode **void**.

The last phrase of a serial clause must always be a unit. Each serial clause must therefore contain a unit but may or may not contain declarations. In the degenerate case a single unit can constitute a serial clause. If a serial clause does contain declarations these should (at least for present purposes) precede the use of the corresponding identifiers in units or in other declarations.

3.3.1. Value associated with a serial clause
Since the last phrase of a serial clause must always be a unit it is possible to associate with a serial clause a value and a mode. The value and mode are just inherited from the last unit.

Example 3.3.1a. Value associated with a serial clause.
In each of the examples below it is assumed that all declarations have been made and that all mode requirements, etc. are satisfied.
  (i) Suppose x is of mode **ref real** and

$$\textbf{int } n = 4; \; x := y + z; \; print \; (x); \; 6.2$$

is a serial clause. The value associated with this is 6.2 and the mode is **real**.
  (ii) Suppose x has mode **ref real** and

$$read \; (a); \; x := a + b$$

is a serial clause. The value associated with this serial clause is just the value associated with the unit $x := a + b$. It is therefore x of mode **ref real**.

3.3.2. Voiding
In some of the examples of serial clauses there are unitary clauses with an associated value and conveniently this value seems to have been ignored. In example 3.3.1a (i) for instance the assignation

$$x := y + z$$

57

has an associated value of mode **ref real**. What happens to this value? One wishes to treat this assignation as a statement similar to read and print statements. But read and print statements have an associated mode **void**. Formally, the mode **ref real** delivered by the assignation will be converted to mode **void** and this will be achieved by means of coercions.

Each unitary clause in a serial clause (apart from the last, which will be considered later) is in a strong syntactic position. There is available in strong positions only (not in firm, weak, meek or soft positions) a coercion called *voiding* which converts the mode of an object to **void**. It thus effectively turns an expression into a statement. After a unit has been voided, no other coercion can be applied to that unit.

Example 3.3.2a. Voiding.
See example 3.3.1a(i). The phrase $x := y + z$ has an associated value of mode **ref real**. The value is just x. But the assignation occupies a strong syntactic position since it is a unit but not the last unit in a serial clause. Hence voiding can take place and the assignation is treated as a statement. The phrase $print(x)$ is already a statement.

In summary, a statement is a unit appearing in a strong syntactic position in which the a posteriori mode is **void**.

3.4. Closed clauses

A closed clause is merely a serial clause enclosed by means of **begin** and **end** or (and). Closed clauses can appear wherever unitary clauses can appear. These brief remarks will extend considerably the shape and nature of the programs that can be written in ALGOL 68. Closed clauses are used to construct units from serial clauses.

Example 3.4a. Closed clauses.
(i) Each of the programs in examples 1.3a to 1.3c is a closed clause.
(ii) In the program in example 1.3c the clauses $(n + 1)$ and $(2 \times n + 1)$ appear in the expression $n \times (n + 1) \times (2 \times n + 1)$. Each is a closed clause whose constituent serial clause consists of a single unitary clause.

3.4.1. Value associated with a closed clause
Example 3.4a(ii) above demonstrates one of the main uses of closed clauses; overriding the priority of operators in formulae. In such

cases there is, naturally enough, a value associated with the closed clause, namely the value of the expression within the brackets. In general one associates a value with a closed clause, the value being that of the enclosed serial clause. This has far-reaching effects as will be demonstrated.

First, however, consider where a closed clause can appear in a program. Apart from its use as an operand a closed clause can appear in almost the same positions as a variable or a constant. Thus it can appear as the source in an assignation or as an actual parameter in a print statement. In fact, if it yields a result of the required mode a closed clause can even appear as the destination in an assignation or as an actual parameter in a read statement.

Example 3.4.1a. On the use of closed clauses.

(i) Consider the assignation

$$x := (\textbf{int } n; read(n); n + 1)\uparrow 2 + 1.6$$

where x has mode **ref real**. In this case the value of the closed clause is just the value delivered by $n + 1$.

(ii) Consider the rather artificial assignation

$$(read(n); sum +:= n; x) := y + pi$$

where x and y have mode **ref real** and n has mode **ref int**. The value delivered by the closed clause is just x and has mode **ref real**.

The introduction of closed clauses adds a further dimension to the concept of an operand and an assignation. Starting from fairly humble beginnings it has been possible to extend these concepts almost beyond recognition. Most of the extensions have resulted from associating a value with an object. For instance, values have been associated with assignations, serial clauses and now closed clauses. A second remark to be made as a result of example 3.4.1a concerns the problem of collateral evaluation – the following sets of items will be elaborated collaterally: operands, the various elements in the data list of a read or print statement and the sources and destinations of assignations. Since closed clauses can now be very complex the problem of avoiding constructions whose effect is undefined is substantially increased.

3.4.2. Closed clauses and coercions

Since a closed clause can appear as, for example, an operand in a formula or as the source in an assignation it follows that it may become necessary to perform coercions of some kind. But it is very important to realise the relative order of two events that have then to take place. The two events are: performing the necessary coercion; and delivering the result from the closed clause. The relative order is as stated above, i.e. the coercions are performed and then the result is delivered. Viewed another way the coercions actually apply to the last unit of the enclosed serial clause. They therefore move inside the brackets. If one imagines that there is an operator **coerce** which performs all the necessary coercions then it would not act as

coerce (. . . ; *final unit*)

but rather as

(. . . ; **coerce** *final unit*)

Of course, one cannot apply just any coercion. The allowable coercions depend on the syntactic position of the closed clause together with the a priori mode and a posteriori mode of the result delivered by the closed clause. In effect then the strength of the syntactic position together with any coercions pass inside the final closing bracket to the last unit of the enclosed serial clause.

Example 3.4.2a. Closed clauses and coercions.
Consider

real $x = ($**int** $n; read(n); sum +:= n; n)$

The closed clause here occupies a strong syntactic position since it is on the right hand side of the equals symbol. The final unit n is de-referenced and widened and an appropriate real number delivered as the result of the closed clause.

A partial answer can now be given to a question left unanswered during the discussion of serial clauses. This is related to the strength of the syntactic position of the last unit of a serial clause. Whenever a serial clause appears as part of a closed clause the strength of the position of the last unit is inherited from the strength of the position of the closed clause itself.

3.5. Ranges and reaches

It has been pointed out that identity and variable declarations serve to introduce identifiers and in some sense give them a value. In the case of variable declarations space is made available and the identifier becomes a means of accessing the location. Basically declarations serve to augment in some way the standard environment.

60

But at certain stages of the execution of a program the programmer can arrange that identifiers and the space they may require become inaccessible. The effect is then to have the program's store requirements expanding and contracting within the computer. This section is concerned with examining the availability and accessibility of space.

The programs written so far have all been closed clauses. The constituent parts of a closed clause are declarations and unitary clauses. Now it could happen that some of these unitary clauses are in turn closed clauses; a closed clause is a perfectly good example of a unitary clause. Such a closed clause is again a serial clause enclosed by **begin** and **end** or (and). This serial clause, if it exists, will contain other units and, possibly, other declarations. These units might be closed clauses; and so the argument continues.

Example 3.5a. A skeleton program.
Using the above argument, a program may have a structure whose skeleton is indicated below. The declarations are written explicitly but units have been represented by horizontal lines.

begin real $e = 2.718$;	# **begin** 1 #
———	
———	
———	
begin real x, y; **int** n;	# **begin** 2 #
———	
———	
———	
end;	# **end** 2 #
———	
begin ———	# **begin** 3 #
———	
begin bool $t = $ **true**;	# **begin** 4 #
———	
———	
end;	# **end** 4 #
———	
———	
end	# **end** 3 #
end	# **end** 1 #

The various **begin**–**end** pairs match and their association is indicated by the numbering in the comments to the right. Thus the first

begin, labelled in the comment $\#$ **begin** $1\#$, and the last **end** match since they delimit the closed clause which forms the program. Similarly the fourth **begin** and the **end** labelled in $\#$ **end** $4\#$ match. The serial clause bracketed by **begin** number 3 and **end** number 3 consists of unitary clauses only. This is quite permissible.

In order to understand the later discussion it is necessary to introduce two definitions:

a *range* is a serial clause;

a *reach* is a range with the exclusion of all its constituent ranges. (With the introduction of more advanced features of ALGOL 68 this definition of range will have to be modified.)

Example 3.5b. On ranges and reaches.
In the program below the various ranges and reaches are depicted. R1, R2 and R3 denote ranges, r1, r2, and r3 reaches.

```
begin
      int n = (                        }r1
            int r; read (r); r         }r2, R2
      );                               } r1
      real result = n × (             } r1
            n + 1                      }r3, R3
            )/2;                       } r1
      print (("result is", result))
end
```

(the above bracketed on the right by R1)

For the purpose of the following discussion it will be convenient to think of the declarations that form the standard environment as being present within a closed clause which contains a particular program as a unit. These declarations come before the user's program. This gives the following skeleton:

```
begin # the declarations forming the standard environment
        appear between the end of this commentary and the
        begin which starts the program to be executed
   #  .
        .
        .
   # particular program to be run now follows #
   begin
        .
        .
        .
   end
```

62

this ends the particular program being run; other phrases may come before the final **end**

.

.

.

end

Returning now to the original problem observe again that in a variable or identity declaration an identifier is introduced and after the elaboration, i.e. execution, of this declaration the identifier is associated with a specific value and a specific mode. In the usual way the environment is augmented.

Identifiers so introduced retain their meaning and identity throughout the statements that constitute the smallest range enclosing that declaration. Having left a particular range no use can be made of identifiers declared within that range. Moreover if a local generator generates space for a variable as a result of a declaration this space will no longer be available on leaving that range. Thus terminating a particular serial clause is one way of relinquishing space obtained by invoking a local generator. It is local to that serial clause. Hence the use of the term 'local' and the abbreviation **loc**.

This situation is usually described formally in terms of the concept of scope. Each value manipulated by an ALGOL 68 program has a scope and this is the largest serial clause throughout which that value will still exist. The scope of a name introduced by a declaration and created by a local generator is therefore the smallest enclosing range.

The subject of scopes of values will be revisited in chapter 7 and the ideas extended.

Example 3.5c. Scopes and availability of identifiers.
Consider the skeleton program in example 3.5a and assume that no other declarations are present.

(i) *e* is available throughout the entire program.

(ii) *x*, *y* and *n* are available only between **begin** number 2 and **end** number 2. On leaving this range all the space generated by these declarations is relinquished. The scope of these names is just this range.

(iii) *t* is available only between **begin** number 4 and **end** number 4.

There are some examples which require further clarification. In the skeleton program below the various ranges and reaches are labelled, using digits and letters respectively, in comments.

63

begin # start of range 1 and reach A #
   int m, p, r;
   .
   .
   .

   begin # start of range 2. reach A ends here but starts
            again later in the program #
       real $r = 3$; **int** m;
       .
       .
       .

       # end of range 2. reach A restarts #
   end;
   .
   .
   .

   # end of range 1 and reach A #
end

Further explanation is required since m and r have been declared within different ranges, one range being nested within the other. Nothing has been said so far to exclude this possibility. Indeed it is perfectly permissible (but see example 2.3d).

Within range 2, m and r will have the meanings demanded by the declarations of m and r in that range. Since the declaration of m involves the use of a local generator, the space used for m is different from the space required by the m declared at the start of range 1. The space created at the start of range 1 still exists throughout the time that the actions in range 2 are being executed (the space is not relinquished until the end of range 1). This space, however, cannot be accessed by means of the identifier m. The m declared at the start of range 1 is accessible, using identifier m, only in reach A.

In the case of identifier r the story is similar. If used within range 2 it will identify the real constant 3. The space generated for the integer variable r declared at the start of range 1 cannot be accessed within range 2 using r. In reach A r will always identify this integer variable and not the real constant.

Example 3.5d. On the availability and accessibility of space. Consider the program

   begin int $m := 3$; **int** *five* $= 5$;
      print $((m, five))$; # first print statement #
      begin int $m := 100$; **char** *five* $= "5"$;
         print $((m, five))$; # second print statement #
         $m +:= 1$
      end;

print ((m, five)) # third print statement #

end

Ignoring spaces, initial signs, etc. produced on printing, the three print statements cause the printing of the integers 3 and 5, the integer 100 and the character 5 and finally the integers 3 and 5. Thus the statement following the second print statement adds 1 to the variable in the inner range, not the variable declared at the start of the program.

3.5.1. 'Equivalence' in ALGOL 68

Suppose that x is of mode **ref real** and consider the identity declaration

ref real $y = x$

Like any other identity declaration, such as **int** $n = 4$, this serves to introduce y and associate with it the mode **ref real**. This results in x, which of mode **ref real**, being ascribed to y. The effect of this declaration is then to have x and y as different identifiers for the same variable and accessing the same space which was generated at the time x was declared. (This facility in other programming languages such as FORTRAN is called 'equivalence'.) Both $x := 7$ and $y := 7$ have the same effect.

Example 3.5.1a. Equivalence.

Consider the program

```
begin int m := 3; ref int p = m;
    print ((m,p));    # first print statement #
    begin int m := 100;
        print ((m,p));    # second print statement #
        m -:= 1; p +:= 1
    end;
    print ((m,p)) # third print statement #
end
```

The first print statement causes the integers 3 and 3 to be printed; the second causes 100 and 3 to be printed and the third causes 4 and 4 to appear. Within the inner range the space generated for the m declared in the outer range is not accessible by means of the identifier m. However it still exists and is accessible using the identifier p.

Note that there is an analogous situation in the day-to-day use of words in the English language. In branches of science terms are defined (their definition corresponds to the ALGOL 68 declaration) and within a particular environment they have the meaning given by this definition. In another environment the words might have some entirely different meaning.

3.5.2. Defining and applied occurrences

A better understanding of what has been described so far in this
section may be obtained by considering the process that the compiler
goes through in determining which declarations are to be used in
different parts of a program. This process will show that there is
one rule to cover all the cases already discussed.

In order to do this consider where identifiers occur in programs.
They may occur as the identifier being defined in declarations. These
occurrences are said to be *defining occurrences* of the identifier.
Other occurrences are said to be *applied occurrences*.

Example 3.5.2a. Defining occurrences and applied occurrences.
Consider the program

> **begin int** n; **int** *ten* $= 10$;
> $\quad n := (\textbf{int } r; \; read \, (r); \; r) + ten$;
> $\quad print \, (n)$
> **end**

and all occurrences of the identifiers r and *print*. Consider first the
identifier r: **int** r contains a defining occurrence of r; *read* (r) contains
an applied occurrence of r; and r is an applied occurrence of r. The
statement *print* (n) contains an applied occurrence of *print*.

A problem that the compiler has to solve is that of relating each
applied occurrence of an identifier to the appropriate defining
occurrence of that identifier. To do this the following algorithm is
applied.

Step 1. Start at the particular applied occurrence and call it A.

Step 2. Look for a defining occurrence of this identifier in the
current reach. If it is found call it B. A is then related to the
defining occurrence B. Stop.

Step 3. If no defining occurrence is found consider the reach which is
immediately outside the reach that has just been searched
and go to step 2. If there is no such reach the identifier has
not been declared. Stop.

The algorithm amounts to a search out through successive reaches
nested within each other.

3.5.3. Results delivered by closed clauses

To return to the questions of availability and accessibility consider the declaration

> **int** $n = ($**co** start of range 1 **co**
> **int** r; *read* (r); r
> **co** end of range 1 **co**$)$

The declaration of r implies that this r exists and its space is available only within range 1. A question that arises is: does the space disappear before the value referred to by r is delivered, does it disappear after the value is delivered or is the order of the two events undefined (e.g. due to collateral elaboration)?

Consider, in detail, what happens. The coercions do not apply to the closed clause but instead they move inside the brackets and apply to the last unit of the enclosed serial clause. Thus the final unit, i.e. r, is dereferenced. The result delivered is the value referred to by r, not r itself. The sequence of events is: the value referred to by r is delivered and then the space associated with the variable r is relinquished. Consequently the above declaration is satisfactory and does as was intended.

On the other hand consider the (supposed) declaration

> **real** $x = ($**real** r; *read* (r); $r)$ **divab** n

where n is of mode **int**. The closed clause (**real** r; *read* (r); r) must deliver a result of mode **ref real** since this is the mode required by the left hand operand of **divab**. No coercions therefore act on r. The actions that would take place would therefore be as follows: the result delivered by the closed clause is of mode **ref real** (and is just r), the space required by r is relinquished and then an attempt is made to reference the space as a result of the action of **divab**. This causes trouble and should give an error.

This section has dealt with the problem of describing when identifiers can be used and when space introduced by local generators is relinquished. It follows that sensible use of closed clauses can result in less demands in terms of the space used by programs.

3.6. Collateral phrases

In previous sections it has been mentioned that certain items within a program, e.g. the operands in a formula, are elaborated collaterally. In this section the possibility of performing the collateral elaboration of several statements or several declarations is investigated.

3.6.1. Void-collateral-clauses

It sometimes happens that certain statements within a program can be elaborated collaterally. To take a simple illustration consider the problem of differentiating an expression of the form ax^b with respect to x. The result is px^q where $p = a \times b$ and $q = b - 1$. In writing a program to perform this it does not matter whether p is evaluated before q, whether q is evaluated before p or indeed whether p and q are evaluated at the same time. This being the case it is convenient to have a method of telling the compiler that it can have these statements executed in whatever order it chooses. If the machine is sufficiently powerful it may decide to perform some of the statements at the same time. The time taken to run the program may therefore be reduced, perhaps considerably. On the other hand careless use of this facility can result in programs whose effects are undefined.

Collateral elaboration of statements can be performed by means of a construction known as a *void-collateral-clause*. This takes the form of a sequence of units enclosed by **begin** and **end** or (and) and separated from each other by commas. As the name suggests the mode associated with such a clause is **void**.

To illustrate the concept consider the void-collateral-clause

$$((\textbf{int } n; read(n); m := n), z := x \uparrow 10 + 7 \times y)$$

This collateral consists of two unitary clauses namely

$$(\textbf{int } n; read(n); m := n)$$

and the assignation

$$z := x \uparrow 10 + 7 \times y$$

These two units are elaborated collaterally. Note that the use of n is restricted to the closed clause which constitutes the first unit of this pair.

Example 3.6.1a. Void-collateral-clauses.
Assuming suitable declarations of the identifiers

$$(a := b, ((c1 := d1; b1 := e1), (c2 := d2; b2 := e2)),$$
$$print(b))$$

is an acceptable void-collateral-clause. Note that it contains another void-collateral-clause, namely

$$((c1 := d1; b1 := e1), (c2 := d2; b2 := e2))$$

and this in turn contains two other closed clauses in which the relative order of the assignations is defined by means of a semi-colon. Thus one can say that $c1 := d1$ is performed before $b1 := e1$ but one can say nothing about the relative order of elaboration of $c1 := d1$ and $b2 := e2$. The relative order in which the various statements are performed can be conveniently depicted in diagram 3.1.

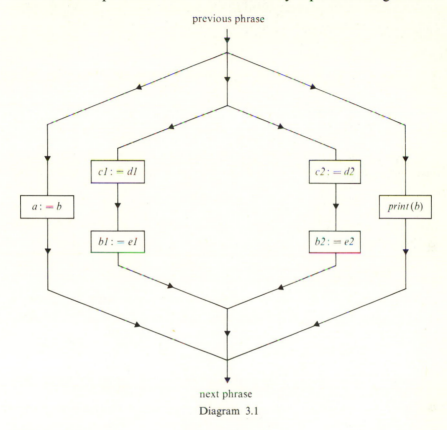

Diagram 3.1

The elaboration of a void-collateral-clause is terminated only when all the different constituent units have been elaborated. Only when these have all been completed is the elaboration of the void-collateral-clause complete and only then is the next statement performed.

The form of these collateral clauses tends to suggest that a comma indicates collateral elaboration whereas a semi-colon indicates serial elaboration. This is in fact the case and this distinction is used in several places in ALGOL 68 programs. Apart from void-collateral-clauses the various items of print or read statements are separated by commas indicating the collateral elaboration of the various items in the data lists.

3.6.2. Collateral declarations.

Declarations such as

$$\textbf{real } x, y, z$$

have already been discussed. The commas indicate that the various generators are invoked collaterally. Consider however

$$\textbf{real } x, y, z; \textbf{int } n$$

The semi-colon implies that the space for n is generated after the space for x, y and z has been generated. This restriction is unnecessary and the semi-colon could and should be replaced by a comma. When this is done the declarations can be elaborated collaterally and the space for x, y, z and n could be generated at the one time.

However, as with all collateral elaboration one should take special care that some undefined element does not appear. In the declaration

$$\textbf{int } n := 4, m := n$$

there is no guarantee that, after this has been elaborated, m will refer to the value 4.

3.7. Loop clauses

By means of loop clauses it will be possible to exploit for the first time the power and speed of the computer. This new concept, another form of unit, is introduced by means of some examples.

3.7.1. Illustrative examples

Consider first a program to read 100 real numbers supplied as data and print the average of these numbers:

$$\textbf{begin real } x, sum := 0;$$
$$\textbf{to } 100 \textbf{ do } read\ (x); sum +:= x \textbf{ od};$$
$$print\ ((\textit{"average of } 100 \textit{ numbers is"}, sum/100))$$
$$\textbf{end}$$

All loop clauses contain **do** and **od** and deliver a result of mode **void**.

$$\textbf{to } 100 \textbf{ do } read\ (x); sum + := x \textbf{ od}$$

is an example of a loop clause. The effect of this statement is to repeat 100 times the statements in the serial clause between **do** and **od**. Thus

$$read(x); sum +:= x$$

is repeated 100 times. If successive numbers in the data are 2, 3, 5, 7, 11,

... then successive values of x are $2, 3, 5, 7, 11, \ldots$ Since the statement $sum + := x$ implies that the current value of x is added to an old value of sum to give a new value of sum the successive values of sum are $0, 2, 5, 10, 17, 28, \ldots$ Thus the total of the 100 numbers is gradually accumulated in the variable sum.

Consider now the similar problem of finding the average of a set of positive real numbers supplied as data. Assume that there is at least one positive number in the data and that the list of positive numbers is terminated by a negative number. A possible program is:

> **begin real** x, $sum := 0$, **int** $count := 0$;
>   **while** $read\,(x)$; $x > 0$
>   **do** $(sum + := x$, $count + := 1)$ **od**;
> $print\,(("average\ of\ the", count, "numbers\ is", sum/count))$
> **end**

Consider the loop clause

> **while** $read\,(x)$; $x > 0$ **do** $(sum + := x$, $count + := 1)$ **od**

The effect of this is to execute the serial clause between the **while** and the **do**. If the result delivered is **true** the serial clause enclosed by **do** and **od** is executed. In this case the clause between the **do** and the **od** consists of a void-collateral-clause since the relative order of elaboration of the two constituent units is irrelevant. On completion of the collateral clause the serial clause between the **while** and **do** is again executed and if the result is **true** the serial clause between **do** and **od** is again executed. This happens repeatedly. Only when the result delivered by $read\,(x)$; $x > 0$ is **false** will the elaboration of the loop clause terminate. The next statement in the program, in the above case the print statement, is then executed.

As another example take the problem of finding the sum of the fourth powers of the integers $1, 2, 3, \ldots, 20$:

> **begin int** $sum := 0$;
>   **for** i **to** 20 **do** $sum + := i \uparrow 4$ **od**;
> $print\,(("sum\ of\ the\ fourth\ powers\ of\ 1\ to\ 20\ is", sum))$
> **end**

The effect of the loop clause in this program is as follows. i is set to 1 and the serial clause between **do** and **od** is executed. In this case the serial clause consists of the single statement $sum + := i \uparrow 4$. Then i is increased by 1 and the statement is again executed. This happens repeatedly until i reaches the value 20. At that stage the statement is executed as usual and the loop clause is then terminated. The next statement in the program, here the print statement, is then executed.

Note that there is no declaration of *i*. The fact that *i* appears after the
for acts as its declaration and it has mode **int**.

As a final example in this introduction to loop clauses consider
the problem of finding the sum of the fourth powers of 3, 5, 7, 9, . . . ,
19:

>**begin int** *sum* := 0;
>
>　　　**for** *i* **from** 3 **by** 2 **to** 19 **do** *sum* + := *i*↑ 4 **od**;
>
>　　　*print* (("*sum of fourth powers of the odd digits between* 3
>　　　　　　　*and* 19 *inclusive is*", *sum*))
>
>**end**

The loop clause in this program has the following effect. *i* is set to 3
and the statement after the **do** is executed. *i* is then incremented by 2
and the statement is again executed. *i* is repeatedly incremented and
the statement repeatedly executed until *i* reaches 19. At this stage the
statement is executed once more and the elaboration of the loop
clause then terminated.

3.7.2. General form of loop clauses

It might appear from the previous examples that loop clauses come
in many shapes and forms. In fact there is only one general form,
namely

>**for** *a* **from** *b* **by** *c* **to** *d* **while** *e* **do** *f* **od**

a is an identifier and its appearance after **for** acts as a declaration.
This identifier, often called the control integer, has mode **int**. *a* can
be accessed only within *e* and *f* and, since it is of mode **int**, cannot be
altered in either place. Now **for** *a* can be and should be omitted if
identifier *a* is not used in the remainder of the loop clause.

b is a unitary clause delivering an integer. The integer can be
negative, zero or positive but *b* will be evaluated once and once only.
This evaluation takes place before the first evaluation of the clause
to be executed repeatedly. The part **from** *b* can be omitted. If it is
omitted a value of 1 is assumed for *b*.

c is a unitary clause delivering an integer. Again *c* is evaluated
only once. The part **by** *c* can be omitted and in this case *c* is taken
to be 1.

d is a unitary clause delivering an integer. *d* is evaluated only once.
to *d* can be omitted and in this case *d* is taken to be plus infinity.

e is, at least for present purposes, a serial clause delivering a result
of mode **bool**. *e* is evaluated before each evaluation of the repeated
clause *f*. The first time *e* delivers the result **false** the execution of the

loop clause is terminated. (To be precise e is an enquiry clause. See later for a full explanation.) **while** e can be omitted and in this case e is assumed to have the value **true**.

f is a serial clause which is executed repeatedly. This, together with **do** and **od**, cannot be omitted.

The effect of the loop clause can be described as follows. f is repeatedly executed but before each evaluation a test is made on a and the value delivered by e. If either a exceeds d (or, if c is negative, a is less than d) or e delivers **false** then f is not executed and elaboration of the loop clause is terminated. If the limit is exceeded e is not evaluated. After each evaluation of f, a is incremented by c.

Before e (and therefore f) is first evaluated each of b, c and d are elaborated collaterally. Since b, c and d are evaluated only once, changes to variables which might alter the result delivered by b, c and d can be made within e and f. These changes will not alter the number of times that f is executed. f occupies a strong syntactic position.

Example 3.7.2a. Loop clauses.

(i) The program

> **begin int** $p := 10$, $q := 12$;
>   **from** p **to** q **do** $print\ ((p+:=1, q+:=1))$ **od**
> **end**

will print the integers 11, 13, 12, 14, 13 and 15. The p and q occurring in **from** p and **to** q are evaluated once and once only.

(ii) The statement

> **do** f **od**

where f is some serial clause is legal. Everything which could be omitted from the general form of a loop clause has been omitted. This causes an infinite loop unless instructions are inserted within f to cause termination (see section 3.9 for such instructions).

(iii) If f denotes some serial clause the following is legal:

> **for** i **to** 100
> **do for** j **from** 2 **by** 2 **to** 100
>   **do** f **od**
> **od**

i is set to 1 and the loop clause

> **for** j **from** 2 **by** 2 **to** 100
> **do** f **od**

performed. Then i is set to 2 and this clause again performed. Continuing in this way the loop clause **for** j . . . is itself repeated 100 times.

Occasionally it seems necessary to perform a repetitive statement using increments which are not integral. This is not allowed directly and it is necessary therefore to find some method of overcoming the problem.

Example 3.7.2b. Non-integral increments.
Write a program to read from the standard input values for a, b and c. Then tabulate for $x = 0$, 0.1, 0.2, . . ., 1 the values of $ax^2 + bx + c$.
The first solution is:

```
begin real a, b, c, x; read ((a,b,c));
      print (("value of x   value of expression", new line));
      for i from 0 to 10
      do x := i/10;
         print ((x, a × x↑2 + b × x + c, new line))
      od
end
```

A second solution is obtained by initialising x and replacing the above loop clause by

```
while x < 1.05 do print ((x, a × x↑2 + b × x + c, new line));
                 x +:= 0.1
      od
```

In the second solution note the use of 1.05 in testing if x has reached its upper limit. The reason for this lies in the fact that reals are not, usually, held accurately in a computer and the addition of 0.05 to the upper limit takes care of inaccuracies in x.

3.7.3. Use of 'skip'
In the discussion on the general form of a loop clause in section 3.7.2 it was mentioned that the serial clause f must be present. But it can happen that it would be convenient to omit it.

The problem can be resolved by using **skip**. **skip** can be used only in syntactically strong positions and it delivers some undefined value of the required mode whatever it may be. In many cases **skip** is used as a dummy statement, that is, it appears as a unit in a serial clause and causes no significant action on the part of the computer.

Example 3.7.3a. Using **skip**.
Write a piece of program which, starting at the present position in

74

the standard input, reads until it receives the first non-blank character.

char *ch*; **while** *read* (*ch*); *ch* = " " **do skip od**

3.7.4. Ranges associated with loop clauses

In discussing the general form of a loop clause in section 3.7.2 it was mentioned that the appearance of an identifier following a **for** constituted a declaration of that identifier and associated with it the mode **int**. It follows that there are certain ranges associated with a loop clause and many relevant questions can be asked. For example, in

for *a* **from** *b* **by** *c* **to** *d* **while** *e* **do** *f* **od**

can *a* be used within the units *b*, *c*, *d*, *e* or *f*? Can declarations occur in *b*, *c*, *d*, *e* or *f*? If so what is the range associated with these? There are other questions concerning the strength of the syntactic position occupied by *b*, *c*, *d* and *e* (*f* occupies a strong position).

Most of these questions can be answered by appealing to knowledge already gained in previous sections. Thus identifiers declared within *b*, for instance, can be used only within *b*. Similarly for *c* and *d*. But there are some seemingly strange though useful rules:

the identifier *a* can be used within *e* or *f* (or both) but not within *b*, *c* or *d*;
any identifier declared in the serial clause *e* can be used also in *f* but not in *b*, *c* or *d*;
any identifier declared in *f* can be used only within *f*.

These ranges are shown in diagram 3.2. Declarations in each box are accessible only to the pieces of program inside the box and any inner boxes.

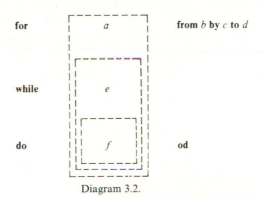

Diagram 3.2.

If the **for** or **while** part is absent the corresponding range is also absent.

Example 3.7.4a. Ranges associated with loop clauses.
(i) The following is an acceptable loop clause.

for i **while** $i \uparrow 3 + 3 \times i \uparrow 2 + 2 < 40$ **do** ... **od**

since the identifier i can be used within the **while** part of the clause.
(ii) The skeleton

while real $x; ...$ **do real** $x; ...$ **od**

is acceptable just as

begin real $x; ...$ **begin real** $x; ...$ **end end**

is acceptable. The scopes involved are similar.

Each of b, c, d and e occupies a meek syntactic position. These constitute the first examples of positions of this strength. For the moment the only relevant coercion that can be applied in these positions is dereferencing.

3.8. Choice clauses

Choice clauses allow the selection and execution of one of several possibilities depending on some condition. Since a special case of a serial clause is a single unit this serial clause might be just an expression, an assignation or even **skip**. To begin with, certain simplifying assumptions will be understood. The various alternative possibilities from which a choice has to be made will all deliver results of the same mode and this will be the mode required by the particular context; the mode may even be **void**. Thus there will be no coercions involving choice clauses.

Two forms of choice clause are considered here. In the first type, called conditional clauses, the choice depends on the value of a boolean. In the second type, called case clauses, the choice depends on the value of an integer.

3.8.1. Conditional clauses
if-then-else-fi will be the first type of conditional clause to be considered. Having studied this the introduction of the other kinds of conditional will be relatively straightforward.

Example 3.8.1a. Using **if-then-else-fi**.
max and *min* have mode **ref real** and x and y have mode **real**.
(i) *max* := **if** $x > y$ **then** x **else** y **fi**
If the boolean expression $x > y$ delivers the result **true** the value of x

is delivered and assigned to *max*; otherwise the value of *y* is assigned to *max*.

(ii) **if** $x > y$ **then** *max* **else** *min* **fi** $:= x$

If $x > y$ delivers **true**, *max* becomes the destination of this assignation; otherwise *min* is the destination.

(iii) **if** $x > y$ **then** (*max* $:= x$, *min* $:= y$) **else** (*max* $:= y$, *min* $:= x$) **fi**

If $x > y$ delivers **true** the collateral between **then** and **else** is elaborated; otherwise the collateral between **else** and **fi** is elaborated.

The general form of the **if-then-else-fi** form of conditional is

if *a* **then** *b* **else** *c* **fi**

a is, at least for the moment, a serial clause which delivers a result of mode **bool**; the syntactic position of *a* is meek and, of the coercions so far introduced, only dereferencing can be applied. *b* is a serial clause which is executed provided that *a* delivers that result **true**, whereas *c* is a serial clause which is executed provided *a* delivers the result **false**.

There is an alternative way of writing the **if-then-else-fi** form of conditional; namely,

$(a|b|c)$

This latter form, although more appropriate in expressions and formulae, can be used when the last units of *b* and *c* are either expressions or statements.

The next example illustrates the fact that conditionals can be used to validate, to some extent at least, the correctness of data supplied to a program. The testing of data can be tedious but in programs to be used repeatedly it is essential that such tests should take place.

Example 3.8.1b. Simple wages program.
This program accepts as data a non-negative integer *n* representing the number of hours a man works per week (assume $n < 100$) and a real number *rate* representing the number of pounds per hour the man is paid when working at his basic rate. It then prints out a man's wage assuming that for the first 50 hours a man is paid at his basic rate and for overtime he is paid at twice the basic rate.

```
begin int n, real rate; read ((n, rate));
    if n < 0 or n > 100 or rate < 0
    then print ("data invalid")
    else real wage = rate × (n > 50|2 × (n − 50) + 50|n);
        print (("for working", n, " hours at", rate,
                " pounds per hour the man's wage is", wage))
    fi
end
```

Conditionals can appear in the same kind of positions as constants, variables, etc. provided that they deliver objects of a suitable mode. Moreover, they constitute yet another example of a unitary clause and consequently they can appear wherever units can appear.

It often happens, especially when forming statements rather than expressions, that one would like the second alternative of an **if-then-else-fi** form of conditional to be **skip** as in **if** a **then** b **else skip fi**. **skip**, when considered as a statement, acts as a dummy statement and performs no significant action. This can be written as

if a **then** b **fi**

or in its abbreviated form as

$(a|b)$

In all respects this behaves like an **if-then-else-fi** form of conditional with the **skip** supplied in the **else** part.

Example 3.8.1c. Using **if-then-fi**.
If x, y and *max* have the same modes as in example 3.8.1a, the following is acceptable

$max := x$;
if $x < y$ **then** $max := y$ **fi**

Repeated use of the two forms of conditionals leads to such complicated constructions that an abbreviation is advisable. To introduce this an example is considered. Needless complication will be avoided by assuming that *sc1*, *sc2* and *sc3* denote suitable serial clauses and that *b1* and *b2* are clauses delivering results of mode **bool**. Suppose that it is required to write a conditional which does the following:

if *b1* delivers **true**, *sc1* is elaborated;
if *b1* delivers **false** and *b2* delivers **true** *sc2* is elaborated;
if *b1* and *b2* deliver **false** *sc3* is elaborated.

Using only the forms of conditional already introduced a possible conditional would be

```
if b1
    then sc1
    else if b2
            then sc2
            else sc3
            fi
    fi
```

The problem of matching the **ifs** and **fis** becomes rather tedious. To overcome this any construction of the general form

else if p **then** q **else** r **fi fi**

can be replaced by

elif p **then** q **else** r **fi**

Similarly any construction of the form

else if p **then** q **fi fi**

can be replaced by

elif p **then** q **fi**

Using only the first of these abbreviations the number of **ifs** and **fis** in the earlier example can be reduced to a single matching pair. That conditional could be written as

if $b1$ **then** $sc1$ **elif** $b2$ **then** $sc2$ **else** $sc3$ **fi**

Earlier a notation involving brackets and vertical bars was introduced as an alternative to **if-then-else-fi** and **if-then-fi**. A similar notation exists for conditional clauses involving **elif**. This together with the earlier notation can be summarised as follows.

(	replaces	**if**
)	replaces	**fi**
|	replaces	**then**
|	replaces	**else**
|:	replaces	**elif**

Using this notation the above conditional involving $b1$, $sc1$, etc. can be written as

$(b1|sc1|:b2|sc2|sc3)$

3.8.2. Case clauses

The other kind of choice clause to be considered here is the case clause. It often happens that one wishes to select one of several unitary clauses depending on the value of some integer. As with conditional clauses there are two forms of case clause.

The first form of case clause is

case $sc0$ **in** $uc1$, $uc2$, . . . , ucn **out** t **esac**

or, using the alternative notation for this first form,

$$(sc0 | uc1, uc2 \ldots, ucn | t)$$

Each of *uc1*, *uc2*, ..., *ucn* denotes a unitary clause, *t* denotes a serial clause and *n* should be at least 2. For the moment *sc0* can be regarded as a serial clause; it occupies a meek syntactic position and should deliver a result of mode **int**.

The effect of this case clause is to cause *sc0* to be elaborated. Suppose it delivers an integer *i*, say. If $i = 1, 2, \ldots, n$ then unitary clause *uci* is elaborated. Otherwise serial clause *t* is elaborated. Thus if *i* lies between 1 and *n* one of the listed unitary clauses is elaborated and if it is outside this range *t* is elaborated. One can think of the case clause producing an effect similar to the effect produced by

> (**int** $i = (sc0)$;
> **if** $i = 1$ **then** *uc1*
> **elif** $i = 2$ **then** *uc2*
>
> . . .
>
> **elif** $i = n$ **then** *ucn*
> **else** *t* **fi**)

However one should not carry this analogy too far. One should not assume for instance that all the tests on *i* are performed. The compiler should arrange that the case clause is executed efficiently.

The second form of case clause is similar to the above. The only difference is that the **out** *t* part is omitted. There is thus a similar relationship between the two forms of case clause as there is between the **if-then-else-fi** and **if-then-fi** forms of conditional. This form of case clause is, assuming $n > 2$,

> **case** *sc0* **in** *uc1*, *uc2*, *uc3*, ..., *ucn* **esac**

or, in the alternative notation,

> $(sc0 | uc1, uc2, uc3, \ldots, ucn)$

and these are equivalent to

> **case** *sc0* **in** *uc1*, *uc2*, ..., *ucn* **out skip esac**

Again *sc0* is in a meek position and delivers an integral result.

Case clauses can be used within expressions or statements in the same way as the conditional clauses considered earlier. Consequently case clauses themselves can appear as the final unit of some of the various alternative unitary clauses within a case clause. For instance, *uc1* and *uc2* could both be case clauses. This can lead to case clauses producing a two-dimensional (in the general situation an *n*-dimensional) effect.

Example 3.8.2a. Using case clauses.

(i) Consider a print statement which causes the season of the year to be printed depending on the value of the integer i. $i = 0, 1, 2$ or 3 should cause the printing of, respectively, *"spring"*, *"summer"*, *"autumn"* or *"winter"*.

> *print* (**case** $i + 1$ **in** *"spring"*, *"summer"*, *"autumn"*, *"winter"*
> **esac**)

(ii) Write a program which reads an integer m and tests if it is divisible by 3, 5, 7 or 11.

> **begin int** $m = ($**int** n; *read* (n); $n)$;
>   **bool** *divisible* $:= $ **false**;
>   **for** i **to** 4 **while not** *divisible*
>   **do int** $k = (i|3, 5, 7, 11)$;
>   *divisible* $:= m$ **mod** $k = 0$
>   **od**;
>   *print* $((m, ($*divisible*$|$*"is"*$|$*"is not"*$)$
>   *" divisible by* 3, 5, 7 *or* 11*"*$))$
> **end**

At the corresponding stage of the study of conditionals the abbreviation **elif** was introduced. A similar abbreviation can be used in a case clause, namely **ouse**. To be precise consider

> **case** $sc0$ **in** . . . **out case** $sc00$ **in** . . . **esac esac**

Note that the case clause starting **case** $sc0$ . . . does contain an **out** part and the clause beginning **case** $sc00$ **in** . . . may or may not contain an **out** part. The above can be abbreviated to

> **case** $sc0$ **in** . . . **ouse** $sc00$ **in** . . . **esac**

Thus a single **case** and **esac** remain. If **case** and **esac** appear as brackets and **in** and **out** as vertical bars then **ouse** should appear as $|$:

3.8.3. Ranges associated with choice clauses
Take the general form

> **if** a **then** b **else** c **fi**

of a conditional. The **if-then-fi** form will be regarded as the special case in which the **else** part is just **skip**. For this purpose abbreviations involving **elif** will be expanded. The rules concerning ranges are as follows:

any identifier declared in a can be used also in serial clauses b and c;

any identifier declared in b can be used only in b;
any identifier declared in c can be used only in c.

These can be expressed diagrammatically as

if ... **then** ... **else** ... **fi**

For case clauses a similar rule applies. All case clauses can be expressed in the general form

case $sc0$ **in** $uc1, uc2, \ldots, ucn$ **out** t **esac**

The relevant rules are:

any identifier declared in $sc0$ can be used in $uc1, uc2, \ldots, ucn$ or in t; any identifier declared in $uc1$ can be used only in $uc1$; similarly for $uc2, \ldots, ucn$ and t.

Example 3.8.3a. Ranges associated with choice clauses.
The conditional below prints the largest integer less than the cube root of n; it is assumed that n is supplied as data and is positive.

```
if int n; read (n); n > 0
then int i := 0;
     while i↑ 3 < n do i + := 1 od;
     print (i − 1)
fi
```

3.8.4. Balancing

In considering choice clauses that deliver values it has been assumed so far that all the alternatives deliver objects of the same mode. This is not necessary but deviating from it raises extra complications, namely considerations of modes and a topic called *balancing*. The problem of having alternatives which deliver objects of different modes will now be considered.

The problem to be discussed stems from two prerequisites. First, at compile time, i.e. before the program has even been executed, the compiler wants to be able to associate a single unique mode with the object delivered by a choice clause. Secondly, coercions cannot be applied to the result delivered by a conditional or case clause. This should be reminiscent of the earlier study of closed clauses.

When all the alternatives deliver objects of the same mode and this is the mode required in that particular position there is no problem since the mode of the object delivered is just the common mode. As mentioned above, this need not be so but in the general case a suitable mode has still to be found and this is achieved by applying coercions to some or all of the alternatives. The mode that is found is called the *balanced mode* and the process of applying the coercions is called *balancing*.

Example 3.8.4a. Choice clauses requiring balancing.
Let x, y and z have mode **ref real**, m and n have mode **int** and b have mode **bool**. Then the following are acceptable assignations:
    (i) $x :=$ **if** b **then** y **else** 3 **fi** $+ 6.7$
    (ii) **if** b **then** x **else** y **fi** $:= 6$
    (iii) $x :=$ **if** b **then** n **else** m **fi**
    (iv) $x :=$ **if** b **then** n **else** m **fi** $+ 6$
What happens then? The coercions are not applied to the result but, as with closed clauses, they move inside the brackets, the **if** and **fi** or **case** and **esac** whichever is relevant, and apply to the individual alternatives. In general different coercions may have to apply to different alternatives.

To be more explicit the following process is performed. The syntactic position of the choice clause is considered. One of the alternatives is coerced to the balanced mode using only coercions available in such a position. All the other alternatives can be strongly coerced if necessary to the balanced mode. Note that the balanced mode is the a posteriori mode required in that position.

It can happen that several of the alternatives of the choice clause can adopt the strength of the syntactic position of the clause. If this is so it is immaterial which is chosen. But in many situations there is only one possibility and this can be found by trial and error.

Example 3.8.4b. Balancing.
The balancing that occurs in each of the situations listed in example 3.8.4a is discussed below.
    (i) $x :=$ **if** b **then** y **else** 3 **fi** $+ 6.7$
Since the conditional appears as an operand in a formula the syntactic position of the conditional is firm. Therefore either 3 accepts the firm position and y a strong position or y accepts the firm position and 3 a strong position. Another relevant observation is that the dyadic operator $+$ will expect a left hand operand of mode **real** or **int** and consequently one would expect the balanced mode to be **real** or **int**. But there is no way in which an object of mode **real** can be coerced to an object of mode **int**. So one would expect the balanced mode to be **real**. This is in fact the case. Consider the coercions involved. If 3 has to be coerced to an equivalent object of mode **real** it must adopt a strong position and hence y must adopt the firm position. So in this example y is firmly coerced (by dereferencing)

to mode **real** and 3 is strongly coerced (by widening) to mode **real**. The balanced mode is therefore **real**.

(ii) **if** b **then** x **else** y **fi** := 6

No balancing or coercions are necessary. The mode of the result delivered by the conditional is **ref real**.

(iii) $x :=$ **if** b **then** n **else** m **fi**.

Since x is of mode **ref real** the source of the assignation must deliver a result of mode **real**. The conditional here is in a strong position and consequently both alternatives can be strongly coerced to the balanced mode which is **real**. Thus both alternatives are widened.

(iv) $x :=$ **if** b **then** m **else** n **fi** + 6

The conditional appears in a firm position. The balanced mode is **int** and it is not necessary to apply any coercions to either m or n. In this case then the coercion widening acts on the result delivered by the dyadic operator + .

This ends the present discussion of choice clauses and of balancing. It will be necessary to return to both of these at a later stage.

3.9. Jumps

The subject of jumps and their use causes much controversy among computer scientists. Some people argue that programs which use jumps are badly designed and hence the use of jumps should be severely limited. People with extreme views argue that they should never be used. This matter will be discussed further in section 3.10.

In the meantime jumps will be discussed. Fortunately, perhaps, their use in ALGOL 68 is fraught with danger. Although jumps themselves are very simple constructions the repercussions of their use are many.

3.9.1. Labelling and jumping

Labels are just identifiers used to mark unitary clauses within a program. A unit is marked by preceding it with an identifier and a colon (or with several identifier–colon pairs if there is a need to attach more than one label to a statement). Note that labels mark units. They do not mark declarations. Moreover, labels act as markers and consequently they are not associated with any particular mode or any particular value.

Example 3.9.1a. Labelling units.
Consider the (arbitrary) unit

$$x := n \uparrow 2 + (m := n + 1) \times 4$$

This is marked by the label *calc* by writing

$$calc: x := n \uparrow 2 + (m := n + 1) \times 4$$

and marked by the three labels *calc*, *repeat* and *again* by writing

$$calc: repeat: again: x := n \uparrow 2 + (m := n + 1) \times 4$$

Normally when a program is being executed, unitary clauses are elaborated in the order in which they appear on the printed page. This last remark is, of course, subject to modification in the light of loop clauses, collateral clauses, choice clauses, etc. But this normal flow of control can be altered by means of jumps. Thus executing **goto** *calc* within a program causes the statement labelled *calc* to be the next statement executed. The machine will execute the statement labelled *calc* and they proceed from *calc* in the usual way. This jump may also be written as **go to** *calc* or even just *calc*.

Example 3.9.1b. Using jumps.
The effect of the loop clause

> **for** *a* **from** *b* **by** *c* **to** *d* **while** *e* **do** *f* **od**

can be expressed using jumps. Of course, one should not perform loops using jumps but the following is instructive since it describes the effect of a loop clause.

```
begin int j := b, int k = c, m = d;
    next: if (k > 0 and j ≤ m) or (k < 0 and j ≥ m) or k = 0
        then int i = j;
            if e
            then f; j +:= k; goto next
            fi
        fi
end
```

Jumps may appear only in strong syntactic positions, where they yield any suitable mode. When used as statements this mode is **void**. But there are other possibilities.

Consider the following statement which, assuming *x* is of mode **real** and *sqx* of mode **ref real**, attempts to square *x* and assign the result to *sqx*.

$$sqx := \textbf{if } x > 1 \textbf{ then } x \uparrow 2 \textbf{ else goto } error \textbf{ in } x \textbf{ fi}$$

The mode associated with this jump is **real**, the required balanced mode. If $x > 1$ yields **true** the expression $x \uparrow 2$ is elaborated and the result assigned to *sqx*. If $x > 1$ yields **false** no value is assigned to *sqx* – it thus retains its previous value – and statements are elaborated starting at the label *error in x*. The effect is thus equivalent to

if $x > 1$ **then** *sqx* $:= x \uparrow 2$ **else goto** *error in x* **fi**.

3.9.2. Restrictions on jumps

So far a rather simplistic view has been taken of jumps. On looking at some details there are several points which require clarification. For example, can one jump from any one point of a program to any other point in that program? The answer to this question is 'no'. A first set of restrictions will follow from a description of the process of relating an applied occurrence of a label with its defining occurrence. Other considerations will lead to further sets of restrictions.

It is convenient to be able to distinguish easily between identifiers used for labels and identifiers declared in identity or variable declarations. The latter set of objects have modes and values associated with them and are hence called 'mode identifiers'. Identifiers used for labels are called 'label identifiers'.

Label identifiers are defined merely by their appearance as a label. No other form of declaration is possible. Thus if in a program the (labelled) statement

$$calc : x := n \uparrow 2 + (m := n + 1) \times 4$$

appeared then this alone would act as a declaration of *calc*. This occurrence of *calc* is therefore a defining occurrence.

Applied occurrences of labels appear in jump statements. Thus in the statement **goto** *calc* or in **if** $x < 0$ **then** *calc* **fi** an applied occurrence of *calc* appears (in the latter case **goto** is omitted).

When applied occurrences and defining occurrences of label identifiers appear it is necessary to relate each applied occurrence to its defining occurrence. This is necessary since several defining occurrences of the same label identifier may occur within a single program though it would certainly be wrong if more than one appeared within a single reach.

Applied occurrences are related to their defining occurrences by means of the process described earlier for mode identifiers. Thus, given an applied occurrence, a defining occurrence in the same reach is sought. If it is not found then one must search out through surrounding reaches until a suitable defining occurrence is found. The fact that one starts with an applied occurrence and searches out through successive reaches has important consequences and limits in a convenient way the set of allowable jumps.

Example 3.9.2a. Erroneous jumps.

In each of the skeleton programs below the jump statement is illegal. It should be noticed however that it is natural to exclude these jumps.

(i)   ...

   goto *label*;

   ...

   begin real x;

      ...

      label: $n := m \div 2$;

      ...

   end

If such a jump were permitted, it would mean bypassing the declaration of x.

(ii)   ...

   goto *label*;

   ...

   for i **to** 100

      do

      ...

       label: $n := m \div 2 + 1$;

      ...

      od;

   ...

If this jump were legal some assumptions about the declaration of i and the value of i would have to be made.

Jumps and declarations

Consider a serial clause which contains constant or variable declarations together with defining occurrences of label identifiers and some jumps. A programmer must not be able to use jumps so that identity or variable declarations are encountered several times before leaving the enclosing serial clause. Otherwise several invocations of a generator, for example, would produce different addresses or names, all to be accessed by the same identifier.

The necessary restriction is imposed by insisting that if a serial clause with declarations is entered then these declarations must be encountered at most once before leaving the serial clause. This is achieved by enforcing the rule that no statement can be labelled if it appears before the last declaration in the serial clause. Thus all defining occurrences of labels must come after all other kinds of defining occurrences. Even the last unit of a serial clause may be labelled.

Jumps and void-collateral-clauses
The use of jumps to leave one of the constituent units of a void-collateral-clause should not be attempted. Its effect is undefined. What effect would one expect from a void-collateral-clause containing three constituent units one of which terminated naturally and the other two of which contained jumps to different labels?

Jumps from within a constituent unit of a void-collateral-clause to another part of that same unit are permitted. But the rule relating defining and applied occurrences will prevent any attempt to jump between constituent units.

Enquiry clauses
Enquiry clauses were mentioned briefly in the discussion of conditionals. It was pointed out that in

    if a **then** b **else** c **fi**

a could be regarded as a serial clause. But it is a serial clause with a difference, a difference which now becomes significant with the introduction of labels and jumps.

Enquiry clauses occur also in other positions. These tend to be parts of larger constructions where a test of some kind has to be performed; hence the term 'enquiry clause'. In

    case $sc0$ **in** $uc1, uc2, \ldots, ucn$ **out** t **esac**

$sc0$ is an enquiry clause; in

    for a **from** b **by** c **to** d **while** e **do** f **od**

e is an enquiry clause. In fact any clause following an **if, elif, case, ouse**, any of the abbreviated versions of these, or **while** is an enquiry clause.

What distinguishes enquiry clauses from serial clauses is the following. An enquiry clause must not contain any defining occurrences of labels in its outermost reach. The reason for this restriction is to prevent anyone attempting to write statements such as

    if ... *label*: ... ; *condition* **then** ... ; **goto** *label*; ... **else** ... **fi**

Without the restriction this would have been legal due to the special ranges associated with conditionals. Similar constructions in loop and all forms of choice clauses would have been possible due to the special ranges associated with these.

3.9.3. Special cases of jumps
There is a special label, *stop*, which is automatically positioned just

88

after the final symbol in every program. Thus if a programmer wishes to terminate his program all he has to do is write *stop*, **goto** *stop*, or **go to** *stop*. This label is part of the standard environment.

The use of the symbol **exit**, called the 'completion symbol', will be illustrated by means of the following rather artificial example. (A similar effect could be obtained by using a case clause.)

Let m and n have mode **ref int** and y and z have mode **ref real**. Consider the piece of program

$$z := y + \quad (\# \text{ start of serial clause A } \#$$
$$\text{if } n \geq 0 \text{ then goto } pos \text{ or } zero \, n \text{ fi};$$
$$m := n \uparrow 2 + n + 1; n + 4 \text{ exit}$$
$$\# \text{ first exit is above } \#$$
$$pos \text{ or } zero \, n : \quad \text{if } n = 0 \text{ then goto } zero \, n \text{ fi};$$
$$m := n \uparrow 2 - n - 1; n - 4.5 \text{ exit}$$
$$\# \text{ second exit is above } \#$$
$$zero \, n : \quad m := n \uparrow 2; n$$
$$\# \text{ end of serial clause A } \#);$$
$$print \,((\text{"the values of } z \text{ and } m \text{ are"}, z, \text{"and"}, m))$$

To understand the effect of this it will be necessary only to describe the effect of serial clause A. The rest should be straightforward.

If the value referred to by n is negative, the initial enquiry, $n \geq 0$, yields **false** and no jump is performed. Hence the assignation $m := n \uparrow 2 + n + 1$ is elaborated. Then $n + 4$, modified by coercions (see later), is delivered as the value of the serial clause and the elaboration of **exit** causes the completion of the elaboration of the serial clause. This result is then added to the value referred to by y, assigned to z and the final print statement then executed.

When $n \geq 0$ yields **true**, a jump to label *pos or zero n* is performed. If $n = 0$ yields **false** the assignation $m := n \uparrow 2 - n - 1$ is elaborated and $n - 4.5$ is delivered as the result of the serial clause. This is added to the value referred to by y, assigned to z and the print statement is then performed. If the test $n = 0$ had produced **true** a jump to label *zero n* would have been performed and the serial clause would have been completed in the usual way. The value referred to by n would have been delivered as the result of the serial clause.

By means of the completion symbol a serial clause can be made to deliver one of several different values. These values may be of different modes, but the compiler will always expect a result of one particular mode. Consequently balancing must take place between the a priori modes of the different results that could be delivered by the serial clause. In the above example it is necessary to balance objects of mode **int**, **real** and **ref int** and the syntactic position of the serial clause is firm. The balanced mode in this case is **real**. Thus the serial clause always delivers a result of mode **real**. As one would expect (since a closed clause will never deliver a result that is coerced but rather the coercions take place first and then the result is delivered) the coercions move inside the brackets and the necessary coercions are applied to the different units $n + 4$, $n - 4.5$ and n.

When an **exit** is encountered, it causes completion of the execution of its enclosing serial clause. The unit immediately before an **exit** may be delivered as a result of the serial clause. An **exit** must always be followed immediately by a defining occurrence of a label for otherwise there would be no means of reaching the phrase following the **exit**.

As a result of the above properties associated with the completion symbol there are several observations that can be made and several restrictions that must be imposed:

> **exit** replaces, in a sense, the semi-colon;
> **exit** cannot immediately follow a declaration;
> after the first occurrence of **exit** in a serial clause no defining occurrences other than those of label identifiers can appear in its outermost reach;
> **exit** cannot occur in the outermost reach of an enquiry clause.

Note however that **exit** can be used in the constituent units of a collateral. Its use there merely completes the elaboration of the particular unit in which it occurs.

Although all the uses of **exit** have centred around serial clauses delivering values, **exit** can also be used when its preceding unit is a statement, i.e. units producing results of mode **void**. In this case the effect of the completion symbol is merely to cause a jump to the end of the smallest enclosing serial clause.

3.10. Programs in ALGOL 68

The purpose of this section is to provide some notes on the actual process of writing programs. Before starting it would first be advisable to investigate just what constitutes an ALGOL 68 program.

3.10.1. Enclosed clauses

All the programs that have been written so far have taken the form of closed clauses. But in fact any closed, choice, loop or collateral clause would constitute a legitimate ALGOL 68 program. These kinds of clauses are grouped together under the title of enclosed clauses, a suitable name since each of these is delimited by some form of bracketing.

Example 3.10.1a. Enclosed clauses.

(i) **if int** n; *read* (n); $n \geqq 0$ **then** *print* $(n \uparrow 2)$ **fi**

is a legitimate program.

(ii) *print* $(\textit{"illegal"})$

is not an acceptable program.

3.10.2. General remarks about programs

Perfect programs, if such things exist, are not easy to produce. In general, the more complex the task which a program has to perform the longer the program will be and the more difficult it will be to produce a 'good' program, whatever the word 'good' means in this context.

Giving a complete set of rules for the writing of 'good' programs to perform any task whatsoever is impossible. Not only is the set of problems too large but there are even certain tasks which cannot be programmed. For instance it is impossible to write a program A which, given as data any other program B, will decide whether or not program B if allowed to run would ever stop. The point, however, is that one cannot give a complete set of rules for producing programs just as one cannot give a set of rules for solving mathematical problems. Consequently these notes can act only as a set of guidelines.

The word 'good' when applied to programs includes the following: the program should be properly structured and efficient, it should be well documented and the layout should be neat. In general the meaning and intention of each part of the program should be quite clear to any other programmer. Ideally, each part of a program should contain a proof of its correctness but this involves a branch of the theory of programming and is beyond the scope of this book.

Some of the suggestions which have been scattered throughout these pages are listed below for ease of access. Other remarks are added.

Mode identifiers and label identifiers should be chosen in such a way that they indicate the purpose for which they are used.

The use of jumps should be limited. Excessive use of jumps often betrays a misunderstanding of the basic constructions in a language. For instance their use might betray a lack of thorough understanding of loop clauses.

Layout (i.e. use of the facilities for displaying programs) can make the difference between a program being readable and a program being extremely difficult to follow. Sensible use should be made of this. For instance matching **begin** and **end** and (and) should be easily located. Matching **begin** and **end** might occur at the same level of indentation. Similarly matching **if** and **fi**, **case** and **esac** should all be easily located.

Comments should be used sensibly, e.g. to outline the purpose of different parts of a program. In this way programmers should be able to read (easily!) each other's programs.

Programs should do what they are intended to do. The data should, if necessary be verified in some appropriate way. Data validation is a fairly complex subject. But when an error occurs within data some attempt at recovery should be made. This procedure is not always possible but if it can be done then several errors can be caught with a single run of the program. To take what should be a well-known example a compiler will come across syntax errors in programs. When it meets such errors it should not abandon all hope but it should attempt to find any other errors in the program.

As far as output is concerned one should always attempt to make the results produced on the line-printer readable and understandable to someone knowing nothing about the workings of the program itself. It is also helpful if within the results produced on the printer there is a copy, in some sense, of the information which appeared as the data. As far as the data itself is concerned the program should aim at allowing some degree of freedom in the form that the data should take.

There are further points which are worthy of mention. It should be apparent that ALGOL 68 is a language which is very particular about the concept of modes and consequently with coercions, balancing, etc. This aspect of the language can be and should be used to the benefit of the programmer. If it is known in advance that a particular value is to remain constant throughout a certain part of a program then it should be treated as a constant and a suitable declaration should reflect this. Any attempt to alter the value of the object will then result in a syntax error. This gives an element of protection which would not otherwise exist.

It has also been remarked that in declarations local generators introduce space which remains in existence until the end of the smallest enclosing serial clause. This allows the programmer to create and relinquish space as he chooses. This facility should be used to good effect. Not only can one delay declarations until the smallest serial clause containing that object but even within serial clauses themselves one can delay declarations until just before they are used for the first time. One can follow these suggestions but they must be tempered with a certain amount of common sense. It may happen on some poor implementations that following this delaying philosophy blindly may lead to inefficient programs, space being repeatedly created and deleted.

Within a loop clause the same action might be performed several times but it should have been performed only once, outside the loop itself. Consider the task of calculating the volume and the surface area of spheres of different radii r. (Volume $= \pi r^3\ 4/3$ and surface area $= 4\pi r^2$.) Ideally the values of 4π and $4\pi/3$ should be calculated once, at the start of the program.

3.10.3. Structured programming

In preparing a program to perform a complicated task it is usually convenient to first of all break the task into several different subtasks. The subtasks should be chosen in such a way that the pieces of program to perform these have a clean and not very complicated interface. The subtasks themselves can again be subdivided into even smaller subtasks which can be themselves further subdivided and so on. In this way a hierarchy is built up and the end product should be a carefully structured program.

Building well-structured programs requires considerable care, thought and practice. This is achieved only by constantly thinking about problems and by writing large programs. There is no fixed way of dividing large tasks into smaller subtasks, etc. Performing this process effectively requires considerable insight into the problem in hand.

The above approach to programming starts with a single task and one then works one's way downwards through smaller and smaller subtasks to the final level which is the ALGOL 68 coding. This approach to programming is called the *top-down* approach. This will be used in most of the programs given in these notes. But there are other approaches.

When one is performing a very intricate task or subtle piece of programming the approach adopted is often to write the piece of program one instruction at a time in order to achieve the desired effect. Note that there is a desired effect. This process is just the converse of the earlier approach and consequently is called the *bottom-up* approach.

Most programs will usually be written using a combination of the two approaches. The initial task can be broken down into subtasks by the top-down approach but at a certain level it might be necessary to write the piece of program for a particular subtask using the bottom-up approach.

There is not even any consensus of opinion about what constitutes a well-structured program. The interested reader should refer to the Association of Computing Machinery Computing Surveys Volume 6, Number 4, December 1974 for further discussion.

3.10.4. Miscellaneous examples on programming

In the remainder of this section some common programming techniques are illustrated. Where appropriate an attempt is made to provide well-structured programs and to make use of the suggestions described earlier for the production of 'good' programs.

The term 'iteration' will be used to describe the process of repeating a set of statements several times. In other programming languages the equivalent of a loop clause is called an iterative statement, a do statement, a repetitive statement, etc.

Interchanging values

The first example illustrates one method of interchanging the values of integer variables. This and variations on this theme are used frequently in programming. Although the discussion here uses integer variables the method is quite general and can be applied to real variables, character variables, etc.

The following piece of program has the effect of interchanging the values of the integer variables m and n.

$$\textbf{int } temp = n; n := m; m := temp$$

Note that $temp$ is of mode **int**. Since its value is never altered it is natural to use mode **int** rather than mode **ref int** and so offer some degree of protection. Moreover, $temp$ cannot be used outside the enclosing serial clause. If m and n referred to 3 and 5 before the elaboration of this clause they would refer to 5 and 3 respectively after its elaboration.

Prime numbers

The above example did not involve the writing of a program and hence there was no necessity for the design of a structure for a program. The next example does involve the writing of a program. In order to indicate the structure step 1, step 2 and step 3 will be used to denote the first set of subtasks. When subtask step 1 is itself divided into subtasks these will be denoted by step 1.1, step 1.2, etc. If these had to be further subdivided the subtasks of step 1.1 would be step 1.1.1, step 1.1.2, etc. This notation will prove convenient in many of the later examples.

Consider the problem of writing a program to read a positive integer n greater than 1 and test if it is a prime number. (A prime number is a positive integer, greater than 1, which is divisible only by itself and 1.)

The top-down approach is used to determine the structure of the program. A first division into subtasks yields:

Step 1.   read and check data (i.e. *n*);
Step 2.   perform calculations to test if *n* is prime;
Step 3.   print appropriate message.

Consider now further divisions of step 1. This gives:

Step 1.1.   read integer *n*;
Step 1.2.   check that *n* is greater than 1 – otherwise terminate the
              program with a suitable error message.

Step 2 is more complex and breaking this task down into smaller subtasks involves a study of the approach that will be adopted in deciding whether *n* is prime or not. *n* will be put through a series of tests which will be satisfied if *n* is prime. If *n* fails any of these tests then *n* is not prime. Of course having failed one test there is no point in carrying out further tests. For this purpose a boolean variable *factor found* will be used. If ever *n* fails a test this is set to **true** and execution of step 2 is terminated. Step 2 is thus refined as follows:

Step 2.1.   check either that *n* is odd or that $n = 2$ – otherwise *n*
              is not prime;
Step 2.2.   test if *n* is divisible by 3, 5, 7, 9, 11, ..., $n-1$ (the criterion
              for *n* being divisible by *i* is that *n* **mod** $i = 0$); if *n* is
              divisible by any of these numbers then *n* is not prime.

Step 2.2 can actually be improved but this will be demonstrated after a first version of the program has been written. Step 3 requires no further refinement. The resulting program follows.

```
begin int n = if int m; read (m); m ≥ 2
              then m
              else print (("program terminated because",
                              m, " is less than 2."));
                   goto stop
              fi;
      bool factor found := not (odd n or n = 2);
      for i from 3 by 2 to n − 1 while not factor found
      do factor found := n mod i = 0 od;
      print ((n, (factor found|" is not prime"|" is prime")))
end
```

It was remarked earlier that an improved version of this program could be produced by refining step 2.2. In fact it would be sufficient to test if *n* is divisible by only 3, 5, 7, ..., *r* where *r* is the largest integer which is less than or equal to the square root of *n*. But since square roots have not yet been introduced in these notes this refinement is not made. The reason for the refinement being possible lies in the following observation. If n has two factors p and q and if $n = p \times q$ then either $p \leq \sqrt{n}$ or $q \leq \sqrt{n}$. For if both $p > \sqrt{n}$ and $q > \sqrt{n}$ then $p \times q > n$ and this contradicts the assumption that $n = p \times q$. Hence if n is not prime it has a factor between 2 and $\sqrt{n}$.

Further refinements are also possible but these involve a study of prime numbers. This completes the investigation of the problem posed.

Using iterative formulae

The particular problem of finding the square root of a non-negative integer will be discussed here. But this is one special example from an entire family of similar problems with similar solutions.

If x_0 is an approximation to $+\sqrt{a}$ then $x_1 = \frac{1}{2}(x_0 + a/x_0)$ is a better approximation and using this value of x_1, $x_2 = \frac{1}{2}(x_1 + a/x_1)$ is an even better approximation. Continuing in this way x_0, x_1, x_2, ... where

$$x_{n+1} = \frac{1}{2}\left(x_n + \frac{a}{x_n}\right)$$

is a sequence of better and better approximations to $+\sqrt{a}$. Note, and this is important from the programming point of view, that there is no need to remember all the previous approximations. To calculate x_{n+1} one need know only x_n, i.e. to calculate a better approximation one need know only an approximation. Thus a single variable can be used to take at different times the various values x_0, x_1, x_2, x_3, ...

It is important to decide on some criterion for terminating the calculation of x_0, x_1, x_2, ... One possible criterion is to terminate the iteration when successive approximations are very close, e.g. they differ by less than *small real*. This is the criterion to be adopted below but it is not the only criterion or even the best criterion. Discussion of the most suitable criterion involves a topic called numerical analysis, a branch of mathematics.

From the above discussion it follows that it will be possible to iterate to a satisfactory solution by using a statement whose structure might be

> **while** the better approximation, as calculated from the formula, and the approximation itself differ by more than *small real*
>
> **do** approximation := better approximation **od**

The entire program will then be given the following structure.

1. read and check the data, i.e. a

1.1. read data
1.2. check that the number read is non-negative; otherwise terminate the program with a suitable error message
2. find the square root of a
   2.1. obtain an initial approximation to $+\sqrt{a}$ (for example use $\frac{1}{2}(1+a)$)
   2.2. iterate to the final approximation using the loop clause described earlier
3. print the results

A possible program reflecting this structure is:

```
begin real a = if real x; read (x); x ≥ 0
              then x
              else print (("program terminated because", x,
                          " is negative"));
                   goto stop
              fi;
         real approx := (1 + a)/2, better approx;
         while better approx := (approx + a/approx)/2;
               abs (better approx − approx) > small real
         do approx := better approx od;
         print (("square root of", a, " is", better approx))
end
```

Nested multiplication

This subsection introduces a technique known as nested multiplication. It can be used when one has to calculate the value of a polynominal. The polynomial

$$a_n x^n + a_{n-1} x^{n-1} + \ldots + a_1 x + a_0$$

can be rewritten as

$$((\ldots((a_n x + a_{n-1}) x + a_{n-2}) x + a_{n-3}) x + \ldots + a_1) x + a_0$$

Evaluating a polynomial by the method suggested by this rearrangement is nested multiplication. It is much more efficient than the straightforward approach and is easily programmed as will be shown.

The program to perform nested multiplication will at successive times round a loop have as the value of the real variable *sum*, say,

$$a_n, a_n x + a_{n-1}, (a_n x + a_{n-1}) x + a_{n-2}, ((a_n x + a_{n-1}) x + a_{n-2}) x + a_{n-3}, \text{etc.}$$

Thus one value is obtained from the previous value by:

$$sum := sum \times x + next \; coefficient.$$

Consider then a program to perform the following calculations: read a real number x followed by a non-negative integer n; then read $n + 1$ real numbers corresponding to $a_n, a_{n-1}, \ldots, a_2, a_1, a_0$, and print the value of the polynomial

$$a_n x^n + a_{n-1} x^{n-1} + \ldots + a_2 x^2 + a_1 x + a_0$$

evaluated using nested multiplication. A possible program is given below. The check that n is non-negative is omitted since it may distract the reader from the proper structure of the program.

> **begin real** $x = ($**real** y; $read \, (y)$; $y)$, **real** $sum := 0$;
>   **to** (**int** n; $read \, (n)$; $n) + 1$
>   **do** $sum := sum \times x + ($**real** $coeff$; $read \, (coeff)$; $coeff)$**od**;
> $print \, ((''value \; of \; the \; polynomial \; when \; x = '', x, '' \; is'', sum))$
> **end**

Exercises for chapter 3

1. Give, using the identifiers *real width* and *exp width*, the number of character positions required by:
   (i) *print (pi)* when printing begins at the start of a line;
   (ii) *print (pi)* when printing is not at the start of a line.

2. What are the (a priori) modes associated with the following serial clauses?
   (i) **int** n; $read \, (n)$; n
   (ii) **int** n; $read \, (n)$; $n = 2$
   (iii) **int** n; $read \, (n)$; **repr** n
   (iv) **int** n; $read \, (n)$; $n +:= 4$

3. Assume that y is of mode **ref real**. Describe and explain the various coercions occurring in
   $$real \; x := (\textbf{int} \; n; \; read \, (n); \; y := n + 10; \; n) + 7$$

4. In ALGOL 68 commas tend to indicate collateral elaboration. Does it follow therefore that
   $$print \, ((x, y))$$
   will result in the values delivered by x and y being printed in a random order? If not, what is implied?

5. Assuming the declarations
   $$real \; x, y, \textbf{int} \; n$$

is the following legal?

if $x > y$ **then** x **else** n **fi** := 4

Give reasons for your answer.

6. Write closed clauses which would deliver **true** if the integer n is:
   (i) a perfect square,
   (ii) a power of 2,
   (iii) zero,
   (iv) a prime number.

7. Is

   begin int n; n **end** := 4

   a legal assignation? Give reasons for your answer.

8. What are the results produced by the following program?

   ```
   begin real x := 4.7; print (x);
         begin int x := 7; print (x); x +:= 1 end;
         print (x)
   end
   ```

9. Assuming that *sum* has already been declared to be of mode **ref real**, structure the following piece of program properly, giving each variable its correct scope.

   ```
   begin int n; read (n); real x;
         to n do read (x); sum +:= x od;
         print (sum)
   end
   ```

10. What is the output produced by this program?
    ```
    begin int n := 1; ref int m = n;
          begin int n = 7;
                print (n);
                m := n + 4
          end;
          print (n)
    end
    ```

11. What are the results produced by the following piece of program, assuming that the value read is 5?
    ```
    int n := 10;
    to (int n; read (n); print (n); n) do print (n) od;
    print (n)
    ```

99

12. What is the effect of each of the following loop clauses assuming the initial value of the integer variable n is 0?
    (i) **from** 4 **by** $-$ 1 **to** 10 **do** $n + := 1$ **od**
    (ii) **from** $-$ 4 **to** $-$ 10 **do** $n + := 1$ **od**
    (iii) **from** $-$ 4 **by** 0 **to** $-$ 10 **do** $n + := 1$ **od**

13. What is the effect of the following piece of program?

    > **int** $n := 0$;
    > **while char** ch; $read\ (ch)$; $ch/ = " + "$ **or** $ch/ = " - "$
    > **do** $n := n \times 10 + $ **abs** ch **od**;
    > $print\ (n)$

14. n is of mode **ref int**.
    (i) $n := 10$; **by** 2 **to** n **do** $n + := 1$ **od**
    How often is the statement $n + := 1$ elaborated?
    (ii) $n := 10$; **by** 2 **to** n **plusab** 1 **do** $n := 4$ **od**
    How often is the statement $n := 4$ elaborated?

15. Is it ever legal to have the following sequence of characters occurring in an ALGOL 68 program (not in commentary, pragmatic remarks, or within quotes)?

    > $\ldots$; $n := 1$; **do** $n + := 1$; $\ldots$

    The dots indicate other phrases which for the purposes of this question are irrelevant.

16. Indicate the coercions that take place in the following assuming the declarations

    > **real** x, y, **int** n, m, **int** $i = 1$, $j = 2$

    (i) $x := $ **case** i **in** 2, 3, j **out** 0 **esac** $+ 2$
    (ii) $x := $ **case** i **in** pi, y, 0 **esac**
    (iii) **case** i **in** x, y **esac** $:= $ **case** j **in** n, m **esac**

17. Point out the syntax error in the following piece of program

    > (**if** $x > y$ **then exit fi**;
    > $z := x$; $x := y$; $y := z$)

18. Would it be legal to write

    > **real** $x = 4 + $ **if** $p > q$ **then** 4 **else goto** $error$ **fi**

    where p and q are suitable integers?

Programming problems for chapter 3

1. Write a program which accepts an integer in base b (where $b > 0$

and $b < 10$) and prints out the decimal equivalent of the integer. The program should incorporate suitable checks against errors.

2. Write a program which reads an integer expressed in hexadecimal and prints its decimal equivalent. Use the letters $A, B, \ldots, F$ for $10, 11, \ldots, 15$.

3. In writing arithmetic expressions or programs one frequently makes use of opening and closing brackets, "(" and ")". In these applications the brackets must match. Write a piece of program which accepts any piece of text (terminated by some character not in the text) and decides if the opening and closing brackets match.

4. Write programs to
   (i) differentiate with respect to x
   (ii) integrate with respect to x
   a sum of terms of the form az^n where a and n are suitable integers and z is some character, e.g. x or perhaps u, v, w, etc.

5. There are four positive integers a, b, c and d each less than 10 for which

$$a^3 + b^3 + c^3 = d^3$$

Find the four integers with the aid of a suitable program.

6. The integer 153 has the property that

$$153 = 1^3 + 5^3 + 3^3$$

For which other 3-digit integer is this the case? Write a suitable program to solve this problem.

7. A positive integer is said to be perfect if the sum of the divisors of the integer is equal to twice the integer itself. Thus 6 is perfect since $1 + 2 + 3 + 6 = 2 \times 6$, and 28 is perfect since $1 + 2 + 4 + 7 + 14 + 28 = 2 \times 28$. Find the first perfect number greater than 28 by writing a suitable program.

8. (i) Write a program to read three positive integers, a, b and c and find all pairs of integers x and y with the property that

$$ax^2 + by^2 = c$$

   (ii) Adapt the above to print out the solutions of

$$ax^2 + by^2 + cz^2 = d$$

9. Write a program to generate the first 100 elements of the Fibonacci series $[f_i]$ defined as follows:

$$f_0 = f_1 = 1$$
$$f_{n+1} = f_n + f_{n-1} \text{ for all } n \geq 1.$$

10. If x_n is an approximation to the cube root of a then x_{n+1} as given by

$$x_{n+1} = \frac{1}{3}\left(2x_n + \frac{a}{x_n^2}\right)$$

is a better approximation to the cube root of a. Write a program to read a real number a and to iterate to the cube root of the real number using the above formula. As an initial approximation use the number itself.

11. Any positive integer $n \geq 2$ can be expressed uniquely in the form

$$n = p_1^{a_1} p_2^{a_2} \ldots p_r^{a_r}$$

where each a_i is a positive integer and each p_i is a prime. Moreover

$$p_1 < p_2 \ldots < p_r$$

Write a program which reads an integer n and prints n in the form described above.

12. Write programs to find the sum of each of the following series.

(i) $\sum_{n=1}^{100} \frac{1}{n^2}$ (ii) $\sum_{n=1}^{\infty} \frac{1}{n^2}$

(iii) $\sum_{n=1}^{\infty} \frac{1}{(n!)^2}$ (iv) $\sum_{n=1}^{\infty} \frac{(-1)^n n!}{(2n)!}$

(v) $\sum_{n=1}^{\infty} \frac{x^n}{(n!)^2}$ x being supplied as data

13. Write a program to read and evaluate an arbitrary arithmetic expression involving:
   (i) only integers;
   (ii) the dyadic operators $+$, $-$ and $\times$;
   (iii) an implied bracketing as in ALGOL 68; and
   (iv) no brackets.

4

MULTIPLE VALUES AND SIMPLE STRUCTURES

In previous chapters the modes that were used were of a relatively simple nature. The purpose of this section is to introduce modes of a more complex nature. In particular a study will be made of modes which allow the introduction of objects which can be manipulated like arrays in mathematics. These will be called multiple values. Another set of objects that will be introduced are structures. These will allow the setting up of records which can contain different kinds of information. For example a single structure might contain all the relevant information about a particular student in a university.

Having introduced these concepts and some related ideas it will be possible for the first time in this book to use a computer as a means of manipulating large quantities of information.

4.1. Multiple values

In ALGOL 68 it is possible at one extreme to manipulate entire arrays and at the other extreme to manipulate individual elements of any array. Between these extremes it is possible to select subsets of multiple values.

The individual elements of an array can be accessed by means of what is called *subscripting*. Subscripted variables are frequently used in many branches of mathematics. They can be used in a similar way in programming although one should in this case be aware of the possibility of a distinction between subscripted variables and subscripted constants.

The uses of subscripted variables in programming can be introduced by means of some examples from mathematics. In statistics observations are often represented as $x_1, x_2, \ldots, x_n$; large sets of simultaneous equations are often expressed using subscripted variables for both the coefficients and the variables; and polynomials are often written in the form

$$a_n x^n + a_{n-1} x^{n-1} + \ldots + a_2 x^2 + a_1 x + a_0$$

There are other examples which involve the use of arrays of

characters. A person's name, for instance, can be regarded as a one-dimensional array of elements all of which are characters. Similarly the name of a street, the name of a town, a district or a country, the name of a day of the week or a month of the year can all be regarded as one-dimensional arrays of characters.

Arrays of booleans also have their uses. For instance, one could regard a computer word as a one-dimensional array of booleans. In this way the main store of a computer could itself be simulated by program, the program making use of a boolean array.

4.1.1. Declarations and subscripting

The effect of the declaration

$$[0:5] \textbf{ int } p$$

is to allow the use of 6 integer variables which can be written as $p[0]$, $p[1]$, ..., $p[4]$ and $p[5]$. Each of these has mode **ref int**.

Take, for the moment, $p[3]$. 3 is called a subscript and $p[3]$ is the ALGOL 68 version of a subscripted variable. Subscripts can in fact be any unit delivering a result of mode **int**. The syntactic position occupied by subscripts is meek and consequently only dereferencing, of the coercions so far introduced, can be applied.

Throughout this discussion of multiple values the brackets [and] can if necessary both be replaced by (and) respectively. This alternative method of representation can be useful when one is dealing with card-punches, etc. with a very limited character set. However the square brackets are much clearer and no further mention will be made of the alternative representation.

In the above declaration of p the integers 0 and 5 are called the lower and upper bounds respectively. In both cases, as with subscripts, any unit can appear provided the result delivered is of a posteriori mode **int**. The syntactic position is again meek and the bounds are elaborated collaterally. A special abbreviation is allowed when the lower bound is 1. If the lower bound and its accompanying colon are omitted a lower bound of 1 is automatically assumed.

Example 4.1.1a. Declarations.
(i) $[-4:0]$ **char** arr makes available five character variables $arr[-4]$, $arr[-3]$, ..., $arr[0]$.
(ii) $[0:r]$ **int** nn where r is of (a priori) mode **ref int** makes available integer variables $nn[0]$, $nn[1]$, ..., $nn[r]$.
(iii) Assuming the number read is 5 the declaration

$$[(\textbf{int } n; \; read \; (n); \; n)] \textbf{ real } xx$$

makes available real variables $xx[1], xx[2], \ldots, xx[5]$.

Example 4.1.1b. Program using multiple values.
Write a program to read a set of ages in the range 0 to 119 inclusive. The data should be terminated by a negative integer. Count the number of ages in each of the ranges 0 to 9, 10 to 19, 20 to 29, $\ldots$, 110 to 119 and print out the number of ages occurring in the most common age group.

The program uses the fact that if i is any integer between 0 and 9 then $i \div 10$ yields 0; $freq[0]$ counts the number of ages in this range. Similarly $freq[1]$ counts the number of ages in the range 10 to 19 since if i lies in this range then $i \div 10$ yields 1.

It would be appropriate to include in the program checks that no integer greater than 119 occurred. The following program could easily be modified to cater for such occurrences.

```
begin [0:11] int freq; for i from 0 to 11 do freq[i] := 0 od;
      while int n; read (n); n ≥ 0 do freq[n ÷ 10] +:= 1 od;
      int max := freq[0];
      for i to 11 do if max < freq[i] then max := freq[i] fi od;
      print (("maximum frequency is", max))
end
```

The mode of the results and the strength of the syntactic position of lower bounds, upper bounds and subscripts are similar. These three are grouped together under the collective title of *boundscripts*.

In example 4.1.1a. some of the bounds which were used, e.g. r in part (ii), were not constants but their value depended on the value of a particular variable. In such cases the term *dynamic* is often applied to the bounds of the multiple value or array so introduced. But once a declaration such as this has been elaborated the bounds of that multiple value remain fixed thereafter. Thus if in example 4.1.1a (ii) the value of r was 4 at the time of elaboration of the declaration any subsequent change in the value of r would not then alter the bounds of that multiple value.

Just as the declaration

int n, m, p

introduces three variables of mode **ref int**, so the declaration

[0:5] **int** nn, mm, pp

allows the use of variables $nn[0], nn[1], \ldots, nn[5], mm[0], \ldots, mm[5], pp[0], \ldots, pp[5]$. The effect is thus equivalent to the effect of

[0:5] **int** nn, [0:5] **int** mm, [0:5] **int** pp

105

There are, however, cases where such an equivalence no longer holds. As a result of the piece of program

> **int** $n := 4$;
> $[0:n +:= 1]$ **int** nn, mm, pp

each of nn, mm and pp will have associated bounds of 0 and 5. The bounds are elaborated once and once only.

4.1.2. Modes associated with multiple values

Consider now in more detail the declaration

> $[0:5]$ **int** p

The mode associated with p as a result of this declaration is reference-to-row-of-integral. This can be written in abbreviated form as **ref** [ ] **int**.

A multiple value has a mode which begins with row-of. An object of mode row-of-integral, i.e. [ ] **int**, is a multiple value. Similarly objects of mode [ ] **real** or [ ] **char** are also multiple values. p as declared above is therefore a reference to a multiple value, in this case a row-of-integral. If 2, 3, 5, 7, 11 and 13 had previously been assigned to $p[0]$, ..., $p[5]$ respectively p would then refer to the multiple value consisting of just these 6 integers.

The effect of following p by a subscript, e.g. 3, is to produce from an object, i.e. p, of mode **ref** [ ] **int** an object, i.e. $p[3]$, of mode **ref int**. Thus subscripting has the effect of removing a row-of from the mode of the object subscripted.

There are two monadic operators **lwb** and **upb** which when applied to multiple values of the kind so far introduced give their lower and upper bounds respectively.

Example 4.1.2a. Monadic **lwb** and **upb**.
  (i) Using the declaration of p given above

> **lwb** p gives a result of 0 and
> **upb** p gives a result of 5.

Note that p is dereferenced in both cases; this is acceptable since p occupies a firm syntactic position as an operand in a formula. Both **lwb** and **upb** then operate in this case on objects of mode [ ] **int**, not objects of mode **ref** [ ] **int**.
  (ii) The results produced by

> **begin int** $n := 4$; $[n]$ **int** a; *print* (**upb** a);
> $n := 6$; *print* (**upb** a)
> **end**

106

are 4 and 4.

4.1.3. Multiple values of several dimensions

All the multiple values introduced so far have been one-dimensional. Consider

$$[0:10, -4:100] \textbf{ real } xx$$

This is again a variable declaration and declares xx to be of mode reference-to-row-row-of-real. This can be abbreviated to **ref** [,] **real**. Note that the number of occurrences of 'row' in the mode is one more than the number of commas between [and] and gives the number of dimensions of the multiple values. Thus xx refers to a two-dimensional multiple value.

The declaration has the effect of making available the real variables $xx[i,j]$ where $0 \leq i \leq 10$ and $-4 \leq j \leq 100$. In total there are 11×105 real variables. Note that there are two subscripts, namely i and j, and as was pointed out earlier a single subscript removes a single occurrence of 'row' from the mode of xx (the 'of' is removed when no occurrences of 'row' remain). Hence the a priori mode of each $xx[i,j]$ is **ref real**.

Again lower and upper bounds are present but there is now a separate pair for each dimension. The first dimension has as lower and upper bounds 0 and 10 respectively. The second dimension has lower bound -4 and upper bound 100.

In general **lwb** and **upb** can be used as either monadic or dyadic operators (like $+$ and $-$). When used as monadic operators they give, respectively, the lower and upper bounds of the first dimension of the multiple value. When used as dyadic operators they take the form r **lwb** $array$ and r **upb** $array$ and these give the lower and upper bound respectively of the rth dimension of the multiple value. Their standard priority is 8.

Example 4.1.3a. Dyadic **lwb** and **upb**.
Using the earlier declaration of xx,

    (i) 1 **lwb** xx gives 0, the same value as is delivered by **lwb** xx;

    (ii) 1 **upb** xx gives 10, the same value as **upb** xx;

    (iii) 2 **lwb** xx gives -4;

    (iv) 2 **upb** xx delivers 100.

Note that in each case xx has to be dereferenced and this can be achieved since being an operand the syntactic position occupied by xx is firm.

Again all boundscripts are in meek syntactic positions and they deliver an integer. The collateral declarations

[$n1 : m1, n2 : m2$] **int** a, b

make available integer variables $a[i,j]$ and $b[i,j]$ where $n1 \leq i \leq m1$ and $n2 \leq j \leq m2$. Each of $n1$, $m1$, $n2$ and $m2$ is evaluated once for each elaboration of the declaration. If either $n1$: or $n2$: is omitted the lower bound of that dimension is taken to be 1. The subscripts in $a[i,j]$ are elaborated collaterally.

All these remarks can be generalised and applied to multiple values of higher dimensions. For example

[$10, n : m, 0 : 4, p$] **int** $aaaa$

is a variable declaration of $aaaa$ which has mode reference-to-row-row-row-row-of-integral. Again each $aaaa[i,j,k,l]$ where $1 \leq i \leq 10$, $n \leq j \leq m$, $0 \leq k \leq 4$ and $1 \leq l \leq p$ is an integer variable of mode **ref int**. Each subscript removes a single 'row' from the mode of $aaaa$; when no occurrences of 'row' remain the 'of' is omitted. Thus a single subscript involves reducing the number of dimensions by one. The monadic and dyadic operators **lwb** and **upb** can be used in the usual way.

Finally in this subsection consider the various objects that have been subscripted. These have all been references to multiple values and their syntactic position is weak. Therefore none of the coercions so far described can be applied. But one can replace these references-to-multiple-values by certain constructions which deliver as a result references to multiple values. These constructions must be enclosed clauses (it will be seen later that others not yet introduced are also allowed).

Example 4.1.3b. Another use of enclosed clauses.
Suppose that b is of mode **bool**, i and j are of mode **int** and assume the declaration

[10] **real** x, y, z, w

Then one could write
   (i) **if** b **then** x **else** y **fi** [i]
   (ii) **case** i **in** x, y, z **out** w **esac** [j]
In each example the balanced mode delivered by the choice clause is **ref [ ] real**.

4.1.4. Slicing
The process of slicing involves the application of the basic processes

108

of subscripting and trimming. These may be applied separately or together. Subscripting has already been introduced in the previous section. Trimming is the process of selecting a subarray, i.e. a smaller array, from a larger array. But whereas a subscript involves reducing the number of dimensions by one, trimming alone will leave the number of dimensions unaltered.

Consider the declaration

$$[-4:100] \textbf{ int } nn$$

As a result of this declaration nn is of mode **ref** [ ] **int**. Suppose it is required to introduce a reference to a multiple value consisting of the elements in $nn[-2], nn[-1], \ldots, nn[9]$. Writing $nn[-2:9]$ yields an object of mode **ref** [ ] **int** with the required properties. The multiple value to which this refers will have its own lower and upper bounds. The lower bound is taken to be 1. Since there are 12 elements in the multiple value the upper bound will be 12. Note that the number of dimensions of $nn[-2:9]$ is equal to the number of dimensions of the original nn. $-2:9$ is called a *trimmer*; it trims the original multiple value. As one might expect, -2 and 9 occupy meek syntactic positions and they can be replaced by any unit provided it delivers a result that can be coerced to an integer.

Example 4.1.4a. Trimming (giving a lower bound of 1).
Since $nn[-2:9]$ has mode **ref** [ ] **int** it can be subscripted or even trimmed. Thus
    (i) $nn[-2:9]$ [1] is equivalent to $nn[-2]$ and has mode **ref int**,
    (ii) $nn[-2:9]$ [10] is equivalent to $nn[7]$,
    (iii) $nn[-2:9]$ [1:2] [1] is equivalent to $nn[-2]$.

A lower bound obtained by trimming is called the *revised lower bound* of that slice. It is sometimes not convenient to have the selected subarrays having a revised lower bound of 1. Suppose it is required to have a reference to a multiple value such as $nn[-2:9]$ but instead of giving the multiple value a revised lower bound of 1 a revised lower bound of 10 is required. This can be achieved by writing $nn[-2:9$ **at** 10]. Again the 10 occupies a meek syntactic position and can be replaced by any unit delivering a posteriori an integer. The symbol **at** can also be written as @.

Example 4.1.4b. Trimming (giving a revised lower bound).
Using the above declaration of nn,
    (i) $nn[-2:9$ @ 10] [12] is equivalent to $nn[0]$;

(ii) $nn[1:9 @ n][n+3]$ is equivalent to $nn[4]$.

The time has now come to consider some special cases which result from omitting the lower and upper bounds from the trimmer. In general either the lower or the upper bound may be omitted and in such cases the lower or upper bound of the multiple value being trimmed is assumed. The revised lower bound is normally 1 but in the very special case when both the lower and upper bounds are omitted, when there is no **at** or @ present and when the colon is omitted the revised lower bound is that of the multiple value being trimmed. Some examples should help in clarifying the position.

Example 4.1.4c. Trimming, special cases.
Consider the previous declaration of nn, i.e. $[-4:100]$ **int** nn. Then the following pairs of slices are equivalent:
   (i) $nn[-2:]$ and $nn[-2:100]$ (when the upper bound is omitted the upper bound of the multiple value being trimmed is assumed);
   (ii) $nn[-2:@-2]$ and $nn[-2:100 @-2]$;
   (iii) $nn[:9]$ and $nn[-4:9]$;
   (iv) $nn[:9$ **at** $-2]$ and $nn[-4:9 @-2]$;
   (v) $nn[:]$ and $nn[-4:100 @ 1]$;
   (vi) $nn[@1]$ and $nn[-4:100 @ 1]$;
   (vii) $nn[\,]$ and $nn[-4:100 @ -4]$.

From the previous remarks it should be apparent that in obtaining a slice of a one-dimensional multiple value there can appear between [and] a subscript, a trimmer or an @ part, sections of which may be omitted, or nothing at all. The term *trimscript* is used to include all these possibilities. Moreover the object being sliced is called the *primary* of the slice. Thus in $nn[-2:9]$, nn is the primary and $-2:9$ the trimscript of the slice.

In trimming multiple values of dimension greater than one the same rules as were mentioned for one-dimensional multiple values can be applied to each dimension separately.

Example 4.1.4d. Trimming a three-dimensional multiple value.
Consider the declaration

$$[0:10, 0:11, 0:12]\ \textbf{char}\ a$$

Then a is of mode **ref** $[,\,]$ **char**. In the construction
   (i) $a[2:4, 3:5$ **at** $0, 2:][i,j,k]$
i, j and k would have to satisfy $1 \leq i \leq 3$, $0 \leq j \leq 2$ and $1 \leq k \leq 11$.

(ii) $a[, , \textbf{at } 1][i, j, k]$
i, j and k would have to satisfy $0 \leq i \leq 10$, $0 \leq j \leq 11$ and $1 \leq k \leq 13$.

In multiple values of dimension greater than one subscripting and trimming can both take place. This is just what is required in selecting a particular row or column of a two-dimensional multiple value (using the terms 'row' and 'column' in the sense of matrices).

Consider for instance

$$[0:9, 0:10] \textbf{ real } xx$$

Then $xx[0,]$ yields a reference to the multiple value consisting of the (ordered) values referred to by variables of the form $xx[0,j]$ where $0 \leq j \leq 10$. Thus writing $xx[0,][j]$ is equivalent to writing $xx[0,j]$, as one should expect. It was seen earlier that a single subscript would remove a single 'row' from the mode of the multiple value. Since the mode of xx is $\textbf{ref}[,]\textbf{real}$ the mode of $xx[0,]$ is $\textbf{ref}[ ]\textbf{real}$. The bounds produced by the trimmer are 0 and 10. Thus $xx[0,]$ yields a reference to the zero[th] row of the multiple value referred to by xx. In a similar way $xx[,0]$ yields a reference to the zero[th] column. Writing $xx[,0][i]$ is equivalent to writing $xx[i,0]$.

With multiple values of dimension greater than two the same principles hold. These are illustrated in the example below.

Example 4.1.4e. Slicing.
Given the declaration

$$[10, 0:100, -4:20] \textbf{ bool } bb$$

$bb[7,,][4,][3]$ is equivalent to $bb[7,4,3]$ and
$bb[7,@10,-3:]$ is equivalent to $bb[7,0:100@10,-3:20@1]$.

4.1.5. Assignments involving multiple values
The ability to manipulate multiple values is greatly increased by the fact that one can have assignments involving multiple values. A reference to a multiple value can be delivered as the destination in an assignment provided that a suitable (unit delivering a) multiple value appears as the source.

To illustrate suppose that the declaration

$$[100] \textbf{ int } a, b$$

appeared in a program. Then it would be feasible to have at a later stage of the program the assignment

$$a := b$$

The usual mode considerations are satisfied since a is of mode **ref** [ ] **int** and b after dereferencing produces a multiple value of mode [ ] **int**. But when such assignations are involved it is also necessary that the bounds associated with both sides of the assignation are identical. In this example this condition is satisfied, the bounds being 1 and 100. For assignations involving multiple values modes must match implying that the number of dimensions must be the same, and for each dimension the bounds must be identical. (See however 4.1.9.)

Example 4.1.5a. Assignations involving multiple values.
Given the declarations

$$[0:10] \textbf{ int } a1, a2, a3, [0:100] \textbf{ int } a4, \textbf{ int } i, \textbf{ bool } b$$

the following assignations are legal.
  (i) $a1[1:3] := a2[8:10]$
  (ii) **if** b **then** $a1$ **else** $a2$ **fi** $:=$ **case** i **in** $a1, a2, a3$ **out** $a4[0:10 @ 0]$
      esac
  (iii) $a1[2:4] := a1[1:3]$

The example given in part (iii) above deserves closer inspection since there is a hidden difficulty. The assignation is legal since the mode conditions are satisfied and since the bounds are identical, both being 1 and 3. But look at the effect of the assignation. If prior to the assignation

$$a1[1] = 2, a1[2] = 3, a1[3] = 5 \text{ and } a1[4] = 7$$

then after the assignation

$$a1[1] = 2, a1[2] = 2, a1[3] = 3 \text{ and } a1[4] = 5$$

Note that this is not equivalent to the three assignations

$$a1[2] := a1[1]; a1[3] := a1[2]; a1[4] := a1[3]$$

for this would result in each element being given the value 2.
   The point of this investigation has been to show that when slices overlap the programmer is entitled to assume that the correct action takes place. The problem of performing the assignation correctly rests with the compiler writer and need not concern the programmer.

Example 4.1.5b. Overlapping slices.
Suppose that aa has been declared as follows

$$[n] \textbf{ int } aa$$

112

n being of mode **int**. Write a piece of program to rotate cyclically to the right by one place all the elements of the multiple value referred to by *aa*.

A possible solution to this is

> **begin int** $a = aa[n]$;
> $aa[2:n] := aa[1:n-1]$;
> $aa[1] := a$
> **end**

4.1.6. Row displays

Since assignations have now been considered it is natural to consider initialisation of multiple values. For this and for the declaration of multiple values whose elements are constants it is convenient to have available some method of writing explicitly a particular multiple value. This is made possible by a special kind of collateral clause known as a *row display*. A row display containing the integers 2, 3, 5 and 7 is written as $(2, 3, 5, 7)$. The lower bound is 1 and since there are four elements in the row display the upper bound is 4; the lower bound of a row display is always 1 unless there is other information to the contrary (see below). One could thus write

> $[4]$ **int** *primes* $:= (2, 3, 5, 7)$

and this would make available four integer variables *primes* [1], *primes* [2], *primes* [3] and *primes* [4] initialised to 2, 3, 5 and 7 respectively.

At a later stage in the program these values could be changed to 11, 13, 17 and 19 respectively by means of an assignation

> *primes* $:= (11, 13, 17, 19)$

Row displays can occur only in syntactically strong positions. Each constituent element can be any unit. As the commas suggest these units are elaborated collaterally. Moreover row displays must contain (either zero or) at least two elements otherwise a certain kind of ambiguity occurs in looking at constructions such as (3). If row displays could contain only one element then this could be interpreted as either a closed clause or a row display, i.e. a closed clause or a collateral clause. This would lead to problems for the compiler. (See chapter 7 for further remarks on row displays with zero elements.)

Note that row displays are something more than multiple value denotations; hence the special term 'row display'. Admittedly one can write constructions such as $(2, 3, 4)$ but one could equally well write displays such as

$$((\textbf{int } n;\ read\ (n);\ n),\ 3,\ (x := (y := (z := 6.3) + 7;\ 4)))$$

For the purposes of dealing with coercions involving row displays the various units comprising the display are inspected and a balanced mode derived. The a posteriori mode of the multiple value is then row-of-the-balanced-mode. As one might expect coercions cannot be applied to the row display itself but like other collaterals and other enclosed clauses the coercions move inside the brackets and apply to the individual elements of the row display.

Example 4.1.6a. Balancing applied to row displays.
In the declaration

$$[4]\ \textbf{real } x2 := (6, 7, 8, 9)$$

the integers $6, 7, 8$ and 9 are all widened. In these circumstances the further assignation

$$x2 := (0, 0, 0, 0)$$

would be acceptable.

Row displays whose elements are other row displays can be used for multiple values of dimension two or more. Since multi-dimensional multiple values are rectangular in shape one must ensure that the row display is also rectangular in shape; rows of varying sizes will lead to error.

Example 4.1.6b. Multi-dimensional row displays.
Each of the following declarations is legal.
    (i) $[2, 3]\ \textbf{int } aa := ((1, 2, 3), (4, 5, 6))$
    (ii) $[2, 3, 4]\ \textbf{real } bb := (((1, 2, 3, 4), (5, 6, 7, 8), (9, 10, 11, 12)), ((13, 14, 15, 16), (17, 18, 19, 20), (21, 22, 23, 24)))$

The previous examples illustrate just some of the methods for performing the initialisation of, and assignations involving, references to multiple values. In general any unit delivering a suitable multiple value can be the source of the declaration or assignation.

Example 4.1.6c. Further row displays.
Given the declaration

$$[4]\ \textbf{int } a, b$$

one could have at a later stage
    (i) $[4]\ \textbf{int } c := a,\ d := (1, 2, 3, 0)$
    (ii) $[2, 4]\ \textbf{int } ab := (a, b),\ cd := ((0, 0, 0, 0),\ b)$

114

With the introduction of row displays and the mode associated with these it becomes convenient to introduce constant multiple values. Just as the identity declaration

> **int** $n = 4$

introduces n and ascribes 4 to it so the identity declaration

> [ ] **int** $nn = (2, 3, 5, 7)$

introduces nn and ascribes to it the multiple value $(2, 3, 5, 7)$. There are thus four constants $n[i]$, $1 \leq i \leq 4$. Each $nn[i]$ is of mode **int** and any attempt to alter its value by assignation would lead to a syntax error. This declaration could also have been written as

> [:] **int** $nn = (2, 3, 5, 7)$

The colon has no significance.

As with other declarations involving multiple values the right hand side of the equals symbol can deliver any multiple value. For present purposes (but see section 4.1.9) the number of dimensions of this multiple value should be the same as the number of dimensions of the mode on the left hand side, but the bounds delivered by the right hand side are inherited by the identifier being declared. It is for this reason that nn has bounds 1 and 4, the row display has these bounds and these are passed to nn.

Example 4.1.6d. Multiple values.
Given the declaration

> [10] **int** a, b

each of the following introduces a constant multiple value with bounds as indicated.
  (i) [ ] **int** $c = b$ the bounds being $1 : 10$.
  (ii) [: ,] **int** $ab = (a, b)$ bounds being $1 : 2$ and $1 : 10$.
  (iii) [ ] **int** $p = ($ [ ] **int** $q = (1, 2, 3); q[@0])$ the bounds of p being $0 : 2$.

4.1.7. Character manipulation

The string $"ABCD"$ is a denotation for a multiple value of mode [ ] **char** and the bounds associated with it are 1 and 4. Character strings are the only multiple values for which there are special denotations. These have been used frequently in print statements where their appearance merely indicates that they should be printed on the standard output.

In general the null string is written as $""$ and all other string denotations must contain two or more characters. As in character denotations a repeated quote must be used in string denotations to denote the character".

String denotations can be subscripted. Consequently

$$"abcdefghijklmnopqrstuvwxyz"[i]$$

would produce an object of a priori mode **char**, the ith letter of the alphabet. Indeed constructions such as this can be used to overcome the uncertainty about the relative order of characters in the character set. Remember that **abs** applied to an object of mode **char** produces an implementation-dependent result.

It is convenient to introduce at this stage some standard operators which can be used for the manipulation of characters and strings of characters.

Arithmetic operators

The dyadic operator $+$ can be used between characters or strings of characters in any combination. The operator essentially performs concatenation of the character strings and gives a result of mode [ ] **char**. The bounds of the operands are immaterial but the result produced will always have a lower bound of 1.

Example 4.1.7a. Concatenation.
  (i) $"a" + "bc"$ produces $"abc"$
  (ii) $"a" + ""$ produces $"a"$ of mode [ ] **char**

The dyadic operator $\times$ can be used with one operand of mode **char** or [ ] **char** and the other operand of mode **int**. The effect is that the character or string of character is duplicated as often as the integer operand requires. The string produced has a lower bound of 1. If the integer happens to be non-positive the upper bound will be 0.

Example 4.1.7b. Multiplication.
  (i) *print* $(2 \times "ma")$ will produce $"mama"$ on the standard output.
  (ii) [ ] **char** *line* $= 80 \times blank$ will cause *line* to consist of 80 space characters.
  (iii) $1 \times "a"$ produces a result of mode [ ] **char**, the bounds being 1 and 1.

Comparison operators

The comparison operators $<, \leq, =, \neq, \geq, >$ and their alternative representations allow comparisons between arbitrary combinations

116

of characters and strings of characters of any length. Their effect is to create an ordering of the set of all character strings, the ordering being determined by comparisons between individual characters.

Two character strings of the same length are compared by comparing the individual characters from the lower to the upper bound (the bounds of the two operands are immaterial). The first pair of characters which are unequal determine the result of the comparison. When two character strings are of differing lengths a similar comparison is performed. However, if the larger string is just the shorter string with some characters added then the shorter will come before the longer in an alphabetic ordering.

Example 4.1.7c. Comparing strings.
(i) Provided that $"b" < "c"$ delivers **true**, $"ab" < "ac"$ will also deliver **true**.
(ii) $"ab" < "abaa"$ delivers **true**.
(iii) $"" < "a"$ delivers *true*.

4.1.8. Simple transput involving multiple values
It is possible to make use of statements such as
        $read\,(a1),$ $read\,((b1,c1,d1))$
or
        $print\,(a2),$ $write\,((b2,c2,d2))$

where $a1,b1,c1$ and $d1$ are references to multiple values and $a2,b2,c2$ and $d2$ are a posteriori multiple values. Thus the data lists of transput procedures can involve multiple values.

The transput of rows of integers, reals, characters or booleans are all essentially similar. On reading, the items are read one at a time, new lines being taken automatically as necessary, into the various elements of the multiple value. On printing, the items are printed one at a time in the manner indicated in section 2.11.2, new lines being taken automatically as required. Of course, *newpage, newline, space,* etc. all play their usual roles but the conversion routines *whole, float* and *fixed* can be used only for transput of multiple values element by element. Some examples will serve to illustrate the process.

The piece of program

    $[10]$ **int** p; $read\,(p)$

causes ten integers to be read from the standard input and placed in the multiple value to which p is a reference. $p[1]$ is given the value of the first integer, $p[2]$ is given the value of the second integer, etc.

and $p[10]$ is given the value of the tenth integer.

Given the declarations

$$[0:10, 0:100] \text{ \bf bool } c, [0:10, 0:20] \text{ \bf int } d$$

then $read(c[0,])$ causes 101 booleans to be read and placed in $c[0,0]$, $c[0,1], \ldots, c[0,100]$. $read\, c[,0]$ causes 11 booleans to be read into $c[0,0], \ldots, c[10,0]$. $read(d)$ causes 11×21 integers to be read and placed in, successively, $d[0,0]$, $d[0,1]$, $d[0,2], \ldots, d[0,20]$, $d[1,0]$, $d[1,1], \ldots, d[10,20]$. With multiple values of higher dimension a similar pattern is followed. Thus the rightmost subscript varies most frequently. Another way of looking at this is to say that the multiple value is read a row at a time.

Printing of multiple values is relatively straightforward. The elements are merely printed in the order suggested from the discussion of the read statement.

4.1.9. Rowing

In discussing row displays it was mentioned that row displays had to contain either zero or at least two items. They could not contain one element. Yet in certain circumstances it may be desirable to have the effect of such a situation.

There is a coercion called 'rowing' which makes this possible. The effect of rowing is to add an extra 'row' to the mode of the item being coerced. Thus it adds one extra dimension and repeated applications add several dimensions. The bounds of the newly created dimensions are always 1 and 1. Thus repeated applications of rowing applied to an item of mode **int**, say, can lead to equivalent items of mode [ ] **int**, [,] **int**, [,,] **int** and so on. Rowing items of mode **ref int** can lead to items of mode **ref** [ ] **int**, **ref** [,] **int**, etc.

Rowing can be applied in strong syntactic positions only. Therefore it may be applied in declarations, assignations, etc.

Example 4.1.9a. Rowing.

(i) In $[1:1]$ **int** $a := 2$, 2 is rowed to mode [ ] **int** and the bounds associated with it are 1 and 1, thereby making the assignation legal.

(ii) In [,,] **real** $x = 3$, the 3 is widened and then rowed three times. The bounds associated with x are $1:1$, $1:1$, $1:1$.

(iii) The declaration

$$[\,] \text{ \bf int } p = ([\,] \text{ \bf int } q = 4; q[@\,0])$$

gives to p bounds of 0 and 0.

(iv) If y is of mode **ref real** the declaration

ref [,] real $x = y$

results in y being rowed twice.

(v) As a result of [, ,] **char** $a = ("abcd", "bcde")$, the bounds associated with a are $1:2$, $1:1$, $1:4$. For rowing, like any other coercion, cannot be applied to a row display itself but only to the constituent units. Each of $"abcd"$ and $"bcde"$ is rowed thus giving the required bounds.

4.1.10. Variable declarations and equivalent identity declarations revisited

The earlier remarks that variable declarations had an equivalent form of identity declaration still hold. Consider the variable declaration

$[0:10]$ **real** xx

This has an equivalent identity declaration, namely

ref [ ] real $xx = $ **loc** $[0:10]$ **real**

Take **loc** $[0:10]$ **real**. The local generator invoked by **loc** generates space for eleven real numbers, attaches lower and upper bounds and delivers as a result a reference to the multiple value that is to hold the eleven real numbers. The result is therefore a reference to a multiple value: xx is simply the identifier the programmer can use to access this reference to the multiple value. Since the generator is local the space exists only within the smallest range.

Note that the bounds are present after the **loc** for the generator has to know just how much space to generate. It must also know the bounds that have to be attached to the multiple value. The right hand side of the identity declaration is then said to contain an *actual declarer* – in fact it consists of **loc** followed by an actual declarer. Thus actual declarers for multiple values contain bounds.

The term 'actual parameter' has been used earlier. When considering the print and read statements it was pointed out that actual parameters appeared between the open and closing brackets. That the word 'actual' is used in this context and also when talking about declarers is no coincidence. The significance will become clearer when operator and procedure declarations are considered in chapter 5.

Example 4.1.10a. Actual declarers.

(i) In the identity declaration

ref int $n = $ **loc int**

the actual declarer is **int** and in

$$\textbf{ref} [\,] \textbf{int}\ p = \textbf{loc}\ [-4:10]\ \textbf{int}$$

the actual declarer is $[-4:10]$ **int**.

(ii) Neither of the identity declarations

$$\textbf{int}\ n = 4,\ [\,]\ \textbf{int}\ p = (2,3,5)$$

has an actual declarer since no generator is involved to the right of the equals symbol.

Consider now the left hand side of the equals symbol in an identity declaration. In the earlier declaration of *xx* the left hand side took the form

$$\textbf{ref} [\,] \textbf{real}\ xx$$

This is said to consist of a *formal declarer*, in this case **ref** [ ] **real**, followed by an identifier, here *xx*. Formal declarers do not contain bounds.

The duty of the formal declarer is to specify the mode of the object identified by the identifier it precedes. In general a formal declarer is necessary, for consider the identity declaration

$$\textbf{real}\ x = 4$$

in which the a priori and a posteriori modes of the right hand side differ.

In a declaration such as

$$[\,]\ \textbf{int}\ n = (1,2,3)$$

n is a mode identifier to which is ascribed the multiple value $(1,2,3)$. In this case the right hand side of the identity declaration is a multiple value. In general the right hand side can be any unit and is called the *source* of the declaration since it has properties similar to the source in an assignation. It must deliver an object whose a posteriori mode is that specified by the formal declarer.

The general form of an identity declaration can be expressed as

formal-declarer identifier = unit

The unit constitutes the source.

Example 4.1.10b. Formal and actual declarers and sources.
Table 4.1 gives several examples of identity declaration.

One can regard a variable declaration as an abbreviated form of an identity declaration. To obtain a variable declaration from a

TABLE 4.1.

Identity declaration	Formal declarer	Actual declarer	Source
int $n = 4$	**int**	none	4
ref int $m = $ **loc int**	**ref int**	**int**	**loc int**
ref [ ] int $nn = $ **loc** [2:100] **int**	**ref [ ] int**	[2:100] **int**	**loc** [2:100] **int**
[ ] int $mm = (2, 3, 4)$	**[ ] int**	none	$(2, 3, 4)$

suitable identity declaration not involving initialisation take the source of the declaration and follow it with the identifier on the left of the equals symbol. If desired the symbol **loc** can be omitted from the resulting text. Thus from

ref [ ] real $xx = $ **loc** [0:10] **real**

one obtains

loc [0:10] **real** xx

a perfectly good variable declaration. **loc** is optional in the position and omitting it leads to the usual form of variable declaration.

[0:10] **real** xx

The abbreviation is reflected in the fact that [0:10] **real** in [0:10] **real** xx or **loc** [0:10] **real** in **loc** [0:10] **real** xx is called a *sample generator*. Thus sample generators contain actual declarers. Moreover **loc** can be omitted from sample generators.

Example 4.1.10c. Equivalent declarations.
The identity declaration

ref real $x = $ **loc real**

has equivalent identity declarations

loc real x or **real** x

The next example illustrates some important points regarding the copying of multiple values.

Example 4.1.10d. Declarations involving multiple values.
Suppose that a is declared as in

[2:10, 0:4] **int** a

Then the following declarations could be made.

121

(i) [,] **int** $n = a$

a is dereferenced and the resulting multiple value copied; any change to an element of a will not cause the corresponding element of n to be altered.

(ii) **ref** [ ] **int** $nn = a[5,]$

any change to $nn[i]$ causes a similar change to $a[5,i]$ and vice versa.

4.1.11. Programming using multiple values

Before giving specific examples note that multiple values should be used only if there is good reason to do so. Their use could involve the need for a considerable amount of space and this might not be necessary. But if it is necessary one should be conscious of generating and relinquishing space at the correct time.

In using multiple values the programmer should be aware that subscripting itself is often relatively costly. If this can be avoided, or if the number of subscripts can be reduced, more efficient programs result. To this end declarations of the type given in example 4.1.10d (ii) can be used.

An example of the use of multiple values was given in example 4.1.1b. The next introduces sorting. A typical problem in sorting is the problem of arranging into some prescribed order the various elements of a multiple value. This prescribed order might be, in the case of sets of numerical items such as integers or real numbers, ascending order or descending order. In the case of characters it might be alphabetical order.

To illustrate suppose that a is declared by

$[n]$ **int** a (n is of mode **int**)

and that the elements of the multiple value have to be arranged in ascending order. Thus before sorting a might refer to the multiple value (in this case $n = 5$)

    5   4 -2 -7 0

and after sorting the multiple value should be

  -7 -2 0   4   5

One common method of sorting is the bubble sort. Essentially the method involves looking at adjacent elements in the sequence and interchanging them if they are out of order. The elements of the set are scanned in this way several times (if necessary). After the first scan the set

    5   4 -2 -7 0

122

would be altered to

$$4 \quad -2 \quad -7 \quad 0 \quad 5$$

Note that the largest element is now in its correct place, having been compared directly or indirectly with every other element via some intermediate largest element. It has bubbled to the top (hence the name for this technique) and therefore can be ignored in subsequent scans. This could be programmed as follows.

```
for i to n − 1
do if a[i] > a[i + 1]
    then int temp = a[i];
        a[i] := a[i + 1];
        a[i + 1] := temp
    fi
od
```

The piece of program to perform the second scan is similar to that for the first scan but with $n − 1$ replaced by $n − 2$. To perform the third and fourth scans $n − 1$ is replaced by $n − 3$ and $n − 4$ respectively.

A piece of program to perform the bubble sort is therefore as follows.

```
for j to n − 1
do for i to n − j
    do if a[i] > a[i + 1]
        then int temp = a[i];
            a[i] := a[i + 1];
            a[i + 1] := temp
        fi
    od
od
```

Note that j stops at $n − 1$. At this stage $a[n]$, $a[n − 1]$, ..., $a[3]$ and $a[2]$ are all in their correct positions and hence $a[1]$ must also be in its position.

In a sense the above piece of program is rather crude, but it can be improved. Observe that if a complete scan is performed and in the course of that scan not a single interchange takes place then the elements are in their correct order. This observation can be incorporated in the program by using a boolean variable called *altered*, say. At the start of each scan this is set to **false**. If ever an interchange takes place it is set to **true**. At the end of the scan if *altered* refers to the value **false** then the elements are in the correct order and no further scans are required.

This completes the present discussion on sorting. Many other methods are available, many of these being superior in various ways to the bubble sort.

4.2. Simple structures

Structures are a means of manipulating collections of items not all of which need be of the same mode. In one guise they resemble what one usually calls a record. In a university, for example, each student might have a record in the university computer. This might contain such items as the student's name, date of birth, marital status, student number, course number, examination passes, etc. One could represent such information by means of a structure in ALGOL 68.

Other examples of the use of records come readily to mind. Each book in a library could be represented by means of a structure containing such information as the name of the book, the name of the author, the book number, the classification number and some code indicating whether or not the book is out on loan and if so who has it and when it is due to be returned.

Entries in a telephone directory can be represented by means of structures; so also can flights of aeroplanes. Structures may be used for the purposes of payrolls, tax returns, stock control, etc. At another level a term in an arithmetic expression could be represented by a structure containing information about, for example, the coefficient, the variable and the power to which the variable is raised.

4.2.1. Declarations and selection

To illustrate the idea of a simple structure consider the books in a library. It will be assumed that the following information about each book has to be held in the computer:
   (a) the author's name, at most 30 characters long;
   (b) the name of the book, also at most 30 characters long;
   (c) the book number;
   (d) a classification number.

These pieces of information are all separate yet they are grouped together by the fact that in a specific case they are associated with one particular book. Each book will be represented by a structure consisting of four fields, one field for each of the above pieces of information. The author's name and the name of the book would be strings of characters and the book number and classification number would be integers.

The declaration of a variable called *new book* referring to such a structure might look like

124

struct ([1 :30] **char** *author*, [1 :30] **char** *name*, **int** *book no*,
int *class no*) *new book*

This can be shortened to

struct ([30] **char** *author, name,* **int** *book no, class no*) *new book*

This declaration introduces the mode identifier *new book* and gives to it a mode which, in a simplified form, is a reference to a structure. The structure has four fields which can be accessed through the various selectors *author, name, book no* and *class no*. The selector *author* selects the first field of the structure. More precisely

author **of** *new book*

is of mode **ref [ ] char** and thus gives the name of the author of the book. Since this mode is a reference to a multiple value the field can be changed. Thus one could write

author **of** *new book* := 20 × *blank* + ″*R. J. SMITH*″

Similarly *name* **of** *new book* is of mode **ref [ ] char** and gives the name of the book. This could be changed by an assignation such as

name **of** *new book* := 18 × *blank* + ″*ABC OF ALGOL*″

Again *book no* **of** *new book* is of mode **ref int** and one could write

book no **of** *new book* := 122718

Similarly for *class no* **of** *new book*.

Thus, just as subscripting of a reference to a multiple value of elements of mode **mode** gives an object of mode **ref mode**, so selecting from a structure gives a reference to an object of the appropriate kind.

Note that no selector can appear twice within the one structure even for fields of different modes. At compile time the compiler wishes to be able to deduce the mode of the object being selected and without the above restriction confusion would result.

Example 4.2.1a. Declarations of references to structures.
(i) The declaration

struct (**int** *coeff*, **char** *var*, **int** *power*) *first term*

introduces the mode identifier *first term*. The structure to which it refers has three fields which can be accessed by the three selectors *coeff, var* and *power*. Each of *coeff* **of** *first term*, *var* **of** *first term* and *power* **of** *first term* are variables.

(ii) The declaration

   struct (**int** *num*, *den*) *fraction*

introduces the mode identifier *fraction*. The structure to which it
refers has fields which can be accessed by means of the selectors
num and *den*. The above declaration could have been written as

   struct (**int** *num*, **int** *den*) *fraction*

In the last of the above examples note that the structure contains
two fields, both of which are integers. This is quite acceptable. Indeed
it is meaningful and sensible to do this rather than to declare *fraction*
to be a reference to a multiple value containing two integers. When
structures are used the appropriate field can be selected at compile
time. With multiple values subscripting would normally take place
at run time, i.e. when the program is actually running. There is
therefore a gain in efficiency in using structures.

   Although it is illegal to have two identical selectors within the
one structure it is possible to use as a selector an identifier which is
used elsewhere within that reach as a mode identifier or as a label.
Thus declarations of the kind

   int *num* = *num* **of** *fraction*

where *fraction* is declared as in example 4.2.1a(ii), are perfectly
acceptable and indeed often desirable. Such declarations can conveniently be used as abbreviations.

4.2.2. Modes associated with structures

Consider again the declaration

   struct (**int** *coeff*, **char** *var*, **int** *power*) *first term*

It was pointed out earlier that *first term* is a reference to a structure.
More precisely it has mode

   reference-to-structured-with-integral-field-coeff-character-field-
   var-integral-field-power-mode.

Note that the mode is essentially reference-to-structured-with- . . . -
mode. In the section represented by dots there appears for each field of
the structure three quantities: the mode of the object in that field;
the word field itself; the identifier which is used as the selector for
that field. The above mode is written in abbreviated form as

   ref struct (**int** *coeff*, **char** *var*, **int** *power*)

Note that in these modes the order in which the fields occur is significant and that the selectors themselves are part of the mode. These observations will be very important when assignations involving structures are considered; if a variable of mode **ref a** appears as the destination, a unit of a posteriori mode **a** must appear as the source.

Example 4.2.2a. Equivalent modes.

(i) **struct** (**int** *a*, **char** *b*, **int** *c*) and **struct** (**int** *a*, *c*, **char** *b*) do not represent the same mode.

(ii) **struct** (**int** *a*, **int** *b*) and **struct** (**int** *a*, *b*) do represent the same mode.

(iii) **struct** (**int** *a*, **char** *b*) and **struct** (**int** *c*, **char** *b*) do not represent the same mode.

The declaration of *first term* given above is in the usual way an abbreviation of

> **ref struct** (**int** *coeff*, **char** *var*, **int** *power*) *first term*
> = **loc struct** (**int** *coeff*, **char** *var*, **int** *power*)

Thus space to hold an integer, a character and another integer is generated in a single action by the local generator. The space remains in existence until the end of the smallest enclosing range.

To take a more complex example the declaration

> **struct** ([30] **char** *name*, **int** *age*, *weight*) *x*

introduces the mode identifier *x* and associates with it the mode

reference-to-structured-with-row-of-character-field-name-integral-field-age-integral-field-weight-mode.

Using the usual abbreviation the mode is

> **ref struct** ([ ] **char** *name*, **int** *age*, *weight*)

The declaration itself is an abbreviation of

> **ref struct** ([ ] **char** *name*, **int** *age*, *weight*) *x*
> = **loc struct** ([1 : 30] **char** *name*, **int** *age*, *weight*)

Note that the bounds appear only in the actual declarer, not in the formal declarer. This is just what was encountered in investigating multiple values themselves.

4.2.3. Building more complex structures
Structured modes can be made more complex in several ways. Until now structures have been built from objects of mode **int**, **char**, **real**, etc.

but they can also be built from other structures. To take a simple example consider the declaration of the mode identifier called *term*:

struct (**struct** (**int** *num*, *den*) *rational*, **char** *var*, **int** *power*) *term*

In the usual way one can now write *var* **of** *term* or *power* **of** *term*. But also one might want to select the *num* field of *rational* **of** *term*. This could be done by writing *num* **of** *rational* **of** *term*. Note that the implied bracketing here is *num* **of** (*rational* **of** *term*). This idea can be extended so that it is possible to build structures which are built of structures which in turn are built from other structures and so on. The implied bracketing in expressions such as *a* **of** *b* **of** *c* **of** *d* **of** *z* is *a* **of** (*b* **of** (*c* **of** (*d* **of** *z*))).

Building structures from structures is one possible extension of the simple idea of a structure. Another possibility is the idea of introducing multiple values all of whose elements are structures. These arise perfectly naturally in some of the examples already described. One might for instance view a polynomial as a row of terms, each term being a structure of the kind already introduced. A telephone directory might be represented by a multiple value all of whose entries are structures. The books in a library might be held in the computer as a multiple value all of whose elements are structures of a kind already described.

Taking this last example for illustration, suppose that it was necessary to declare a multiple value variable containing 1000 structures each of which represented a book. This could be done by the declaration

[1000] **struct** ([30] **char** *author*, *name*, **int** *book no*, *class no*) *books*

This declaration makes available, in the usual way, 1000 variables *books* [1], *books* [2], . . . , *books* [1000]. Each of these variables is a structure variable and, consequently, one can write pieces of program such as

author **of** *books* [100] := 20 × *blank* + "*R. J. SMITH*"

The implied bracketing of the source of this assignation is *author* **of** (*books* [100]). The situation can be described by saying that subscripting binds more tightly than **of**, i.e. than selecting. But in the usual way brackets can always be used to override the implied bracketing. Taking again the example of the library one might wish to access the first letter of the name of the 200th book. This can be done by writing

(*name* **of** *books* [200]) [1]

If the brackets had been omitted a syntax error would have resulted.

In the examples given above only one-dimensional multiple values

128

have been considered. However, multiple values of higher dimensions can be used and trimming and selecting of these can take place in the usual way.

Example 4.2.3a. Equivalent declarations.
The declaration

> [10] **struct** ([30] **char** *name*, **int** *age*) *q*

has an equivalent identity declaration

> **ref** [ ] **struct** ([ ] **char** *name*, **int** *age*) *q*
> = **loc** [10] **struct** ([30] **char** *name*, **int** *age*)

4.2.4. Multiple selection
Multiple selection is the process of selecting from an array of structures to obtain an array containing all the entries of one particular field. Consider the declaration

> [1000] **struct** ([3] **char** *alpha*, **int** *no*, **char** *year*) *reg no array*

designed to hold car registration numbers. The selection *year* **of** *reg no array* will produce a result of a priori mode **ref** [ ] **char**, the multiple value having bounds of 1 and 1000. In general the structures may be elements of multiple values with an arbitrary number of dimensions and multiple selection will produce associated multiple values with the same number of dimensions. The bounds of each dimension are inherited from the bounds of the multiple value from which selection is made.

4.2.5. Assignations involving structures
Consider the declaration

> **struct** ([30] **char** *author*, *name*, **int** *book no*, *class no*) *x*, *y*, *z*

Later in a program containing such a declaration it would be quite acceptable to write an assignation such as

> *x* := *y*

or even

> *x* := *y* := *z*

In the first of these examples *y* is dereferenced in the usual way and the assignation takes place. In the second example the value referred to by *z* is assigned to both *x* and *y*. As with previous assignations it is important that the mode requirements are satisfied. Thus if the destination is of mode **ref amode** the source must give, after possible coercion, a result of mode **amode**. With structures **amode** would be just **struct** (...) or perhaps a multiple value of objects of mode **struct** (...).

4.2.6. Structure displays

Structure displays are analogous to row displays. They can appear only in syntactically strong positions. This implies that the mode of a display will always be known from the context and in particular no confusion can ever arise over whether a display is a row display or a structure display. Furthermore coercions apply not to structure displays themselves but they move inside brackets and apply to individual units. The various elements of the structure display can be any unitary clauses delivering results of the required mode. A structure display must contain at least two fields.

Example 4.2.6a. Declarations of constant structures.
The declaration

> **struct** (**int** *day, month, year*) *indep day* = (4, 7, 1776)

introduces the constant structure *indep day*. Each of the objects *day* **of** *indep day*, *month* **of** *indep day* and *year* **of** *indep day* is of mode **int** and consequently cannot be changed.

The next example demonstrates a further application of multiple selection.

Example 4.2.6b. Another example of multiple selection.
The declaration

> [ ] **struct** (**char** *letter*, **int** *integer*) *roman*
> = (($''I''$, 1), ($''V''$, 5), ($''X''$, 10), ($''L''$, 50), ($''C''$, 100))

introduces the multiple value *roman* whose elements are structures.
   (i) *letter* **of** *roman* is of mode [ ] **char** and contains the five letters *I*, *V*, *X*, *L* and *C*.
   (ii) *integer* **of** *roman* is of mode [ ] **int** and contains 1, 5, 10, 50 and 100.

With structures there is no coercion analogous to rowing. An analogous coercion would be meaningful only if structures with single fields were being used. Such structures are of limited value but there is one situation (see section 5.2.3) in which their use is beneficial. For the moment consider

struct (**real** *value*) *x*

One could initialise this only by writing an assignation such as

value **of** *x* := *initial value*

Example 4.2.6c. Rowing and structure displays.
Consider the declaration

[ ] **struct** ([ ] **int** *a*) *r* = (1, 2, 3)

The following problem arises: is *r* a row of three structures each with a single field or is it a row consisting of one structure?

The answer is determined from the basic properties of coercions. As usual a display itself cannot be coerced but the coercions move inside the brackets and apply to the individual elements. No set of coercions will produce either of the above possibilities and the declaration would be flagged as illegal.

One final example in this section introduces constant declarations involving both multiple values and structures.

Example 4.2.6d. Multiple values and structures.
The following declaration is legal:

[ ] **struct** ([ ] **char** *name*, **int** *age*) *family* =
(("*JOHN*", 3), ("*ROBERT*", 1), ("*CATHERINE*", 4))

Note that the character strings are of differing lengths. This would have been illegal in a variable declaration but is acceptable in the above identity declaration.

4.2.7. Transput involving structures

Transput can be dealt with by noting that if *p* is a structure then *print* (*p*) or *write* (*p*) causes the fields to be printed in order to the standard output and if *q* is a reference to a structure *read* (*q*) causes the appropriate number of items of the appropriate modes to be read from the standard input. These remarks are illustrated in the following example.

Example 4.2.7a. Transput involving structures
 (i) The data for the program below consists of the name, age (in years) and weight (in kilograms) of several people. The data is arranged in such a way that each line consists of a name occupying the first 30 character positions followed by two integers representing

the age and weight of that person. The data is terminated by an entry with a negative age followed by a blank line. The program should reproduce the table but mark with the word "DANGER" all people whose age is over 90 and who are also over 90 kilograms in weight.

```
begin print ("health danger list follows:");
      while struct ([30] char name, int age, weight) a;
            read ((a, newline)); age of a >= 0
      do bool danger = age of a > 90 and weight of a > 90;
         print ((newline, a, (danger |" DANGER" |" ")))
      od;
      print ((newline, "list terminated"))
end
```

The effect of the read statement following the **while** is to read from *standin* the first 30 characters and assign these to the first field. Then the two integers are read. The first is given to the second field and the second is given to the third field.

The print statement involving *a* causes the first field to be printed, then the second field and finally the third field. Thus a name appears followed by the 2 integers representing the age and weight of that person.

(ii) The next example is, in a sense, rather trivial but it does illustrate transput involving both multiple values and structures. Consider

```
begin [5, 8] struct (int num, den) a;
      read (a);
      for i to 5 do print ((a [i, ], new line)) od
end
```

The read statement causes 5×8 pairs of integers to be read from *standin*; each structure corresponds to a single pair of integers. In the print statement $a[i,]$ is used to select the ith row of *a* thus illustrating trimming. The numbers are therefore printed in such a way that there are eight pairs of integers to each line. (It is assumed that the lines are long enough.)

4.2.8. Programming using simple structures

The structures that have been introduced have been of a limited nature. In particular it has been necessary to have within fields character strings with fixed bounds. In many situations this is natural. Items such as postal codes, national insurance numbers, student identity numbers, car registration number, etc. are all items of a standard format and size. This limitation is in general rather restricting. The number of characters involved in the names of people or towns, titles of books, etc. varies from item to item. ALGOL 68 does allow the manipulation of such character strings but they must be treated with a certain amount of understanding and respect. This and other more advanced aspects of structures will be dealt with in chapter 7.

The proper use of structures is a very complex subject. The study of this is variously known as data processing, data structures, data bases, etc. No attempt is made here to cover the topics thoroughly. But basically structures should be such that (i) they reflect the relevant properties of the item being represented, and (ii) frequently performed operations are relatively efficient. Note that (i) implies that one must abstract from a physical object the relevant details. This is by no means an easy matter and indeed the same object may be represented in different ways for different purposes.

The rest of this section is concerned only with certain aspects of the efficiency of using structures. A detailed study of structures is material for another volume.

Assignations involving structures themselves have been discussed. In general, if the structures themselves happen to contain a great deal of information then the process of copying involves the computer in a great deal of work. The more information the structure holds the more the work required.

Certain algorithms can involve a considerable amount of copying of information. Such an algorithm is that given earlier for performing the bubble sort. When the items of information being sorted are integers or real numbers then the amount of copying is acceptable but if they happen to be large structures the amount of copying is prohibitive and, indeed, unnecessary. In this section a modified version of the bubble sort will illustrate the point.

In the above discussion there is an implicit assumption being made that structures can be compared in some way. Usually this comparison will take the form of a comparison between certain fields of the structure. To take an example, the entries in a telephone directory are ordered, at a crude level, by means of alphabetical order of surname. At a more sophisticated level entries with identical surnames are ordered by means of initials of first names and then, if necessary, by alphabetical order of the name of the road or street in which a person lives.

For the purposes of illustrating a sorting algorithm which avoids excessive interchanges consider a multiple value all of whose elements are structures. Suppose that each structure consists of two fields one of which represents a person's name and the other of which represents their age. The multiple value of structures has to be sorted in order of increasing age.

The following declaration is therefore assumed:

$[n]$ **struct** ($[30]$ **char** *name*, **int** *age*) *a*

Since the structures have to be arranged in order of increasing age the straightforward bubble sort would require the comparison of successive ages *age* **of** $a[i]$ and *age* **of** $a[i+1]$ with subsequent inter-changes of $a[i]$ and $a[i+1]$ if necessary. The modified method must involve some comparisons but must overcome the problem of the interchanges. In fact the same set of comparisons are made but instead of interchanging the structures themselves pointers to the structures are interchanged. To help in this task an auxiliary multiple value *b* is introduced. Each $b[i]$ is initialised to the value *i*. The algorithm then proceeds by comparing successively the values of *age* **of** $a[b[i]]$ and *age* **of** $a[b[i+1]]$ and if the entries are out of order the values of $b[i]$ and $b[i+1]$ are interchanged. This results in:

```
[n] int b; for i to n do b[i] := i od;
for j to n − 1
while bool altered := false;
        for i to n − j
        do if age of a[b[i]] > age of a[b[i + 1]]
            then int temp = b[i];
                  b[i] := b[i + 1];
                  b[i + 1] := temp;
                  altered := true
        fi
    od; altered
do skip od;
    # put sorted elements into temporary array c #
a := begin [n] struct ([30] char name, int age) c;
            for i to n do c[i] := a[b[i]] od;
        c
    end
```

This completes the algorithm for sorting structures. Note that it is worthwhile going to the trouble of specially programming the above sort only if the more straightforward method would be much less efficient. The decision on this would in general depend on the size of *n* and on how much interchanging would have to be done.

4.3. Simple mode declarations

By means of mode declarations it will be possible for the programmer to introduce his own modes. There are several reasons for this being desirable. Writing declarations involving structures with several fields can become tedious. If the mode involving such structures has to be written several times there is a danger of making errors in typing or in interchanging the positions of fields, etc. In declarations involving structures which have been built from other structures these remarks become even more relevant.

Mode declarations allow such problems to be overcome. But note that, for the moment, they are being used as a matter of convenience, not necessity.

4.3.1. Examples of mode declarations

As an example of a simple mode declaration consider

> **mode ratn = struct** (**int** *num*, *den*)

as a result of this declaration **ratn** could be used wherever

> **struct** (**int** *num*, *den*)

could be used. In particular the following declarations would be acceptable.

> **ratn** *half* = (1, 2), *quarter* = (1, 4)
> [10] **ratn** *a*
> **struct** (**ratn** *coeff*, **char** *var*, **int** *power*) *first*

Indeed after this mode declaration one could later introduce another mode declaration which made use of the mode already defined. Thus the declaration

> **mode term = struct** (**ratn** *coeff*, **char** *var*, **int** *power*)

would be acceptable and it would be equivalent to

> **mode term = struct** (**struct** (**int** *num*, *den*) *coeff*, **char** *var*, **int** *power*)

The use of mode declarations need not be restricted to structures.

Example 4.3.1a. Simple mode declarations.
Each of the following is an acceptable mode declaration.

> **mode integer = int**
> **mode z = int, r = real, b = bool, v = void**
> **mode array1 = [100] int, array2 = [10, 2 :9] real**

The means of denoting a new mode is an indicant, any bold

sequence of letters and/or digits starting with a letter. The bold sequence must not be already used in ALGOL 68 for another purpose. Thus **in** for example could not be used as a new mode since it is already used in case clauses. No typographical display features can be used to separate the various letters and digits of the new mode. The new mode itself can be used only within the smallest enclosing serial clause, in the usual way.

All new modes introduced by mode declarations can be used like any of the standard modes such as **int**, **real**, etc. Thus one can introduce identity declarations, variable declarations, multiple values, structures, new mode declarations, etc. all involving objects of the new mode.

Note that in the declarations involving multiple values the bounds were present, the lower bound in some cases being implicit. This must always be the case but any units delivering results of (a posteriori) mode **int** can be present as the lower and upper bounds. Their syntactic position is meek.

Consider then

> **mode m** $= [p : q]$ **int**

A problem arises over when the bounds p and q are elaborated. In fact they are elaborated when **m** is involved in a declaration which requires their elaboration.

Example 4.3.1b. Dynamic arrays revisited.
Consider the piece of program

> **int** $p := 2, q := 10$;
> **mode m** $= [p : q]$ **int**;
> **m** a; *print* $((\textbf{lwb } a, \textbf{upb } a))$;
> $q := 4$;
> **m** b; *print* $((\textbf{lwb } a, \textbf{upb } a, \textbf{lwb } b, \textbf{upb } b))$

The results produced are 2, 10, 2, 10, 2 and 4 respectively. Moreover note that one could write a declaration such as

> **m** $c = (1, 2, 3, 4)$

and c would have bounds 1 and 4 respectively. For this purpose the mode **m** is [ ] **int**. The bounds are ignored and p and q not elaborated.

4.3.2. row-of-row-of-modes
As a result of the remarks in the previous section the following would be acceptable

> **mode a** $= [10]$ **int**

136

and it could be followed by a declaration such as

   [2:100] **a** x

This would then have the same effect as the declaration

   [2:100][10] **int** x

Such declarations have not been previously encountered. Yet they are legal and the above would result in x having mode reference-to-row-of-row-of-integral. One could write, after this declaration, $x[i]$ where $2 \leq i \leq 100$ and $x[i]$ would have mode **ref a**. Similarly $x[i][j]$ where $1 \leq j \leq 10$ would have mode **ref int**.

Note that the multiple value referred to by x is only one-dimensional. Its mode is quite different from that of y introduced by the declaration

   [2:100, 10] **int** y

x has mode reference-to-row-of-row-of-integral and y has mode reference-to-row-row-of-integral.

Example 4.3.2a. Rows of integers.
The declaration

   [ ][ ] **int** $g = ((1, 2, 3), (4, 5), (6, 7, 8, 9))$

is legal. On the other hand

   [,] **int** $h = ((1, 2, 3), (4, 5), (6, 7, 8, 9))$

is illegal since each row of h must be the same size.

Although modes of row-of-row-of-integral have been introduced above one can have many occurrences of 'row-of' included in the mode. And instead of **int** one could have any of the standard modes or indeed any mode including those introduced by the programmer by means of a mode declaration.

4.3.3. Rowing revisited
In previous cases rowing caused the addition of an extra, or several other, occurrences of 'row' to the mode of the object being coerced. In the declaration

   [,] **int** $a = (1, 2, 3)$

for instance the right hand side is coerced to mode [,] **int** (each item of the display is rowed) and one can write $a[i,j]$ where $1 \leq i \leq 3$ and $j = 1$.

137

With the introduction of the modes involving 'row-of-row-of' the coercion rowing takes on an added significance. Consider the identity declaration

$$[\ ][\ ] \textbf{int } b = (1, 2, 3)$$

This is acceptable and rowing will move inside the brackets and produce from $1, 2$ and 3 equivalent objects of mode [ ] **int**. Thus an extra 'row-of' is added to the mode. Then one can write $b[i][j]$ where $1 \leq i \leq 3$ and $j = 1$.

The precise effect of rowing is therefore derived from the context. Extra occurrences of 'row' or 'row-of' are added as required.

Exercises for chapter 4

1. Express each of the following declarations as an identity declaration.
   (i) [10] **int** *nn*
   (ii) [10, 4, 6] **int** *nnn*
   (iii) [ ] **bool** $p =$ (**true, false, true**)

2. Given the declaration

   $$[-7:100, 0:10] \textbf{ int } n$$

   what multiple value is referred to by each of the following?
   (i) $n[0:10, 1:5][1,]$ (ii) $n[0:10, 1]$
   (iii) $n[@1, @2][\ ,2]$ (iv) $n[\ ,@2][1,]$
   (v) $n[:5, @0][\ ,1]$

3. Is it (a) necessary, (b) advisable to make use of multiple values in writing programs to perform each of the following tasks?
   (i)   Find the maximum of a set of numbers.
   (ii) Find the maximum and minimum of a set of numbers.
   (iii) Find the position of the (first) maximum of a set of numbers i.e. find the value of i where the maximum is the ith number in the sequence.
   (iv) Find the number of times the maximum appears in a sequence and the position of the last occurrence of this maximum.
   (v)   Find the standard deviation of a set of observations $x_1, x_2, \ldots x_n$; standard deviation is defined as

   $$\frac{1}{n}\sqrt{(n \sum_{i=1}^{n} x_i^2 - (\sum_{i=1}^{n} x_i)^2)}$$

4. Write pieces of program to accomplish each of the tasks outlined

138

in (i) and (iii) in the previous example.

5. Suppose that an array of 32 booleans, *array*, holds the binary representation of an unsigned integer. How would you print that integer in decimal notation? (Assume that **false** denotes 0 and **true** denotes 1.)

6. Is it legal to label the subscript of a slice? What ambiguity might result?

7. Let *n* be a positive integer and assume *a* is declared as

   [*n*] **int** *a*

   Write a section of program to move the first *r* elements ($1 \leqq r \leqq n$) of the multiple value referred to by *a* into the last *r* places and replace the remaining $n - r$ entries by 0.

8. The declaration

   [10, 100] **int** *mark*

   is made with the intention that the multiple value referred to by *mark* contains the marks of 100 students each of whom takes 10 different subjects. For this purpose the subjects are numbered from 1 to 10 and the students numbered from 1 to 100. With this convention *mark* [*i, j*] holds the mark obtained by student *j* in subject *i*.
   (i) Give a closed clause whose value is the maximum mark obtained in subject 1.
   (ii) Write a closed clause whose value is the maximum of the complete set of 1000 marks.
   (iii) Trim *mark* in such a way that the trimming yields a reference to a one-dimensional multiple value consisting of the marks in subject 7. The revised lower and upper bounds should be 1 and 100 respectively.
   (iv) Write a closed clause which gives a multiple value delivering the class average in each of the examinations.

9. Improve the efficiency of the following piece of program which tests if two integer multiple values *a* and *b* are identical

   ```
   (bool equal := lwb a = lwb b and upb a = upb b;
   if equal
   then for i from lwb a to upb a
        do equal := equal and a[i] = b[i] od
   fi;
   equal)
   ```

10. Assume the declaration

   [n] **int** q

   Write a section of program to rotate cyclically to the right r places the elements of the multiple value referred to by q. Do not use a loop clause.
   How would the program be altered to cause rotation to the left rather than to the right?

11. One way in which the computer can evaluate $x \uparrow n$ is to perform, effectively, the closed clause

   begin real *prod* := 1; **to** *n* **do** *prod* × := *x* **od**; *prod* **end**

   Are n multiplications necessary? To what extent can this number be reduced?

12. Write separate pieces of program to perform the addition, subtraction and multiplication of two matrices.

13. Under what circumstances would a set of numbers of the same mode be held as a structure rather than as a multiple value?

14. To what are these identity declarations equivalent?
    (i) **struct** (**int** a, b) x := (2, 3)
    (ii) **struct** ([5] **char** x, **int** a) y
    (iii) **struct** ([4, 7] **real** x, [7] **bool** t) z

15. Given the declaration

   struct (**int** a, b) x, **struct** (**int** c, d) y, [2] **int** z, **bool** b

   are any of the following legal? Give reasons for your answer.
    (i) $x := y$ (ii) $x := z$ (iii) $z := x$
    (iv) **if** b **then** x **else** y **fi** := (2, 3)
    (v) **if** b **then** x **else** z **fi** := (2, 3)

16. Each of the following items can be represented in the computer by means of a structure. Indicate what form these structures might take:
    (i) a rational number   (ii) a point in x, y plane
    (iii) a polygon   (iv) a circle
    (v) a straight line
    Give mode declarations for each of these structures.

Programming problems for chapter 4

1. Write a program which accepts sentences (terminated by a

140

period) and indicates whether or not they are palindromic, i.e. read the same forwards as backwards. Spaces should be ignored and the data should start with some integer which indicates the maximum size of the sentence to follow.

2. Write a piece of program to take two sets of integers both in increasing order and merge them together to give a third set also in increasing order and containing all the elements in the first two sets. Your program should make use of the fact that the given sets are already sorted. Assume that elements may be repeated on input but not on output.

3. Frequency counts can be performed on various sets of data. Some examples include:

   (i) count the number of ages (these appear as integers in the range 0–119 inclusive) in each of the ranges 0–9, 10–19, ..., 110–119;

   (ii) as in (i) except that the ranges are 0–5, 6–15, 16–25, ..., 86–95, 96–125;

   (iii) count the number of heights (these appear as real numbers denoting centimetres in the range 30–250) in the ranges 30–35, 35–40, ..., 245–250.

   In each case the lower bound is included in the range and the upper bound is excluded from the range.

   Indicate in each case what form the program would take.

4. Write a piece of program to decide if one multiple value can be obtained from a second multiple value merely by interchanging two elements of the first multiple value.

5. Write a piece of program to take a matrix and produce its transpose.

6. Let a be an array of integers sorted into increasing order. It is required to test if the integer x is in the set.

   Write a piece of program which performs this task by using a binary chop thus: a comparison of x and the central element will yield one of three results; either x is not present in the array or, if present, it is in either the top half or lower half of the array. In the latter two cases the technique is repeatedly applied to the top/lower part of the array. (Often arrays are sorted so that fast searches such as binary chops can be performed.)

7. Write a program to print out the first n rows of Pascal's triangle. n is supplied as data.

8. If m is a positive integer the m-generalised Fibonacci numbers

$f_0, f_1, f_2, \ldots$ are defined as follows:

$$f_0 = f_1 = f_2 = \ldots = f_{m-2} = 0, f_{m-1} = 1 \text{ and for each } n > 0$$

$$f_{n+m} = f_{n+m-1} + f_{n+m-2} + \ldots + f_{n+1} + f_n$$

i.e. each term is obtained by adding together the m previous terms.

Write a program to read two positive integers m and p and to print out the first p m-generalised Fibonacci numbers. Assume that $p > m$ but incorporate suitable checks on the values of m and p in your program.

9. Show how new modes **name** and **address** as described below could be introduced by means of mode declarations. **name** is a structure consisting of two fields; the first is a row of 20 characters and has selector *surname*, the second is a row of 15 characters and has selector *firstname*. **address** is a structure consisting of four fields defined as follows:

(i) the first is an integer denoting the number of the house in a street and has selector *no*;

(ii) the second is a row of 20 characters denoting the name of the street and has selector *street*;

(iii) the third is a row of 15 characters denoting the town, city or county and has selector *town*;

(iv) the fourth is a row of 7 characters denoting the postal code and has selector *pc*.

The mode **record** is a structure consisting of a name and a corresponding address. Indicate how an object of this mode might be printed for the purposes of addressing an envelope.

10. Consider a set of records each of the form indicated by the previous example. Write a program to print out these records in alphabetical order of surnames (if two surnames are identical then the first names should give the alphabetical ordering). Assume if necessary that no two names are identical.

11. Devise a program which will remove all comments and pragmatic remarks from an ALGOL 68 program.

12. Design a program which will keep an updated version of a football, squash, or hockey league. Your program should read in the current state of the league together with a set of results and produce an updated league table. State clearly any assumptions you make.

5

PROCEDURES AND OPERATORS

In ALGOL 68 expressions involve a wider range of operators than one would usually encounter in mathematics. The expressions could include assignations and the concept of mode was always to the fore. However there are certain mathematical ideas (functions, for instance) which have a counterpart in ALGOL 68 and have still to be described.

In mathematics one often makes use of functions such as *sin, cos, log, cosh*, etc. Their meaning is understood in the same kind of way that the usual meaning of the operators $+$, $-$, etc. is understood.

In this chapter it will be seen that *standard functions*, as they are often called, can be used in ALGOL 68 programs. Their definition is included in the standard environment and they can be used in expressions.

Apart from their more traditional use, functions are themselves objects that can be manipulated within a program in the same kind of way as integers, characters, multiple values, structures, etc. As with all such objects ALGOL 68 requires that a mode be associated with functions. It is then possible to introduce variables whose values are functions. For instance, it will be possible to have a variable *f* whose value at one point in a program is *sin* and at another point is *cos*.

Now the standard functions, and indeed the standard operators, will not in general provide a sufficiently comprehensive set to cover the needs of all programmers. A facility is therefore available to allow the programmer to declare his own functions and operators. Objects so declared can then be used in a similar way to those in the standard environment.

Besides functions such as *sin* and *cos* there are available objects such as *print* and *read*. These are in many respects similar to functions except that they deliver a result of mode **void**. Functions together with objects such as *print* and *read* are called procedures.

5.1. Procedures

5.1.1. The standard procedures

The set of standard procedures can be divided conveniently into three subsets. The first includes the standard mathematical functions, the second functions used for generating random numbers and the third contains a solitary function used for character manipulation.

The few standard procedures which require a more advanced knowledge of ALGOL 68 will be considered in later chapters.

The mathematical functions

The standard mathematical functions are listed in table 5.1. Each has a single parameter, e.g. $sin(x)$, and delivers a result of mode **real**. The syntactic position of the parameter x is strong and x should deliver a result of (a posteriori) mode **real**. (Note that the actual parameters of print and read statements should be regarded as exceptional in this respect.)

TABLE 5.1.

Function	Effect	Remarks
sqrt	square root	$sqrt(x)$ is defined only for $x \geq 0$
exp	exponential	$exp(x) = e^x$ where $e = 2.718\ldots$
ln	natural logarithm	$ln(x)$ is defined only for $x > 0$
sin	sin	
cos	cos	
tan	tan	
arcsin	inverse sin	$arcsin(x)$ is defined only for **abs** $x \leq 1$; **abs** $arcsin(x) \leq pi/2$
arccos	inverse cos	$arccos(x)$ is defined only for **abs** $x \leq 1$; $0 \leq arccos(x) \leq pi$
arctan	inverse tan	**abs** $arctan(x) \leq pi/2$

Example 5.1.1a. On the use of the standard procedures. Assume that x is of mode **real**.

(i) $sin(x) + 4.7$

is a legal arithmetic expression delivering a result of (a priori) mode **real**. The operand $sin(x)$ is a call to procedure sin and it delivers a result of mode **real**. The result of adding two reals is a real.

(ii) $sin(x) \uparrow 2 + sqrt(pi)/ln(7) + cos(pi/5)$

is a legal arithmetic expression delivering a result of (a priori) mode **real**; note that the 7 is widened.

(iii) In the expression

$$sin\,(sqrt\,(ln\,(pi/4 \times x)) + pi/4.7)$$

note that the actual parameter of *sin* makes use of an expression involving *sqrt* and *ln*.

In general the parameter of these functions can be an arbitrary unit delivering a result of (a posteriori) mode **real**.

Random number generators

By writing *random* in an expression a programmer obtains some real number in the range 0 to 1, 0 being included but 1 being excluded. Repeated calls, i.e. requests to activate the procedure, yield numbers which are uniformly distributed over the range 0 to 1. A procedure such as *random* is often called a random number generator.

Using *random* one can obtain random real numbers or random integers distributed uniformly over other ranges. To illustrate, a random integer in the range 1 to 10 is produced by the expression

entier $(10 \times random + 1)$

Random numbers are used in programs whenever some element of uncertainty is required. A simple example is given below.

Example 5.1.1b. Using *random*.
Write a program to generate ten questions in simple arithmetic involving the addition of two integers in the range 1 to 10. The results should be printed on a new page.

```
begin [10] int result;
    for i to 10
    do int m = entier (10 × random + 1);
       int n = entier (10 × random + 1);
       result [i] := m + n;
       print (("question", whole (i,0),". ", whole (m,0),
                " +", whole (n,0)," = ?", newline))
    od;
       print ((newpage, "results for questions 1 to 10 are",
               result))
end
```

Note that more sophisticated uses of *random* could produce questions involving the addition of a variable number of integers. In this case the number of integers generated is obtained by using *random*.

One must always ask if random numbers are reproducible, i.e. if a program is executed twice will the same sequence of numbers be

145

generated? Some random number generators make use of the time on a clock in the computer and consequently there is only a remote chance of the same numbers being reproduced on successive runs. The procedure *random* will in general produce the same numbers although the programmer can alter this state of affairs if he so chooses (see section 5.1.3).

The conversion routines revisited

The conversion routines *whole*, *fixed* and *float* have been used in conjunction with the print or write statements to obtain a greater degree of control over the manner in which integers or real numbers are printed. These routines however are just standard procedures each giving a result of mode [ ] **char**. They may be used outside the confines of transput procedures.

Example 5.1.1c. Using the conversion routines.

(i) An integer is said to be a palindrome if the number remains unaltered when the order of its digits is reversed. Thus 1221, 77 and 7 are palindromes but 32 is not. Write a piece of program which delivers **true** if the integer *n* is a palindrome and **false** otherwise.

```
begin [ ] char number = whole (n, 0);
      int ub = upb number, bool pal := true;
      for i to ub ÷ 2 while pal
      do pal := number[i] = number[ub + 1 − i] od;
      pal
end
```

(ii) If *coeff* and *pow* are of mode **int** the statement

$$print \ (whole \ (coeff, 0) + "x\uparrow" + whole \ (pow, 0))$$

is acceptable. The operators + perform the concatenation of character strings and the resulting string is printed to the standard output.

The standard procedure *char in string*

char in string tests if a particular character is present in a string of characters. The procedure has to be supplied with three quantities: the character to be sought, an integer variable and the character string to be searched. It returns the value **true** or **false** indicating the presence or absence of the character and the integer variable is given a value indicating the position of the first occurrence of the character.

Example 5.1.1d. *char in string*.
Assume that *p* has been previously declared and is of mode **ref int**.

146

(i) *char in string* (*"a"*, *p*, *"abc"*) returns **true** and *p* is set to 1.

(ii) *char in string* (*"a"*, *p*, *"def"*) returns **false** and *p* is unaltered. See also example 5.1.3c(i).

5.1.2. Modes associated with procedures

Each of the procedures appearing in table 5.1 has the property that it takes as parameter a real number and produces as result a real number. Their mode is said to be

> procedure-with-real-parameter-yielding-real

This is abbreviated to **proc (real) real**.

The introduction of this mode allows in the usual way the declaration of constants and variables whose values are functions.

Example 5.1.2a. Procedure declarations I.

Assuming suitable declarations of *x*, *y* and *i*, the following are acceptable declarations:

(i) **proc (real) real** *f* = **if** *x* > *y* **then** *sin* **else** *cos* **fi**,
$\qquad\qquad$ *g* = **case** *i* **in** *exp*, *ln*, *sqrt* **esac**

(ii) **proc (real) real** *h* := **if** *x* > *y* **then** *arcsin* **else** *arccos* **fi**

Note that *h* has mode

> **ref proc (real) real**

(iii) **proc (real) real** *h1*, *h2*

Consider the declaration of *f* given in (i) above. This is an identity declaration and its effect is to introduce *f* and to ascribe to *f* either *sin* or *cos* depending on whether *x* is greater than *y* or not. In an environment containing this declaration one could write a call such as $f(x \uparrow 2 + y)$ and, assuming *x* > *y* when the declaration of *f* is encountered, this would have the same effect as the call $sin (x \uparrow 2 + y)$.

Consider however the declaration of *h* given in the second part of the previous example. One would like to be able to write expressions such as *h*(0.5). The intended effect would be that the parameter 0.5 would be supplied to the procedure which at that time was the value referred to by *h*. Indeed this is possible. Formally, the syntactic position occupied by *h* is meek and dereferencing of *h* takes place. *h* is said to be the *primary* of the call *h*(0.5). In a similar way *sin* is the primary of the call *sin* (*pi*/4) though in this case no coercion is required.

An assignation of the form

$\qquad$ *h* := *arctan*

147

can occur. Note that the mode considerations normally encountered in assignations are satisfied. The mode of *h* is **ref proc (real) real** and the mode of *arctan* **proc (real) real**. Also allowed are assignations of the form

$$h1 := h2$$

where *h1* and *h2* are declared as in (iii) above. In this case *h2* must be dereferenced. If *h2* had the value *sin* then the effect of the assignation would be to give to *h1* the value *sin*.

Thus functions can themselves be used in assignations in the same kind of way as integers, booleans, characters, multiple values, structures, etc. The assignation is a construction by means of which an object of a particular mode can be assigned to a variable which can accept values of that mode. Objects of any mode other than **void** can be manipulated by assignation.

The mode associated with the standard mathematical procedures was **proc (real) real** indicating that the procedure took a real parameter and delivered a real result. Thus the mode took the form

proc (mode of parameter) mode of result

This is a particularly simple case. In more complex examples the procedure might have no parameters, e.g. *random*, or it might have several parameters, e.g. *char in string*. If there are no parameters but the result is of mode **p** the mode of the procedure is **proc p**. Thus *random* is a procedure of mode **proc real** since it delivers as a result a real number. If there are several parameters of modes **p1, p2, . . . , pn** and if the result is of mode **p** then the mode of the procedure is **proc (p1, p2, . . . , pn) p.** In particular, *char in string* has mode **proc (char, ref int, [ ] char) bool.**

The example below illustrates the variety of possibilities that are now open. The variety arises from the fact that each **pj** and **p** can be any of the modes already encountered with the following reservations:

if multiple values are involved then formal declarers should be used; thus bounds are never present;

the mode of the result could be **void** indicating that no result is delivered;

no **pj** can be of mode **void**.

Example 5.1.2b. Modes associated with procedures.
The following are all possible modes of procedures.

(i) **proc (ref real, int) char** would be the mode of a procedure with two parameters, the first being of mode **ref real** and the second being of mode **int**. The result delivered by a call of the procedure would be of mode **char**.

(ii) **proc (ref real, ref real) int** would be the mode of a procedure with two parameters both of mode **ref real** and delivering a result of mode **int**.

(iii) **proc void** would be the mode of a procedure with no parameters delivering as result the **void** value.

(iv) **proc (real, int) struct (real** *r*, **int** *j*) wculd be the mode of a procedure having two parameters of modes **real** and **int**. The result is of mode **struct (real** *r*, **int** *j*).

(v) **mode fn = proc (real) real** is a mode declaration which allows **fn** to be used where one would use **proc (real) real**.

(vi) **proc (real, proc (int) char) bool** would be the mode of a procedure having two parameters the second of which is itself a procedure with an integer parameter and a result of mode **char**.

5.1.3. Routine texts

At the corresponding stage of investigating multiple values or structures the next step was to consider the possibility of introducing some form of multiple value denotation or structure denotation. This led to row displays and structure displays. The intention now is to consider the corresponding construction for procedures, *routine texts*. These will enable the programmer to define his own procedures.

To illustrate the construction of routine texts consider the problem of writing a routine text for the factorial function. This function has to take an integer parameter and deliver an integer result. Its mode is therefore **proc (int) int**. Before writing the routine text itself consider the problem of writing a unitary clause whose value is just *n*!. In the following illustration of such a clause there should be a check made on the fact that *n* is non-negative. This is omitted in the interests of simplicity and clarity.

> **begin int** *product* := 1;
>   **for** *i* **to** *n* **do** *product* ×:= *i* **od**;
>   *product*
> **end**

The corresponding routine text is then

> **(int** *n*) **int**: **begin int** *product* := 1;
>   **for** *i* **to** *n* **do** *product* ×:= *i* **od**;
>   *product*
>   **end**

The brackets (and) cannot in this case be replaced by **begin** and **end** though in the usual way **begin** and **end** can be replaced by (and).

In the routine text the unitary clause was preceded by

(mode and identifier of parameter) mode of result:

The effect of the mode of the result followed by the colon, **int**: in the factorial example, is to force a coercion. The syntactic position of the unitary clause is strong and the result it delivers is strongly coerced to the required mode. In the above example the coercions move inside the brackets in the usual way and dereferencing of *product* takes place.

Since the factorial function has mode **proc (int) int** the following identity declaration could be made.

> **proc (int) int** $f =$ (**int** n) **int**:
> > **begin int** *product* $:= 1$;
> > > **for** i **to** n **do** *product* $\times := i$ **od**;
> > > *product*
> **end**

The effect of such a declaration is similar to the effect of other identity declarations. As a result of this declaration, f can be used as if it were a standard function. Thus in a program one could write $f(4)$ and this would have the effect of evaluating 4!. One could even write expressions such as

$$7 \times f(4) + f(6 + (\textbf{int } n; \textit{read } (n); n))$$

and each call of f would result in the appropriate factorial being evaluated. As with previous procedures the parameter occupies a strong position and can be any unit provided it delivers a result of the required (a posteriori) mode.

The declaration of f given above contains some redundant information. The fact that f takes a single parameter of mode **int** and delivers a result of mode **int** is contained in both **proc (int) int** and in (**int** n) **int**: . . . The redundancy can be removed by employing an abbreviation which allows the removal of everything between the **proc** and the f on the left hand side of the equals symbol. Using this abbreviation f can be declared by writing

> **proc** $f =$ (**int** n) **int**:
> **begin int** *product* $:= 1$;
> > **for** i **to** n **do** *product* $\times := i$ **od**;
> > *product*
> **end**

150

This would be the usual form of the declaration of f. The abbreviation is allowed only when the right hand side of the identity declaration or variable declaration is a routine text. This implies that the equals symbol above could have been replaced by the becomes symbol giving

proc $f := ($**int** $n)$ **int**: ...

Example 5.1.3a. Using the factorial function in a program.
Write a program to tabulate the values of $r!$ for $r = 1, 2, 3, \ldots, 8$.

```
begin proc f = (int n) int:
        begin int product := 1;
                for i to n do product ×:= i od;
                product
        end;
        print ((''value of r  factorial r'', newline));
        for r to 8 do print ((newline, r, 8 × '' '', f(r))) od
end
```

In the declaration of f the parameter that appears is n. The n is said to be a formal parameter. It is formal in the sense that it appears only in the declaration of f. When a call of f is made, as in $f(4)$, the 4 is in the usual way an actual parameter. It is an actual parameter in the same way that it is an actual parameter in the procedure calls $print(4)$, $sin(4)$, etc. The terms formal and actual parameter were also used earlier in the discussion on identity declarations. That the same terms were used in two different contexts is no coincidence. The connection will be discussed thoroughly in section 5.1.4.

Example 5.1.3b. Procedure declarations II.
In several of the procedures declared below it would be advisable to incorporate a check on the value of the parameter. To avoid repetition this is done only in the first case.

(i) $log\ 10$ is used to evaluate the logarithm to the base 10 of a real number.

```
proc log 10 = (real x) real:
(if x ≦ 0
then print ((newline, ''parameter of log 10 is'', x,
                ''positive parameter required. program terminated.''));
    stop
fi;
ln(x)/ln(10)
)
```

(ii) Three new mathematical functions *cosec*, *sec* and *cot* are declared below.

$$\textbf{proc } cosec = (\textbf{real } x) \textbf{ real}: 1/sin(x),$$
$$sec = (\textbf{real } x) \textbf{ real}: 1/cos(x),$$
$$cot = (\textbf{real } x) \textbf{ real}: 1/tan(x)$$

Note the abbreviation employed in (ii) above. **proc** appears just once. This can be used for any number of procedures, and their modes need not all be the same. Moreover the equals symbol could have been replaced at each of its occurrences by the becomes symbol if procedure variables were required.

The procedure declarations given so far have been of a rather simple nature in that they make use of only a single parameter. Moreover the parameters could not change value within the unitary clause since their modes were **real**, **int**, etc. To be altered their modes would have to be **ref real**, **ref int**, etc. The next example illustrates several possible extensions of the earlier ideas. Several parameters are employed and their modes can be more complex than before. Checks are again omitted for simplicity and clarity.

Example 5.1.3c. Procedure declarations III.

(i) The standard procedure *char in string* has as its definition in the ALGOL 68 Report:

```
proc char in string = (char c, ref int i, [ ] chars) bool:
begin bool found := false;
      for k from lwb s to upb s while not found
      do (c = s[k]|i := k; found := true) od;
      found
end
```

(ii) *swap* interchanges the values of two integer variables, the variables being supplied as parameters.

```
proc swap = (ref int a, b) void:
begin int r = a; a := b; b := r end
```

Note that the formal parameter part

$$(\textbf{ref int } a, b) \textbf{ void}$$

is an abbreviation for

$$(\textbf{ref int } a, \textbf{ ref int } b) \textbf{ void}$$

(iii) *sum and average* calculates the sum and the average of the elements of a one-dimensional multiple value which is supplied as parameter (see also section 5.1.4).

```
proc sum and average = ([ ] real x, ref real sum, average) void:
begin int lb = lwb x, ub = upb x; sum := 0;
    for i from lb to ub do sum + := x[i] od;
    average := sum/(ub − lb + 1)
end
```

(iv) *hcf* finds the highest common factor of two positive integer parameters using Euclid's algorithm.

```
proc hcf = (int m, n) int:
begin int a := m, b := n;
    if a < b then int c = a; a := b; b := c fi;
    while b ≠ 0 do int c = b; b := a mod b; a := c od;
    a
end
```

The design of tasks suitable for expressing as procedures is relatively simple when only a simple program has to be written. But when large programs are involved this becomes a major hurdle. It is difficult even to give rigorous guide-lines that should be followed for there are exceptions to all the usual rules. In general one should try to design procedures that perform one specific task and, if possible, do not make use of variables declared by the programmer outside the procedure. Usually, procedures should not perform both transput and calculations, though the printing of an error message could be regarded as an exception – the parameters supplied may have been in an unexpected form.

The standard procedure *random* does, however, make use of a variable declared outside the procedure though within the standard environment. A look at the standard procedure *next random* will clarify the situation.

Example 5.1.3d. *next random.*

(i) The procedure *next random* has a declaration in the standard environment and it starts:

```
proc next random = (ref int a) real: ...
```

The effect of a call of *next random* is that the value of the integer variable *a* is altered to some other integer in the range 0 to *max int*, both 0 and *max int* being included. The successive values of *a* are uniformly distributed over this range. Real numbers produced by *next random* are derived from some function which maps the integers in the range 0 to *max int* into the real numbers between 0 and 1, 0

153

being included and 1 being excluded. The resulting real numbers are uniformly distributed. The value of this function when applied to a is the result delivered by *next random*.

(ii) The definition of *random* in the standard environment is:

> **int** *last random* : = **round** (*max int*/2);
> **proc** *random* = **real**: *next random* (*last random*)

Each of *random, next random* and *last random* can be accessed by the programmer.

5.1.4. The ALGOL 68 calling mechanism

This section explains exactly what happens when a procedure is called. The explanation is important since it shows the connection between the various uses of the terms formal parameter and actual parameter, for both these terms were used in discussing identity declarations and in discussing procedure calls. To illustrate, two examples will be used: the factorial procedure and the *sum and average* procedure (see 5.1.3c (iii)).

Consider first the factorial function f. When a call such as $f(4)$ takes place the following clause is in effect elaborated.

> **begin int** $n = 4$;
>   **begin int** *product* : = 1;
>   **for** i **to** n **do** *product* ×: = i **od**;
>   *product*
>   **end**
> **end**

This produces after coercion (in this case dereferencing of *product*) the required result. Note that n is initialised by means of an identity declaration on whose right hand side the appropriate actual parameter appears. This is the reason for the terms formal and actual parameter being used in (apparently) different contexts.

Consider now the call *sum and average* (*data, s, a*) of the procedure *sum and average* declared in example 5.1.3c (iii). Assume suitable declarations of *data, s* and *a*. The effect of this call is the elaboration of

> **begin** [ ] **real** $x = data$, **ref real** *sum* = *s*, *average* = *a*;
>   **begin int** $lb = $ **lwb** x, $ub = $ **upb** x; *sum* : = 0;
>   **for** i **from** lb **to** ub **do** *sum* + : = $x[i]$ **od**;
>   *average* : = *sum*/$(ub - lb + 1)$
>   **end**
> **end**

Note the initialisation of x. In poor implementations this identity

154

declaration may cause the copying of all the elements from *data* into a new multiple value namely *x*. If *data* is large this is an expensive operation. In a sense the expense of copying is needless though logically the correct action has been taken. To overcome this expense one could make the mode of *x* **ref** [ ] **real** rather than [ ] **real** but then the protection given by the modes is sacrificed.

The calling mechanism is similar for items of other modes. Where large amounts of information have to be copied the expense can be overcome by placing **ref** in front of the offending modes at the risk of sacrificing protection. This risk is usually unnecessary.

5.1.5. Recursive procedures

The word 'recursion' has a meaning in programming analogous to the meaning of the word 'induction' in mathematics. Recursion is an extremely powerful tool and its proper use can lead to neat and elegant solutions to seemingly difficult problems. On the other hand the use of recursion does involve overheads in the form of computer time and space and often non-recursive procedures are more natural and more desirable than their recursive counterparts.

When one talks of recursion in programming one usually means the process of declaring a procedure in terms of itself. This is called *recursive definition* of procedures.

A procedure can be defined in terms of itself in one of two ways. It can be defined in terms of itself directly, when the recursion is usually called *simple recursion,* or it can be defined in terms of other functions which in turn are defined in terms of the first function, when the recursion is called *mutual recursion.* Most of the examples below involve only simple recursion.

The writing of recursive procedures involves no essentially new ideas. Consider a procedure *hcf* for finding the highest common factor of two non-negative integers *m* and *n*, not both zero. The value of *hcf*(*m,n*) can be defined as follows: if $m < n$ then *hcf*(*n,m*); if $n = 0$ then *m*; otherwise *hcf*(*n, m* **mod** *n*). This is effectively a statement of Euclid's algorithm for finding the highest common factor of two integers and can be written as

> **proc** *hcf* = (**int** *m, n*) **int** :
> **if** $m < n$ **then** *hcf*(*n, m*) **elif** $n = 0$ **then** *m* **else** *hcf*(*n, m* **mod** *n*) **fi**

This declaration could appear in a program. This definition of the *hcf* procedure is very natural and easier to follow than the definition of *hcf* given in section 5.1.3. A feature of recursive procedures is the fact that they always contain a conditional clause or case clause of some kind. Moreover, one of the alternatives of the choice clause should not involve a call to the procedure being declared.

Example 5.1.5a. Recursive procedures.

(i) Consider the function f defined for non-negative integers m and n as follows:

$$f(m, 0) = m \text{ for all values of } m$$
$$f(m, n) = f(n, m) \text{ if } m < n$$

and $f(m, n) = mf(m \div n, n - 1) + nf(m - 1, n)$ otherwise.

The function f can be expressed as a recursive procedure as follows:

proc $f = ($**int** $m, n)$ **int**:
if $n = 0$ **then** m **elif** $m < n$ **then** $f(n, m)$ **else** $m \times f(m \div n,$
   $n - 1) + n \times f(m - 1, n)$ **fi**

Note that in the expression

$$m \times f(m \div n, n - 1) + n \times f(m - 1, n)$$

there are two calls of the function f. Indeed one could have any number of such calls.

(ii) Consider the function A defined for non-negative integers m and n as

$$A(0, n) = n + 1$$
$$A(m, 0) = A(m - 1, 1)$$

and otherwise

$$A(m, n) = A(m - 1, A(m, n - 1))$$

A is called Ackermann's function after the mathematical logician of that name. This function has an important place in theoretical topics closely related to computer science. The function could be programmed as follows:

proc $A = ($**int** $m, n)$ **int**:
if $m = 0$ **then** $n + 1$ **elif** $n = 0$ **then** $A(m - 1, 1)$ **else** $A(m - 1,$
   $A(m, n - 1))$ **fi**

(Ackermann's function, because its definition depends so heavily on recursion, is often used to test the ability of computers to handle recursion.)

The examples of recursive procedures that have been given so far have been relatively straightforward. Much of the elegance associated with recursion comes from noting that a certain process can indeed be expressed in a recursive manner.

156

Example 5.1.5b. Printing an integer.

Consider the problem of printing in base b the integer n. Assume that both b and n are positive integers and that $b > 1$ and $b < 10$. The number should occupy only as many character positions as are necessary. The case $b = 10$ is dealt with by the standard procedure *whole*.

To obtain a recursive solution note that to print 5467 one has to print 546 followed by 7. The procedure *outpos* could be written, ignoring a check on the sign of the formal parameters n and b, as

> **proc** *outpos* = (**int** n, b) **void**:
> **if** $n \neq 0$ **then** *outpos* $(n \div b, b)$;
>   *print* (*whole* $(n$ **mod** $b, 0))$
> **fi**

This procedure could be used by another procedure to print an integer of any sign. The procedure *out* prints positive, negative or zero integers.

> **proc** *out* = (**int** n, b) **int**:
> **case sign** $n + 2$**in** $(print(" - ")$; *outpos* $(- n, b))$, **co** negative nos **co**
> $print(" 0 ")$,   **co** zero **co**
>   *outpos* (n, b) **co** positive nos **co**
> **esac**

Example 5.1.5c. Nested loop clauses.

Consider the problem of writing a procedure to find a solution in integers $x_1, x_2, x_3, \ldots, x_n$ of the equation

$$a_1 x_1^2 + a_2 x_2^2 + \ldots + a_n x_n^2 = b$$

where b and each a_i is a non-negative integer. It will be assumed that the procedure has as parameters

(i) a, a multiple value whose elements are just the integer values of $a_1, a_2, \ldots, a_n$ (assume each $a_i \neq 0$),

(ii) b, an integer,

(iii) x, a reference to a multiple value through which the results are transmitted.

At first sight one might expect that the solution required only several loop clauses. For instance *i1* might run through the possible values of x_1, *i2* the possible values of x_2, etc. But the trouble is that in general the value of n is not known and such an approach is not immediately applicable.

Note therefore that the solution to this problem could be used in the solution to the more general problem of dealing with an unknown number of nested loop clauses.

The procedure to solve this problem will be called *cansolve*. This will produce a boolean result which will be **true** if a solution is possible. For instance

$$5x_1^2 + 4x_2^2 + 2x_3^2 = 21$$

has a solution $x_1 = 1$, $x_2 = 2$, $x_3 = 0$ and in this case the procedure would return **true**. When a solution is possible the values of x_1, $x_2, \ldots, x_n$ will be found in the corresponding elements of x.

When a result is not possible *cansolve* will return **false**. Such would happen in the case

$$5x_1^2 = 4$$

for there are no integers x_1 which when squared and multiplied by 5 give the result 4.

The recursive solution is obtained by noting that to solve

$$a_1 x_1^2 + \ldots + a_n x_n^2 = b$$

one has only to solve

$$a_1 x_1^2 + \ldots + a_{n-1} x_{n-1}^2 = b - a_n x_n^2$$

for x_n taking successive values $0, 1, 2, \ldots$, **round** $\sqrt{(b/a_n)}$.

The procedure *cansolve* is then as follows:

```
proc cansolve = ([ ] int a, int b, ref [ ] int x) bool:
if int n = upb a; n = 0
then b = 0
else bool soln := false;
    for i from 0 to round sqrt (b/a[n]) while not soln
    do x[n] := i;
        soln := cansolve(a[1 :n − 1], b − a[n] × i↑2, x[1 :n − 1])
    od;
    soln
fi
```

This completes the solution of the problem. Thus the effect of a dynamic number of loop clauses can be achieved by means of recursion.

5.1.6. Deproceduring

The need for deproceduring comes from the existence of procedures without parameters. Consider the procedure *random*. This has mode **proc real** and it can be used in statements such as

proc real $f := random$ or **real** $x := random$

These two uses of *random* are quite different. In the second case *random* is called and the result, of mode **real**, is assigned to x. This occurrence of *random* results in a call and therefore an activation of the procedure *random*. But in the first example above no such activation takes place. f is a variable whose values can be procedures without parameters delivering reals and in this use of *random* the variable f is just given the procedure *random*.

Note however that with procedures which do have parameters these two uses would not cause any trouble. For consider *sin*. If *sin* had to be activated it would be given a parameter as in *sin* (*pi*). Otherwise it would not. So the appearance or otherwise of a parameter would indicate an activation or non-activation of the procedure.

Return now to the problem that arises in using *random*. In

> **real** $x :=$ *random*

random has mode **proc real**. Yet for the usual mode conditions for assignments to be satisfied it follows that there has to be a coercion of some kind. This coercion must alter the mode of *random* to **real**. The coercion is called *deproceduring*. This can be employed in any soft, and therefore any weak, meek, firm or strong syntactic position. It always causes the procedure to be activated. In the above example the source is deprocedured and so *random* is activated, the resulting real value being assigned to the real variable x.

Example 5.1.6a. Deproceduring.

(i) The procedure *random* can be used quite legitimately in each of the following declarations. Deproceduring, and hence activation of the procedure, takes place each time. b is assumed to have mode **bool**.

> **real** $x :=$ *random* $\times 10 + 5$
> **real** $x :=$ **if** b **then** *random* $+ 1$ **else** 0 **fi**
> **int** $n =$ **round** (*random* $\times 10$)

(ii) In this set of examples no deproceduring and hence no activation of *random*, g or h takes place. Assume that g and h have mode **proc real** and b has mode **bool**

> **proc real** $w :=$ **if** b **then** g **else** *random* **fi**
> **proc real** $w :=$ **case int** i; *read* (i); i **in** g, h, *random* **esac**

This completes a first look at deproceduring. All the concepts have been illustrated using the procedure *random*. But equally well they could have been described in terms of any procedure of mode **proc mode** for any **mode** except **void**. This exception leads to some difficulties that will be considered in the next section.

5.1.7. Deproceduring and voiding

Until now voiding has been the coercion which allows unwanted results to be thrown away, i.e. reduced to mode **void**. With the introduction of deproceduring there is now another way, in certain cases, of achieving this. Consider an object of mode **proc void**. Deproceduring of this leaves a result of mode **void**. Unless some rule is stated there would be an element of ambiguity about whether deproceduring or voiding would take place in certain cases. If there is a rule what is the difference, if any, between voiding and deproceduring?

To illustrate what happens consider two examples both involving an object *dump*, say, of mode **proc void**. The first example is an assignation which involves a variable *f* of mode **ref proc void**. The assignation appears in a serial clause as

$$\ldots ; f := dump ; \ldots$$

The mode of the result has to be reduced somehow to mode **void**.

Now *dump* could also appear as follows

$$\ldots ; dump ; \ldots$$

the intention being that the procedure *dump* should be called (and, for instance, it might print out the current values of several objects). But again the mode of *dump* has to be reduced to mode **void**.

These, then, are the two examples. Note that in the first case the intention is not to call the procedure *dump* but merely to assign it to a suitable variable. In the second case a call of *dump* is intended.

Returning to deproceduring remember that deproceduring always causes a call to a procedure. Indeed, in the second case, the a priori mode of *dump* is **proc void** and this is coerced to the a posteriori mode **void** by deproceduring. Thus *dump* is activated.

In the first example the result delivered by the assignation is just *f* and this is of mode **ref proc void**. The a priori mode is therefore **ref proc void** and this is coerced by voiding to mode **void**. Thus there is no activation of *dump* (or of *f*).

How then should one decide in general whether deproceduring or voiding is involved in a mode change? The solution to this dilemma comes from stating more precisely what the coercion voiding entails. Remember that after the coercion voiding, no other coercion can be applied.

Before looking at the precise implications of voiding the following definition is necessary.

160

Definition of NONPROC

If **mode** denotes an arbitrary mode then NONPROC includes all modes other than **proc void**, **proc mode**, and these modes with (any number of occurrences of) **ref** preceding the **proc**, e.g. **ref proc void**, **ref proc mode**.

With this definition the precise meaning of voiding is as follows:

the result delivered by an assignation or a denotation can be reduced immediately to mode **void**;

the result delivered by any other construction so far introduced can (after possible deproceduring and dereferencing) be reduced to mode **void** provided that the a priori mode before voiding is one of the NONPROC modes.

Essentially voiding can be applied to anything provided the object to be coerced is not a procedure without parameters or a variable whose values are parameterless procedures. Deproceduring on the other hand can never be employed in reducing assignations, etc. to mode **void** but is used to reduce other non-NONPROC constructions to **void**.

To summarise the results of this section, deproceduring causes the activation of a procedure, voiding does not. A more comprehensive treatment of this occurs in chapter 7.

5.2. Operators

The introduction of new operators, or new definitions of old operators, is similar in some respects to the introduction of new procedures. However added complexity results from the fact that a single operator symbol such as + or **abs** can have various meanings depending on the particular context in which it is used. The symbol + when operating between two integers will give a result of mode **int**, when used between two reals it will give a result of mode **real**; the monadic operator **abs** will have different meanings depending on the mode of its operands. These operators are said to be *overloaded*, i.e. they can have more than one meaning in a reach.

In this section it will be seen that the standard operators such as +, −, **abs**, etc. can be even more heavily overloaded and can be made to operate on objects of other modes. These other modes might be the usual modes such as **real**, **char**, [ ] **int**, etc. or they might be new modes introduced by the programmer.

Having discussed this it will then be seen that completely new operators can be defined. These can be either monadic or dyadic operators. In the latter case, of course, it will be necessary to attribute a priority to these operators.

To recap, operators are of two basic kinds, monadic and dyadic. Monadic operators act on single objects and in many ways resemble procedures with a single parameter. Dyadic operators have two operands and resemble procedures with two parameters. As a result of this similarity with procedures it should come as no surprise that operator declarations closely resemble procedure declarations.

Operators themselves have a priority which determines, to a certain extent, the implied bracketing in formulae. In cases where several operators (or occurrences of operators) of the same priority appear as in $a + b - c - d$ the implied bracketing is from the left, i.e. it is $(((a + b) - c) - d)$. Dyadic operators have a priority which can be any integral value between 1 and 9 inclusive. Monadic operators have a priority greater than that of all dyadic operators. Similarly with extended or new operators the same rules govern the implied bracketing.

Operands are the objects on which operators act. These occupy, and even with extended or new operators they continue to occupy, a firm syntactic position. Thus dereferencing of operands is allowed but widening is not allowed. So no new ideas on this topic have to be introduced.

The above is an oversimplified view of the situation. There are some complications which will be considered when the more basic ideas on operator declarations have been discussed.

5.2.1. Extending the definition of operators
To illustrate the usual method of extending the definition of an operator consider the problem of extending the meaning of the dyadic operator + in such a way that its operands are one-dimensional multiple values of integers. Assume that the bounds of the two operands are identical and that the result is produced by adding corresponding elements of the operands thus giving as result another multiple value with bounds identical to those of the operands.

The definition of + is extended by means of an operator declaration in which + is defined for objects of mode [ ] **int**. Operator declarations in general consist of the symbol **op** followed by the operator symbol, the equals symbol and a routine text defining the operator. In the case of a monadic operator the routine text would denote a routine with a single parameter; in the case of a dyadic operator it would denote a routine with two parameters.

The declaration of + is as follows:

$$\textbf{op} + = ([\ ]\ \textbf{int}\ a, b)\ [\ ]\ \textbf{int}:$$

begin int *lb* = **lwb** *a*, *ub* = **upb** *a*;
    [*lb* : *ub*] **int** *result*;
    for *i* **from** *lb* **to** *ub* **do** *result* [*i*] := *a*[*i*] + *b*[*i*] **od**;
    result
end

Having made this declaration, + can be used between one-dimensional multiple values of integers just as it is used between, say, integers themselves. The priority of + is just the standard priority, i.e. 6, and this determines the implied bracketing in the usual way.

Example 5.2.1a. Extending the definition of operators.
Extend the definition of × so that it operates on *a* and *b*, two one-dimensional multiple values of integers with identical bounds, and produces as result the scalar product of *a* and *b*.

It will be assumed, to avoid complicating the solution, that the bounds of *a* and *b* are indeed identical. In practice a test should be included to check the truth of this.

op × = ([ ] **int** *a*, *b*) **int** :
begin int *sum* := 0;
    for *i* **from lwb** *a* **to upb** *a* **do** *sum* +:= *a*[*i*] × *b*[*i*] **od**;
    sum
end

× will have its standard priority, i.e. 7.

A remark was made earlier to the effect that the definition of an operator could be extended in several ways thus allowing the one operator to be used for, to give an example, the addition of multiple values of integers, the addition of multiple values of characters together with the addition of integers and reals in any combination.

To show how this can be achieved using a fairly realistic example consider the problem of defining the operator + to operate between integers and rational numbers in any combination. For this purpose suppose that there has been a mode declaration

mode ratn = **struct** (**int** *num*, *den*)

Now + has to be defined between objects of mode **ratn** and **ratn**, **ratn** and **int**, **int** and **ratn** and **int** and **int**. In the latter case a definition already exists for + . Thus three definitions have to be given.

When several operator declarations are required certain abbreviations are allowed. In declaring the above three + operators the following would suffice

op + = (**ratn** *a*, *b*) **ratn** : **begin** . . . **end**,

$+ = (\textbf{ratn } a, \textbf{int } b) \textbf{ ratn} : \textbf{begin} \ldots \textbf{end},$
$+ = (\textbf{int } a, \textbf{ratn } b) \textbf{ ratn} : \textbf{begin} \ldots \textbf{end}$

The obvious generalisation applies. Note the similarity between this and the abbreviation allowed when several procedure declarations are required.

It should be apparent that, unlike other objects declared by means of the identity declaration, operators have to be thought of, not as entities on their own, but as entities with modes attached. Monadic operators have a single mode attached and dyadic operators have two modes attached, these being the mode of the left hand operand and the mode of the right hand operand.

The reader may have become worried by the fact that several operator declarations can appear within the one reach; indeed he should be for this raises some thorny questions. For example, dyadic + could be defined for operands of mode **ref int**. But dereferencing can be applied to operands and this suggests that the compiler is liable to become confused by expressions involving the addition of two integer variables. Questions such as this have to be answered but the answers are left until section 5.2.3.

Finally in this section consider

$$\textbf{op mod} = (\textbf{real } a, b) \textbf{ real} : (\textbf{int } n = \textbf{entier } (a/b); a - n \times b)$$

It will not now follow that $\%\times$ can be used in place of **mod**. It is certainly still the case that $p \textbf{ mod } q$ and $p \% \times q$ have the same meaning when p and q are of mode **int**, for then the operators have their standard meanings. But they do not have the same meaning if p and q are of mode **real**. **mod** has been defined by the above declaration but $\% \times$ has not.

This demonstrates a general principle about operators which are represented by several possible symbols. If a new meaning is attached to one of these symbols it is not automatically attached to the others.

5.2.2. Introducing new operators

Operator symbols
Operators can be represented either by bold words such as **abs**, **round**, etc. or by some combination of characters such as $+, -, \times,$ $:=$, etc. New operators are represented in a similar way. However there are some necessary restrictions.

Bold words – more precisely, any bold sequence of letters and/or digits starting with a letter and containing no typographical display features – cannot be used for new operators if they have already been reserved for some other purpose. It may seem natural to use **in** for a dyadic operator to detect if a character was present in a character string. But **in** is used as part of the **case** ... **in** ... **esac** construction. Consequently it cannot be used as an operator.

Other restrictions apply to the allowable combinations of the characters $+, -, \times, :=$, etc. To understand the reasons for these restrictions consider some examples. Let p and q be of mode **int**. If $++$ happened to be an allowable monadic operator symbol $++p$ would be ambiguous. For it could be interpreted as the operator $++$ operating on p or as $+(+p)$. Similarly $++$ cannot be used as a dyadic operator for $p++q$ could be interpreted as $p+(+q)$.

Both these difficulties arise because the second character of the combination $++$ can be used on its own as a monadic operator. It would seem natural therefore to divide the set of characters $+,$ $-, \times$, etc. into two sets, one of which is the set of characters that can be used as monadic operators. The elements in this set are, for obvious reasons, called *monads*. The rest are called *nomads*. The monads include $\vee, \wedge, \&, \leqq, \geqq, \%, \div, \neq, \neg, \sim, \uparrow, \downarrow, +, -$ and the nomads $<, >, /, =, *, \times$. Any particular implementation may allow only a subset of these or may include other characters not mentioned above. For example, it is quite likely that some implementations will allow only one of $\%$ and $\div$ or $*$ and $\times$. Other characters such as £, !, ?, etc. are classified as monads.

With these definitions the operator symbols that can be used for monadic operators can now be defined. Any of the following will suffice:

(i) a bold word of the kind mentioned earlier;
(ii) any monad;
(iii) a monad followed by a nomad;
(iv) a combination of the form mentioned in (ii) or (iii) above followed by either $:=$ or $=:$ but not by both.

Example 5.2.2a. Monadic operator symbols.

(i) Each of the following is a legal monadic operator symbol:

$$\wedge, \vee, \%, \uparrow, +, -\%:=, \%=:, \%<, \%< :=, \neg =$$

(ii) The following are not acceptable as monadic operator symbols:

$$<<, \quad <>, //, **, <<<, =:$$

Dyadic operators can be represented by:
(i) a bold word of the kind already mentioned;
(ii) a monad or nomad;

165

(iii) a monad or nomad followed by a nomad;

(iv) a combination of symbols of the form mentioned in (ii) or (iii) followed by either := or =:, but not by both.

As before whenever combinations of characters form a single operator symbol the individual characters should not be separated by typographical display features, comments or pragmatic remarks.

Note that all the standard operators conform to the specifications outlined above. Moreover all monadic operators can also be used as dyadic operators, though the converse is not true.

Example 5.2.2b. Dyadic operator symbols.

(i) The following are acceptable dyadic operators:

$$\neg = \qquad **:= \qquad \textbf{abs} \qquad \times =:$$

(ii) The following can be used for dyadic but not monadic operators:

$$< <, *, = =, //, /=, /= =:, = = =:$$

(iii) The following are not acceptable as operator symbols:

$$+ +, \%\%, \leqq \geqq, \vee \wedge, = :, = :.$$

New monadic operators

Introducing new monadic operators now causes no new problems since the new operators can be denoted by one of the suitable operator symbols already described. Each monadic operator automatically has the same priority. To illustrate the process consider the following problem.

Example 5.2.2c. New monadic operator.

Declare $\%/$ so that it takes as its only operand a real number lying in the range 0 to 1. The result should be an integer between 0 and 100 representing a conversion of the value of the actual parameter into a percentage correct to the nearest integer. Thus $\%/0.5$ should yield 50 and $\%/0.333$ should yield 33. The required declaration is:

$$\textbf{op } \%/ = (\textbf{real } x) \textbf{ int}: \textbf{round } (x \times 100)$$

Having made this declaration $\%/$ can now be used like any other monadic operator. If x and y were of mode **ref real** and n was of mode **ref int** one could write

$$n := \%/(x+y) \text{ or } n := \%/x \text{ or } n := \%/x + \%/\textbf{abs } sin(y)$$

In the expressions involving $\%/x$ the x has to be dereferenced and

166

this can be done since x is an operand and therefore occupies a firm syntactic position.

New dyadic operators

The declarations of new dyadic operators introduces the problem of priorities. A priority has to be assigned to dyadic operators in order to determine the implied bracketing in expressions involving the new operator. The priority is given to an operator by means of a *priority declaration*. Priority declarations are extremely simple. For example to give the dyadic operator **min** the priority 3 one has only to write

    prio min $= 3$

Thus the symbol **prio** is followed by the operator symbol, an equals symbol and a digit denoting the priority of the operator. Note that a digit is used for the priority, not a variable or a clause delivering an integer. The priority must be a digit.

The declaration of new dyadic operators can now be accomplished by using both an operator and a priority declaration. Note that one priority declaration suffices although there may be several operator declarations.

Example 5.2.2d. New dyadic operator.
Define the dyadic operator **max** to operate between objects of mode **int** and **real** in any combination. Give **max** priority 3.

    prio max $= 3$;
    op max $= ($**int** $a, b)$ **int**: **if** $a > b$ **then** a **else** b **fi**,
       max $= ($**int** $a,$ **real** $b)$ **real**: **if** $a > b$ **then** a **else** b **fi**,
       max $= ($**real** $a,$ **int** $b)$ **real**: **if** $a > b$ **then** a **else** b **fi**,
       max $= ($**real** $a, b)$ **real**: **if** $a > b$ **then** a **else** b **fi**

Note that with these declarations **max** could now be used in formulae such as

    n **max** m **max** x **max** $(y$ **max** $n)$

where m and n are of mode **int** and x and y are of mode **real**. The operator used in any particular case is determined by the modes of the operands.

Further remarks

The operator declarations given so far have all been of the particular form which necessitates a routine text on the right of the equals symbol. In fact any unit delivering an object of the required mode may appear in place of the routine text. For monadic operators the required mode would be that of a procedure with a single parameter, e.g. **proc (real) int**. In the dyadic case the required mode could typically be **proc (real, real) int**, i.e. that of a procedure with two parameters. In these cases, however, the **op** symbol on the left hand side would be replaced by **op (real) int** and **op (real, real) int** respectively. Several operator declarations can then be concatenated by writing declarations such as

> **op (real) int s1** = . . . , **s2** = . . . , **s3** = . . .

or

> **op (real, real) int s1** = . . . , **s2** = . . .

Priority declarations can be concatenated in a similar way. Thus

> **prio s1** = . . . , **s2** = . . .

Example 5.2.2e. Abbreviations for operator declarations.
Declare operators **s**, **c** and **t** which represent the action of the *sin*, *cos* and *tan* functions respectively. Thus writing **s** x should yield *sin* (x), etc.

> **op (real) real s** = *sin*, **c** = *cos*, **t** = *tan*

The strong similarity between operator and procedure declarations can be carried even further: operators can be defined recursively. No new ideas are involved.

5.2.3. The uniqueness condition for operators
It has been pointed out that operator declarations differ in certain important ways from declarations of objects such as procedures, multiple values, integers, etc. In fact they are essentially different from objects declared by means of the identity declaration or by means of their occurrence as labels. There are two reasons for this difference.

First of all several operator declarations involving the same operator symbol can appear in the same reach. On the other hand the identifier f, for example, if used in a variable or identity declaration to denote a procedure of some kind, cannot be used in any other variable or identity declaration in the same reach. It cannot be used to identify another procedure, a multiple value or an integer, for instance. Moreover if a call is made to f and the modes of the formal and actual parameters are incompatible then a syntax error results.

Another respect in which operators differ from procedures is that there is no such object in ALGOL 68 as a variable whose values are operators. Variables exist for objects introduced by means of the identity and variable declaration but not for objects introduced by means of operator declarations.

As mentioned earlier several operator declarations can appear within the same reach. But unless some restrictions are stated this could lead to trouble. Consider

$$\textbf{op } \textbf{p} = (\textbf{int } a, b) \textbf{ int}: a \times 240 + b$$
$$\textbf{op } \textbf{p} = (\textbf{int } a, b) \textbf{ int}: a + 240 \times b$$

These are bound to lead to confusion since the compiler would not know which definition of **p** was intended whenever an applied occurrence of **p** appeared.

The rule which forbids the above is called the *uniqueness condition* for operators. Operator declarations have to satisfy this condition for a program to be meaningful. The uniqueness condition is designed to prevent the compiler becoming confused by operator declarations such as the pair given above. More complicated cases of two operator declarations which in some sense clash can also arise. The uniqueness condition for operators must also exclude these from meaningful programs.

To illustrate a more complicated case consider

$$\textbf{op } \textbf{q} = (\textbf{int } a, b) \textbf{ int}: a \times 240 + b$$
$$\textbf{op } \textbf{q} = (\textbf{ref int } a, b) \textbf{ int}: a + 240 \times b$$

Now if n and m are of mode **ref int** take the formula $n\,\textbf{q}\,m$. At first sight the second declaration of **q** would presumably be intended since the modes of the formal and actual parameters are identical. But since m and n are in firm syntactic positions both can be dereferenced to produce objects of mode **int** and at this stage the first definition of **q** could be used. There is thus a conflict caused by the coercions that can take place in a firm syntactic position.

Example 5.2.3a. Violating the uniqueness condition for operators.
Each of the following pairs of (skeleton) operator declarations cannot appear in the same reach since the modes of one set of operands can be firmly coerced to the modes of the other set, i.e. only coercions applicable in a firm position can be used.
  (i) $\textbf{op } £ = (\textbf{int } a, \textbf{ref int } b) \textbf{ int}: (\ldots)$
      $\textbf{op } £ = (\textbf{int } a, b) \textbf{ real}: (\ldots)$
The modes in the first declaration can be firmly coerced to the modes

in the second declaration, the second operand being dereferenced.

(ii) Consider the operator declarations involving the modes **ma** and **mb**

$$\textbf{op} \% = (\textbf{ma } x) \textbf{ int}: (\dots)$$
$$\textbf{op} \% = (\textbf{mb } x) \textbf{ char}: (\dots)$$

Suppose further that y is of mode **m** and that **m** can be firmly coerced to either mode **ma** or mode **mb**. Consider $\% y$. Again there is ambiguity and the uniqueness condition must exclude such cases.

Any attempt at specifying the uniqueness condition for operators must forbid operator declarations whose corresponding operands have modes which can be firmly coerced to each other or which have modes having the property outlined in the second part of the above example. Indeed this is just the uniqueness condition.

The above considerations lead to the concept of *firmly related modes*. Two modes are said to be firmly related if there exists a common mode from which both modes can be firmly coerced; the common mode can be one of the two related modes.

Example 5.2.3b. Firmly related modes.
The two modes **int** and **ref int** are firmly related since both modes can be firmly coerced from the mode **ref int**, the first by dereferencing and the second by the empty coercion.

There is one further restriction involving operator declarations. Consider the skeleton

```
begin
    op + = (int a, b) int: ( ... );
        begin op + = (ref int a, b) int: ( ... );
            int n = 4, m = 5; real x = n + m;
                . . .
        end
    end
```

The $+$ used in the formula $n + m$ is presumably intended to invoke the outer definition of $+$. However, any such attempt to use the outer operator in the inner clause is illegal. (The argument in favour of this restriction is that it removes a possible source of confusion for the programmer.) Further explanation of this is given in the next section.

This completes the list of restrictions. Note that between the modes **real** and **struct** (**real** *value*), say, there is no connection that

170

will cause trouble. Consequently one could have separate declarations of, for instance, + between two reals and + between two objects of mode **struct** (**real** *value*) both usable within the same reach. This is one of the few times when structures containing a single field can be useful. The **struct** is used to retain the old definition of + and yet allow a new definition to be accessible.

5.2.4. Identification of operators

In this section the process of connecting applied occurrences of operators with their appropriate defining occurrences is considered. A similar problem has already been discussed for objects declared explicitly by means of identity declarations or variable declarations or implicitly by means of their appearance as labels. For this purpose it is again convenient to consider a program being embedded in a range containing the declarations of all objects in the standard environment. Thus all priority and operator declarations are present in this outer range.

The identification problem for operators is made more complicated than the corresponding problem for identifiers. Apart from the fact that modes have to be considered there should be two defining occurrences of each dyadic operator. For each dyadic operator should appear in both an operator declaration and a priority declaration.

The identification process for monadic operators is relatively straightforward. It is required to link an applied occurrence of an operator symbol to the appropriate defining occurrence of that same operator symbol. A scan out through successive reaches is performed. The first monadic operator declaration (i) which uses the operator symbol under consideration and (ii) whose formal parameter is of a mode firmly related to the a priori mode of the actual operand, i.e. the operand of the applied occurrence of the operator, is considered. If the mode of the actual operand can be firmly coerced to the mode of the formal parameter this is taken to be the required defining occurrence. Otherwise no suitable defining occurrence exists.

Example 5.2.4a. Identification of monadic operators.
Consider the following piece of program.

> **op** £ = (**int** *d*) **int**: *d* ÷ 240;
> **begin op** £ = (**ref int** *p*) **int**: **p** ÷ 100;
>   *print* (£ 40)
> **end**

This will produce a syntax error. In attempting to find an appro-

171

priate defining occurrence for £ the inner declaration is first encountered and this satisfies requirements (i) and (ii) listed above. But the requisite coercions cannot be performed and an error will therefore result. Note that this is what one should expect following the remarks at the end of section 5.2.3.

For dyadic operators a similar kind of scan links the applied occurrence of an operator to its defining occurrence in an operator declaration. A scan out through successive reaches will in the usual way link an applied occurrence of an operator with its defining occurrence in a priority declaration. These two scans will then give respectively the meaning and the priority of the applied operator. However, their relative order is crucial. The priority scan must be performed first for the purpose of determining the implied bracketing. Then, since the a priori modes of the operands are known, the operator scan can be performed. Thus different operators sharing the same operator symbol must share priority.

Example 5.2.4b. Identification of dyadic operators.

> **begin prio** $+ = 7$; *print* $(3 + 4 \times 7)$ **end**

produces a result of 49.

5.3. The use of procedures and operators in programming

The reasons for using procedure and operator declarations are many. Often in programming the same task has to be performed several times. Rather than write the same instructions repeatedly they should be dressed as a procedure or operator which can be used when necessary. Again, the same piece of program might be required in several different programs. Then, as before, the instructions should be wrapped up as a procedure or operator which can be used in the various programs.

Whenever a certain task has a naturally recursive solution, procedure and operator declarations can be used to express the natural solution.

Procedure and operator declarations are very important in structuring programs properly. Complex programs often have scores of operator and procedure declarations. The writing of these often goes hand-in-hand with the designing of modes. When simple modes are defined one may require operators and procedures for the manipulation of objects of these new modes. At a higher level one might design more complex modes in terms of the new modes. Now a new set of procedures and operators may be required for the manipulation

172

of the more complex objects. This process can of course be continued and it leads to layers upon layers of modes and their corresponding operator and procedure declarations.

Essentially by this technique the programmer is building his own instructions and his own language in which to solve his problem. But if he is not careful the computer will spend all its time jumping from one procedure or operator to another and achieving very little.

Exercises on chapter 5

1. What are the (a priori) modes associated with the serial clauses listed below?
   (i) **real** x; *read* (x); *sin* (x)
   (ii) **real** x; *read* (x); $y := x$; *sin*
   (iii) (*sin, cos, tan*)

2. Find the fault in the following call of the *sin* function:

   sin (**real** x; *read* (x); x)

3.   (i) Extend the definition of $\uparrow$ in such a way that one could write $x \uparrow n$ where x and n are of mode **int** and n can be negative. What does this imply about the mode of $2 \uparrow 3$?
   (ii) Extend the definition of $\uparrow$ to allow a positive real number to be raised to a real power.

4. Assuming x and y are of mode **ref real** and **real** respectively define the operator ? in such a way that $x ? y$ has the effect of assigning y to x but the result delivered is the old value referred to by x.

   If p and q are of mode **ref real** what is the effect of the assignation $q := p ? q$?

5. Assume x is of mode **ref real** and y is of mode **real**. Give appropriate declarations for the following operators:
   (i) $+/$; $x +/y$ assign $x + y$ to x but delivers as result the old value of x;
   (ii) $-/$; $x -/y$ assigns $x - y$ to x but delivers as result the old value of x.

   (Note that similar definitions are possible for $\times/$, etc.)

6. Are the following legal operator symbols?

(i) $+ = :$	(ii) $+ = ::=$
(iii) $//$	(iv) $\quad := +$
(v) $+ \times$	(vi) $\times + :=$
(vii) $\% \times$	(viii) $\quad \% \%$

7. Write a procedure which accepts as parameter an integer n and whose result is the largest power of 2 dividing n if $n \neq 0$, and -1 if $n = 0$.

8. Will the procedure

   proc $hcf = ($**int** $a, b)$ **int**:
   $(b = 0 \,|\, $**abs** $a \,|\, hcf\,(b, a \textbf{ mod } b))$

   find the highest common factor of two integers?

9. Is it possible to change by means of an operator declaration involving monadic minus the result produced by $print\,(6e - 4)$?

10. Consider the procedure declaration

    proc $g = ($**int** $i)$ **void**:
        case i **in goto** a, **goto** b, **goto** c **esac**

    What is the effect of calling such a procedure?

11. Consider the declaration

    proc $sum = ($**int** $uplimit$, **proc** (**real**) **real** $g)$ **real**:
    begin real $total := 0$;
        for i **to** $uplimit$ **do** $total +:= g\,(i)$ **od**;
        $total$
    end

    Assuming z is of mode **ref real** what is the effect of

    $z := sum\,(100, sin)$?

12. Is it possible to define to operator $\leqq$ in such a way that if m, n and p are of mode **int** then

    $m \leqq n \leqq p$

    has its usual mathematical meaning?

13. The following declaration is intended to extend the definition of the $\times :=$ operator so that it allows operations involving matrices. Thus $A \times := B$ should have the same effect as $A := A \times B$ where $\times$ denotes multiplication between matrices; assume both matrices are square and of the same size.
    Find the fault in the operator declaration and rectify it.

    op $\times := = ($**ref** [,] **real** a, [,] **real** $b)$ **ref** [,] **real**:
    begin int $l = $**lwb** a, $u = $**upb** a;
        for i **from** l **to** u

```
        do for j from l to u
           do real sum := 0;
              for k from l to u
              do sum +:= a[i,k] × b[k,j] od;
              a[i,j] := sum
           od
        od
     end
```

14. A set of integers is held as multiple value of integers. The zero[th] element gives the number n of integers in the set. The 1st, 2nd, ..., n^{th} elements give the various elements of the set. A function *pred* when applied to a set gives the answer 1 or 0 indicating that a set has or has not a particular property. What is the effect of the following piece of program?

```
proc count = ([ ] int st, proc ([ ] int) bool pred) int:
begin [0 : upb st] int set: = st;
     proc p = ([ ] int s) bool:
     begin [0 : upb s + 1] int t; t [0 : upb s @ 0] := s;
           pred ((t[t[0] + := 1] := set [set [0] + 1]; t))
     end;
     if set [0] = 0
     then abs pred (set)
     else set [0] − := 1;
          int n = count (set [0 : set [0] @ 0], pred);
          int m = count (set [0 : set [0] @ 0], p); n + m
     fi
end
```

15. Is it legal to have, within enclosing reaches, operators which use the same operator symbol and which have associated routines of modes (the first is in the outer reach, the second in the inner) given by
(a) (i) **proc (ref int, ref int) int**   (ii) **proc (int, int) bool**
(b) (i) **proc (int, int) bool**   (ii) **proc (ref int, ref int) int**
(c) (i) **proc (ref int, int) bool**   (ii) **proc (int, ref int) int** ?

16. Write procedures to straighten a
   (i) two-dimensional (ii) three-dimensional
multiple value of integers. Straightening a multiple value p of integers involves producing a one-dimensional array of integers containing all the elements of the original matrix in the order in which they would have been printed by *print* (p).

Programming problems for chapter 5

1. When programmers are typing instructions for a computer it is often convenient to allow them the facility of correcting their typing mistakes. One approach to the problem is to make use of an 'escape character'. For example, @ could be used as an escape character, @ C meaning 'erase the previous character', @ L 'erase the current line', and @@ denoting the @ character itself. Thus

    JOB CE@CAFABC@C@C@CSMITH, (C@C@C :CADU10

    when edited would produce

    JOB CAFSMITH, :CADU10

    Write a program to accept text from *standin* and produce as a result the edited string. Assume that @ C cannot be used to jump to a previous line and that @ Z terminates the input.

2.   (i) Write a procedure to evaluate

$$\sum_{i=0}^{n} a_i x^{i}$$

using nested multiplication. How many additions and multiplications are performed in this evaluation? Compare these figures with the corresponding figures for any other method of evaluating the polynomial.

    (ii) Extend the idea of nested multiplication to the case of polynomials in two variables and thereby obtain a procedure for evaluating

$$\sum_{i=0}^{n} \sum_{j=0}^{n} b_{ij} x^{i} y^{j}$$

3. Let a and b be arrays of integers which have been sorted into ascending order. Use merging (see programming problem 2 of chapter 4) to produce a recursive procedure to sort an array of n elements. Your procedure should split the array into two sub-arrays and merge the sorted subarrays.

4. The printer can be used to produce graphs of functions. This is achieved by using printed characters to indicate the shape of the curves. Write programs to produce graphs of
    (i) $sin(x)$;
    (ii) $sin(x)$ and $sin(4x)$ superimposed on each other.

5. The computer can be used to evaluate numerically some definite

integrals which cannot be evaluated using the usual analytic techniques. Examples of such integrals are

$$\int_0^1 exp\left(\frac{x^2}{2}\right)dx \quad \text{and} \quad \int_0^1 \frac{dx}{\sqrt{(2-x^3)}}$$

The computer can approximate to a solution by dividing the area under the graph of the integrand into small trapezia and adding their areas.

Demonstrate the feasibility of this method by tabulating values of

$$\int_0^a exp\left(\frac{x^2}{2}\right)dx$$

for $a = 0.1, 0.2, \ldots, 2.0$.

6. Random number generators can be used to produce exercises in arithmetic, simple algebra, problems in integration and differentiation, etc. Coefficients, powers, variables, the number of terms in an arithmetic expression, etc. can all be generated randomly. Design a program to produce four exercises each with ten questions in some subject of your choice. The answers to all questions should be supplied on a separate page at the end of each exercise.

7. Write programs to produce:
   (i) all permutations of the digits $1, 2, \ldots, n$;
   (ii) all combinations of i digits from n ($i \le n$).
   Assume that n and i are supplied as data.

8. Recursive definitions often define a function $f(x)$ in terms of $f(y)$ where in some sense, y is less than x. Consider the functions g and h defined as follows

   $g(x) = $ **if** $x > 100$ **then** $x - 10$ **else** $g(g(x+11))$ **fi**
   $h(x) = $ **if** $x > 100$ **then** $x - 10$ **else** 91 **fi**

(g is often referred to as the 91 function.)
Write a program to print out the value of $g(n)$ and $h(n)$ for $n = 1, 2, \ldots, 100$.
Print the corresponding values of $p(n)$ and $q(n)$ where

   $p(n) = $ **if** $n > 100$ **then** $n - 10$ **else** $p(p(p(n+21)))$ **fi**
   $q(n) = $ **if** $n > 100$ **then** $n - 10$ **else** $q(q(q(q(n+31))))$ **fi**

9. Write a program to tabulate in three columns the values of $f(n,m), g(n,m)$ and $h(n,m)$ for $n, m = 1, 2, \ldots, 10$ where

$f(x, y) = $ **if** $x = y$ **then** $y + 1$ **else** $f(x, f(x - 1, y + 1))$ **fi**
$g(x, y) = $ **if** $x = y$ **then** $y + 1$ **else** $x + 1$ **fi**
$h(x, y) = $ **if** $x \geq y$ **then** $x + 1$ **else** $y - 1$ **fi**

10. Write a procedure to insert the character c at the ith position of the multiple value st. All the characters from the ith position upwards should be shifted up to make room for the new character.

11. Write a procedure to calculate the first n prime numbers.

12. Suppose that the point (x, y) is generated randomly in such a way that $-1 \leq x \leq 1$ and $-1 \leq y \leq 1$. The point certainly lies within the square defined by $-1 \leq p \leq 1, -1 \leq q \leq 1$ but it might also lie within the circle whose centre is the origin and whose radius is 1. If *random* does generate numbers randomly, as it should, then the probability of the point (x, y) lying within the circle is $\pi/4$. Turning the argument round, generate $10, 20, 30, 50, 100, 200$ and 400 sets of values for (x, y) and use the above argument to obtain approximations to π.

6

MORE STANDARD MODES

The basic modes that have been used so far have been **real**, **int**, **bool** and **char** (together with **void**). These are basic in the sense that all the other modes so far encountered have been built from these using **ref**, **struct**, **proc** and [ ]. Less basic are other standard modes to be introduced in this chapter.

The first mode to be introduced will be **compl** which allows the manipulation of complex numbers. An object of mode **compl** is a structure with two fields both of which are **real**.

The two new modes **bytes** and **bits** exist to allow the efficient manipulation of particular objects of modes [ ] **char** and [ ] **bool** respectively. To understand the reason for this it is necessary to understand a little about the architecture of computers and about the way in which characters and boolean values are held.

The last section of this chapter is concerned with multiple length working. It can happen that the magnitude of objects of mode **int**, for example, is inadequate for a particular purpose. A suitable implementation of ALGOL 68 would allow the existence of objects of mode **long int**, **long long int** etc. to overcome such problems. Similar facilities may exist for real numbers, complex numbers, objects of mode **bits** and objects of mode **bytes**. Thus one might use modes **long real**, **long compl**, **long bytes**, etc. At the other end of the spectrum there are modes **short int**, **short real**, etc.

6.1. Complex numbers

To understand the manner in which complex numbers can be manipulated one should know that within the standard environment there is a mode declaration

mode compl = **struct** (**real** *re, im*)

This gives all the information necessary about the mode **compl**. Now complex variables can be introduced by means of declarations such as

compl *z, w*

Constants, variables, multiple values of complex numbers, structures with fields which are complex numbers, procedures and operators manipulating complex numbers, etc. can all be used.

Together with the declaration of the standard mode **compl** there are certain standard operators which allow the easy manipulation of complex numbers. Some of the previous operators have their definitions extended to deal with complex numbers.

Applying monadic $+$ or $-$ to a complex number is equivalent to applying the operator to the real and imaginary parts separately; the result is of mode **compl**.

The dyadic operators $+$, $-$, $\times$, $/$ have their usual priorities and now permit the usual addition, subtraction, multiplication and division of integers, reals or complex numbers in any combination; if there is at least one complex operand the result is of mode **compl**. $\uparrow$, which can also be represented as **up** or as $**$, allows a right hand operand of mode **int** and a left hand operand of mode **compl**; the integer may be positive, zero or negative and the result is of mode **compl**.

The comparison operators $=$ and $\neq$ (these can also be represented in various other ways, e.g. **eq**, **ne**, etc.) allow the comparison of integers, reals or complex numbers in any combination.

The assignational operators **plusab**, **minusab**, **timesab** and **divab** (which can also be represented as $+:=$, $-:=$, $\times:=$, $/:=$, etc., respectively) all allow a left hand operand of mode **ref compl** and a right hand operand of mode **int**, **real** or **compl**; the result is of mode **ref compl**.

abs applied to a complex number gives the modulus of the complex number; thus, if z is of mode **compl**, writing **abs** z is equivalent to writing $sqrt$ $((re$ **of** $z)\uparrow 2 + (im$ **of** $z)\uparrow 2)$.

This completes the list of operators whose definitions have been extended to deal with complex numbers. Note that certain operators have been omitted. The operators $\div$, **mod**, etc. associated with integer division have no counterparts and are therefore not extended. Similarly $>$, $\geq$, etc. are not defined and again this is natural since these are not normally defined in mathematics. But as usual the programmer can introduce his own operator declarations and therefore his own interpretation of these if he so wishes.

There is a further set of new operators to augment those already mentioned. There is only one dyadic operator, namely **i** (it can also be written $+\times$, $+*$ or $\perp$). This has standard priority 9, the highest possible for a dyadic operator, and is usually referred to as the *plus-i-times symbol*. The left and right hand operands can be reals or integers in any combination. The result is a complex number whose real part is the left hand operand and whose imaginary part is the right hand operand. Thus one could write

> **compl** $z1 = 4\mathbf{i}5$, $z2 = 0\mathbf{i}pi$

The operator **i** joins the real and imaginary parts of complex numbers and allows a kind of denotation for complex numbers. A structure display could also be used but only in strong syntactic positions.

All other standard operators which allow the manipulation of complex numbers are monadic.

re produces the real part of its complex operand, the result being of mode **real**.

im also produces a result of mode **real**, the imaginary part of its complex operand.

conj produces the complex conjugate of its complex operand, an object of mode **compl**.

arg gives the argument of its complex operand; the result is of mode **real** and lies between $-pi$ and $+pi$; $-pi$ is excluded from the range.

Example 6.1a. Expressions involving complex numbers.
  (i) **abs** $(3 \mathbf{i} 4)$ is a legal expression and gives a result 5 of mode **real**.
 (ii) $3 \mathbf{i} 5 \uparrow 4$ has implied bracketing $(3 \mathbf{i} 5) \uparrow 4$.
(iii) **arg** $(1 \mathbf{i} 1)$ gives as result $pi/4$;
     arg $(4 \mathbf{i} 0)$ gives as result 0 of mode **real**;
     arg $(-4 \mathbf{i} 0)$ gives as result pi

With the introduction of complex numbers the coercion widening takes on an added meaning. Just as an object of mode **int** can be widened in a strong syntactic position to an object of mode **real** so an object of mode **real** can be widened in a strong syntactic position to an object of mode **compl**. Indeed, by a double application of widening an integer can be converted to a corresponding complex number.

Example 6.1b. Widening and complex numbers.
The following declarations are perfectly legal.
  (i) **compl** $z1 = 4$, $z2 = pi$, $z3 = (\mathbf{int}\ n; read\ (n); n)$
 (ii) **compl** $z := \mathbf{if}\ \mathbf{real}\ x, y; read\ ((x, y));\ x > y\ \mathbf{then}\ x\ \mathbf{else}\ y\ \mathbf{fi}$
(iii) $[1]$ **compl** $z := 0$

An actual parameter of a procedure is usually a strong syntactic position and there widening will again take place if necessary. The apparent exceptions to this rule are, of course, the transput procedures, in particular *print* and *write*. In these cases the syntactic position should be regarded as firm.

When a complex number has to be read and made the value of a complex variable that complex variable should appear in the data list of the read statement at the appropriate position. The input file should contain two real numbers separated by either the symbol *i* or the symbol⊥. The first of the pair of numbers becomes the real part and the second the imaginary part of the complex number referred to by the complex variable. The real numbers can appear on the input file in any of the usual forms. An arbitrary number of spaces can occur on either side of the *i* or ⊥ symbol. (Note that a single integer or real is not sufficient.)

Arbitrary units delivering complex numbers can appear in the data list of a print (or write) statement. The usual rules apply. If the entire complex number will not fit on the current line a new line is taken automatically. If the number is printed at the start of a line no initial spaces are left, otherwise one space is automatically left. The real part of the number is printed in just the manner one would expect of a real number. Then a space followed by the plus-*i*-times symbol and the imaginary part are all printed. The imaginary part is again printed as a real number would be printed.

The routines *whole*, *fixed* and *float* cannot be used immediately for the transfer of complex numbers. But by printing the real parts and imaginary parts separately a high degree of control can be obtained.

Transput of multiple values or structures involving complex numbers involves the transput of the individual items in the usual way.

6.2. The modes 'bytes' and 'bits'

As mentioned earlier the reason for the existence of these two modes requires some understanding of the way in which values are held in the computer. Unfortunately this will vary from computer to computer and from compiler to compiler, but a typical arrangement is outlined below.

Locations within a computer are generally arranged in terms of words. Words are often subdivided into a fixed number of bytes, each byte holding a fixed number of bits. Here the terms *byte* and *bit* are used in a non-ALGOL 68 sense. A bit is a binary digit, i.e. a 0 or a 1. With suitable coding a bit can hold a boolean value and a byte will usually hold a character. Typically there may be 8 bits per byte and 4 bytes per word.

Returning now to ALGOL 68, a declaration such as

int *q*,　　　**char** *q*,　　　or　　　**bool** *q*

might cause a word to be made available and *q* will then be the means within the program of accessing this word. The declaration

real *q*

might cause two words to be made available so that a real number of a reasonable size can be held to a satisfactory degree of accuracy.

Notice that with character and boolean values, especially large multiple values of these, there is a considerable inefficiency in terms of storage space. In fact several characters or several boolean values can be packed into a single word. Using the figures of the above example, 4 characters or 32 booleans could be placed in a word. In such a case an object of mode **bytes** would correspond to a multiple value of four characters. An object of mode **bits** would correspond to a multiple value of 32 booleans. The numbers of characters per **bytes** value and booleans per **bits** value may vary from computer to computer and indeed from implementation to implementation.

6.2.1. Bytes

The mode **bytes** is a standard mode and can be used in a program in the same way as other standard modes such as **real**, **bool**, etc. However to understand the significance of **bytes** one should imagine that within the standard environment there is a mode declaration

mode bytes = **struct** ([1 : *bytes width*] **char** ℵ)

The selector ℵ cannot be typed by a programmer and consequently there is no way in which he can break open the structure by selection. He can access the various characters only by means of the standard operators which exist for this very purpose. Indeed since **bytes** is designed for the efficient manipulation of characters it is natural that this restriction should exist.

bytes width is an integer constant declared in the standard environment. It allows an environment enquiry to discover how many characters are packed into an object of mode **bytes** in a particular implementation.

The standard comparison operators $<, \leq, =, \neq, \geq, >$ and their alternative representations **lt**, etc. all have their definitions extended to operate between two objects of mode **bytes**. Their effect is similar to the comparisons on the corresponding rows of characters.

One new dyadic operator **elem**, of standard priority 7, permits the selection of a single character from an object of mode **bytes**. The integral left hand operand selects from the right hand operand of mode **bytes**. The result is of mode **char**. If b is of mode **bytes**, 1 **elem** b chooses the leftmost character, 2 **elem** b the next leftmost, etc.

The coercion widening will in a strong syntactic position convert an object of mode **bytes** to an object of mode [ ] **char**. To perform the reverse operation requires use of the standard procedure *bytespack* which takes as its only parameter a multiple value of characters and gives as result an object of mode **bytes**. Of course the number of characters in the multiple value should be at most the magnitude of *bytes width*; otherwise the effect of the procedure is undefined. If there are less than *bytes width* characters the characters are placed in order at the left hand end of the object of mode **bytes**. The remainder is padded with copies of some arbitrary character, the null character. (The null character will vary from implementation to implementation.) Note that there is no stipulation that the lower bound of the character string, which is the parameter of *bytespack*, should be 1.

Input of objects of mode **bytes** can be achieved by converting from multiple values of characters. **bytes** values can be printed using *print* by performing the reverse conversion.

6.2.2. Bits

As with the mode **bytes**, one should imagine that within the standard environment there is a mode declaration

mode bits = struct ([1 :*bits width*] **bool** ℵ)

Again the structure cannot be broken open by selection and *bits width* indicates the number of boolean which can be packed into a single object of mode **bits**.

Bits denotations

ALGOL 68 admits denotations for objects of mode **bits**; no denotations exist for **bytes**. These denotations can be expressed in base (or radix) 2, 4, 8 or 16. A denotation expressed in base 2 would take the form $2r1001$. The $2r$ indicates that 2 is the base or radix being used. 1001 is then treated as a set of booleans with 0 corresponding to **false** and 1 corresponding to **true**. A denotation in base 8 would be $8r452$. Each of the digits 4, 5 and 2 represents three booleans. The digits can be expressed in base 2 so yielding three digits which are each 0 or 1. The conversion 0 to **false** and 1 to **true** can then be performed. Since base 8 is being used note that it would be meaningless and indeed wrong to use the digits 8 or 9 in a bits denotation using base 8.

In bits denotations using base 4 each digit must be 0, 1, 2 or 3 and each represents two booleans. In denotations using base 16 the letters a, b, c, d, e and f are used to represent 10, 11, 12, 13, 14 and 15 respectively. Thus the denotation $16r4f$ is equivalent to $2r1001111$ or $4r1033$.

Note that in general it will happen that these denotations do not produce precisely *bits width* booleans. Producing more than the requisite number would be similar to writing a denotation of an integer whose value exceeds *max int*. Producing less than the required number results in the leftmost section of the packed multiple of booleans being filled with **false**.

Within a bits denotation no typographical display features such as spaces, new lines or new pages can appear.

Operators and procedures for manipulating bits
The standard operators for manipulating objects of mode **bits** are more numerous than the standard operators for manipulating objects of mode **bytes**. The operations are typical of the kind of basic instructions which computers perform.

The operators **and**, **or** and **not** and their alternative representations can operate on objects of mode **bits** and produce a result of mode **bits**. In effect the operations are performed on the individual booleans. The operator **not** results in each **true** being changed to **false** and each **false** to **true**. The operator **and** (or **or**) must have both operands of mode **bits** and then **and** (or **or**) is applied to each pair of corresponding booleans. In each of the three cases the result is of mode **bits**.

Example 6.2.2a. Using **and** and **or**.
    (i) $2r111$ **and** $2r101$ produces $2r101$ of mode **bits**.
    (ii) If x is of mode **bits**, x **and** $2r111$ selects the rightmost three booleans from x. The operation of examining parts of words by using **and** in this way is usually called masking.

Certain comparison operators have also been extended to operate on **bits** and produce a result of mode **bool**. The operators $=$ and $\neq$ and their alternative representations operate between two objects of mode **bits**. $=$ yields **true** only if the corresponding booleans in each operand are identical. If a and b are of mode **bits**, the effect of $a \neq b$ is equivalent to the effect of **not** $(a = b)$.

The only other comparison operators that have been extended are $\leq$ and $\geq$ (and their alternative representations). Again if a and b are of mode **bits** then $a \leq b$ yields **true** only if for every boolean in a which is **true** the corresponding boolean in b is also **true**. Moreover $a \geq b$ is equivalent to $b \leq a$.

Example 6.2.2b. Comparing objects of modes **bits**.

(i) $2r1010 \leqq 2r1110$ produces **true**

(ii) $4r331 \geq 8r74$ produces **true**

(iii) $2r100 \geq 2r011$ produces **false**.

Note that (iii) above demonstrates that the effect of the comparison operators cannot be achieved by treating objects of mode **bits** as integers and then performing the appropriate comparison between the integers.

The priority 7 operator **elem**, introduced when discussing **bytes**, also allows the selection of an arbitrary boolean from an object of mode **bits**. Thus if i is of mode **int** and b of mode **bits**, i **elem** b selects the ith boolean from b, i.e. the result is of mode **bool**, counting from the left.

Two new operators, both of standard priority 8, allow objects of mode **bits** to be shifted an arbitrary number of places to the left or right. These operators are respectively **shl** with alternative representations **up** and ↑ and **shr** with alternative representations **down** and ↓. The right hand operand is of mode **int** and this gives the size of the shift that has to be performed on the left hand operand which is of mode **bits**. If the right hand operand is negative the direction of the shift is reversed. In other words, if b is of mode **bits** and i of mode **int** then b **shl** $- i$ is equivalent to b **shr** i. Similarly b **shr** $-i$ is equivalent to b **shl** i. When shifting occurs booleans drop off one end and **false** fills the vacant places at the other end (Note **abs** $i \leqq bitswidth$.)

In some implementations the operations associated with **shr**, **shl** and **elem** may be performed much more quickly than some more common operations such as multiplication or division. Consequently when efficiency is of the essence it is often advisable to check if their use would be appropriate. (See example 6.2.2c.)

The conversion of objects of mode **bits** to other modes is achieved by coercions and by operators. In strong positions a bits value can be widened to an object of mode [ ] **bool**. The monadic operator **abs** converts a suitable object of mode **bits** to an equivalent integer, obtained by treating false as 0 and true as 1 and regarding the result as the binary representation of this integer. The integer obtained by use of **abs** should be non-negative, hence **abs** should only be applied to suitable bits values. Thus **abs** 8r77 yields 63.

The reverse operation, i.e. conversion of a non-negative integer to an object of mode **bits**, is achieved by means of the new monadic operator **bin**.

Example 6.2.2c. Using **bin**.

(i) **bin** 7 produces $2r111$.

(ii)   Assuming *i* is a suitable integer

(**bits** $b = $ **bin** i; **abs** (b **shl** 3) $+$ **abs** (b **shl** 1))

causes *i* to be multiplied by 10.

Having discussed all these operators there still remains the problem of how to convert a multiple of booleans to an object of mode **bits**. There is a standard procedure *bitspack* which does just this. Of course the number of elements in the multiple should not exceed *bits width*. If the boolean multiple (whose lower bound need not be 1) contains less than *bits width* elements the booleans fill the right hand end of the object of mode **bits** and the left end (i.e. elements $1, 2, \ldots$) is padded with **false**. The procedure *bitspack* has mode **proc** ([ ] **bool**) **bits**.

Transput involving bits

As far as transput is concerned an object of mode **bits** is treated as a multiple value of *bits width* booleans. Thus on output the various values are transferred one after the other without intervening spaces but with new lines being taken as needed. The symbols printed are the *flip* and *flop* symbols mentioned in section 2.11.2.

On input the data list must contain an element of mode **ref bits**. The requisite number, i.e. *bits width*, booleans are read in and assigned to the appropriate elements of the object of mode **bits** referred to by the variable in the data list. Spaces and new lines can separate the various *flip* and *flop* symbols on the input file.

6.3.   Multiple length facilities

In the introduction to this chapter it was mentioned that the mode **long int** may be used to allow the manipulation of integers larger in magnitude than the integers which can be manipulated using only the mode **int**. Typically an object of mode **long int** might be held in two computer words (rather than in a single computer word which might be used for integers).

A particular implementation may indeed allow objects of modes **long long int**, **long long long int**, etc., objects of these modes occupying three, four, etc. computer words. But in any implementation there will be some limit to the number of significant occurrences of **long** which can appear. This limit will be greater than or equal to 0 but in any particular case it can be obtained by means of an environment enquiry involving the predeclared identifier *int lengths* which is of mode **int**. *int lengths* is $1 +$ the maximum number of significant **long**s that can appear. If more than (*int lengths*-1) **long**s are present the programmer will gain no extra accuracy, though the modes still differ.

At the other extreme it can happen that the space automatically allocated for an integer is larger than necessary; it may happen that the integers to be used are all relatively small in magnitude. A suitable implementation of ALGOL 68 will allow objects of mode **short int** to enable the programmer to make use of this information. An object of mode **short int** might occupy half a computer word. An implementation might even allow objects of mode **short short int**, these being held in perhaps one byte of the computer. Indeed **short short short int**, etc. are all legal modes. The integer identifier *int shorths* indicates the number of significant occurrences of **short** that are allowed. The value of *int shorths* is 1 + the number of significant occurrences of **short** that can appear. Its value will be at least 1 and extra occurrences of **short** will have no effect except that modes with different numbers of **short** are not the same mode.

6.3.1. Environment enquiries associated with multiple length facilities

Associated with the new modes **long int**, **short int**, etc. are predeclared identifiers which give the largest integer of that mode in the particular implementation. Thus just as *max int* gives the largest object of mode **int** so *long max int* gives the largest integer of mode **long int**, *short max int* gives the largest integer of mode **short int**, *long long max int* gives the largest integer of mode **long long int**, and so on. As one would expect *long max int* is of mode **long int**, *short max int* is of mode **short int**, etc.

Similar multiple length facilities are associated with real numbers, complex numbers and objects of modes **bytes** and **bits**.

For real numbers the modes **long real**, **short real** and **long long real**, **short short real**, etc. are available. To allow appropriate environment enquiries there is a set of predeclared identifiers in the standard environment:

real lengths is of mode **int** and its value is 1 + the number of significant occurrences of **long** that can precede **real**; its minimum value is 1;

real shorths is of mode **int** and its value is 1 + the number of significant occurrences of **short** that can precede **real**; its minimum value is also 1;

long max real is of mode **long real**, and gives the largest real number of this mode; similarly there are identifiers *long long max real* of mode **long long real**, etc; there is also *short max real* of mode **short real**, *short short max real* of mode **short short real** and so on;

long small real is of mode **long real** and gives essentially the number of significant decimal places to which an object of mode **long real** is held; if there are n such places then *long small real* has a value of approximately 10^{-n}; there is a similar identifier *short small real* and other identifier *long long small real, short short small real*, etc.

Objects of mode **long compl, short compl**, etc. are effectively of mode **struct (long real** *re, im***)**, **struct (short real** *re, im***)**, etc. There are no special identifiers available for performing environment enquiries on objects of these modes. All the necessary information can be obtained from information about real numbers.

Associated with the mode **bytes** one can have the usual modes **long bytes, short bytes**, etc. The pattern that is developing should by now be predictable. There are predeclared identifiers which allow environment enquiries:

bytes lengths and *bytes shorths* have value $1 +$ the number of significant occurrences of **long** and **short** that can precede **bytes**; these are of mode **int** and in both cases their minimum value is 1;

long bytes width, short bytes width, etc. give the number of characters which are packed into each object of mode **long bytes, short bytes** etc. respectively.

For mode **bits** there are corresponding identifiers *bits lengths* and *bits shorths* both of which are of mode **int** and have a minimum value of 1. The identifiers *long bits width, short bits width*, etc. tell the number of booleans per object of mode **long bits, short bits**, etc. respectively.

6.3.2. Multiple length denotations and related topics
Before looking at the various denotations it is convenient to introduce the concept of *size* when talking about multiple length facilities. The size of an integer or real is

    0 if its mode does not begin with **long** or **short**,

    $+ n$ if its mode starts with n occurrences of **long** and

    $- n$ if its mode starts with n occurrences of **short**.

The generalisation of the concept to other items is straightforward.

Example 6.3.2a. Size.
  (i) Objects of mode **int, real**, etc. are of size 0.
 (ii) Objects of mode **long int, long real, long compl, long bytes** or **long bits** are of size 1.
(iii) Objects of mode **short int**, etc. are of size $- 1$.

Multiple length denotations exist only for integers, real numbers and multiple length **bits**. To achieve the necessary effect the denotation of size 0 must be preceded by the appropriate number of occurrences of **long** or **short**. Of course these size 0 denotations can now be larger in magnitude, contain more digits of accuracy, etc. than before. Thus **long** 2345 is a denotation for an integer of mode **long int** and **short** 2.4 is a denotation for a real number of mode **short real**.

Usually in denotations it happens that typographical display features cannot be used to break up the denotation. However spaces, newlines and new pages (but not comments or pragmatic remarks) can be used to separate **long**s or **short**s from each other or the rest of the denotation.

The ability to write only these multiple length denotations would be rather restricting. Fortunately there are available two operators **leng** and **shorten** which help in overcoming many of the difficulties. The operator **leng** effectively adds 1 to the size of the mode of its operand the operand being an integer, real number, complex number or a set of packed characters or booleans. The operator **shorten** reduces the size of the mode of its operand by 1.

Example 6.3.2b. Using **leng** and **shorten**.
The following are acceptable declarations:
    (i) **long int** *constant* = **leng** (**int** *n*; *read* (*n*); *n* + 1)
    (ii) **short int** *index* = **shorten abs** *"A"*

Finally in this section coercions are considered. The widening coercion still applies only in strong syntactic positions but its meaning is extended to cover the conversion of an integer of any size to a real number of that same size, a real number of any size to a complex number of that same size or a bytes or bits value of any size to a corresponding object of mode [ ] **char** or [ ] **bool** respectively.

6.3.3. Extensions of standard operators
In previous sections certain standard operators were introduced. Many of these have been extended to deal with objects of mode **long int**, **short real**, etc. But there are certain exceptions. Consequently the various categories of operators will be considered in turn and the restrictions, which are all perfectly natural, will be mentioned.

Take first the arithmetic and comparison operators. These include the monadic operators such as + and − and the dyadic operators +, −, ×, /, ÷, **mod**, ↑, >, ≥, =, ≠, ≤, < and their alternative representations, if any. The monadic operators have been extended in the natural way. All the dyadic operators apart from ↑ have been extended to allow suitable operations between objects (integers, reals or complex numbers) of the same size. The size of the result is the common size of the operands. As an example if a and b are of mode **long int** then $a \div b$ is defined and gives a result of mode **long int**. Similarly $a \times b$, $a + b$, etc. all give a result of mode **long int**. The quotient a/b gives a result of mode **long real**.

The operator $\uparrow$, together with any of its alternative representations, is exceptional. The right hand operand must be of mode **int**, not **long int** or **short int**. The mode and size of the result is just the mode and size of the left hand operand. If the left hand operand is an integer of any size then the right hand operand must be non-negative.

The arithmetical assignational operators have all been extended in a straightforward manner. The sizes of the right hand operand and the value referred to by the left hand operand must be identical. There are no exceptions to this rule.

The operators for performing mode changes have been extended in a natural way. Consider for instance **round** or **entier**. When applied to a real number of a particular size these give as result an integer of that same size. For example, an operand of mode **long real** produces a result of mode **long int**.

The operator **abs** has been defined for integers, reals and complex numbers of arbitrary size. It produces results of the same size as its operand. **odd** operates on integers of arbitrary size and produces a result of mode **bool**. **sign** operates on integers or reals of arbitrary size and produces a result of mode **int**.

It has been seen that the operator $\times$ allows the multiplication of integers and characters or strings. The standard environment does not include extensions of $\times$ which would allow the multiplication of character strings and integers of any size other than size 0.

The only operators still to be considered are those used for objects of mode **bytes** and **bits** together with the operator **i**, **re**, **im**, **conj** and **arg** which are used for complex arithmetic. The latter set are considered first.

In every case **i**, **re**, **im**, **conj** and **arg** give results which are the same size as their operands; **i** is the only dyadic operator and its operands must be of equal size. The effect of the operators is as before: **i** combines integers or reals in any combination to give a complex number; **re** produces the real part and **im** the imaginary part of the complex operand; **conj** gives the complex conjugate and **arg** the argument of the complex operand.

The comparison operators all allow the comparison of two bytes values of the same size. The result is always of mode **bool**. The left hand operand of **elem** must be of mode **int** but its right hand operand can be of any size. The result is always of mode **char**.

Finally the operators associated with mode **bits** all extend in the natural way. The comparison operators are defined only for operands of the same size. **and** and **or** (and their alternative representations) operate on bits values of the same size and give as result an object whose mode is the common mode of the operands. **not** and its alternative representations operate on bits values of arbitrary size and give a result of the mode of its operand. Right and left shift operators must have their right hand operand of mode **int**. The left hand operand can be of arbitrary size and its mode is the mode of the result. **abs** converts packed booleans of arbitrary size to integers of that same size. **bin** converts integers of arbitrary size to bits values of the same size. **elem** must have a left hand operand of mode **int** and it delivers the appropriate boolean from its right hand operand which is of arbitrary size.

This completes the description of the various extensions which exist in the standard environment. Of course, the programmer can as usual introduce and declare his own operators and his own extensions if he so chooses.

Example 6.3.3a. Multiple length arithmetic.
Extend the definition of the operator + in such a way that a **long int** and **long long int** can be added to produce a result of mode **long long int**.

A suitable declaration would be

$$\textbf{op} + = (\textbf{long int } a, \textbf{long long int } b) \textbf{ long long int}: \textbf{leng } a + b$$

6.3.4. Standard constants and functions

Corresponding to many of the constants and standard functions available in the standard environment for operating on objects of size 0, there are similar constants and functions for operating on quantities of arbitrary size.

Consider first *pi*. There are predeclared identifiers *long pi* and *short pi* of modes **long real** and **short real** respectively and these give the most accurate value of *pi* subject to the limitations of that particular mode. In a suitable implementation there would also be *long long pi*, *short short pi*, etc.

The standard mathematical functions include also the functions *long sqrt*, *long cos*, *long sin* etc. all of mode **proc (long real) long real** together with *short sqrt*, *short cos*, *short sin*, etc. all of mode **proc (short real) short real**. The standard functions therefore include appropriate functions corresponding to *sqrt, exp, ln, cos, arccos, sin, arcsin, tan* and *arctan* and applicable to reals of any size. The results are objects of the same size as the parameter.

192

There is also a set of functions *long random, random, short random,* etc. for generating real numbers of an arbitrary size. Typical of this set of functions is *long random* which gives a result of mode **long real**. Just as *random* depends on the procedure *next random* and the integer variable *last random* (see example 5.1.3d) so *long random* depends on the procedure *long next random* and the integer variable *long last random* of mode **long int**. The mode of *long next random* is **proc (ref long int) long real**. There is thus a family of procedures corresponding to *next random* and a family of integer variables corresponding to *last random*.

The procedures *bytespack* and *bitspack* also typify families of related procedures. Thus *long bytes pack* produces from a parameter of mode [ ] **char** a result of mode **long bytes**. Similarly *short bits pack* produces from a multiple of booleans a result of mode **short bits**.

6.3.5. Transput

On reading information into variables of mode **ref long int**, etc. the data takes the same form as it did previously. There are no new difficulties. In particular the data will not contain any indication of the size of the variable into which it will be fed.

On output integers and real numbers of any size are printed in as much space as would be required by the largest integer or real of that mode. As with objects of size 0, a space automatically precedes each number unless it appears at the start of a line; and if the number will not fit on the current line a new line is automatically taken.

The number of character positions required by the various objects can be determined by examining the values of certain identifiers declared in the standard environment for this very purpose. These identifiers correspond to *int width, real width* and *exp width* and are typified by *long int width, long real width* and *long exp width* respectively.

Complex values, bytes values and bits values of arbitrary size are transmitted as before with suitable modifications. The number of character positions required by a complex number can be obtained from the number of positions required by the real and imaginary parts.

The standard conversion routines *whole, fixed* and *float* can be used to obtain greater control over the layout of numbers. The various parameters are used for the same purpose as before.

Programming problems for chapter 6

1. Write procedures to:
    (i) take a row of characters and pack these to produce an object of mode [ ] **bytes**;

(ii) take a row of bytes and unpack these to give a row of characters.

2. Extend the definition of the exponential operator to allow:
    (i) a complex number to be raised to a real power;
    (ii) a complex number to be raised to a complex power.

3. Write procedures to calculate:
    (i) the square root of a complex number;
    (ii) the *sin*, *cos*, *tan* of a complex number;
    (iii) logarithm and exponential functions applied to complex numbers.

4. Write programs to read the real numbers a, b and c and to print out the roots of
    (i) $az^2 + bz + c = 0$
    (ii) $az^4 + bz^2 + c = 0$
    (iii) $z^{10} = a$.

5. The binary representation of an integer can be regarded as an object of mode **bits**. Use this fact to write efficient procedures to
    (i) determine if an integer is divisible by 16;
    (ii) find the largest integer $\leq log_2 n$ (assume $n \geq 1$);
    (iii) decide if a positive integer is of the form $2^n - 1$;
    (iv) decide if a positive integer is of the form $2^n + 2^m$ ($n \neq m$).

6. Write procedures to simulate the action of very simple hardware addition, subtraction and multiplication of positive integers by performing the appropriate actions on objects of mode **bits**. Produce a suitable message in the event of the result being too large.

7. Write programs to read an integer n and to express:
    (i) $sin\,(2n + 1)x$ as a polynomial in $sin\,x$;
    (ii) $cos\,2nx$ as a polynomial in $cos\,x$.

8. Take a simple computer with which you are familiar. Write a program to simulate the action of the set of machine-code instructions of the computer.

7

ADVANCED FEATURES ASSOCIATED WITH MODES

For the most part the advanced features considered in this chapter arise from more complex forms of modes. By means of these modes it will be possible to have, for instance, references to multiple values of varying size, variables whose values are in some cases integers and in other cases real numbers or even characters, and variables whose values are variables. These new facilities will lead to applications in algebraic manipulation, information retrieval, record manipulation, list processing, etc.

It should be mentioned at this stage, however, that once objects of these new modes have been introduced the programmer can assume that all the facilities introduced in previous chapters automatically become available. For instance multiple values of such objects can be introduced together with procedures and operators to facilitate their manipulation. This aspect of ALGOL 68 is usually referred to as the *orthogonal design* of the language (or sometimes just *orthogonality*). At the appropriate stage the precise meaning of this term will have to be considered.

7.1. Flexible names

In all the various kinds of multiple values or arrays so far considered the bounds could not be altered once the declaration involving the multiple value had been elaborated. Indeed this is always the case in ALGOL 68; a multiple value can never change its bounds. Moreover references to multiple values have been associated with multiple values all of which have the same bounds. Even with dynamic arrays the elaboration of their declaration results in the various sets of bounds being fixed.

A special kind of reference can be used to refer to multiple values of different sizes. These references or names are described by the adjective 'flexible'. Such a reference to a one-dimensional multiple value whose elements are integers would have mode reference-to-flexible-row-of-integral. In its abbreviated form, and in programs, this is written as **ref flex [ ] int**.

The facility offered by flexible names is in some cases absolutely necessary. Consider the problem of reading an identifier and storing it as a multiple value of characters. There is no way of knowing in advance the size of the multiple value that is required. Flexible names can be used to solve this problem.

But before proceeding further it should be stated that flexible names should be regarded as something of a luxury. Their use can involve considerable overheads as will be seen shortly. Consequently they should be used with a certain amount of care and understanding.

7.1.1. Declaring flexible names

Consider the declaration

flex [2 : 6] **int** p

This introduces the mode identifier p and gives it the mode **ref flex** [ ] **int**. Initially space is generated for a multiple value of five integers, the multiple value having bounds of 2 and 6. One can then write an assignation such as

$$p := ([\ ] \textbf{int} \ b = (1, 2, 3, 4, 5); b[\ @ \ 2])$$

At a later stage one may wish to assign to p a multiple value of three integers. This could be done by

$$p := (6, 7, 8)$$

The effect of this assignation would be that a new multiple value now with bounds 1 and 3 would be referred to by p. The bounds of the multiple value referred to by p have thus been altered.

The example just given illustrates the only way of changing the bounds of the multiple value referred to by a flexible name. One must perform an assignation with the flexible name as destination. It is for this reason that undisciplined use of flexible names can be expensive. When an assignation takes place a copying operation has essentially to be performed. Large numbers of copying operations of large multiple values can be costly.

Example 7.1.1a. Declarations of flexible names.

    (i) **flex** [1 : 0] **int** n

gives to n the mode **ref flex** [ ] **int**. Initially no space is generated for elements of n. The lower and upper bounds associated with the multiple value are 1 and 0 respectively.

    (ii) **flex** [4, 6] **int** p

gives to p the mode **ref flex** [,] **int**. The bounds of both dimensions can be altered.

In part (i) of the above example note that the lower bound exceeded the upper bound. This resulted in no space being generated. Any two units delivering integers such that the lower bound is greater than the upper bound could have been used with a similar effect. When introducing arrays of more than one dimension, or arrays of arrays, it is necessary only to have one upper bound less than the corresponding lower bound and no space will be generated.

To alter the bounds of the multiple value referred to by a flexible name it is convenient to have null row displays and null string denotations. These are represented by ( ) and ″″ respectively and have bounds of 1 and 0 (see also section 7.1.5).

Example 7.1.1b. Null row displays and string denotations.
In the reach of the declaration

flex [4] **int** a, **flex** [4, 6] **int** b, **flex** [10] **char** c

the assignation
(i) $a := ( )$ makes a refer to a multiple value with lower and upper bounds of 1 and 0 respectively;
(ii) $b := (( ),( ))$ is legal;
(iii) $c := ( )$ or $c := ″″$ is acceptable.

7.1.2. Deflexing
Consider again the variable declaration

flex [2 :6] **int** p

This has an equivalent identity declaration

ref flex [ ] **int** $p = $ **loc flex** [2 :6] **int**

The local generator as usual takes the form of **loc** followed by an actual declarer, in this case **flex** [2 :6] **int**. The generator causes the creation of a certain amount of space and delivers a result of mode **ref flex** [ ] **int**. All the usual rules about identity declarations are therefore satisfied. Indeed one could write any identity declaration of the form

ref flex [ ] **int** $p = unit$

provided that *unit* delivered a result of a posteriori mode **ref flex** [ ] **int**.

Now return to the assignation

$p := (6, 7, 8)$

introduced in section 7.1.1. The a posteriori mode of the source is [ ] **int** and the mode of the destination is **ref flex** [ ] **int**. The usual mode considerations associated with assignations are no longer satisfied. Yet such assignations are indeed acceptable. To overcome the problem the idea of *deflexing* is introduced. Deflexing is not a coercion but in many respects it behaves in this way. As the term suggests deflexing allows certain occurrences of **flex** to be dropped from the required mode.

To be precise, deflexing produces mode **b** from mode **a** by removing from **a** all occurrences of **flex** which are not also contained in the mode of some name, i.e. some variable, included in **a**.

The next example illustrates some applications of deflexing. Some of the modes which appear in this example cannot themselves appear as declarers. However these modes can occur as parts of more complicated modes.

Example 7.1.2a. Deflexing.
The process of deflexing produces:
- (i) [ ] **int** from **flex** [ ] **int**;
- (ii) [,] **char** from **flex** [,] **char**;
- (iii) [ ] **struct** ([ ] **char** *name*, **int** *age*) from **flex** [ ] **struct** (**flex** [ ] **char** *name*, **int** *age*).

Deflexing will not produce
- (iv) **ref** [ ] **char** from **ref flex** [ ] **char** (the latter being the mode of a name).

Deflexing is applicable in only a limited number of places. It can be applied in sources and these can occur on the right hand side of assignations, the becomes symbol in identity or variable declarations, the equals symbol in identity declarations and certain kinds of operator or procedure declarations, i.e. those in which no routine text is present. In these circumstances the required mode **a** can be deflexed to give a new mode **b**. An object delivering an a posteriori mode **b** is then adequate for that position.

Deflexing occurs in the performing of certain kinds of dereferencing. When a flexible name is dereferenced not only is the **ref** removed but deflexing also occurs. (See also section 7.1.4.)

With these new rules the earlier assignation $p := (6, 7, 8)$ can be justified. At first sight the required mode is **flex** [ ] **int** but deflexing gives [ ] **int**.

Example 7.1.2b. Applications of deflexing.
Consider the declaration

198

flex [10] **int** a, b

(i) In the assignation $a := b$, b will be dereferenced and in the process **flex** will be removed to give a result of a posteriori mode [ ] **int**.

(ii) In the statement *print* (a) a will be dereferenced and in the process deflexed.

7.1.3. Transient names

Flexible names can be sliced, by trimming or subscripting, in the same way as ordinary references to multiple values. But there is now a new danger associated with this. Suppose that q is declared as

flex [2 :6] **int** q

and assume that it was possible to perform the following sequence of operations:

(i) trim q by means of q [4 :6]

(ii) remember the resulting reference in some way e.g. by means of the declaration

ref [ ] **int** $r = q$ [4 :6]

(iii) alter the bounds of q by, for instance,

$q := (1, 2, 3)$

If the above were possible r would then be left as a reference to a multiple value which now no longer exists since the bounds of q have been altered. Some restriction must therefore be introduced to prevent this happening.

To overcome the stated difficulty the concept of *transient names* is used. The operation of slicing a flexible name produces a transient name. To be precise trimming an object of mode **ref flex** [ ] **int** produces an object of mode transient-reference-to-row-of-integral. Subscripting such an object would produce a transient-reference-to-integral.

Slicing is only one means of producing transient names. They arise also from multiple selection from flexible names and from the rowing of flexible names.

ALGOL 68 is designed in such a way that transient names can never be remembered. Assuming that no dereferencing, etc. occurs transient names can never appear on the right hand side of an identity or variable declaration, be passed as parameters to procedures or operators, be remembered by suitable variables or yielded as the result of a procedure or operator. (It was mentioned briefly at the start of this chapter that variables whose values are variables are possible in ALGOL 68. These values can never be transient names.)

Syntactically the restrictions outlined above are imposed quite simply. There is no abbreviated form of, and therefore no way of writing in a program, a declarer of any mode beginning with 'transient-reference-to-...'.

It is important to realise that it is the transient names which cannot be remembered. The values to which these names refer can be remembered in the usual way. Dereferencing an object of mode transient-reference-to-row-of-integral, for example, produces an object of mode row-of-integral with the appropriate bounds attached.

Example 7.1.3a. Transient references and declarations.
Let p be declared as in

> **flex** [4, 6] **int** p

Consider the following subsequent declarations in the reach of p.

(i) [ ] **int** $q1 = p[3,]$ is legal since the transient name produced by $p[3,]$ is dereferenced giving a result of mode [ ] **int**.

(ii) **ref** [ ] **int** $q2 = p[3,]$ is illegal since an attempt is being made to remember a transient name; suitable coercions do not exist.

(iii) **ref** [,] **int** $q3 = p$ is illegal; p cannot be suitably deflexed since its mode begins **ref flex**.

(iv) **ref flex** [ ] **int** $q4 = p[3,]$ is illegal again for the same reason as given in (ii).

(v) **ref flex** [,] **int** $q5 = p$ is legal and p and $q5$ are different ways of accessing the same name.

It is of interest to look at another example involving transient names but on this occasion they are used with procedures or operators.

Example 7.1.3b. Transient names and procedures or operators.
Let r be declared as in

> **flex** [10] **int** r

and consider the subsequent statements.

(i) *print* ($r[1:4]$) is legal since the transient name is dereferenced.

(ii) *read* ($r[1:4]$) is illegal since an attempt is made to pass a transient reference as a parameter of a procedure.

(iii) $r[i] + := 4$ is illegal since $r[i]$ is a transient name and cannot be passed as the operand of $+ :=$. Note however that $r[i] := r[i] + 4$ is legal, assuming suitable i.

With the introduction of transient names it is necessary to look again at assignations and coercions. In assignations the mode of the destination, and hence the mode of the assignation itself, can begin with either reference-to-amode or transient-reference-to-amode. The a posteriori mode of the source is then **amode** and if necessary deflexing can occur in the usual way.

In dereferencing either a reference or a transient reference can be removed and deflexing performed as necessary. Related to coercions is the idea of balancing. Whenever a transient name is involved in a balance with other names and the expected result is a name then the result of the balance will be a transient name.

Example 7.1.3. Assignations, coercions and transient names. In the reach of the declarations

> **flex** [10] **int** a, b, [10] **int** c, **int** m, n

each of the following assignations is legal.

(i) $a[i] := 4 + b[i]$, since $b[i]$ is dereferenced to give a result of a posteriori mode **int**.

(ii) $a[2:4] := (1, 2, 3)$

(iii) **if** $m > n$ **then** $a[1]$ **else** $c[1]$ **fi** $:= b[1]$

In case (iii) the balanced mode of the destination is a transient name.

7.1.4. 'flex' and declarers

Whenever **flex** appears in a declaration there is always an implicit or explicit **ref** preceding it. In the declaration

> **flex** [4] **int** p

for example, the **ref** is implicit since p has mode **ref flex** [ ] **int**. This is in keeping with the fact that flexibility is a property of a name and not of the multiple value to which it refers. Consequently one would not expect to be allowed to write declarations such as **flex** [ ] **int** $b = (1, 2, 3)$, and indeed this is illegal. One should write instead

> [ ] **int** $b = (1, 2, 3)$

In writing mode declarations it has been pointed out that for multiple values the bounds must be present. Thus

> **mode a** $= [n]$ **int**

is legal and omitting the bounds would be illegal, i.e. actual declarers must appear in mode declarations. Yet it is possible to then write

> **a** $x = (1, 2, 3)$

the bounds associated with **a** being conveniently ignored. With the introduction of **flex**, mode declarations can become even more complicated. **flex** can now appear in mode declarations (since it can occur in actual declarers) and in appropriate cases this together with bounds can be ignored. In fact the process of deflexing removes the relevant occurrences of **flex**.

Note that a more pronounced difference between the concepts of mode and declarer is starting to appear. At the start it was not necessary to distinguish between these but this is now less advisable. A declarer is used to specify a mode. In obtaining the mode from the declarer it may be necessary to ignore bounds and possibly perform deflexing. Note that there are no declarers from some modes (e.g. transient names).

Example 7.1.4a. flex and mode declarations.
Given the mode declaration

> **mode a** = [*n*] **int**

the declaration

> **mode b** = **flex a**

is legal. One could then have declarations such as
(i) **b** *p1* and *p1* would have mode **ref flex** [ ] **int** and initially space would be generated for *n* integers;
(ii) **b** *p2* = (1, 2, 3) and conveniently the **flex** and bounds associated with **b** are ignored;
(iii) **proc** *ex* = (**b** *par 1*, **ref b** *par 2*) **b**: *unit* and the **flex** and bounds associated with the first and third occurrences of **b** are ignored; the bounds associated with the second occurrence of **b** are also ignored.

7.1.5. The standard mode 'string'
In the standard environment there is a mode declaration

> **mode string** = **flex** [1 :0] **char**

This mode can therefore be used as if it were a standard mode and it can be included in declarations, etc. in the usual way.

Together with the mode declaration there are certain standard operators which allow the manipulation of objects of this mode. The operators $+$, $\times$ and the comparison operators were all introduced in section 4.1.7. But an additional set of assignational operators are also available.

The operators $+ :=$, $\times :=$ and their alternative representations,

plusab and **timesab** can be used to operate on characters and character strings:

plusab and $+:=$ can take a left hand operand h of mode **ref string** and right hand operand r of mode **char** or **string**; $h + := r$ has in the usual way the same effect as $h := h + r$ but now the $+$ indicates concatenation of strings of characters;

timesab and $\times:=$ can take a left hand operand h of mode **ref string** and a right hand operand r of mode **int**; $h \times := r$ is equivalent to $h := h \times r$.

There is one further priority 1 operator which has been included to facilitate character manipulation:

plusto, and its equivalent representation $+ =:$, takes a right hand operand r of mode **ref string** and a left hand operand h of mode **string** or **char**; $h + =: r$ is equivalent to $r + := h$

Example 7.1.5a. Assignational operators for strings.
If s is declared as

string s

then $"ma" + =: s$ produces $"ma"$ in s. $s \times := 2$ would then produce $"mama"$ in s

Using the read procedure strings of characters can be read from *standin* into an object of mode **ref string**. Used in a straightforward manner the input will be terminated by the end of line or the logical end of file, whichever comes first.

Example 7.1.5b. Reading strings of characters.

string s, t; *read* $((s, t))$

results in t being assigned the empty string since reading into s leaves the current reading position at the end of a line or the logical end of file.

7.2. United modes

In ALGOL 68 all the values that one manipulates are of one specific mode. But there are occasions when one wishes to write pieces of program to deal with objects of several possible modes.

Occasions when this arises occur in various contexts. One of these has already been encountered, namely the use of the elementary transput procedures *read* and *print*. Take for this discussion the

203

print procedure and consider *print* (*x*). The actual parameter *x* may deliver a result of mode **real**, **int**, **char** or **bool**, it might involve multiple values or even structures of varying degrees of complexity. In fact since *newline*, *backspace*, etc. are themselves procedures and can also be used, one has to include the possibility of the parameter being another procedure. The declaration of the *print* procedure, which occurs in the standard environment, must take account of all the possibilities. In particular the mode of the formal parameter must be rather special.

Another case where one wishes to deal with objects of varying modes is in polynomial manipulation. One might wish to manipulate, say, polynomials in the variable *x*. For simple polynomials the coefficients might be integers, in more complicated cases they might be rational numbers, real numbers, complex numbers or even polynomials in other variables. Again if one wishes to write general procedures one must allow the possibility of the coefficients being one of several different modes.

ALGOL 68 allows the possibility of features such as those described above by allowing *united modes*. These resemble unions of sets in elementary mathematics. Before discussing these united modes in detail it is important to remember that values of united modes do not exist. The values are always of some particular non-united mode.

7.2.1. Uniting
The mode **union** (**int**, **real**) is a declarer specifying a united mode. In longhand this is described as union-of-integral-real-mode. The modes that are united are integral and real and these are called the *alternative* or *component* modes of the union. In the usual way the declaration

>   **union** (**int**, **real**) *ir*

is a shorthand for

>   **ref union** (**int**, **real**) *ir* = **loc union** (**int**, **real**)

and *ir* becomes a variable whose values can be of mode **int** or of mode **real**. In particular one can now write assignations such as

>   *ir* : = 3

and *ir* now refers to the integral value 3. Or one could write

>   *ir* := 2.718

and *ir* would then refer to the real value 2.718. In a similar way the declaration

204

union (int, bool, char) *ibc*

would allow one to write

ibc := 4 or *ibc* := **true** or even *ibc* := *"A"*

These assignments are all perfectly legal. But before the introduction of these united modes assignments had always to satisfy certain mode restrictions. In the simple case one assigned to a variable of mode **ref x** an object of a posteriori mode **x**. This rule still holds, even if united modes are involved. This requires the introduction of another coercion, known as *uniting*.

Consider the assignation *ir* := 3 described above. The 3 is united to mode **union (int, real)**. In this way the rule about the mode requirements in assignations still holds. Similarly in *ibc* := *"A"* the mode **char** (the a priori mode of the source of this assignation) is united to mode **union (int, bool, char)** and the mode condition again holds.

(Having seen that values can by assigned to united variables it should be immediately stated that these values and their original modes can be extracted from such variables. But this cannot be done by dereferencing in the usual way; instead a *conformity clause* must be used. See section 7.2.3.)

Take again the coercion uniting and the assignation *ir* := 3. It was stated that the right hand side was coerced to give an a posteriori mode of **union (int, real)** and that *ir* then referred to the value 3 of mode **int**. But in stating this it follows that there must be some restriction to forbid widening 3 to **real** – after all, the 3 does occupy a strong syntactic position – and then uniting thereby making *ir* refer to the value 3.0 of mode **real**. This is resolved by imposing certain rules. Uniting is a coercion that can be applied in any firm or strong syntactic position. It must occur before all strong coercions (i.e. the coercions widening and rowing which are applicable only in strong syntactic positions) and after the application of all other coercions, i.e. deproceduring and dereferencing. With this restriction the 3 could not be widened and then united.

A united mode can be formed by combining any of the modes so far introduced, including **void, ref flex [ ] int, ref [ ] int**, etc. (subject to some restrictions to be outlined in the next section). The various modes are always expressed as formal declarers. When user defined modes are used in a union **flex** and/or bounds are ignored as required.

Since **void** can occur in united modes it is convenient to have a denotation for the **void** value. The denotation is **empty**.

With the introduction of united modes one immediately gains access to many other facilities. One can define multiple values, structures, operators, procedures, mode declarations, etc. all involving united modes. It is worth mentioning specially that since uniting is possible in firm syntactic positions and since operators whose operands have united modes can be introduced one can partially overcome the problem of having several different declarations involving the same operator. In this way also procedures can be defined to manipulate objects of different modes. However, there are certain drawbacks to these practices (see section 7.2.4).

It was earlier remarked that the actual parameter of a procedure call occupies a strong syntactic position. It has been suggested that there was an exception to this rule in that the actual parameter of the print or write statement and the conversion routines could not be widened and consequently should be thought of as a firm position. However, even with print or write statements the syntactic position is strong. But only now can some light be shed on the reason for this slight, but at an earlier stage necessary, deception.

The mode of the parameter of a print or write statement is essentially

[ ] **union** (**int**, **real**, **compl**, **char**, . . .)

the dots indicating that other modes are also included. When an object of a priori mode **int** is supplied as parameter it has to be converted to an a posteriori mode of [ ] **union** (**int**, **real**, . . .). This happens by uniting and then rowing. Note that widening could not be followed by uniting and rowing. Within the print statement itself the mode of an object to be printed is disentangled (using a conformity clause – see section 7.2.3) and the appropriate action taken.

The mode of the parameter of a read statement is similar to the above. It is of the form

[ ] **union** (**ref int**, **ref real**, . . .)

This whole argument can now be inverted. By using parameters of mode row-of-united-mode note that objects of different modes can be passed either as single items or as multiple values to procedures and indeed operators. Of course, row displays and structure displays can appear only in strong positions and not therefore as operands.

7.2.2. Component modes
Consider

      union (**int**, **bool**, **char**)
      union (**bool**, **char**, **int**)
      union (**bool**, **union** (**int**, **char**))
      union (**union** (**char**, **bool**), **int**)

206

These are four ways of writing or spelling the same mode, namely union-of-integral-boolean-character-mode. Thus the order of the component modes in a union does not matter (i.e. the component modes in a union are commutative) and inner unions can be removed (i.e. the component modes in a union are associative). Other ways of spelling this mode are **union (union (int, bool), union (int, char))** and **union (union (int, bool), char, union (int, char))**.

The component modes of **union (int, bool, char)** are **int**, **bool** and **char**. A union of a subset of these does not constitute a component mode. In particular **union (int, bool)** is not a component mode of **union (int, bool, char)**.

To prove that two spellings lead to the same mode it is only necessary to show that the set of component modes in both cases are identical.

Example 7.2.2a. Component modes.
The component modes of
    (i) **union (union (int, bool), union (int, char))** are **int**, **bool** and **char**;
    (ii) **union (struct (int** a, **real** b), **[ ]int)** are **struct (int** a, **real** b) and **[ ] int**.

The fact that uniting occurs after other coercions imposes certain limitations on the modes that can be components of a united mode. For example, if the modes **int** and **ref int** could be united there would be ambiguity in considering assignations such as $x := n$ where x is a variable of such a united mode and n is of mode **ref int**. Should n be dereferenced and then united or just united?

The general rule for forming unions can now be stated. One can form a union of a set of component modes provided that any component mode cannot be firmly coerced to one of the other component modes, or to a union of the other component modes.

Example 7.2.2b. On united modes.
    (i) Each of the following is an illegal mode:

        union (int, real, ref proc ref real)

since **ref proc ref real** can be dereferenced, deprocedured and then dereferenced to give **real**, one of the other component modes;

        union (ref union (int, real), union (int, real, bool))

since **ref union (int, real)** can be dereferenced and then united to give a union of the other component modes.
    (ii) Each of the following is legal:

union (int, real, compl)
union (union (int, real), union (int, bool))
and   union (ref [ ] char, ref string)

In the light of the restriction that unions can have only components that cannot be firmly coerced to another component or to a union of the other components it is natural to ask about modes such as **union (int, union (int, real))**. It was earlier implied that this is an acceptable way of expressing the mode **union (int, real)** and indeed it is. Yet **int** can be firmly coerced by uniting to **union (int, real)**. The apparent anomaly can be resolved by noting that the rule about formation of modes was phrased in terms of component modes. **union (int, real)** is not a component mode of **union (int, union (int, real))**.

There is another distinction here between modes and declarers. The declarer **union (int, union (int, real))** specifies the mode union-of-integral-real-mode. There is no such mode as union-of-integral-union-of integral-real-mode-mode.

Having discussed the form of the component modes in a union consider again the coercion uniting. Uniting will do one of the following:

(i) take a mode **m**, not a united mode, and produce a united mode one of whose component modes is **m**, i.e. **union (. . ., m, . . .)**;

(ii) take a mode **union (. . .)** and produce another united mode whose component modes include all the components of the first union plus some other modes not contained in that first union.

Example 7.2.2c. Uniting.

(i) Under the appropriate circumstances **union (int, real)** can be united to **union (union (int, bool), union (real, bool))** since the latter is another way of expressing **union (int, real, bool)**.

(ii) Under no circumstances could **union (int, real)** be coerced to **union (real, bool, char)**.

(iii) **int** cannot be coerced to **union (real, char)**.

7.2.3. Conformity clauses
Conformity clauses are used to recover the mode of a value that has previously been united. For instance as a result of the declaration

union (int, real) *ir* := 3

the value 3 is assigned to *ir* and the mode associated with the value is remembered. At a later stage in the program one may wish to discover the mode of the value and perform some action accordingly. The conformity clause allows the programmer to do this.

The conformity clause takes the form of another kind of **case** clause. In this form however the choice is determined by the original mode of the value that was united. Being a case clause one can make use of the usual abbreviations, i.e. (for **case**,) for **esac**, |for **in** and **out** and | : for **ouse** and one must be consistent about what form one uses. Moreover the usual rules about no defining occurrences of labels appearing in the enquiry clause between the **case** and the **in** still hold together with the fact that any identifier declared in the enquiry clause is also available in the units between the **in** and **out** and the **out** and **esac** but not vice versa. The a priori modes of the various alternative units of the conformity clause are, when necessary, balanced in the usual way. So in many respects these conformity clauses behave like case clauses where the choice is determined by the value of an integer. However, in a conformity case clause the number of alternatives that appear must be at least one. Note that in case clauses involving a choice by integers the number of alternatives had to be at least two.

To demonstrate the conformity clause suppose one had to take the variable *ir* introduced above and to print *"integer"* or *"real"* depending on the mode of the current value. This could be done as follows:

> *print* (**case** *ir* **in**
>   (**int**): *"integer"*,
>   (**real**): *"real"*
>   **esac**)

The mode of the current value of *ir* is tested. If it is an integer then the unit preceded by (**int**): is chosen, in this instance *"integer"*. If the current value happens to be of mode **real** the unit preceded by (**real**): is chosen. Each of the alternatives between the **in** and **esac** or, if **out** (**ouse**) is present, between the **in** and the **out** (**ouse**) is of the form

> (declarer): unit

The bracketed declarer and colon is called a *specification part* of the conformity. The declarer must specify a mode which can be united to give the mode of the result delivered by the enquiry clause. Thus it can specify a component mode or a union of the component modes.

The various alternatives in the conformity clause can also take a slightly different form that is illustrated by the next example. Take the same variable *ir* but in this case suppose the sum of the value of the integer or real and 1 or *pi* respectively is to be produced. This can be accomplished by

209

```
    case ir in
        (int i) : 1 + i,
        (real x) : pi + x
    esac
```

Here if *ir* is an integer then the first alternative is chosen as before. But now the integer value referred to by the variable is ascribed to *i* and *i* can be used anywhere within the following unit. This occurrence of *i* acts as a defining occurrence. Here the different possibilities have the alternative form of specification part indicated by

(declarer identifier): unit

In both cases the declarer is a formal declarer and both kinds of specification part can be mixed within the one conformity clause.

The choice in a conformity clause is determined by the clause between the **case** and the **in**. The mode of this clause must be, a posteriori, a united mode. The syntactic position of this clause is meek and so deproceduring and dereferencing can be performed in any order.

The declarers attached to the different alternatives must realise modes that the component modes or a union of a subset of these component modes. If this is not so there is no way in which the unit associated with that alternative can ever be executed. By performing an appropriate mode check the compiler can detect errors of this kind. Thus an element of security is provided. Note that the philosophy here is similar to the philosophy that insists that an **exit** is followed by a label.

In writing conformity clauses it can happen that one specifies in one case a mode **m** and in another case either **m** or a united mode one of whose components is **m**. In such cases the effect of the conformity clause is undefined for there would be uncertainty about which unit had to be elaborated. Less obvious examples can also appear.

Example 7.2.3a. Conformity clause whose effect is undefined.
Let *irb* be of mode **union (int, real, bool)**. The following piece of program is faulty since ambiguity results from *irb* having been assigned a boolean, for example

```
    case irb in
            (int i): print (i + 4),
            (union (bool, int)): read (space),
            (union (bool, real)): print ("no value")
        out print ("error occurred")
    esac
```

210

To end this section on conformity clauses consider **ouse**, or its abbreviated version|:, occurring in such clauses. This is in part an abbreviation for **out case** and its presence indicates that another case clause has been elided with the first. ALGOL 68 insists that if the first case clause is a conformity clause then the second and any subsequent such cases must also be conformities. There is also a corresponding rule regarding case clauses in which the choosing is done on the basis of integral values. Here again the second and subsequent case clauses must involve choosing on the basis of integral values.

7.2.4. Overheads in using united modes

Consider the declaration

$$\textbf{ref union (int, real, char) } irc = \textbf{loc union (int, real, char)}$$

The generator has to generate space to hold values. Since the values can be of one of several modes, in this case real, integer or character, the space generated must be the maximum that would be required for an integer, a real or a character. Further, attached to the value must be some information about the mode so that when a conformity clause is executed in the running program the mode of the current value can be determined. Note that in general this mode cannot be determined at compile time and a conformity clause is nothing more than a check on the mode of a value. In fact a programmer performs his own mode checks explicitly in this way. No mode checking is hidden from him.

United modes impose a double penalty in terms of the space they occupy. They require the maximum space that would be occupied by any of the possible values and they require the space for mode information.

7.3. Orthogonality – modes and constructions

It has been mentioned that ALGOL 68 is designed in such a way that all the facilities available for objects of any one mode are automatically available for objects of any other mode. As a bald statement this is too general. Thus although the *read* procedure allows integers and real numbers to be read it does not allow the reading of objects such as integer variables, procedures and so on. Similarly although + is defined for any combination of integers and reals it is not defined for multiple values of integers, for instance. A clearer definition of the

211

meaning of orthogonality is therefore necessary.

7.3.1. Modes

Orthogonality of modes allows the programmer to have new modes resulting from having:

multiple values whose objects are of any legal mode, excluding **void**;

structures with fields of any mode, excluding **void**;

references to objects of any mode, excluding **void**;

flexible names referring to multiple values of any mode except **void**;

procedures whose parameters, if any, and result are of any mode (results but not parameters may be of mode **void**);

united modes involving any modes subject to the usual restrictions.

Orthogonality will allow the construction of new modes from already existing modes by using **ref**, **struct**, **proc**, [ ], **flex** and **union**. These new modes can in turn be used in the construction of even more complex modes. One must remember however that when **flex** is used in a declarer it must be preceded either explicitly or implicitly by at least one **ref**.

Example 7.3.1a. Allowable modes.
The following modes are all acceptable.
   (i) [ ] **ref int**
  (ii) **ref ref ref int**
 (iii) [ ] **string**
  (iv) **ref flex** [ ] [ ] **int**
   (v) **ref flex** [ ] **ref flex** [ ] **int**

User defined modes introduced in a program by means of mode declarations can also be used in the construction of more complex modes. As usual **flex** and the bounds will be omitted automatically from the declarers.

This covers many of the allowed modes but it does not include them all. Mode declarations can be introduced in which actual declarers specifying any of these new modes can appear on the right hand side. But, as before, such mode declarations are used as a convenience rather than a necessity. Later in this chapter the remaining set of modes will be introduced. It will be possible to introduce these modes only by means of mode declarations (see section 7.6).

7.3.2. Actual, formal and virtual declarers

The introduction of these new modes will increase considerably

212

the types of objects that can be manipulated in programs, but one must first be able to introduce such objects by means of declarations. In this subsection such declarations will be discussed. This requires a closer look at declarers.

Actual declarers have been used in variable declarations, in generators and in mode declarations. Formal declarers have appeared in identity declarations, in specifying the modes of parameters and of the result of a routine (as used in operator and procedure declarations), within united modes and in the specification parts of conformity clauses.

Now it is possible to introduce a row of ten objects each of which has mode **ref** [ ] **int**. This would be achieved by a variable declaration such as

$$[10] \textbf{ ref } [\ ] \textbf{ int } a$$

This variable declaration has as an equivalent identity declaration

$$\textbf{ref } [\ ] \textbf{ ref } [\ ] \textbf{ int } a = \textbf{ loc } [10] \textbf{ ref } [\ ] \textbf{ int}$$

In these cases **ref** [ ] **int** consists of a **ref** followed by a virtual declarer and in virtual declarers the bounds are never present. Virtual declarers are always immediately preceded explicitly by a **ref** or a **ref flex** and they can appear in either actual or formal declarers. The converse of this statement is also true, i.e. whenever a **ref** or **ref flex** appears explicitly in an actual or formal declarer it precedes a virtual declarer and in this declarer no bounds will be present.

Example 7.3.2a. Virtual declarers.
[ ] **int** appears as a virtual declarer in each of the following variable declarations.
    (i) **ref** [ ] **int** s
introduces s and gives it mode **ref ref** [ ] **int**.
    (ii) **struct** ([10] **int** a, [4] **ref** [ ] **int** b) c
    (iii) **union** (**ref flex** [ ] **int**, **proc** (**int**) **int**) t

It is of interest to look at some of the declarations that can appear in a program.

$$\textbf{flex } [4] [3] \textbf{ int } a$$

is acceptable and gives to a the mode **ref flex** [ ] [ ] **int**. Its equivalent identity declaration is, in the usual way,

$$\textbf{ref flex } [\ ] [\ ] \textbf{ int } a = \textbf{loc flex } [4] [3] \textbf{ int}$$

Each $a[i]$ is of mode transient-reference-to-row-of-integral and each has (fixed) bounds 1 and 3. Initially space is reserved for four of these but the space requirements can be altered if necessary.

On the other hand

[4] **flex** [3] **int** b

gives to b the mode **ref** [ ] **flex** [ ] **int**. Each $b[i]$ is of mode **ref flex** [ ] **int**. The number of $b[i]$s is fixed at four. The above is equivalent to the declaration

ref [ ] **flex** [ ] **int** b = **loc** [4] **flex** [3] **int**

7.3.3. Constructions

Having introduced these new modes it is now natural to make the following observation. If one can have declarations such as

int $p = 4$ and **int** $p := 4$

(though not in the same reach) and given that

ref int $p = n$

(where n is of mode **ref int**) is legal, is it then possible to have declarations such as

ref int $m := n$?

The answer is 'yes' and in the usual way this is equivalent to

ref ref int m = **loc ref int** $:= n$

The effect of the declaration is to introduce m as a variable whose values are other variables, the latter being of mode **ref int**. As a result of the above declaration one could write (assuming $n1$ and $n2$ of mode **ref int**) assignments such as $m := n1$ or

$m :=$ **if bool** b; *read* (b); b **then** $n1$ **else** $n2$ **fi**

Note that the usual mode condition for assignments is satisfied in each case. Thus m is of mode **ref ref int** and its values are of mode **ref int**.

Many of the ALGOL 68 constructions which have been used for the manipulation of objects of particular modes can in fact be used for objects of any mode. Thus one can have mode declarations, constant and variable declarations, assignments, procedure and operator declarations, formulae, calls, slices of multiple values, selections, generators which make space available, and choice clauses, conformity clauses, etc. acting as expressions or statements for objects of any allowable mode. (See also Appendix B, p. 339.)

214

Having stated this, the standard environment supplies a particular set of declarations which the programmer assumes. These include the standard definitions of the operators $+$, $-$, $\times$, etc., the mode declarations for **string** and **compl**, the procedure declarations of *read* and *print*, and so on.

This is a convenient place to make a general observation. In a formula such as $a + b - c - d \times e$ the implied bracketing can be decided without knowledge of the modes of a, b, c, d and e. Only information about the relative priorities of the operators is required. In fact the implied bracketing in a **of** b **of** c and $n(i)(j)$ can again be determined without knowledge of the modes of the constituent elements. Indeed ALGOL 68 is designed in such a way that the implied bracketing can always be determined without knowledge of the modes of the constituent elements. In more technical jargon one would say that it admits *mode independent parsing*.

7.3.4. Pointers
In some programming languages variables whose mode begins with at least two successive occurrences of **ref** are called 'pointers', e.g. **ref ref int**, **ref ref ref real**, **ref ref [ ] char**, etc.

Suppose that r and s are variables whose values are structures of some kind, eg.

> **mode man** = **struct** (**string** *name*, **int** *age*); **man** r, s

The declarations of r and s involve invoking a generator to generate space for the two structures referred to by r and s. A variable declared as in

> **ref man** p

could be given the value r by the assignation $p := r$. The effect of this is to allow p to point to the space referred to by r. The assignation $p := s$ causes p to point instead to the structure referred to by s.

In this way p can be made to point to different areas of store – hence the term 'pointer'. The fact that the term 'pointer' has been used suggests that these variables are the means of having pointers to structures or from structures to other structures, multiple values, etc. Indeed this is the case.

There is one special value which is a name and is often used to initialise pointers. **nil** has a mode beginning with **ref** and it can occur only in strong syntactic positions (so that its mode can be fully determined). It cannot be made to refer to a value by means of an assignation and it can never be dereferenced.

7.3.5. Casts

Assume that p is of mode **ref ref int**. Suppose that p refers to some integer variable and that this integer variable has to be given the value 4. One cannot assign 4 to p directly since the only objects which can be assigned directly to p are objects whose (a posteriori) mode is **ref int**. Naturally there is no coercion which will alter an object of mode **int** to a corresponding object of mode **ref int**. After all, what would this mean? Nor can an object of mode **ref ref int** be coerced by dereferencing in a soft position – the left hand side of an assignation is a soft position – to an object of mode **ref int**.

Previously whenever a mode change was required it was performed either by a coercion or by a routine (an operator or procedure), but both of these are inappropriate here. A new kind of construction called a *cast* is better suited to this application.

Casts are used to force mode changes. They take the form of a formal declarer followed by an enclosed clause; the formal declarer specifies the required mode and the enclosed clause delivers the object whose mode has to be altered. The syntactic position of the clause is strong and consequently all coercions can be applied in order to obtain the required mode.

A cast is exactly what is required in the above example. The necessary assignation can be performed by

ref int $(p) := 4$

The effect of a cast is essentially to provide a strong syntactic position in a position in which this would not otherwise be the case.

Example 7.3.5a. Casts.
Each of the following is an example of a cast.

real (3)
union (**int**, **real**) (3)
[ ] **int if bool** b; *read* (b); b **then** 1 **else** 0 **fi**

In the third example the enclosed clause is a conditional.

Casts themselves can appear in almost any syntactic position. If they deliver results of the appropriate kind they can be sliced, be selected from or appear as a source, destination or operand.

7.3.6. Identity relations

With the introduction of the new modes it has been seen that it is possible to have, in effect, variables whose values are other variables. Thus one could make the following declarations

216

$$\textbf{int } n := 3, m := 3; \textbf{ref int } w := n$$

When comparing the values of variables of the appropriate kinds for equality one usually writes expressions such as $p = q$ and this gives the appropriate result. Here p and q occupy firm syntactic positions since they are operands in a formula and in the usual way any necessary dereferencing takes place.

Consider then what happens in writing $w = m$, using the above declarations. Equals is an operator defined between objects of mode **int**. Consequently in this expression w will be double dereferenced to give a result 3 and m will be dereferenced once to give also the result 3. The expression therefore yields **true**. But w is a variable and has as its value another variable, namely n. m is a different variable from n and so one would hope that a comparison could be made at this level and a result **false** delivered. But neither operators nor casts can be used for this purpose.

Comparisons of the kind mentioned above can be achieved by means of a construction known as an *identity relation*. Identity relations make use of the symbols $:= :$ (which has **is** as an alternative representation) and $: \neq :$ (which can also be represented as $:/= :$ or **isnt**). These symbols are not operators; they are called the *identity relators*.

Consider $p := : q$. Both p and q are elaborated collaterally and they must deliver as results variables of the same mode. This identity relation then delivers **true** provided that both sides of the identity relation deliver the same variable; otherwise the result is **false**. Both p and q can be any type of construction that can appear as the destination part of an assignation. Thus they can be any type of unit excluding essentially assignations and identity relations themselves.

The coercions that can be applied to the two sides of an identity relation are rather peculiar. Either p occupies a soft position and q occupies a strong position or p occupies a strong position and q occupies a soft position. Thus one side of an identity relator is soft and the other is strong. The coercions are applied in such a way that the variables delivered by both sides are of the same mode. In effect balancing occurs.

The construction involving $: \neq :$ or **isnt** is similar to that involving $:= :$ or **is**. Thus $p : \neq : q$ or p **isnt** q delivers **false** provided that p and q both yield the same variable; it delivers **true** otherwise.

Example 7.3.6a. Identity relations.
Consider the declarations

$$\textbf{int } n := 3, m := 3; \textbf{ref int } w := n, z := n, \textbf{ref int } y = n$$

(i) $y := :n$ delivers **true** since y and n deliver the same variable of mode **ref int**: no coercions take place.

(ii) $n := :w$ delivers **true**; here w is dereferenced to yield n. The right hand side of the identity relator $:=:$ is taken to be strong since dereferencing cannot occur in a soft position. Similarly $w := :n$ delivers **true** and in this case w is again dereferenced. Here the strong position is the position on the left of $:=:$.

(iii) y **isnt** m delivers **true**; no coercions take place.

(iv) **ref int** $(w) := :z$ delivers **true** though $w := :z$ delivers **false**. Note that the cast causes dereferencing of w and of z.

Whenever an attempt is made to compare two names which result from slicing, the effect is rather curious. In the first place it is illegal to compare two transient or flexible names by means of an identity relation. Moreover whenever a slice is performed unless all the trimscripts (see section 4.1.4) are subscripts, the programmer should not make any assumptions about the uniqueness of the resulting name.

Example 7.3.6b. Identity relations and slices.
a is of mode **ref** [ ] **int**.

(i) The yield of $a[2:3] := :a[2:3]$ is undefined;

(ii) $(a[1] := :a[1])$ and $(a[1] : \neq :a[2])$ are both defined and yield **true**.

7.4. Orthogonality – coercions

It was remarked earlier that there are no new coercions or rules for applying coercions although many new modes have been introduced. The aim of this section is not only to gather together the various rules that are scattered throughout the earlier pages but also to mention in more detail some of the rules that were of necessity incomplete when they were first encountered.

7.4.1. NONPROC modes revisited

In suitable positions calls are of the form $f(\ldots)$ or f depending on whether or not f has parameters – the latter example is a call of a parameterless procedure. In the case where f does have parameters f occupies a meek syntactic position. One can parameterise only an object of a posteriori mode starting with **proc**. Therefore, if as can now happen, f has mode starting with **ref proc**, **ref ref proc** or **ref ref ref proc**, etc., dereferencing and deproceduring can take place yielding a result of the required mode.

For procedures without parameters it is necessary to become involved in a discussion about deproceduring and voiding. To a large extent this has already been discussed in section 5.1.7. The modes covered by the NONPROC modes however have to be extended. A complete definition of these modes now follows.

Let **m** denote an arbitrary mode. Then NONPROC includes all modes with the exception of

(i) the modes **proc m** including **proc void**;

(ii) the modes in (i) preceded by any number of **ref**s.

Whenever a COMORF (i.e. an assignation, an identity relation, a generator, a cast or a denotation of some kind) produces a result whose a posteriori mode must be **void** then the necessary mode change is performed by voiding immediately. As a result no activation of the procedures involved takes place.

In the case of MORFs, i.e. all other kinds of constructions excluding jumps, **skip** and **nil**, the story is not so simple. If the construction yields a result of a priori mode NONPROC then it will be voided. If, after possible dereferencing and deproceduring, it again yields a result of mode NONPROC then again voiding will take place. In all other cases deproceduring will be involved if necessary and activation of the procedures will ensure. As usual deproceduring implies activation of procedures, voiding does not imply such activation.

It is possible to declare procedures that give as a result other procedures. If f is such a procedure then expressions such as $f(i)(x)$ become meaningful. For in this case $f(i)$ might yield as a result a procedure such as *sin* which takes a single parameter. In the above example the actual parameter is x. Thus $f(i)$ (x) is merely a call to the procedure given by $f(i)$. The implied bracketing here is therefore $(f(i))(x)$. Of course, not only two but several parameters can appear. Thus expressions such as

$$f(i)(j)(k) \ldots$$

may be meaningful and in these cases the implied bracketing is from the left.

7.4.2. Weak dereferencing
One aspect of multiple values and structures is the implied bracketing in expressions such as

a **of** $b[i]$
a **of** b **of** c **of** d
$n[i][j]$

and so on. These have all been discussed in earlier sections and the rules introduced there apply in general. Note that in the last of the above three examples the implied bracketing is as for procedure calls. Indeed one is allowed to use the round brackets (and) in place of the square brackets [and] in slices and declarers. In these circumstances it is only possible to decide whether a construction such as $p(i)$ or $r(i)(j)$ is a procedure call or a slicing of a multiple value from the modes of p and r. In both cases the implied bracketing is the same.

With the introduction of the new modes it is natural to ask if one could subscript, for example, objects of mode **ref ref** [ ] **m**, **ref flex** [ ] **ref** [ ] **m**, etc. and structures of a similar nature. To answer these questions consider slices and selections such as $nn[i]$ and a **of** b. Both nn and b occupy weak syntactic positions. These are the only weak positions. In such positions only deproceduring and a special kind of dereferencing (see below) can be applied. Now slicing can be applied only to (references to) multiple values and selecting only to (references to) structures or multiple values. Consequently if nn or b happens to have mode which begins reference-to-reference-to-etc. then since dereferencing can take place in a weak position the nn or b will be automatically dereferenced. But only a limited form of dereferencing called *weak dereferencing* can take place. Weak dereferencing allows for the removal of any initial **ref** apart from the last with appropriate modifications for flexible and transient names. The final **ref** can never be removed by weak dereferencing. (The modification necessary for flexible and transient names are no different from those outlined in section 7.1.3.)

Example 7.4.2a. Weak dereferencing.
In the reach of the declarations

>   **ref** [ ] **int** n, **flex** [4] **ref** [ ] **int** m, **int** i, j

(i) $n[i]$ yields a result of a priori mode **ref int** for n is of mode **ref ref** [ ] **int** and is weakly dereferenced to give a result of mode **ref** [ ] **int**.

(ii) $m[i]$ yields a result of a priori mode transient-reference-to-reference-to-row-of-integral.

(iii) $m[i][j]$ yields a result of a priori mode **ref int**. The transient name yielded by $m[i]$ is weakly dereferenced to yield a result of mode **ref** [ ] **int**.

It is of interest to look at an example in which casts are used to overcome the effects of weak dereferencing.

Example 7.4.2b. Casts and weak dereferencing.

Suppose x is of mode **ref m** where
  mode m = struct ([20] **char** *name*, **ref int** *n*)

(i) In n **of m**(x) a cast is used to force dereferencing of x.

(ii) In **ref int** $(n$ **of** $x)$ the result delivered by n **of** x is of mode **ref ref int**. The cast forces this to be dereferenced.

Note that both (i) and (ii) deliver the same result.

7.4.3. Review of coercions and syntactic positions

ALGOL 68 admits a total of six coercions all of which have been encountered at various stages. However, there are limitations on the way in which these coercions can be applied. Each type of position will now be considered in turn.

The soft positions are destinations in assignations, and one side of an identity relation (remember that one side is strong and the other soft). In soft positions only deproceduring can be applied, repeatedly if necessary.

Examples of weak positions are mentioned in the discussion on weak dereferencing, i.e. the object being selected from in selections and the primary of slices (see section 4.1.4). The coercions that can be applied are dereferencing and deproceduring. They can be applied repeatedly and in any order but weak dereferencing imposes the restriction that a final **ref** cannot be removed.

Examples of meek syntactic positions are all enquiry clauses, i.e. the clauses following occurrences of **if**, **case**, **while** etc., boundscripts in actual declarers and slices including lower bounds or subscripts; the **from**, **by** and **to** parts of a loop clause; and the primary of a call (see section 5.1.2). In meek syntactic positions deproceduring and dereferencing can be applied repeatedly if necessary and in any order.

The only firm syntactic position is the position occupied by an operand in a formula. In firm positions dereferencing and deproceduring can be applied repeatedly and in any order. A single application of uniting can then be performed if required.

The strong syntactic positions can be listed as: actual parameters in procedure calls; sources in assignations and declarations; the **do** part of a loop clause; the enclosed clause in casts; and statements. Strong positions appear also on one side of an identity relation, in balancing and in routine texts.

The coercions available in strong positions include widening, rowing and voiding. Repeated applications, if necessary, of widening can be preceded by any of the coercions available in a meek position. Widening allows the following changes of mode: **int** to **real**; **real** to

compl; **bits** to [ ] **bool**; and **bytes** to [ ] **char**. Similar changes exist when multiple length objects are involved.

Rowing allows the following mode changes, assuming that **m** is an arbitrary mode: **m** to [ ]**m**; [ ]**m** to [,] **m**, [,]**m** to [,,]**m**, etc; **ref m** to **ref** [ ]**m**; and **ref** [ ]**m** to **ref**[,]**m**, **ref**[,]**m** to **ref**[,,]**m** etc. Whenever rowing is involved the coercions are applied in the following order: the repeated application if necessary of meek coercions, i.e. deproceduring and dereferencing; one application of uniting if necessary; repeated applications of widening if necessary; and finally repeated applications of rowing if necessary. Note therefore that the various coercions are applied in a particular order. They are applied from the weakest through to the strongest.

The final coercion available only in a strong position is voiding. The discussion of section 7.4.1 contains all the information about voiding and, in particular, how this differs from deproceduring.

Some examples are now given to illustrate the way in which coercions are applied.

Example 7.4.3a. Complex coercions.
Strong syntactic positions allow (assuming suitable constructions)
(i) an a priori mode of **proc ref int** and an a posteriori mode of **real**. The coercions applied are, in order, deproceduring, dereferencing and widening.
(ii) an a priori mode of **ref proc ref ref int** and an a posteriori mode of **ref** [ ] **int**. The coercions are dereferencing, deproceduring, dereferencing and rowing. By further applications of rowing a posteriori modes **ref** [ ][ ] **int** or **ref** [ ][,,] **int** could be produced.
(iii) an a priori mode of

transient-reference-to-procedure-yielding-integral

could produce an a posteriori mode of

[ ] **union** (**int, char**)

by dereferencing, deproceduring, uniting and rowing.

7.5. Orthogonality – scope

This is a convenient place to reconsider in more detail the idea of a local generator and the idea of scope. Another kind of generator, the global generator, will also be introduced.

7.5.1. Scope revisited
Typical assignations used so far have been of the form (assuming

222

x, y and z to be of mode **ref real**),

$$x := y \text{ or } x := z + 4.7 \times y$$

In these assignations the value delivered by the source is, since x is of mode **ref real**, of a posteriori mode **real**. This value is then assigned to the variable x in the usual way. In particular there is no difficulty about the assignation $x := y$ no matter what the scope of y happens to be. y is dereferenced and the real result is assigned to the variable x.

Note that this happy state of affairs can no longer be assumed to be true if one now takes into account objects of the new modes introduced by orthogonality considerations. To be more explicit consider the assignation $xx := y$ where xx is of mode **ref ref real** and y is, as before, of mode **ref real**. This assignation seems correct but its strict correctness depends on the relative scopes of xx and y. Suppose the scope of y is strictly smaller than that of xx. When the space associated with y is relinquished xx will suddenly have an undefined value.

To overcome the problem illustrated above ALGOL 68 insists that all assignations satisfy a scope requirement: the scope of the result delivered by the source of an assignation is always at least as great as the scope of the result delivered by the destination.

The scope requirement has arisen as a result of the new modes introduced. It has arisen also from associating a scope with variables. From the earlier discussion about the design of ALGOL 68 one should now expect two consequences: (a) the scope requirement should apply to all assignations, even those of the form $x := 4.7$; (b) scopes have been associated with variables; a scope should be associated with objects of any mode, even constants.

These two demands are met by associating with all values of mode **real**, **int**, **bool**, **char** and **void** together with their multiple length counterparts a scope which includes the entire user program. In assignations in which the source or destination can deliver one of several values, as can happen by using conditionals, cases or multiple exits from a serial clause, the smallest of the scopes of the result delivered by the source must be at least as great as the greatest scope of any of the results delivered by the destination.

For multiple values and structures the scope is defined to be the smallest of the scopes of all the individual elements. In particular multiple values of integers, characters, reals and booleans have a scope which extends over the entire program, and similarly for structures involving these objects.

The above discussion of scopes has been conducted purely in terms of assignations. A similar situation will arise in variable, identity, procedure and operator declarations and indeed similar restrictions must be enforced in these cases (see section 7.5.3).

So, a scope is associated with all values in a program. For constant values and variables involving local generators the scope is straightforward. **nil** has a scope which extends over the entire program. But there are other possibilities to be considered. For example, a scope must be associated with a routine (see section 7.5.4).

7.5.2. Local generators revisited

Until now local generators have been used only in variable (or their equivalent identity) declarations. The space they generate has remained available throughout the smallest enclosing range (serial or enquiry clause). In this section some new uses of local generators will be investigated. These arise as a result of the wealth of new modes now available. Consequently some of the earlier ideas about generators will have to be modified. In particular it will be seen that generators need not appear as parts of declarations.

First consider a use of generators in which the generator does appear as part of a declaration but in a manner somewhat different to the earlier use. Suppose it is required to introduce a new mode called **gasmeter** containing the serial number and the reading of a gasmeter. In this case the two integers are different in nature. The serial number will presumably be constant and will never change. The meter reading will vary as more gas is used. With this in mind the serial number would presumably be of mode **int** and the meter reading of mode **ref int** – hence the declaration

$$\text{\textbf{mode gasmeter} = \textbf{struct} (\textbf{int} \textit{ serial no}, \textbf{ref int} \textit{ reading})}$$

Consider now the declaration of an object x of mode **gasmeter**. A possible (identity) declaration of x would be

$$\text{\textbf{gasmeter} } x = (23146, \textbf{loc int})$$

The serial number is 23146; to initialise the meter reading to 0 the declaration could be altered to

$$\text{\textbf{gasmeter} } x = (23146, \textbf{loc int} := 0)$$

As required, one field is of mode **int**, the other is of mode **ref int** and space has been created by **loc**. The generator acts in the usual way, i.e. it generates space to hold an integer and returns as result the name or address of the space. This can then be accessed by *reading* **of** x. The scope of the variable is as usual the smallest enclosing range. Moreover the meter reading can be altered by an assignation such as

$$\textit{reading} \textbf{ of } x := 10$$

since *reading* **of** x is of a priori mode **ref int**.

This example is a special case of a more general situation. By similar means one can introduce structures some of whose fields are variables and some of whose fields are constants.

Another use of local generators arises from considerations of (usually large) multiple values of special kinds. It frequently happens in mathematical and other applications that one has to deal with multiple values many of whose elements either do not exist or are zero. The zeros often lie in convenient places and then the multiple values are called by special names, e.g. upper triangular, diagonal, tridiagonal, etc.

Consider the special case of a two-dimensional array v of size $n \times n$ having the property that there are only elements $v[i,j]$ for $j \geq i$. The previous kinds of multiple values could be used for this but there would be, for large values of n, considerable wasted space. But the above array is just a row of vectors and space can be generated using **loc** for each of these vectors.

Let w be declared as

$[n]$ **ref** [ ] **int** w

Then $w[1]$ is of mode **ref ref** [ ] **int** and can be assigned a value of mode **ref** [ ] **int**.

$w[1] := $ **loc** $[n]$ **int**

will be a legal assignation and results in space being generated for the top row of the array. Moreover this space can be accessed via $w[1]$. For $w[1][j]$ where $1 \leq j \leq n$ will be of a priori mode **ref int** since $w[1]$ is weakly dereferenced.

The space for the entire multiple value can be generated as follows:

$[n]$ **ref** [ ] **int** w;
for i **to** n **do** $w[i] := $ **loc** $[i:n]$ **int** **od**

The required effect is thereby achieved. By replacing i and n in **loc** $[i:n]$ **int** by expressions, subscripted variables, function calls, etc., arrays of strange shapes can be generated. Only as much space as is required is generated and the bounds can always be obtained using **upb** and **lwb**.

The space generated for the multiple value above has a scope which is just the scope of w. This remark requires some further explanation since until now local generators have created space which exists only within the smallest enclosing range. This rule will now have to be modified. In the meantime, however, note that **loc** followed by an actual declarer results in the generation of the appropriate amount of space and the result returned is the name or address of this space. This in turn can be assigned to other variables.

When one elaborates a local generator the space so created remains available usually until the end of a particular range. In the usual way one looks out from the generator through successive reaches. If in so doing one encounters the **for** part of a loop clause, the specification part of a conformity clause, or a serial or enquiry clause containing, at most, label or priority declarations then one moves out to the next reach and investigates this. When one can move out no further the resulting serial or enquiry clause gives the scope of the space generated by the local generator. It is for this reason that the earlier uses of local generators in loops were valid.

There is one exception to the above set of rules. If space is created by a local generator appearing in the unit associated with a procedure or operator declaration or in a routine text then this space will disappear either at the end of the elaboration of this or at the end of the range obtained by the above rules, whichever is sooner.

Example 7.5.2a. Using local generators.
A common use of local generators is in passing dummy variables to routines. The call

$$char\ in\ string\ (ch,\ \textbf{loc int},\ str)$$

will determine whether the character *ch* is in the string *str*. It is assumed that the position of the character, if it is present, is irrelevant.

7.5.3. Global or heap generators
In this section a new kind of generator, the *global* or *heap* generator as it is called, will be studied. The difference between these new generators and local generators is that space generated by global generators remains available for as long as required. The programmer should think of the space being available to him throughout the entire program.

The new generator is invoked by using **heap** in place of **loc**. Thus

$$\textbf{ref int}\ n = \textbf{heap int}$$

is an acceptable identity declaration. The space so created remains available as long as necessary. But it should be stressed that the identifier *n* can be used only, as before, within the smallest enclosing range. Just as

$$\textbf{ref int}\ n = \textbf{loc int}$$

has an equivalent variable declaration, namely **loc int** *n* or the more

226

usual form **int** n, so the above identity declaration has an equivalent variable declaration

> **heap int** n

In this case the **heap** can never be omitted so that confusion cannot arise between declarations involving the different kinds of generator.

Example 7.5.3a. Declarations involving global generators.
  (i) **heap int** $n := 5$
  (ii) **heap** [10] **int** nn
  (iii) **heap flex** [4] **int** p
  (iv) **heap string** s
  (v) **struct** (**int** a, **ref int** b) $x = (4,$ **heap int** $:= 0)$

Global generators create space which can be used in the same way as space generated by local generators with the added benefit that no scope problems arise in constructions such as

> **begin ref real** xx;
>   **begin heap real** $x := 4$;
> $xx := x$
>   **end**;
> $print(xx)$
> **end**

The assignation $xx := x$ is legal; the scope rule is satisfied because the scope of the name generated as a result of the declaration

> **heap real** $x := 4$

is the entire program. Had a local generator been used at this stage an error would have arisen as was pointed out in section 7.5.1. Note that the statement $print(xx)$ in the above piece of program will cause the real number 4.0 to be printed. xx is double dereferenced. Moreover this print statement could not have been replaced by a statement $print(x)$, for x can be used only within the inner serial clause.

By using a pointer the space generated in the inner serial clause can be accessed in the outer reach. This facility will prove to be very powerful though this power will not be illustrated until after recursive modes have been introduced in section 7.6.

Example 7.5.3b. Using heap generators.
If xx is declared as in **ref real** xx note that $xx := 4.5$ is illegal. xx occupies a soft position and cannot be dereferenced. Yet $xx :=$ **heap real** $:= 4.5$ is legal.

It would appear from the previous discussion that using heap generators in preference to local generators would cure all ills arising in scope problems. However, the use of heap variables will often involve considerable overheads. Although by means of heap generators more space can be requested it can also happen that the programmer no longer needs certain space previously generated. In ALGOL 68 the programmer has no means of indicating that space generated by a heap generator can be relinquished and used for other purposes. Therefore this space must be recovered automatically. A piece of program known as a *garbage collector* is usually available for this purpose. The programmer should expect that if he uses heap variables the execution of his program will be suspended every so often and the garbage collector called into action. The use of heap variables can therefore lead to less efficient programs: the space requirement is increased since there must be room for the garbage collector and the time requirement is increased since the garbage collector must have time to act.

7.5.4. Scope of routines
Defining the scope associated with a routine is made more complex by the fact that the definition of routines will in general contain applied occurrences of variables and other quantities which themselves have scopes associated with them.

Consider the piece of program

```
      . . .
    begin int t;
          proc f = (int x, y) void: t := x + y;
          begin int t, p, q; read ((p, q));
                f(p, q)
          end
    end
      . . .
```

The procedure f is declared in such a way that it alters t. But there are two different defining occurrences of t. The question arises as to which t is altered by the call of f? The answer is that the first occurrence of t is altered. The second is unaffected. (Note that similar questions can arise in using operators.)

The situation can be explained by saying that one associates with a routine an environment, the environment *necessary* for the routine. In general the necessary environment will contain a subset of the identifiers, modes, operators, etc. contained in the environment in which the procedure or operator is declared. This subset includes all the objects used by, but declared outside, the routine. In the above example the declaration of f introduces a procedure which has a necessary environment which includes t, the t declared in the reach in which f was declared. (The necessary environment will include also the definition of $+$.)

One should think of a routine as consisting of two quantities: the instructions required for carrying out the task and the environment necessary for the routine.

When a routine is activated via a procedure call or use of an operator it is important to be aware of the variables, etc. that are used. To understand precisely what happens one should imagine that the routine call is replaced by a closed clause. At the start of this clause the necessary environment is established and then the routine instructions are activated.

The idea of a necessary environment enables the scope of a routine to be defined. Each of the objects in the necessary environment will have been declared in a particular serial or enquiry clause. From the identification rules of section 3.5 the set of such clauses will all be nested and the innermost such clause is the scope of the routine. Note that it is the position of the declarations that is important.

Example 7.5.4a. Scope of routines.

(i) The scope of the f declared in the above example is equal to the scope of t, the first t declared.

(ii) The scope of g declared by

$$\textbf{proc } g = (\textbf{int } n)\ \textbf{int}: (n = 1 | 1 | n \times g(n-1))$$

is, assuming the standard operators $=$, $\times$ and $-$, the entire program.

(iii) Consider the declaration

$$\textbf{proc int } h = (\textbf{heap int } count := 0;$$
$$\textbf{int}: count +:= 1)$$

This declaration is wrong. The routine text

$$\textbf{int}: count +:= 1$$

has a necessary environment which includes $count$. The scope of the routine is the serial clause in which $count$ is declared. It is therefore illegal to pass it out of the serial clause since the scope rule would thereby be violated.

7.6. Recursive modes

To show the need for recursive modes, consider a structure with fields containing information about a person's name, age, weight and height. A declaration of *x*, a reference to such a structure, might take the form

> **struct** (**string** *name*, **int** *age*, **real** *weight*, *height*) *x* :=
> (*"IAN"*, 25, 160.1, 68.5)

Or one could write using mode declarations

> **mode person** =
> **struct** (**string** *name*, **int** *age*, **real** *weight*, *height*);
> **person** *x* := (*"IAN"*, 25, 160.1, 68.5)

Suppose now that one wanted records of several people. They might be the people in a family, for example. Such a record might have a field containing a pointer to the person's spouse; in the case of an unmarried person this would be **nil**. Then in attempting to write down a mode for a person without using mode declarations one would write a mode resembling

> **struct** (**string** *name*, **int** *age*, **real** *height*, *weight*,
> **ref struct** (. . .) *spouse*) *x*

Note the second occurrence of **struct**(has to be followed by **string** *name*, **int** *age*, **real** *height*, *weight*, **ref struct**(and this last occurrence of **struct**(has to be followed by a similar list of modes and selectors, and so on. In fact one can never write the mode in this way.

Fortunately mode declarations come to the rescue and by their means one can write

> **mode person** = **struct** (**string** *name*, **int** *age*, **real** *height*,
> *weight*, **ref person** *spouse*)

Note that this mode declaration is recursive. One can now write

> **person** *x*, *y*

and later

> *spouse* **of** *x* := *y*; *spouse* **of** *y* := *x*

These assignations are legal since the destinations have mode **ref ref person** and the sources have mode **ref person**.

This example has demonstrated the use of recursive modes and the essential importance of mode declarations. It also introduces a new concept in programming. In general, structures can be intro-

230

duced and can contain pointers, more than one if necessary, to other structures which can in turn contain pointers to yet other structures and so on. These ideas constitute the tip of an iceberg. The underlying subject matter is usually known as 'data structures' and is concerned with the best ways of representing either abstract or real-world objects in a computer so that the representations can conveniently be manipulated by a program.

7.6.1. Well-formed modes

Before looking at practical applications the full power of recursive modes has to be investigated. The mode **person** declared earlier was a legal mode. On the other hand, one would not expect

mode a = [100] **a**

to be a legal declaration since this defines an object of mode **a** to occupy 100 times the space of an object of mode **a**. These examples are reasonably straightforward, but there are other less obvious cases. For example, do the declarations

mode b = **proc (b) bool** and **mode d** = **proc d**

define acceptable, or well-formed, modes? It is desirable to have some rules to determine whether or not a certain (recursive) mode declaration defines a well-formed mode.

Mode declarations often involve combining several modes to form a more complex mode. For example, **struct** combines the modes of the different fields; **union** combines the different component modes involved in the union; **proc** (...) ... combines the modes of the parameters and the mode of the result; **proc** ... adds **proc** to the mode of the result; **ref** ... adds **ref** to the mode of its successor; and [ ],[,], etc. together with **flex** are used in manipulating multiple values whose elements are of particular modes. These items are called *heads* and they play an important part in determining the legality of a particular mode declaration. Given a mode declaration one can decompose the mode on the right hand side of the equals symbol by progressively stripping off the heads. Removing one head will leave one or more constituent modes. One can then remove the heads of these constituent modes and so on.

Take a particular mode **a** which is defined recursively. In going from the defining occurrence of **a** to any applied occurrence (i.e. an occurrence on the right hand side of the equals symbol in a mode declaration) heads are progressively removed. The declaration is well formed provided that in so doing one ignores bounds and passes over

(i) a **struct** and a **ref**, in either order,

(ii) a **struct** and a **proc** (the procedure can be with or without parameters), in either order,

(iii) a **proc** where the **proc** has parameters.

Otherwise the declaration is illegal.

The reasons behind these restrictions stem from consideration of coercions and storage allocation. It is essential, to avoid ambiguity about the coercions to be applied in a particular situation, that whenever a coercion occurs the mode changes. If the mode **m** declared as in

> **mode m = ref m**

had to be legal **m** would be essentially an infinite sequence of **ref**s. Dereferencing **m** would then produce **m**. Similar situations arise with the coercions rowing, deproceduring and uniting.

To illustrate the reasoning behind the other restrictions assume the legality of mode **n** where

> **mode n = struct (int** a, **n** b**)**

Let the space occupied by an object of mode **n** be x and by an integer be y. Then from the mode declaration of **n**

$$x = y + x$$

and this implies $y = 0$ which is false. Note that for this purpose an object of mode **amode** and a variable whose values are of mode **amode** occupy different amounts of store.

Example 7.6.1a. Well-formed modes.

(i) Each of the following mode declarations provides a well-formed mode.

> **mode a = proc (a) bool**
> **mode a = proc (a) a**
> **mode a = proc struct (a** *test*, **int** n**)**
> **mode a = struct (int** n, **proc a** *test*)

(ii) None of the following mode declarations is acceptable.

> **mode a = struct (int** n, **a** *test*)
> **mode a = union (real, bool, a)**
> **mode a = [100] union (real, bool, a)**
> **mode a = proc a**

Just as it is possible to declare mutually recursive procedures so it is possible to declare mutually recursive modes, e.g.

232

mode a = struct (int *n*, **b** *test*), **b = ref c, c = a**

Here **a** is declared in terms of **b**, **b** is declared in terms of **c** and **c** in terms of **a**. To test the well-formedness of the declarations one has to continually remove heads and check that an allowable set of heads has been removed. The above declarations pass the test since in going from **a** to **b** a **struct** has to be removed and in going from **b** to **c** a **ref** is removed. Also **struct** and **ref** form an allowable set of heads.

This completes the description of what constitutes a well-formed mode. The reader should note that mode declarations such as

mode a = [4 : (**a** *p* . . . ; . . .)] **int**

define well-formed modes. But their use requires some care. Whenever **a** appears as an actual declarer in an identity or variable declaration its bounds have to be elaborated. In such cases the unit

(**a** *p* . . . ; . . .)

has to be elaborated and if **a** appears in this unit as an actual declarer this will in turn involve the elaboration of the bounds of a. A loop will result. However when **a** is used as a formal declarer its bounds are ignored and **a** is essentially the mode [ ] **int**. In more delicate examples **a** could occur in the inner depths of much more complicated clauses involving conditionals, etc.

7.6.2. Equivalent modes
Consider the declarations

mode a = struct (ref a *b*, **int** *n*),
        b = struct (ref struct (ref b *b*, **int** *n*) *b*, **int** *n*)

In fact these are two ways of declaring the same mode. To see this replace the occurrence of **a** on the right hand side of the declaration of **a** by itself, i.e. by **struct (ref a** *b*, **int** *n*).

There is a general method of determining whether or not two modes are equivalent. At all stages of this process any user-defined mode should be replaced wherever and whenever it is encountered by its definition. Then one can proceed as follows (note that the process is recursive).

Look at the heads of the modes. If these are different the modes are different. If they are the same and both are
ref, then test the equivalence of the remaining parts of the modes;

struct, test that (i) the modes of corresponding fields are equivalent, and (ii) the selectors of corresponding fields are identical;

233

[ ], [,], ..., **flex** etc., test that the remaining parts of the modes are identical;

proc with or without parameters, test that the modes of
 (i) corresponding parameters are equivalent
 (ii) the results are equivalent;

union, test that each set of component modes is equivalent to a subset of the other set of component modes and vice versa.

This process must be repeated until either the modes are proved to be not equivalent or it is impossible to distinguish one mode from the other (in which case the modes are equivalent). In practice it can be shown that this is a finite process. It should be assumed, of course, that modes such as **real**, **int**, **bits**, **long int**, etc. are all primitive and independent in that they cannot be expressed in terms of each other. The modes **string** and **compl** have been defined in terms of other modes and as such should be treated like user-defined modes, i.e. they should be replaced by their appropriate definition.

7.7. Programming examples

7.7.1. Using flexible names
Consider the problem of reading into a multiple value the various characters of an ALGOL 68 identifier. Spaces should be removed as the characters are read.
 Assuming the existence of a procedure

> **proc** *letter or digit* = (**char** *c*) **bool**: ...

which yields **true** if *c* is a letter or digit and **false** otherwise, the following piece of program will, if the first character in the standard input is a letter, place in *st*[1 :*count*] the letters of the identifier.

```
flex [10] char st, int count, char ch;
proc next = (ref char c) void:
      while read (c); c = " " do skip od;
st[count := 1] := (read (ch); ch);
while letter or digit ((next(ch); ch))
do if count = upb st
   then st +:= 10 × " "
   fi;
   st[count +:= 1] := ch
od
```

The procedure *next* has been used to remove all insignificant spaces.

234

Note also that since increasing the size of the multiple value referred to by *st* may be a relatively costly operation an attempt has been made to decrease the frequency of this by increasing the size of the multiple value by 10 rather than by 1 whenever an increase is necessary.

7.7.2. Using recursive modes

One of the most frequent uses of recursive modes is in what is traditionally called list processing. The recursive mode declaration

mode cell = struct (char *item*, **ref cell** *rest*)

introduces a simple form of list. Items of this mode are essentially collections of characters but with suitable mode declarations they could be objects of any mode. See diagram 7.1. The arrows indicate the presence of pointers and the diagonal stroke indicates **nil**. To add a new cell containing *"C"* to the start of the list space has to be created, the *"C"* inserted in the appropriate place and the cell linked to the old list. Given that *h* is of mode **ref ref list** this is accomplished by

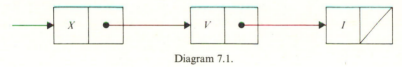

Diagram 7.1.

$h := $ **heap cell** $:= ("C", h)$

These simple lists are often used as stacks. As the name suggests a stack can be visualised as a collection of objects placed one on top of the other. Stacks are characterised by the fact that one can take from the stack only the topmost item or one can place an item on top of the stack.

Example 7.7.2a. Stack manipulating routines.
Given the mode declaration

mode list = struct (char *top*, **ref list** *rest*)

the procedure *push* places an item on the stack and *pop* removes an item.

ref list *null list* = **nil**;
null list makes the program more readable and avoids a cast in the identity relation
ref list *stack* := *null list*;
proc *push* = **(char** *c*) **void**: *stack* := **heap list** := (*c, stack*);

235

```
          proc pop = char:
          if stack := : null list
          then error
          else char c = top of stack;
                    stack := rest of stack;
                    c
          fi
```

It is assumed that *error* is some procedure of mode **proc char** which takes suitable action if someone attempts to remove an item from an empty stack.

Example 7.7.2b. Parenthesis matching.
Given a sequence of brackets (,), [and] write a program to determine whether or not such a sequence could appear in a legal ALGOL 68 program. It is assumed that the data is terminated by £ and that brackets occurring in comments, pragmatic remarks and within character or string denotations will not appear. Thus the sequence ([ ](( ))) is legal but (( )))(is illegal since after the fifth bracket the number of closing brackets exceeds the number of opening brackets.

The piece of program below performs the necessary task. Procedure *br error* takes appropriate action when an illegal sequence is encountered. The declarations given in example 7.7.2a are assumed.

```
      while char ch; read (ch): ch | = "£"
      do if ch = ")" or ch = "]"
         then if stack := : null list then br error fi;
              if char top = top of stack;
                 top = "(" and ch = ")" or top = "[" and ch = "]"
              then pop
              else br error
              fi
         else push (ch)
         fi
      od;
      if stack : ≠ : null list then br error fi
```

The basic idea given in this example can be extended considerably to allow the matching of **begin** and **end**, **if** and **fi**, **case** and **esac**, etc., some of the tasks that have to be performed by a compiler.

Example 7.7.2c. Other uses of recursive modes.
  (i) **mode polyn = struct (int** *coeff, power,* **ref polyn** *rest)*
can be used for the representation of polynomials in one variable.

(ii) **mode person** = **struct** (**string** *name*, **int** *age*, *height*,
ref **person** *spouse*,
flex [0] **ref person** *children*)

can be used for family trees.

(iii) **mode book** = **struct** (**string** *title*, *author*, **int** *class no*);
mode subjectlist = **struct** (**book** *item*, **ref subjectlist** *rest*);
mode library = [1000] **subjectlist**

could be used in organising a program to manipulate information about books in a library.

7.7.3. Using united modes

By using united modes structures of much greater complexity can be considered. Take, for example, lists. Instead of these being a collection of characters as in the previous example they could be a collection of characters, integers and real numbers.

Example 7.7.3a. Lists of different kinds of objects.
Consider the declarations

mode item = **union** (**char**, **int**, **real**),
list = **struct** (**item** *item*, **ref list** *rest*);
ref list *null* = **nil**

Design a procedure *enumerate* to count the number of objects of the different types which are in a list. The integer variables *char*, *int* and *real* will be used to return the necessary results

proc *enumerate* = (**ref int** *char*, *int*, *real*, **ref list** *h*) **void**:
begin *char* := *int* := *real* := 0;
ref list *hh* := *h*;
while *hh* :≠: *null*
do case *item* **of** *hh* **in**
(**char**): *char*, (**int**): *int*, (**real**): *real*
esac +:= 1;
hh := *rest* **of** *hh*
od
end

The definition of **list** can be further extended to allow a collection of items some of which may themselves be lists, as follows

mode atom = **union** (**int**, **ref list**),
list = **struct** (**atom** *item*, **ref list** *rest*)

This would include not only simple lists but lists of the form given in diagram 7.2.

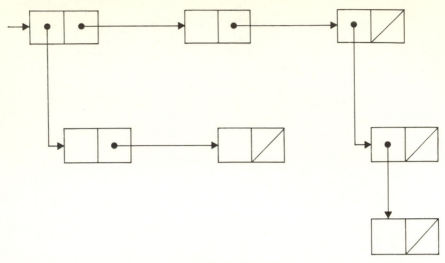

Diagram 7.2.

Example 7.7.3b. Using complex lists.

Given an object of mode **ref list** write a procedure to count the number of integers in the list to which the object refers. Assume that no two pointers point to the same cell (if they did some integers would be counted more than once).

> **mode atom = union (int, ref list),**
>   **list = struct (atom** *item*, **ref list** *rest*);
> **ref list** *null* = **nil**;
> **proc** *size* = (**ref list** *h*) **int**:
> **if** *h* :=:*null*
> **then** 0
> **else** (*item* **of** *h*|(**int**): 1|(**ref list** *k*): *size*(*k*)) + *size*(*rest* **of** *h*)
> **fi**

This completes the discussion on lists. Their range of applicability extends far beyond what has been suggested above. Modes such as those used above occur in many applications. For polynomial manipulation for example one could have declarations

> **mode coeff = union (int, ref poly),**
>   **term = struct (coeff** *coeff*, **char** *var*, **int** *power*),
>   **poly = struct (term** *first*, **ref poly** *rest*)

Exercises on chapter 7

1. Are the following constructions allowed?

(i) *"abcdefg"* [*i*]

(ii) (1, 2, 3, 4, 5) [*i*]

(iii) (*"a"*, *"b"*, *"c"*, *"d"*, *"e"*) [*i*]

Give reasons for your answers.

2. Will deflexing produce
   (i) **ref [ ] char** from **ref string**
   (ii) **[ ] struct (ref flex [ ] int** p, **int** q) from **flex [ ] struct (ref flex [ ] int** p, **int** q)
   (iii) **ref struct ([ ] char** r) from **ref struct (string** r)?

3. If x is declared as in

   [4][6] real x

   (i) how would one obtain the multiple value consisting of all the elements referred to by each of

   $x[1][j]$

   where $j = 1, 2, 3, 4, 5$ and 6?

   (ii) how would one obtain the multiple value consisting of all the elements referred to by

   $x[i][1]$

   where $i = 1, 2, 3$ and 4?

   (iii) could one write, in the reach of x,

   [,] real $y = x$?

4. Given the declarations

   string a, **[4] char** x

   are the following acceptable?
   (i) $a := x := \textit{"ABCD"}$
   (ii) $x := a := \textit{"ABCD"}$
   Give reasons for your answers

5. Is the declaration

   ref flex [ ] int $nn = \textbf{loc}$ **[10] int**

   legal?

6. Given the declaration

   flex [5] int a, b, **[5] int** c, **int** m, n

   are the following legal?
   (i) **if** $m > n$ **then** a **else** c **fi** $:= b$

(ii) **if** $m > n$ **then** a **else** c **fi** $[1:4] := b[1:4]$

(iii) **if** $m > n$ **then** a **else** b **fi** $:= c$

(iv) **if** $m > n$ **then** $a[2:5]$ **else** $c[3:6]$ **fi** $:= b[1:4]$

7. Are the following legal declarers?
  (i) **ref string**
  (ii) **ref[ ]string**
  (iii) **ref flex [ ]string**
  (iv) **ref flex [ ]flex [ ]int**

8. Would it be syntactically correct to write
  (i) **union (int, real)** $ir = $ **loc int** $:= 3$
  (ii) **union (int, char)** $ic = "z"$
  (iii) **union (real, char)** $c1 = "A"$, $c2 = "B"$; $print$ (**abs** $(c1 = c2)$)
  (iv) **ref union (int, real)** $ir = $ **loc real** $:= pi$?

9. Which of the following are legal declarations?
  (i) **union (int, [ ]int)** x
  (ii) **union (int, real, compl)** x
  (iii) **[10] union (int, [ ]char)** y
  (iv) **[10] union (int, [10] char)** y
  (v) **union (string, [ ] char, int)** s
  (vi) **union (flex [ ]char, [ ] char)** t

10. Does

    union ([ ]int, struct (int p, q, r**))**

    specify an acceptable united mode? If so, is

    union ([ ] int, struct (int p, q, r**))** $z := (1, 2, 3)$

    legal? Give reasons for your answer.

11. What would be the result of writing

    union (struct (int a, b**), struct (int** c, d**))** $r := (1, 2)$

    in a program?

12. In the reach of the declarations

    union (int, real) ir, **[4] union (int, real)** irs

    would it be legal to write
    (i) $print ((ir | (\textbf{int } i) : i, (\textbf{real } r) : r))$
    (ii) $print (ir)$
    (iii) $print (irs)$?
    In the legitimate cases indicate the relevant coercions.

13. Consider the declaration

   flex [4] **flex** [10] **char** t, [4] **char** s

Is the assignation

   $t[1] := s$

legal? If so outline the coercions, etc. involved.

14. Given the declaration

   [4][6] **char** x, **flex** [4][6] **char** y,
   [4] **flex** [6] **char** z, **flex** [4] **flex** [6] **char** w

which of the following are syntactically admissible:

   (i) $x[1] := "A"$ (ii) $y[1] := "A"$
   (iii) $z[1] := "A"$ (iv) $w[1] := "A"$
   (v) $x := w$ (vi) $y := z$?

15. Given the declaration

   flex [4] **flex** [6] **string** s

what is the a priori mode of

   (i) $s[1]$ (ii) $s[1][1]$
   (iii) $s[1][1][1]$ (iv) $s[1][1:2]$
   (v) $s[1:2][1]$

16. Is the result produced by the following undefined?

   print (**if string** a; $a = ""$ **then** 0 **else** 1 **fi**)

17. A syntax error would result from the following program. What causes this?

   ([10] **ref int** a;
   print ((*read* (a); a)))

18. Are the following legal mode declarations:
   (i) **mode a** = **flex** [1 : 10] **int**
   (ii) **mode b** = **flex** [ ] **int**   ?

19. Consider the declaration

   mode ratn = **struct** (**int** *num, den*)

It is required to extend the definition of the comparison operator = in such a way that it can be used between integers and rationals, i.e. objects of mode **ratn** in any combination.

Could a single declaration

> **op** = = (**union** (**int**, **ratn**) a, b) **bool** : . . .

be used for this purpose?

20. In the reach of the declaration

    > **flex** [0, 0] **int** x

    which of the following are legal and, in the legal cases, what bounds become associated with x?
    (i) $x := (( ), ( ))$
    (ii) $x := (( ))$
    (iii) $x := ( )$
    (iv) $x := ((( )))$

21. Can p and $(p[\ ])$ be used interchangeably given that p is of a priori mode
    (i)   [ ] **int**
    (ii) **ref** [ ] **int**
    (iii) **ref ref** [ ] **int**
    (iv) **ref flex** [ ] **int**   ?

22. It is sometimes said that **flex** should not occur in ALGOL 68 since its effect can be achieved by using pointers to multiple values and (local) generators. Is there any added advantage in using **flex**?

23. Consider the modes **a** and **b** declared as follows

    > **mode a** = **struct** (**int** p, **ref a** q)
    > **mode b** = **ref struct** (**int** p, **b** q)

    What is the relationship between these modes?

24. Would it be legal to write in a program
    mode fn = **proc** (**real**) **real**;
    proc *compose* = (**fn** f, g) **fn** :
    (**real** x) **real** : $f(g(x))$;
    fn *fourth root* = *compose* (*sqrt*, *sqrt*)   ?

Programming problems for chapter 7

1. Multiplication of a $p \times q$ and $q \times r$ matrix requires pqr multiplications. If matrices A, B and C are of size 1×10, 10×100 and 100×1 respectively what is the most efficient way (in terms of multiplications involved) of multiplying $A \times B \times C$, as $(A \times B) \times C$ or as $A \times (B \times C)$? How do the number of additions involved

in the two methods compare? Deduce a general strategy for efficiently multiplying a set of matrices. Write a procedure which will efficiently calculate

$$M_1 \times M_2 \times \ldots \times M_n$$

where each M_1 is of size $r_{i-1} \times r_i$.

2. A string of characters can be held within a computer as a flexible row of characters or as a simple list. Write separate procedures to perform the following operations using these two methods:
    (i) concatenation of two strings, i.e. joining two strings together to form a third string;
    (ii) insertion of one string within another;
    (iii) deletion of one string from another.
Each procedure should be of mode **proc (ref m, m) ref m** where **m** is of the appropriate mode. Which method of representation do you consider to be better and why?

3. Consider an object *l* of mode **list** where

    mode list = **struct** (**int** *item*, **ref list** *rest*)

Write procedures to
    (i) count the number of integers in *l*;
    (ii) reverse the list *l* leaving the original list unaltered;
    (iii) reverse a list by redirecting the pointers in the original list.
Test your procedures by incorporating them in suitable programs.

4. Assuming that a set is implemented as a simple list write procedures to perform union and intersection. Also write procedures to
    (i) decide if a given element is a member of a set;
    (ii) replace all occurrences of *x* in a set by *y*;
    (iii) copy a set.

5. Consider the declaration

    mode tree = **struct** (**ref tree** *left*, **m** *node*, **ref tree** *right*)

Objects of mode **tree** are of the form given in diagram 7.3(a) below, the circles representing objects of mode **m** (e.g. integers, characters, etc.). A tree can be traversed by following the dotted line given in diagram 7.3(*b*). If each node is processed
    (i) on its first encounter the tree traversal is described as a pre-order tree traversal,
    (ii) on its second encounter then an in-order tree traversal results,
    (iii) on its third encounter then a post-order tree traversal

is obtained.
Write algorithms to perform traversals of the various kinds.

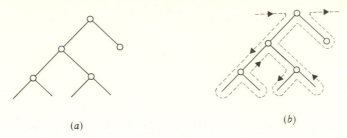

(a)   (b)

Diagram 7.3.

6. (See previous example.) Trees can be used to sort elements of a set. The first element is placed in the tree as the topmost node. The second element will be positioned down the left or right subtree depending on whether it is less than or greater than the top node, etc. Thus 4, 8, 7, 3, 9, 2 would result in the tree of diagram 7.4.

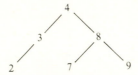

Diagram 7.4.

Write a procedure to sort an array of integers in this way. How would the sorted elements be printed?

7. (See previous examples.) An arithmetic expression can be represented in the computer by a tree; each node with no descendent subtrees is an operand, the other nodes are operators. Thus $a + b \times c$ would be represented as in diagram 7.5.

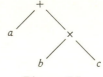

Diagram 7.5.

Devise:
   (i) operators to add, subtract, multiply and divide two expressions;
   (ii) a procedure to evaluate an expression;

244

(iii) a procedure to differentiate an expression with respect to a particular variable.

8. When the tree of an arithmetic expression is traversed in post-order, postfix notation results. Thus traversing diagram 7.6

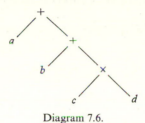

Diagram 7.6.

corresponding to $a + (b + c \times d)$ results in

$abcd \times + +$

Postfix notation can be evaluated using a stack. As the various items are read operands are put on the stack. Operators result in the top two operands being removed, acted on by the operator and the result placed on the stack. When the input stream has been exhausted the result will be left on the stack.

Design an algorithm to take postfix notation (involving only dyadic operators) and evaluate it. The operands should all be integers.

9. Write a program to take a fully-parenthesised arithmetic expression and produce a tree for the expression. Use this to write a program to evaluate fully-parenthesised expressions which are supplied as data.

N. B. a fully-parenthesised expression the bracketing alone (not the priority of the operators, etc.) determines the order of evaluation of the operands.

10. Write a cross-reference program to process ALGOL 68 programs. The idea is that the program should print a (sorted) list of all identifiers, modes and operators together with an indication of the lines on which the various objects were used.

11. Write a program which accepts as data an ALGOL 68 program and indicates whether or not the brackets, **begin–end** pairs, etc. match.

12. Write a program which, in a simplified form, converts abbreviated versions of conditional clauses to their **if-then-else-fi** form.

The data for the program should consist of a sequence of the symbols (,),|,| : (suitably terminated) and the output should be a list of the corresponding bold words. Note the possibility of having conditionals within conditionals.

How might the program be altered to deal also with

(i) closed clauses?

(ii) choice clauses where the choosing is done using integers?

8

PARALLEL PROCESSING

8.1. Introductory remarks

In previous chapters the possibility of the collateral elaboration of different parts of a program was mentioned. Collateral elaboration, or parallel processing as it is sometimes called, can take place on, for instance, operands or the individual elements of displays. Thus the computer may be executing several parts of the same program at the same instant of time. The aim of this chapter is to look in much more detail at the topic of parallel processing from an ALGOL 68 point of view.

In looking at collateral elaboration earlier it was seen that a problem arose in writing expressions such as

$$(n := 5) \times 4 + n \times 7$$

because of the uncertainty over the relative order of elaboration of the operands. The difficulties are caused by the fact that the elaboration of the different pieces of program involve accessing the same variable (i.e. the same resource) and in one of these cases the access is to alter the value of the variable or resource. This is an example of what is called *resource sharing*, the resource in this example being the variable *n*. If one part of the program wishes to access the resource in order to alter it in some way then there is liable to be doubt about the effect of the program unless there is some means by which the programmer can exercise control over the order in which the different parts of program access the resource. In simple cases he can control the order by forcing serial elaboration (by using serial clauses) but there are problems for which this is too slow or not possible. ALGOL 68 has facilities for dealing with these situations. These take the form of semaphores, introduced into computing by E. W. Dijkstra around the mid-1960s. (See section 8.7, reference 3.)

Resource sharing by itself, of course, does not cause problems in parallel processing. One can write, for instance,

int *m1, m2, n*; *read* (*n*); (*m1* := *n*, *m2* := *n* + 4)

and there is no ambiguity involved although the value of *n* is accessed in the elaboration of both $m1 := n$ and $m2 := n + 4$.

In general, if several sets of instructions have to be elaborated collaterally and if the set of variables altered by any one set of instructions is disjoint from the set of variables accessed by any other set of instructions then no trouble will arise. Such sets of instructions are said to be *disjoint* or *non-interacting*. Their use is straightforward. Troublesome cases are caused by the violation of this disjointness criterion.

These new errors one can call time-dependent errors since they are due to uncertainty about the relative order of elaboration of sets of instructions. One serious drawback of this type of error is that often the errors cannot readily be reproduced. In parallel processing the relative ordering of instructions can vary from one run of a program to another. This could depend on what is happening in the rest of the computer at the time. For instance if another program is using the floating-point unit then instructions requiring its use might be delayed until some later time; otherwise they would be performed.

Until now the problems caused by the use of parallel processing have been quite artificial and easily overcome. In fact the problem arose because of errors in the way the programs or statements were written. Proper structuring of the programs and proper sequencing of statements readily produce programs in which these problems do not arise. But there are cases where such an approach will not suffice. In these cases there must be orderly and controlled access to shared variables. The sets of instructions which have to access the shared variables and therefore have to be synchronised are hereafter called *processes*.

8.2. The mutual exclusion and message passing problems

In this section two specific examples will be considered. The first of these is usually referred to as the *mutual exclusion* or *lock-out* problem. It arises whenever only one process has to be granted access to a shared variable at any one time. An example of the kind of situation in which mutual exclusion is required is now given. It is taken from the writings of Brinch Hansen (see references at end of this chapter).

Let P and Q be two processes which have access to a common variable v of mode **ref int**. Process P collects statistics of some kind and, for simplicity, these take the form of incrementing the value of the variable v by 1 whenever P is invoked. Process Q on the other hand periodically prints the value of v and then immediately sets it to zero. One cannot program P and Q by merely writing a collateral clause one of whose units is

248

$$(\ldots; v+:=1)$$

the other being

$$(\ldots; print\,(v); v:=0)$$

(The dots merely indicate that other instructions may be involved in processes P and Q.) The disjointness condition is of course violated and indeed an interleaving of the processes such as

$$\ldots; print(v); v+:=1; v:=0$$

will not produce the desired effect. Thus some rather careful synchronisation must take place. In fact one of the processes must, if necessary, be temporarily suspended while the other has access to the shared variable v. Synchronisation might therefore involve the ability to temporarily suspend processes.

More precisely, mutual exclusion requires that

(i) at most a single process has access to shared resources at any one time.

The following additional requirements should also be stipulated:

(ii) a process will always complete its operations on shared variables within a finite time;

(iii) a process will be able to access a common variable within a finite time if it so wishes.

If the latter condition is not satisfied then a condition known as *deadlock* arises. This is sometimes also called a *deadly embrace* and results from errors in synchronisation.

Apart from the mutual exclusion problem there is also a problem arising from sending messages or signals between processes. The classical example of this type of problem arises when there is a set of processes sending messages and another set of processes receiving and consuming the messages. It is assumed that the messages are placed in a message buffer (e.g. a multiple value whose elements are messages) of finite capacity. At a given instant certain conditions must be satisfied.

(i) The number of messages received cannot exceed the number of messages sent. Consequently the consumers must if necessary be suspended until there are messages to be absorbed.

(ii) The number of messages sent but not yet read from the message buffer cannot exceed the capacity of the buffer. Consequently if the buffer is full the senders might have to be suspended until the receivers absorb some of the information in the buffer.

(iii) Access to the common buffer must be governed by the principle of mutual exclusion.

249

The problems outlined in (i) and (ii) are of a different nature to the mutual exclusion problem although these can all be classified as synchronisation problems. In the mutual exclusion case it is necessary to have semaphores to keep track of whichever process is accessing the shared resource. In the case of the messages being passed the processes have common variables which are necessary to count the messages being passed between the processes.

8.3. Parallel clauses and semaphores

A semaphore is an object of mode **sema**, which is essentially a structure with a single field containing an integer variable. The structure cannot be broken open since the selector is inaccessible to the programmer. (In this respect it resembles the modes **bits** and **bytes**.) Semaphores are special in that there are restrictions on the timing of operations that can be performed on them. These will be discussed later at a more appropriate point.

There are four basic operations that are supplied in the standard environment for the manipulation of semaphores. These are:

(i) **op level = (int n) sema**: . . .

level takes an integer operand and produces as a result a semaphore whose field is initialised to the value of the integer;

(ii) **op level = (sema s) int**: . . .

level takes a semaphore as operand and produces as a result an integer, namely the value of the integer referred to by the integer variable contained within the semaphore;

(iii) **op down = (sema s) void**: . . .

down inspects the integer variable contained within the semaphore. If its value is positive it is decreased by one. If, on the other hand, it is zero the process is suspended temporarily until the variable becomes positive. It is then decreased by 1 and the process awakened i.e. allowed to proceed;

(iv) **op up = (sema s) void**: . . . .

up increments the value of the integer variable contained within the semaphore. Note that this can result in the awakening of other processes temporarily suspended.

Whenever synchronisation has to take place there must be some form of parallel processing in operation. Synchronisation can be performed only between the units of a *parallel clause*. A parallel clause is like a void-collateral-clause except that it must be preceded by **par**. As usual the various units that are being elaborated collaterally are separated by commas and surrounded by open and close brackets or **begin** and **end**. Note that a collateral clause can appear in a program

250

as either a row display, a structure display or a-void-collateral-clause. A parallel clause cannot appear as either a row or structure display.

Two of the four operators, **level**, allow semaphores to be, in effect, broken open and initialised or inspected. **up** and **down** are the operators which permit synchronisation to take place. The **down** operator can involve a potential delay and hence suspension of the process in which it is contained. The **up** operator does not involve a delay but its use can awaken or restart a process that was earlier sent to sleep or suspended as a result of a previous application of **down**.

An important stipulation concerning semaphores is that no two processes can simultaneously access the same semaphore in order to perform either **up** or **down** operations on it. Thus when a process performs an **up** or **down** operation there is a guarantee that no other process is accessing the semaphore at that time with the intention of performing either an **up** or a **down** operation on it. This is of paramount importance and is crucial in obtaining the desired effect from semaphores.

Consider now how these semaphores can be used to solve the mutual exclusion and message passing problems. In dealing with several processes there are often only certain parts of the various processes that have to be synchronised. These will be called the critical regions and are simply the statements at which the shared resources are liable to be accessed. Thus only the critical regions are of interest.

8.4. Solution to mutual exclusion problem

The mutual exclusion problem is solved by introducing a semaphore, traditionally called *mutex*, and initialising its integer variable to 1 by means of **level**. Then each critical region is protected as in

> **down** *mutex*;
> critical region
> **up** *mutex*

The **down** operator will, if the *mutex* semaphore is set at 1, decrease the value of the variable to 0 and then allow the process to enter the critical region. While it is in this region no other process can gain access to it since any other attempt to enter a critical region is also preceded by a statement **down** *mutex* and since *mutex* is now set at zero that critical region cannot be entered. When the process leaves the critical region the **up** *mutex* allows another process to enter its critical region. Note that the validity of the above argument depends on the fact that only a single process can operate on a semaphore at one time.

251

Example 8.4a. Mutual exclusion.

The proper synchronisation of the mutual exclusion problem outlined in section 8.2 can be performed by

```
sema mutex = level 1;
par begin ( . . . ; down mutex;
              v +:= 1;
              up mutex
        ),
        ( . . . ; down mutex;
              print (v); v := 0;
              up mutex
        )
   end
```

Note the position of the dots denoting the other instructions, if any, of the processes. These are outside the critical region and there is no need – in fact it would be needlessly restrictive – to surround these by **down** *mutex* and **up** *mutex*.

Note that in this example the integer variable within the semaphore assumes values of only 0 or 1. Thus a boolean variable rather than an integer variable would have sufficed. This is the only kind of semaphore that is absolutely necessary but the generality of an integer variable within a semaphore is useful as will be seen in discussing the problem of synchronising the passing of messages between processes.

8.5. Solution to message passing problem

That part of the message passing problem dealing with mutual exclusion can be solved at once. A producer, assuming it is in a loop and repeatedly sending messages, could be programmed as indicated below ignoring for the moment the possibility that there is no room in the buffer for the message.

```
do produce message;
   down mutex;
   add message to buffer;
   up mutex
od
```

The various procedures *produce message*, etc. are assumed to have been declared earlier. The semaphore *mutex* is used for mutual exclusion as was done earlier. Its declaration therefore takes the form

```
sema mutex = level 1
```

A consumer can be programmed in a similar fashion as follows

252

ignoring the possibility that there may be no message to consume.

> **do down** *mutex*;
>   *take message from buffer*;
>   **up** *mutex*;
>   *process message*
> **od**

The problems of a producer finding a full buffer or a consumer finding an empty buffer must now be considered. Take a producer first of all. Clearly he should test if the buffer is full before attempting to add a message to it. If it is full the producer should be suspended until it is possible to leave the message in the buffer. Since the operator **down** acting on a semaphore will cause a process to be suspended when the value of the integer variable within the semaphore is 0 it would seem natural that there should be a semaphore indicating the number of empty message positions in the message buffer. Thus if *capacity* is an integer giving the size of the buffer it would seem natural to have a declaration

> **sema** *number empty* = **level** *capacity*

and then

> **down** *number empty*

would cause the producer to be suspended whenever the buffer happened to be full. It is crucial that this operation is performed by the producer at the correct time. If it happens after

> **down** *mutex*

and before the call

> *add message to buffer*

then a deadlock is liable to occur. For if the producer is suspended as a result of

> **down** *number empty*

then no consumer could access the buffer in order to remove a message because the producer itself has already gained sole access to the buffer. Thus the test must come before

> **down** *mutex*

and not after it.

Consider now the possibility of a consumer encountering an empty buffer. An argument similar to that given above suggests that there should be a semaphore *number full* declared as

sema *number full* = **level** 0

and just before the statement

down *mutex*

in the consumer's program there should be a statement

down *number full*

This causes the consumer to be suspended if the buffer should contain no messages to be read.

The two processes have so far used two extra semaphores, namely *number full* and *number empty*. The reason for this lies in the fact that the conditions under which the consumer and producer have to be suspended are different and therefore two different semaphores are required to detect these conditions. But there is a strong connection between the two semaphores in that the number of messages plus the number of empty positions in the message buffer should always equal the capacity of the buffer. If the statements

down *number empty* and **down** *number full*

have to appear then at some stage there must also appear the statements

up *number empty* and **up** *number full*

The first of these will appear just after a consumer has extracted a message from the buffer and the other will appear just after a sender or producer has placed a message in the buffer. The program must therefore have semaphore declarations such as

sema *mutex* = **level** 1, *number empty* = **level** *capacity*,
number full = **level** 0

The program for a single producer and single consumer would look like

```
par begin
        do produce message;
            down number empty;
            down mutex;
            add message to buffer;
            (up mutex, up number full)
        od,
        do down number full;
```

254

down *mutex*;
take message from buffer;
(**up** *mutex*, **up** *number empty*);
process message
od
end

The relative order of some statements is immaterial and collaterals have been used to indicate this. In fact collaterals could have been used more widely but the above seemed to be the sensible compromise.

The example given above made use of a single producer and a single consumer. The problem of coping with several producers and several consumers is no more difficult if one realises that recursive procedures can be used to set many processes in motion simultaneously.

To demonstrate, suppose that several possibly different procedures each of mode **proc void** have to proceed in parallel and that their actions have to be synchronised in some way. The procedures can be placed in a multiple value of mode [ ] **proc void** and they can be started by calling the following procedure.

proc *n in parallel* = ([ ] **proc void** *p*) **void**:
if int *l* = **lwb** *p*, *u* = **upb** *p*; *u* = *l*
then *p*[*u*]
else par (*p*[*u*], *n in parallel* (*p*[*l*:*u* − 1]))
fi

To cause the procedure *p* to proceed in parallel with other versions of itself, those other versions using different parameters, one can proceed as follows. (It is assumed that synchronisation will be required.) If *p* is of mode

proc (ref int) void

the values of the different parameters can be placed in an object of mode

ref [ ] **int**

and one has merely to invoke

proc *parallel p* = (**proc (ref int) void** *p*, **ref** [ ] **int** *parameters*)
　　　void:
if int *l* = **lwb** *parameters*, *u* = **upb** *parameters*;
　u = *l*
then *p* (*parameters*[*u*])

else par (p (*parameters*[u]),
            parallel p (p, *parameters*[l :u − 1]))
fi

8.6. The dining philosophers problem

Though rather artificial, the problem of the dining philosophers is an interesting example of synchronisation. A set of five philosophers spend their entire lives successively thinking and eating. They can think independently, but to eat they must sit in their place at a circular table and they must eat from a bowl containing an infinite supply of spaghetti. There are a total of five forks, one placed between each pair of adjacent table places. To eat a philosopher must use two forks, the fork on his left and the fork on his right. Thus no two neighbours can be eating at the same time. The table can be represented as in diagram 8.1.

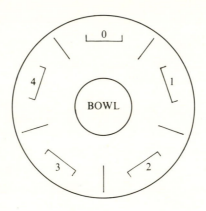

Diagram 8.1.   ⌊ *i* ⌋ indicates the table place of philosopher *i*

         | indicates the position of a fork.

The problem is to write a piece of program which represents the life of a philosopher. The solution should not give rise to a deadly embrace and should ensure the maximum good to the entire community. In particular if a philosopher wishes to eat and the forks are available he should be allowed to eat.

The danger with any solution to the problem lies in the fact that a deadly embrace is liable to result. If, for instance, each philosopher becomes hungry at the same time and each picks up his left fork then

256

each has to wait for his right hand neighbour to return his fork to the table and deadlock occurs.

Each philosopher's life is concerned with successively thinking and eating. Thus ignoring all problems of synchronisation the life of a philosopher is reflected by the piece of program

do *think*; *eat* **od**

Looking at the problem more carefully and heeding synchronisation, eating cannot take place until the forks are available. When eating is finished the forks should be immediately made available to the neighbours and if they wish to eat they should be allowed to do so. It would seem then that there are essentially three states in which a philosopher might find himself: (i) thinking, (ii) wishing to eat, (iii) eating. These states are represented in the program by the integers 0, 1 and 2 respectively. The current states of the five philosophers can then be held in a multiple value consisting of five integers. The complete program therefore contains

int *thinking* = 0, *waiting* = 1, *eating* = 2;
[0 :4] **int** *state*;
for *i* **from** 0 **to** 4 **do** *state* [*i*] := *thinking* **od**

indicating that all philosophers are initially thinking.

When philosopher *i* wishes to eat, certain conditions have to be satisfied. Neither of his two neighbours can be eating. Therefore the condition can be expressed as

$$state \ [i] = waiting \ \textbf{and} \ state \ [(i + 1) \ \textbf{mod} \ 5] \neq eating$$
$$\textbf{and} \ state \ [(i - 1) \ \textbf{mod} \ 5] \neq eating$$

If this condition is satisfied then the state of philosopher *i* must be set to eating indicating that he is now eating. If the condition is not satisfied then philosopher *i* must be suspended. Therefore there is associated with each philosopher a semaphore and performing a **down** operation on this will cause the philosopher to wait provided that the semaphore's integer variable is initially set to *thinking*. Thus the program contains an initial declaration

[ ] **sema** *phil* = [ ] **sema** (**level** 0, **level** 0, **level** 0, **level** 0,
level 0) [@ 0]

where *phil* [*i*] is then the semaphore for philosopher *i*. (Note the use of a cast to provide a strong position for the row display.)

When a philosopher has finished eating he must change his state and check if both his neighbours wish to eat. If the necessary conditions are satisfied this will involve performing an **up** operation on

257

the relevant semaphores and changing the state associated with a philosopher. For convenience therefore a procedure *check* is used to test the condition of a philosopher and perform the necessary changes. Thus

proc *check* = (**int** *i*) **void**:
if *state* [*i*] = *waiting* **and** *state* [(*i* + 1) **mod** 5] ≠ *eating*
                 and *state* [(*i* − 1) **mod** 5] ≠ *eating*
then (*state* [*i*] := *eating*, **up** *phil* [*i*])
fi

The common resource in this discussion is the multiple value referred to by *state*. Consequently any access to it must be governed by mutual exclusion.

With these remarks it is now possible to write the program. Note that, apart from the declaration of the procedure *check*, the declarations include the usual semaphore *mutex* together with the semaphores *phil* [*i*] and the multiple value referred to by *state*.

The process for philosopher *i* can be written as:

do *think*;
  down *mutex*;
  state [*i*] := *waiting*; *check* (*i*);
  up *mutex*; **down** *phil* [*i*];
  eat;
  down *mutex*;
  state [*i*] := *thinking*;
  (*check* ((*i* + 1) **mod** 5), *check* ((*i* − 1) **mod** 5));
  up *mutex*
od

In some respects this piece of program could be improved but this solution suffices.

Further remarks on the dining philosophers problem are contained in Dijkstra [4] and in Hoare [5]. The solution presented here was that of Dijkstra.

8.7. References on parallel processing

[1] Baer, J. L. A Survey of Some Theoretical Aspects of Multiprocessing, *ACM Computing Surveys* vol. 5, no. 1, March 1973, pp. 31–80.
[2] Brinch Hansen, P. Concurrent Programming Concepts, *ACM Computing Surveys* vol. 5, no. 4, December 1973, pp. 223–245.
[3] Dijkstra, E. W. Cooperating Sequential Processes, *Programming*

258

Languages edited by F. Genuys, published by Academic Press 1968, pp. 43–112.

[4] Dijkstra, E. W. Hierarchical Ordering of Sequential Processes, *Operating Systems Techniques* edited by C. A. R. Hoare and R. H. Perrott, published by Academic Press 1972, pp. 72–93.

[5] Hoare, C. A. R. Towards a theory of Parallel Programming, *Operating Systems Techniques* edited by C. A. R. Hoare and R. H. Perrott, published by Academic Press 1972, pp. 61–71.

[6] Holt, R. C. Some Deadlock Properties of Computer Systems, *ACM Computing Surveys* vol. 4, no. 3, September 1972, pp. 179–196.

Programming problems for chapter 8

1. Write an ALGOL 68 procedure to evaluate

$$\sum_{i=1}^{n} a_i b_i$$

making use of parallel processing.

2. To make a program run as fast as possible a programmer attempts to read, compute and print simultaneously. For reading he has an array into which information is read and from which the computing process takes information. Another array is shared by the output and computing processes. Write procedures to indicate what form the various processes must take.

3. Consider processes A and B, both of which require a line-printer and a card-reader. How can one arrange that deadlock will not result?

4. Coroutines are routines which can call each other. But if A and B are coroutines then when A calls B, B will resume execution from the point at which A was previously called, and vice versa. This leads to a flow of control indicated by the arrows in diagram 8.2. (Assume A is called initially.)

   Show how two procedures A and B can be declared and made to behave like coroutines.

5. Consider three processes A, B and C running in parallel. Processes B and C cause actions b and c to occur respectively. At a certain point in the execution of A it is required that execution is halted until

   (a) either b or c has occurred, or

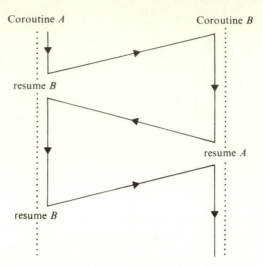

Coroutine *A*   Coroutine *B*

resume *B*

resume *A*

resume *B*

Diagram 8.2.

(b) both *b* and *c* have occurred.

How can these two situations be resolved?

6. Each piece of program or process which might be executed in a computer is assumed to be represented by an object of mode **process**. This can be regarded as a structure of some kind containing identification of the process, its store and device requirements, a pointer to the code, etc. In the computer there is

    (a) a free list containing all the processes free to run, and

    (b) an array of lists each containing halted processes; list *i* contains all these processes halted for reason *i* (the various reasons have been suitably coded).

What declarations would you need for this purpose?

Assuming that parallel computation is possible within the computer design procedures which will allow

    (i) a process to be moved from the free list to halt list *i*

    (ii) a process to be moved from halt list *i* to the free list.

Note that no unnecessary blocking should occur.

7. Consider the declaration

    [*n*] **char** *buffer*

Processes may read from this or write to it subject to the following restrictions:

    (a) a writer can write only if no other writer is writing and no reader is reading;

    (b) a reader can read only if no writer is writing.

Describe procedures for reading and writing which ensure that orderly conduct is maintained.

8. Rearrange the following loop clauses so that they can be executed more efficiently if parallel processing is used (assume suitable declarations)

    (i) **for** i **from** 4 **to** 100 **do** $a[i] := a[i-3] + a[i-4]$ **od**

    (ii) **for** i **to** 5

        do for j **to** 5

            do $b[i,j] := (b[i+1,j] + b[i-1,j] + b[i,j-1]$
                $+ b[i,j+1])/4$

        od

        od

9. A banker has £m which he is prepared to lend, without interest, to his n customers. A customer can request £r, say, and provided that $r \leq m$ and the banker has the money presently available the customer's request will be granted. On the other hand, if the money is not available the customer will be asked to wait until enough money does become available (or if $r > m$ he will be told that there can never be enough money).

Write procedures called *withdraw* and *return* to simulate the action of a customer withdrawing £r and returning £r respectively.

9

TRANSPUT

The intention of this chapter is to look at the full range of transput facilities. Consider possible extensions to the (relatively) primitive facilities offered by *read* and *print*. The *read* procedure allows the transfer of information from *standin*, the standard input, to the program. There is therefore at most one input. One possible extension is to allow the programmer several inputs and to allow him to switch from one to another as he so wishes. Similarly, one might allow several outputs, not just the standard output *standout* offered by using *print*.

For instance, in updating a sequence of student records with examination marks the input might be the old student records and the marks themselves. These two sets of information are distinct and would ideally be held on different inputs. For output the updated records and the pass, resit, and absentee lists might be required, which could constitute four different outputs.

Multiple inputs and/or outputs will be discussed in section 9.1 under 'Books, channels and files' and in section 9.2 under 'Formatless transput'.

The possible extensions by no means end here. In using the *read* procedure special default actions are taken when new lines, spaces, etc. are encountered in *standin*. For instance, if an integer has to be read and the first character on the input is a space then the default action is to skip over the space. If the first character is a letter, the default action might be to abandon the program and supply an error message indicating the offending characters. If a programmer wishes to take some action different from the default action ALGOL 68 allows him to do so by the use of *events*. These will be discussed in section 9.3.

Again when performing transput using the *read* and *print* procedures certain assumptions are made about the form of the input or output. For instance the integer 1,234,567 appearing as input could not be read as an integer without special action to remove and possibly check the existence of the commas. Moreover, the *print* procedure would not produce 1,234,567 unless the commas are explicitly

262

inserted. Commercial programming requires transput of this nature in, e.g., printing bank statements, wage slips, etc. Such applications require a precise control of the transput format. This will be discussed in section 9.4.

All the transput discussed so far can be termed *character transput*. Both the input and the output takes the form of characters which might be letters, digits, points, spaces, etc. But in executing a program a computer does not manipulate characters as such. It manipulates groups of binary digits. Thus when characters are read a conversion from character form to binary form must take place. Similarly on output a conversion from binary form to character form must occur. Now there are situations in which information has to be sent out from one program only to be read in by another (or in some cases the same) program; thus the information is not for the programmer to read and digest. On such occasions the sensible action is not to perform the conversions but just to send out the binary digits and read them back again. This topic will be discussed further under 'Binary transput' in section 9.5.

Yet another extension follows from the observation that the standard input and output files allow only a limited form of access. And it is perfectly natural that this should be so. One would not usually expect to be able to write to the standard input or read from the standard output. But there are occasions when it is convenient to be able to read from and write to the same file, possibly jumping randomly from one part of the file to another. Discussion of kinds of access and all that this entails will commence in section 9.1.

Inevitably certain aspects of transput will depend to some extent on the particular ALGOL 68 system and the environment in which it is running. For instance, the particular operating system will probably have a considerable bearing on the transput. Here some attempt at being implementation independent is made but where it is felt necessary some examples are given from particular systems.

These remarks summarise the various aspects of transput that have to be discussed. It will later be possible to combine certain of the topics mentioned above and, for example, make use of formatted transput involving events and files other than the standard input and output.

9.1. Books, channels and files

A comprehensive study of transput necessitates looking first at the technical meanings to be associated with each of the three terms 'books', 'channels' and 'files'.

9.1.1. Books

As the name suggests, a book consists of a set of pages, each page consists of lines and each line consists of characters. The number of characters per line may vary from line to line and the number of lines per page may vary from page to page.

The most readily available example of a book would be a set of results produced on the line-printer. This book certainly contains pages, namely the pages of the line-printer paper. Each page consists of a certain number of lines of text and each line of text contains characters (possibly blanks). In this case the number of lines per page is usually fixed, as is the number of characters per line (60 and 120 are typical figures).

Another example of a book would be a set of data which, for the sake of familiarity, is assumed to be on cards. Each card can be thought of as a line of the book. The number of cards is then the number of lines in the book – note that the book has only one page. If the trailing spaces on each card are ignored the book will in general have a variable number of characters per line. If the trailing spaces are not ignored each line will have a fixed number of characters (typically 72 or 80).

Books produced by output from ALGOL 68 programs can also have a variable number of characters per line or lines per page (and then the book is said to be *compressible*). On output to a compressible book the use of the procedure *newline* (or *newpage*) would result in the line (or page) being terminated without the addition of any other characters and then being transmitted. In non-compressible books the line (or page) would typically be filled with blanks.

Returning now to the general concept of a book, each character can be identified uniquely by its position within the book. This position is represented by three integers corresponding to the page number p, line number l and character number c. These represent the cth character on the lth line of the pth page of the book. In particular the position beyond the last character of the entire book can be so characterised and this position is referred to as the *logical end* of the book. Also there will be a *current position* associated with a particular book; this is the position at which reading or writing is presently being performed.

Example 9.1.1a. Logical end of a book.

(i) A set of results appearing on line printer paper and occupying 10 complete pages plus an incomplete page with 20 lines, the last line with characters in its first 70 character positions has its logical end at $(11, 20, 71)$.

264

(ii) A set of results occupying exactly one complete page will have a logical end of file at $(1, 60, 121)$, assuming 60 lines to a page and 120 characters to a line.

As example 9.1.1a(i) suggests, the logical end of the book changes as the results are produced. Initially, i.e. before any printing at all takes place, the logical end is at $(1, 1, 1)$. Assuming that the first character is printed on the first position on the first line the logical end then moves to $(1, 1, 2)$, and so on. The logical end, in this case, indicates the position up to which printing has taken place.

So far a book consists of text divided into pages and lines together with a logical end of book characterised by three integers. There are three other quantities which are also associated with a book. The first of these is an identification of some kind taking the form of a string of characters. One could envisage this as being the title of the book but its precise form and function are left undefined (by the ALGOL 68 Report); thus it will be implementation dependent. However the identification string might typically contain in some predetermined form information about the title of the book, the ownership of the book, passwords to be quoted on accessing the book, etc.

To understand the reason for introducing the remaining quantities associated with a book, one has to consider a book in a more general and realistic context: several users may wish to access the one book. If a user can do anything he wants to the book whenever he chooses, mayhem will result. Thus certain restrictions have to be enforced.

A typical situation is the following. A teacher places information on disc as a set of data for a programming exercise given to 200 students. After informing the class of the information's existence, the teacher decides to alter it. There are then 201 users wishing to access the book; the students to read its contents, and the teacher to alter its contents. Sharing has to take place and yet it has to be controlled in an orderly and sensible way.

The remaining two quantities attached to a book are to enable the system to allow sharing of the information in the book. Sharing among several users is possible, and indeed sensible, only if none of them intends to alter the contents of the book. If just one person does intend to alter the contents of the book he can do so only if no other user is using the book at that time. Once he has been allowed access with the intention of altering the contents then access must be denied to all other users wishing to use the book during the time the alterations are taking place. To allow for these circumstances

(i) an object of mode **bool** called *putting* is attached to each book;

this is set to **true** whenever a user gains access to the book with the intention of altering its contents; otherwise it is **false**.

(ii) an integer called *users* which, though initially 0, is incremented by one each time someone accesses the book for whatever purpose; it is decreased by one whenever someone relinquishes access.

Thus no-one can be granted immediate access to a book if *putting* is **true**, for someone already has access and intends altering the contents of the book. If *putting* is **false** then a user intending only to read the book can certainly be granted access but a user intending to make alterations can do so only if *users* = 0.

When a user is not granted immediate access to a book it does not necessarily follow that the program will be abandoned and the user supplied with some appropriate message. Such a situation is left undefined (by the ALGOL 68 Report) and so is implementation dependent. But typically the program may be suspended until such time as the appropriate kind of access can be granted.

Summing up this introduction, a book is characterised by means of text, a logical end, an identification string, together with a boolean *putting* and an integer *users*. In the ALGOL 68 Report there appears the following definition of **book**.

> **mode book** = **struct** (**flextext** *text*,
> **pos** *lpos* ¢ *logical end of book* ¢,
> **string** *idf* ¢ *identification* ¢,
> **bool** *putting* ¢ *true if the book may be written*
>   *to* ¢
> **int** *users* ¢ *the number of times the book is*
>   *opened* ¢)

where **flextext** and **pos** are defined by

> **mode flextext** = **ref flex** [ ] **flex** [ ] **flex** [ ] **char**

and

> **mode pos** = **struct** (**int** *p*, *l*, *c*).

However it should be stressed that these declarations of the modes **book**, **pos** or **flextext** are not part of the standard environment – they exist merely to help in explaining the various concepts. For this reason one cannot access a book by selecting the various fields, etc. Standard procedures are used for this purpose.

9.1.2. Channels

Channels correspond to the physical devices (i.e. peripherals) attached to a computer and their precise form will therefore depend on the particular ALGOL 68 system. A single channel corresponds to one or more physical devices.

Typically there might be a channel associated with each of the following: a card-reader, a line-printer, a bank of paper tape readers, a bank of magnetic tape units or a filestore maintained by an operating system.

Associated with channels are certain objects which reflect relevant properties of the physical devices. Some of these depend only on the channel itself but others depend also on the particular book being accessed via the channel. Since a book has an identification string which may contain information about ownership, passwords, etc. the particular access granted to a user may partly depend on the identification and therefore on the book itself. These last remarks are intentionally vague: the identification string attached to a book is undefined (by the ALGOL 68 Report).

Now consider the properties which depend only on the channel, not on the particular book being accessed. First of all, the channel number, an integer associated with each particular channel, allows one to distinguish between channels with otherwise identical properties. Thus although two different banks of magnetic tape units might have identical properties, their different channel numbers would allow the programmer to choose a particular bank.

All the remaining items associated with channels take the form of routines for determining the channel's properties.

It is convenient to associate with each channel a maximum amount of information that can be accommodated. This takes the form of a procedure (denoted by *max pos*) yielding a triple (p, l, c) indicating the appropriate page number, line number and character number respectively which will be independent of any book. Generally p will indicate the maximum number of pages allowed, l the maximum number of lines per page, and c the maximum number of characters per line. Thus a magnetic tape channel might have a routine which makes use of certain environmental information (such as the density of writing, the length of the tape, etc.) to produce a triple indicating the maximum amount of information that can be written on the magnetic tape.

The last book-independent routine is denoted by *estab* and indicates whether or not a program can make use of the particular channel. In some cases several programs may make use of the one channel (as with the channel associated with a filestore) but in other cases only one program can be allowed to access the channel (e.g. the channel associated with a line-printer).

The remaining properties depend on both the channel and the particular book. In each of these cases the routine has a single parameter of mode **ref book**.

get returns **true** provided the appropriate channel and book can be used for input. Otherwise it returns **false**. Thus a channel corresponding to a card-reader would usually have a *get* routine which delivers **true** whereas the channel corresponding to a line-printer would have a *get* routine delivering **false**.

put returns **true** provided the appropriate channel and book can be used for output. Otherwise it returns **false**. Thus the channel corresponding to a line-printer would normally have a *put* routine which delivers **true**.

bin indicates whether the appropriate channel can be used for binary, as opposed to character, transput.

set indicates whether one can adjust the current position to any specified position within the bounds of the book. If a channel and a book admit this facility then the *set* routine returns **true** and the book is said to be a *random access* book. Otherwise the various characters in the book must be accessed sequentially starting at the first and moving through to the last (possibly with several uses of *backspace*, etc.). Such a book is said to be a *sequential access* book.

Typically a random access book would be held on disc or on drum whereas a sequential access book would be associated with a magnetic tape unit, a card-reader, line-printer, etc.

reset indicates whether the current character position can be returned to the position denoted by (1, 1, 1,), i.e. the start of the book. Such a facility may be allowed when using a magnetic tape: the process of resetting is then a matter of rewinding the tape. Resetting would not usually be allowed when dealing with either a card-reader or a line-printer.

reidf returns **true** if the channel and book allow the identification string attached to the book to be altered. If the identification string contains information about passwords it may be desirable to periodically alter this password as a form of security. Of course, the ability to perform such a change should be reserved for privileged programs. The *reidf* routine should take care of this.

compress returns **true** if, on sending information to the book, the information is liable to be compressed (see section 9.1.1).

The *standconv* routine differs from the others in that its result is a character conversion code, not a boolean. Basically a character conversion code is a table containing two columns, one the external form of each character and the other the corresponding internal form. The translation of a particular character then involves looking through the first column until that character is found. The corresponding entry in the other column gives the internal representation.

There are several common character codes in which characters can be transmitted, e.g. EBCDIC, IBM 029, ASCII, ICL 1900, etc. The *standconv* routine takes as parameter an object of mode **ref book** and delivers as result one of these character codes. In the later section on files it will be seen that the programmer can replace the standard code by a code which, subject to certain limitations, can be of his own choosing.

This completes the list of routines associated with a channel. One could envisage a declaration

mode channel = **struct** (

> **proc (ref book) bool** *reset, set, get,*
> *put, bin, compress, reidf,*
> **proc bool** *estab,*
> **proc pos** *max pos,*
> **proc (ref book) conv** *standconv,*
> **int** *channel number*

)

where **pos** is defined as in the discussion on books and **conv** is described informally above. Though **channel** is another of the standard modes the user cannot use the selectors provided above to access the fields of any object of mode **channel**: like the modes **bits** and **bytes** their selectors are unobtainable. But there are two standard routines which can be applied to channels, *estab possible* accesses and activates the *estab* field and *standconv* delivers the *standconv* field of a channel.

There are three channels which are automatically available to the user: for *standin channel* the *get* routine always returns **true**; for *standout channel* the *put* routine returns **true**; and for *standback channel get, put, set, reset* and *bin* all return **true**. Any implementation will assign suitable routines to the other fields of these channels. Moreover other channels with suitable properties will probably also be provided in the standard environment.

9.1.3. Files

Consider now a program running in a computer and wishing to read or print some information. The information will pass between the program and a book. But before the communication can take place the lines of communication – files – must be established and installed.

The mode **file** can be defined as a structure containing several fields which are the various objects one associates with a file. As for the mode **channel**, standard procedures are provided for the inspection

269

and possible alteration of the various fields. Associated with a file are:

(i) a channel, a reference to a book and a reference to the contents of the book. The book holds the information being read or printed and the channel represents the physical device on which the book is situated. (The reason for including references both to a book and to its contents will be considered in section 9.2.5.)

(ii) a standard character conversion key. It will be seen later that if the standard code happens to be, say, ICL 1900 code then it will be possible to alter this to, say, EBCDIC given that the standard environment provided with the ALGOL 68 system allows such a character code.

(iii) event routines. When transput is taking place certain events can occur (e.g. end of line reached, faulty character read) requiring some special action (e.g. take new line, print error message and stop). The special action will always be preceded by the calling of the appropriate event routine. These can be altered by means of standard procedures but if they are not altered the default actions will take place automatically. Often these default actions are just as required and there is no need to take special precautions. Routines are associated with each of the following events:

end of logical file reached – happens if after input has been exhausted a further attempt to read from the file is made; may also happen as a result of attempting to go beyond the end of a random access book;

end of physical file reached – happens if the current page number exceeds the number of pages in the book and transput is attempted;

end of page reached – happens if the current line number exceeds the number of lines in the current page of the book and transput is attempted;

end of line reached – occurs if the current character position exceeds the number of characters in the current line of the book and transput is attempted;

character conversion has been unsuccessful – happens if, for example, on attempting to read an integer a letter is the first character encountered;

a value error occurs – this happens if on attempting to read an integer one encounters an integer which is too large for the particular machine to hold;

a format error occurs – an explanation of this will be given when formatted transput has been considered.

It will be necessary to return repeatedly to the topic of events and to discuss in more detail the circumstances under which each event takes place and the default action in these cases.

(iv) a string of characters which act as terminators. When reading a variable number of characters, any one of the characters in the string will act as a terminator of the input. This string can be altered by the programmer as necessary.

(v) state of the file. This takes the form of several boolean variables which indicate whether reading or writing is taking place using character or binary information. There are five such variables:

read mood yields **true** if the file is being used for input;
write mood yields **true** if the file is being used for output;
char mood yields **true** if the file is being used for character transput;
bin mood yields **true** if the file is being used for binary transput;
opened yields **true** if the file has been linked to a book.

None of these five variables can be accessed directly by the programmer but they can be altered indirectly using standard routines. Note that when transput is taking place, assuming that the state of the file is not being adjusted just then, one and only one of *read mood* or *write mood* will yield **true**. Similarly one and only one of *char mood* or *bin mood* will yield **true**.

In simple transput the values of these variables will remain fixed for the duration of a program. But in more complex cases it is quite possible that for a suitable file their values will alter as the program progresses. A change would occur in the state of a file if it first received information from a program which later read it back. In the first phase *write mood* would yield **true** and *read mood* **false** and in the second phase *write mood* would yield **false** and *read mood* **true**.

(vi) current position. This is just a triple indicating the current page, line, and character numbers.

This concludes the list of relevant objects associated with a file. In the section on formats, section 9.4, it will be seen that a format and format pointer are also contained in a file. But until that stage is reached they can be considered to have undefined values.

The process of setting up the means of communication between a program and a file is, as from the above, a fairly complex operation. All the various routines and other objects must be made available. The linkage process is described by saying that 'a book is *opened* on a file via a channel'. The converse involves a tidying up operation and occurs when transput between a file and a program has been completed. This is referred to as *closing* a file. Both the opening and closing of files will be discussed in more detail in section 9.2.2.

9.2. Formatless transput

This section considers the routines that allow character transput to be performed between a program and a suitable file without resorting to the use of formats, i.e. the routines which operate on files in general in the same kind of way that *read* and *print* (or *write*) operate on the standard input file and standard output file respectively.

9.2.1. Straightening

Ignoring for the moment procedures such as *newline*, *space*, etc. the number of modes of values involved in transput is limited, all other modes being combinations of these basic modes. Thus multiple values and structures involved in transput are built from simpler objects.

On output the basic modes include

> **short int, int, long int**, etc.,
> **short real, real, long real**, etc.,
> **short compl, compl, long compl**, etc.
> **bool**
> **short bits, bits, long bits**, etc.,
> **char** and [ ] **char**.

On input the basic modes are simply the above modes preceded by **ref** together with the additional mode **ref string**, which uses **flex**.

Values which are more complex than these basic modes will be considered in what follows to have been decomposed into a one-dimensional array of these basic items. This process of decomposition is known as *straightening*. Structures are straightened in the manner one would expect. In simple cases the first field supplies the first element, the second field the second element, and so on. In more complicated cases the elements supplied by the fields may themselves have to be straightened, etc. One-dimensional multiple values are also straightened in the way one would expect. Again the elements of the multiple values may themselves have to be straightened in some cases. With higher dimensional multiple values the straightening takes place row at a time.

Example 9.2.1a. Illustrating straightening.

(i) If *a* is declared as in

> [1 :8, 1 :9, 1 :10] **int** *a*

then it is straightened for input in such a way that the successive variables receiving the data are

272

$$a[1, 1, 1], a[1, 1, 2], \ldots, a[1, 1, 10], a[1, 2, 1], \ldots,$$
$$a[1, 2, 10], a[1, 3, 1], \ldots, a[2, 1, 1], a[2, 1, 2], \ldots$$

(ii) Consider the mode declarations

mode name = **struct** (**char** *initial*, [20] **char** *surname*);
mode address = **struct** (**int** *no*, [20] **char** *street*, *town*);
mode record = **struct** (**name** *name*, **address** *address*)

If x is of mode **record** it is straightened for output into the following sequence of basic items: a character (giving the *initial* field of a name), a row of characters (the *surname* of a name), an integer (giving the *no* field of an address), a row of characters (the *street* of an address) and a row of characters (the *town* of an address).

9.2.2. Linking books to files

The tasks of linking a book to a file and breaking this linkage are complex. Fortunately standard routines are available which allow these tasks to be performed quite simply. Certain default options then become associated with the files. (These options may be altered by using the standard procedures described in section 9.3.)

Fortunately the novice programmer need not concern himself with any of this detail. The three standard files referred to by *standin*, *standout* and *standback* are opened automatically and closed automatically. Only if other files are required need a programmer concern himself with this problem. To be precise each of *standin*, *standout* and *standback* is an object of mode **ref file**.

Opening, establishing and creating files

A book can be linked to a file in one of three different ways: a file can be opened, established or created by the routines *open*, *establish* or *create*. Each of these routines returns a value of mode **int**: zero if the particular task has been performed satisfactorily and, otherwise, a non-zero integer indicating the particular error that has arisen. In general this integer will be implementation dependent and consequently will not be further discussed here.

If a book has to be linked to a file that already exists then the linkage between the book and the program should be accomplished by the procedure *open*. This takes three parameters: a reference to the file, an identification string for the book, and the channel via which the book has to be opened. The declaration of *open* appears in the standard environment (the dots indicating omission of, for the moment, irrelevant details) as

proc *open* = (**ref file** *file*, **string** *idf*, **channel** *chan*) **int**:
begin . . . **end**

The string *idf* should be the identification string of *file* and may have a form peculiar to the particular implementation.

Example 9.2.2a. Opening a file.
In the standard environment the standard input file is opened automatically. This is accomplished by means of the call

> *open* (*standin*, "", *standin channel*)

Thus there is a null identification string and the standard input channel, also introduced in the standard environment, is used. Similarly the standard output file is opened by a call

> *open* (*standout*, "", *standout channel*)

When a book is opened on a file the state of the file (i.e. whether it is being used for input or output, character or binary data) is initialised from information about the book and the channel being used. The character conversion code is a function of both the channel and the book involved. All the event routines are initialised to

(ref file f **) bool** : **false**

except the routine corresponding to a character conversion error which is initialised to

(ref file f, **ref char** a) **bool** : **false**

The current position is set to $(1, 1, 1)$. The request for a file to be opened may be denied for various reasons. For instance, the identifier string may be illegal, e.g. it may contain an illegal file title. But it may also happen that at that time someone else is using the book that has to be linked to the file and the types of access are incompatible.

Some channels allow just one book to be opened on that channel at any one time, e.g. only one person at a time might be allowed to access a particular magnetic tape. But other channels, e.g. filestores, might allow several.

Refusal to open a file can take one of two forms depending on the particular implementation: the program may be temporarily suspended until access can be granted or the *open* procedure could return a non-zero integer whose value would indicate the reason for refusal.

This concludes the discussion about the procedure *open*. Note that its use implies that the book involved already exists. However the programmer might want to produce some output which will

274

form the contents of the book linked to the file. In these circumstances the book has to be brought into existence and the file initialised in the required way.

If the size of the book to be produced is known the routine *establish* should be used to bring the file into existence. The declaration in the standard environment of *establish* is, in skeleton form,

proc *establish* = (**ref file** *file*, **string** *idf*, **channel** *chan*, **int**
p, l, c) **int**: (. . .)

Thus *idf* is used to supply an identification to the book generated and *p, l* and *c* are used to indicate respectively the number of pages, lines per page and characters per line in the book. Note that *establish* results in the invoking of a generator to produce a book of the necessary size.

When established, a file is automatically opened – and opened for writing – and the current position is set at the start of the book. The various event routines are initialised as for the procedure *open* and the conversion code is taken to be a function of the channel and the book now generated.

A request to establish a file can be denied for reasons similar to the reasons for denying a request to open a file. These include: the identification string is illegal, the size of the book requested is beyond the maximum allowed by that channel, writing is not permitted or no more files can be opened on that channel.

If the size of the required book is not known the procedure *create* can be used. *create* is declared in the standard environment as:

proc *create* = (**ref file** *file*, **channel** *chan*) **int**:
begin pos *max pos* = *max pos* **of** *chan*;
    establish (*file*, **skip**, *chan*, *p* **of** *max pos*, *l* **of** *max pos*,
        c **of** *max pos*)
end

Note that the use of **skip** implies an undefined identification string which suggests that *create* will normally be used only for files which are temporary.

If a file is brought into existence by either *establish* or *create* the book referred to will be given a particular size. The lines and pages will all be of one particular size. Subsequent output to compressible books may result in the size of the various lines and pages being altered (or compressed).

Closing, locking and scratching files

The linkage between a book and a file can be broken in one of three different ways: closing, locking and scratching.

Closing a file merely breaks the link and the book may be re-opened in the usual way at a later date.

Locking a file results in the book being maintained but access to it is thereafter denied until the file becomes unlocked; the ALGOL 68 Report does not state how this unlocking is to take place and therefore it will depend on the particular implementation.

Scratching a file removes or deletes the book linked to a file; it will no longer be available.

The three procedures for performing these tasks are respectively *close*, *lock* and *scratch*. Each takes a single parameter of mode **ref file** and give a result of mode **void**.

If a file has not been opened (by any of the three procedures *open*, *establish* or *create*) then there is no point in attempting to close, lock or scratch it. But the procedures *close*, *lock* and *scratch* have no effect; they do not result in an error.

The question of which of the three procedures to use in any particular circumstance is usually easy to answer.

Example 9.2.2b. Opening and closing files.

(i) To create a temporary file to remain in existence only during the time a program is being executed one might use *create* and *scratch*.

(ii) To produce a book for results to be used at a later date one might use *establish* and *close* (assuming the size of the book is known).

After each program there is as part of the standard environment
    stop: *lock* (*standin*); *lock* (*standout*); *lock* (*standback*)
the label *stop* being supplied to show its relative position.

9.2.3. The *get* and *put* routines

The *get* and *put* routines allow formatless character transput to be performed between programs and suitably opened (established or created) files. *get* is in some sense a generalisation of *read*, and *put* a generalisation of *print* or *write*. Both of these procedures take two parameters, the first of which is a reference to the file to be used in transput. The second is a list of variables – the 'data list' – which receives the input items from the file in the case of *get*, and the data list to be printed in the case of *put*. These lists are straightened in the usual way. Of course, before using *get* and *put* one must make sure that the file is opened so as to allow the appropriate kind of transput.

276

Example 9.2.3a. Using *get*

The following would read three integers from the file referred to by *data*

    int m, n, p; *get* (*data*, (m, n, p))

As one might expect, the list of variables to receive values (in the case of *get*) or items to be printed (in the case of *put*) are similar to those used with *read* and *print* (or *write*). In fact *read* $((x, y, z))$ and *read* (z) are equivalent to *get* (*standin*, (x, y, z)) and *get* (*standin*, z), and also *print* $((x, y, z))$ and *print* (z) are equivalent to *put* (*standout*, (x, y, z)) and *put* (*standout*, z). With the *get* and *put* procedures one can use all the facilities that until now have been used with the *read* and *print* (or *write*) procedures, e.g. expressions, (references to) multiple values, (references to) structures and so on. Moreover one can include use of the procedures *whole*, *fixed* and *float* together with *space*, *backspace*, *newline* and *newpage*.

9.2.4. *space*, *newline*, etc. revisited

space, *backspace*, *newline* and *newpage* are procedures of mode **proc** (**ref file**) **void.** When they appear as a parameter in a call of *read*, *write*, *print*, *get* or *put* they are in fact called from within the routine and the appropriate file name is automatically supplied. But calls of *space*, etc. can be made without supplying them as parameters of *put*, etc. Thus *print* (*newline*) is equivalent to *newline* (*standout*) and *get* (*data*, *space*) is equivalent to *space* (*data*).

If the current position is brought beyond the limits of the physical or logical file by a call to a transput routine or to *space*, *newline*, or *new page*, this will not have any immediate consequence. However, before other transput operations, including further calls of *space*, *newline* or *newpage*, the appropriate event routine will be called. If the event routines return **false** the default actions for the events 'line ended' and 'page ended' are to call *newline* and *newpage* respectively. For violating the bounds of the physical or logical file the default actions are undefined.

9.2.5. Association

Under certain circumstances it can be convenient to associate a file with a reference to a particular multiple value of characters, i.e. the multiple value can be regarded as the book linked to a file. All the facilities available for files can then in effect be applied to the character array. Thus *get*, *put*, string terminators, standard routines and so on can be used.

The modes of the character arrays that can be used in association are **ref [ ] char**, **ref [ ] [ ] char** and **ref [ ] [ ] [ ] char** and the lower bound in each dimension must be 1. These correspond to lines, pages and books respectively. Note that flexible names are not included. Before association takes place between a file and one of these objects the file should not have been opened (otherwise the result is undefined).

The standard routine *associate* performs the association: its declaration in the standard environment looks like

> **proc** *associate* = (**ref file** *file*, **ref [ ] [ ] [ ] char** *sss*) **void**: (. . .)

Of course, since a parameter of a routine occupies a strong syntactic position items of mode **ref [ ] char** and **ref [ ] [ ] char** will both be coerced by rowing to objects of the required mode.

When *associate* is called, a book and a channel are brought into existence. A book with the following properties is generated on the heap: its logical end is at (**upb** $sss + 1, 1, 1$) where sss is the reference to the character array; the number of users is set to 1; *putting* is initialised to **true**; and other fields are undefined. Note that, in particular, the pointer to the text of the book is left undefined. This remark is important and will be examined in some detail later in this section.

An object of mode **channel** is introduced. The channel permits setting and resetting together with the reading and writing of characters. It does not permit binary transput, reidentification of books, compressible books or the establishing of other files on that channel. The channel number and standard conversion code are left undefined and *max pos* produces (*max int, max int, max int*).

Association then results in the linking of the above book to the file via the above channel. The file is opened in such a way that only character transput is permitted, the current position is set to $(1, 1, 1)$, the pointer to the text of the book is sss, the string terminator is null, the event routines are initialised to

> (**ref file** f) **bool**: **false** and (**ref file** f, **ref char** a) **bool**: **false**

and the conversion code is undefined.

There is an important point to be considered in connection with scopes and files. In discussing scopes in previous chapters it was remarked that for an assignation such as $x := y$ to be legal the scope of the result delivered by y could not be smaller than the scope of the result delivered by x. When, as a result of calling *associate*, a book is generated on the heap there takes place in effect an assignation of the form

> **heap book** := (. . .)

Care has to be taken that the above scope rule is not violated at this stage. It is for this reason that the reference to the text of the book is undefined, i.e. **skip**. If one included instead *sss* (using the earlier declaration of *associate*) the scope rule would in general be violated. But, of course, it is necessary that via a file the text of a book can be accessed and this is done via a reference to the contents of a book (see section 9.1.3(i)). This provides the very reason for including in the structure **file** references both to the book and to the contents of the book.

Of course, if one is not careful scope rules can still be violated. As a result of a call

$$associate\ (file, sss)$$

there takes place, in effect, an assignation

$$file := (\ldots, sss, \ldots)$$

For this to be acceptable *sss* must not be smaller in scope than *file*.

9.3. Accessing and altering files

In this section the frequently mentioned standard routines for inspecting the state of a file or altering the values of objects associated with files are studied. They are conveniently divided into three groups: file (access) enquiries, the event routines and other routines. Section 9.3 ends with a discussion on assignations, etc. involving the manipulation of files.

In accessing and altering files it is important to realise whether a property of the file or, more precisely, a property of the book or channel is being accessed. In the latter case the standard routines can be invoked only if the file has been opened; the standard routine needs to know about the book or channel linked to the file.

9.3.1. File enquiries
The file enquiry routines can be divided into two sets: one set is used to enquire about the state of a file at a particular instant, the other for enquiring about the current position within a file.

Each routine from the first of these two sets takes as its only parameter an object of mode **ref file** and all except one returns a value of mode **bool**. The corresponding files must be open.

get possible returns **true** if the file can be used for input, **false** otherwise.

put possible returns **true** if the file can be used for output, **false** otherwise.

bin possible returns **true** if the file can be used for binary transput,

false otherwise.

compressible returns **true** if, during output, the lines and pages of the book will be compressed; otherwise **false** is returned.

reset possible returns **true** if the file can be rewound and the current position of the book returned to the start, i.e. the position represented by (1, 1, 1); otherwise the value returned is **false** (see note below).

set possible returns **true** for random access books and **false** otherwise, i.e. for sequential access books; in random access books the current position for reading or writing can be set to any position provided it lies within the bounds of the book.

reidf possible returns **true** if the identification string for the book linked to the file can be altered, **false** otherwise.

chan returns an object of mode **channel**, namely the channel associated with the particular file.

Note that binary and character transput can be intermingled, but this is in general highly undesirable. Discussion of the restrictions enforced to deter programmers from attempting this are deferred until the end of section 9.5.

Each routine available for enquiring about the current position within a file takes as its only parameter a reference to a file. The result returned is of mode **int**. The three routines available are *char number*, *line number* and *page number* giving respectively, the current character position on the current line, the current line number on the current page and the current page number. They should be used only on a file that has been opened. The result delivered is otherwise undefined.

9.3.2. The event routines

It was earlier stated that certain event routines would be called on the occurrence of certain (usually) rare events that arise in transput. The event routines usually take some standard default action but this action can be altered to suit the programmer by means of the on routines *on logical file end*, *on physical file end*, *on page end*, *on line end*, *on format end*, *on value error* and *on char error*. Thus a routine is available for each event that can arise.

With the exception of *on char error*, the on routines are similar in form and in application, their declaration in the standard environment being of the form

> **proc** *on routine* = (**ref file** f, **proc** (**ref file**) **bool** p) **void**:
> **begin** ... **end**

Within the **begin** and **end** the procedure p is then associated with the file referred to by f. Indeed it is this procedure p that is called

280

whenever the appropriate event occurs.

To illustrate consider the following.

```
⁰        on line end (standin,
            (ref file f) bool:
            begin put (f, (new line, line number (f))):
                    true
            end)
```

The routine appearing as the second parameter of *on line end* is introduced to put line numbers before the start of each new line. As a result of this call to *on line end*, the routine appearing as parameter is called each time the event 'line end' occurs in dealing with transput from the file *standin*. Since the supplied procedure delivers a result **true**, the routine is assumed to have cured any likely trouble arising as a result of the event taking place. The main program can then continue as if the event had not taken place at all. On the other hand, if the result delivered had been **false** then the system would assume that the trouble had not been cured and the default action would occur.

For the events corresponding to *on line end* and *on page end* these default actions are that *newline* and *newpage* are called respectively when formatless transput is being employed. For other events corresponding to *on logical file end* and *on physical file end* the action is not defined.

If on reading or printing an object of mode [ ] **char** an end of line is encountered the appropriate event routine will be called (and in the default case a new line taken). On reading into an object of mode **ref flex** [ ] **char** the number of characters read is determined by the terminator string, by the end of line, or perhaps the end of page, end of physical file or end of logical file. If an event routine is called and returns **false** the input of characters is ended (and this is the default case). Otherwise input is continued until a character in the terminator string is encountered or an event routine returning **false** is called.

Within a file there are, in effect, selectors *logical file mended, physical file mended, page mended*, etc. used to identify the corresponding event routines. Invoking an on routine effectively changes the routine referred to by the corresponding selector. If the event routine returns **true** the trouble is assumed to have been mended.

In altering an event routine of a file variable *f* notice that scope considerations are likely to arise. One should assume that within the on routine is an assignation with destination *f* and the source supplies the new event routine. As usual the scope of the source must be at least as great as the scope of *f*. To overcome difficulties in this area it may be necessary to introduce a new variable of mode **ref file** (see example 9.3.2a).

Since the event routines are a property of the file itself the on routines can be invoked without the corresponding file being open.

Example 9.3.2a. Event routines.
Write a program to read a set of positive numbers representing ages in the range 0–119 and count the number of these ages in each of the ranges 0–9, 10–19, 20–29, ... , 110–119

```
begin [0:11] int count;
      for i from 0 to 11 do count [i] := 0 od;
      file st in := standin;
      on logical file end (st in,
          (ref file f) bool: goto print results);
      do count [(int age; read (age); age ÷ 10)] +:= 1 od;
      print results:
      print (("respective frequencies are", count))
end
```

Note that the second loop clause as stated here would continue indefinitely but for the fact that the supply of data becomes exhausted. When this happens the event 'logical file end' occurs, the appropriate event routine is called and as a result of the call control passes to the label *print results*.

This completes the discussion of the on routines except for the case of routine *on char error*. Its declaration in the standard environment is of the form

```
proc on char error = (ref file f, proc (ref file, ref char)
                 bool p) void:
  begin ... end
```

Note the extra parameter in the procedure *p*.

The key to understanding the operation of the *on char error* routine lies in understanding the role played by this extra parameter. And this involves understanding what is meant by saying that one of a certain set of characters is expected when transput is taking place.

Consider in detail the process that *get* or *read* must go through in reading, character by character, a possibly signed integer. First initial spaces are skipped. If the next character is a sign this is read and subsequent spaces are skipped. The next character expected is a digit. If a digit is not present the 'character error' event occurs. The default routine or any other routine supplied by *on char error* is then called into operation. This routine has two parameters, the second of which is, in this case, a character variable initialised to "0". If the event returns **true** the error is assumed to have been fixed and the value of the character variable is supplied as if it had been the character read. Note that the routine and therefore the programmer can alter the value of the variable if required. If the routine returns **false** the default action of the system will occur. The situation described above can be summarised by saying that a digit is expected and if it is not present the event routine corresponding to *on char error* is called with zero supplied as suggestion.

Example 9.3.2b. *on char error*.

Write a program to read data of the form

$$5x - 7x + 16x$$

and print out the sum of these terms. Note that a difficulty arises with terms of the form $+x$ or $-x$.

For clarity, no provision has been made for checking that each variable is indeed an x. Such checks are easily incorporated.

A possible program follows.

```
begin file st in := standin;
      on logical file end (st in,
                (ref file f) bool: goto print results);
      on char error (st in,
                (ref file f, ref char sugg) bool:
                if sugg = "0"
                then backspace (f);
                      sugg := "1";
                      true
                else false
                fi);
      int sum := 0;
      do int coeff, char ch; read ((coeff, ch));
         sum + := coeff
      od;
      print results:
      print (("required answer is", whole (sum, 0),
                "x"))
end
```

Note that the routine supplied by the call of *on char error* checked that the suggested character would be zero. The reason for this was merely to limit the occasions on which the supplied routine would recover from the error. Had this check not been included recovery would have taken place each time a character error occurred. Such a situation would make detection of other errors arising from, for example, the reading of an illegal character needlessly complicated.

It should also be noted that the programmer has no direct control over the character that is supplied as suggestion. The particular *read* or *get* statement will attempt to read an object of some mode and in so doing it will expect one of a certain set of characters with a character supplied as suggestion. The transput routines themselves therefore supply the suggestions.

Apart from the situation described previously digits will be expected at appropriate places during the reading of real and complex numbers. If a digit is not present the event corresponding to *on char error* is called with, in each case, zero supplied as suggestion. In reading complex numbers either ⊥ or *i* is expected; if it is not present ⊥ will be supplied as suggestion in the usual way. In reading booleans and therefore bits values *flip* or *flop* will be expected; if they are not present *flop* is supplied as suggestion.

During input each character is converted to an internal form. Now, a character could occur which is not present in the character key table, making it impossible to obtain a corresponding internal value. Such a situation is described by saying that character conversion was unsuccessful. In this case again the event routine corresponding to *on char error* is called with a space being supplied as suggestion. The converse situation can arise on output; the same event can occur and the same character is supplied as suggestion.

9.3.3. Altering identification of books, terminator strings and character conversion codes

To alter the identification of a book the relevant routine is *reidf*. Note that the identification string is primarily a property of the book that is linked to the file. Therefore the file must be opened (established or created) and the routine *reidf possible* must return **true** before the identification of the file can be altered. Even when the conditions are satisfied note that the new title of the book may be subject to local (i.e. peculiar to the particular implementation) restrictions such as being of a certain length, containing passwords, etc.

The declaration of *reidf* in the standard environment looks like

> **proc** *reidf* = (**ref file** *f*, **string** *idf*) **void**:
> **begin** ... **end**

Between the **begin** and **end** the string *idf*, assuming that the file is opened and that a suitable change in the title of the book linked

284

to the file is allowed, is made the new title of the book.

The routine *make term* allows the programmer to attach a string of terminators to the file. When this is done then any single character of that string (or the end of line, etc.) will act as a terminator when a request is made to read an unknown number of characters. In the standard environment the definition of *make term* looks like

proc *make term* = (**ref file** *f*, **string** *t*) **void**:
begin ... **end**

A terminator string is attached to neither a book nor a channel but to the file itself. Therefore a call to *make term* can be performed successfully without the file being opened, i.e. without the linkage between the book, channel and file being made.

The last routine to be considered here is *make conv*. A successful call to this necessitates the file in question being opened since the character conversion code is a property of the channel and of the particular book.

One peculiarity of *make conv* is that certain codes must be supplied in the standard environment, and only one of these codes can take the place of the standard conversion code. In general different implementations will supply a different set of character codes.

make conv has two parameters, one of mode **ref file** and the other, in effect, a conversion code. Thus in a call of *make conv* the first parameter indicates the appropriate file to be altered and the second indicates the code that has to replace the standard conversion code.

9.3.4. Setting and resetting files
The three routines *set char number*, *set* and *reset* will be discussed here.

The routine *set char number* can be used with any opened file; *set possible* or *reset possible* need not return **true**. The routine can be used only to place the current reading or writing position at a particular point in the current line. But it should not be used to jump beyond the bounds of the book for the effect would be undefined. The *set char number* routine has a declaration in the standard environment of the form

proc *set char number* = (**ref file** *f*, **int** *c*) **void**:
if not *opened* **of** *f* **then** *undefined* **else** ... **fi**

The parameter *c* indicates the new setting of the character part of the reading or writing position. If the file has not been opened some undefined system action will occur.

The *set char number* routine can be conveniently used to produce tables, graphs, etc. by using it to move the printing position to the appropriate column.

The two standard procedures *reset* and *set* allow files to be reset and set respectively. But they can be used only on certain kinds of files. A file which can be reset, i.e. a file for which *reset possible* yields **true**, would typically be a file on magnetic tape. A file which can be set, a random access file, is a file for which *set possible* yields **true**. Skeleton declarations of *reset* and *set* are

> **proc** *reset* = (**ref file** *f*) **void**:
> (. . .)

and

> **proc** *set* = (**ref file** *f*, **int** *p*, *l*, *c*) **void**:
> (. . .)

Resetting a file is straightforward. The file must previously have been opened and the parameter of *reset* is a reference to the file to be reset.

Setting also requires the file to be already opened. The parameter *f* is merely a reference to the file to be used and the parameters *p*, *l* and *c* are integers representing the page number, line number and character number of the position at which the current position variable is set. Of course as one would expect *set* cannot be employed to jump beyond the logical end of a book or outside the physical bounds of the book.

If an attempt is made to jump beyond the logical end of the book the appropriate event routine will be called. But before this it is arranged that the current position is at the logical end of the book. If, using *set*, an attempt is made to otherwise go beyond the bounds of the book the effect is undefined.

Example 9.3.4a. Using *set*.

Consider a program for updating a master file by means of a file of alterations. Such a situation might arise in adding examination marks to student records in a university environment or adding overtime to the records associated with a payroll in an industrial environment.

Assume that the master file and alterations file are referred to by *master* and *updates* respectively. Assume also that each entry on *updates* takes the form of a structure, one of whose fields, selected by *key*, gives the position to be altered in the master file. The position is represented by three integers representing the page, line, and character numbers.

286

To help in writing the program it will be assumed that the following items have been declared: the mode **posn** declared as in

mode posn = **struct** (**int** p, l, c)

which is used for the current position; the variable *item* whose values in the form of structures run through the various items in the alteration file; and the procedure *alter* which performs the necessary alterations on the master file using the items from the alterations file. Then, assuming that the selector *key* selects from *item* the position in the master file to be updated, a loop to perform the necessary task would look like

> **do** *get* (*update, item*);
> **posn** *cp* = *key* **of** *item*;
> *set* (*master, p* **of** *cp, l* **of** *cp, c* **of** *cp*);
> *alter* (*master, item*)
> **od**

It is presumed that the loop is terminated in a sensible manner, e.g. by the use of a suitable event routine.

Peculiarities of a rather weird nature would result unless special care was taken to deal with the possibility of both reading and writing to the same file within the one program. It will be assumed in the following discussion that the file admits the necessary operations.

For sequential access files output causes the logical end of file to be moved to the current position. In effect, then, input may not follow output unless the file is first reset (assuming this is possible). After each resetting the programmer can once again decide whether to read or write. Note that it is possible for writing to follow reading without resetting.

On random access files the programmer may read and write as he so wishes (assuming again that these operations are permitted). If the logical end of file is encountered on writing it is moved to accommodate the information being sent to it. If it is encountered on reading the appropriate event routine is called.

These restrictions will be further discussed when the added complexity of binary, as well as character, transput becomes possible (see section 9.5).

The various restrictions combine to give the following highly desirable effects. Information which remains undefined cannot appear between the start and the logical end of a file. Nor is there any way in which the programmer can read or write at positions beyond the logical end or outside the physical bounds of the book.

9.3.5. Manipulating files

It has already been stated that **file**, and also **channel**, are standard modes. Due to orthogonality it becomes possible to introduce multiple values of files, structures with files appearing as fields, procedures and operators involving files, and so on. Moreover files can be manipulated by assignments. This latter possibility raises many pertinent questions. Would one expect for instance to be able to write

$$standin := standout$$

in a program? To illustrate further complications consider the piece of program

> **file** *in 1*, *in 2*; *open* (*in 2*, "*initial data*", *chan 3*);
> *in 1* := *in 2*

After this has been executed does it follow that the file referred to by *in 1* is now opened? If so, what properties of the file referred to by *in 2* are thereby passed across to the copy, i.e. the file referred to by *in 1*? Does altering the conversion code of one file alter the conversion code of the copy? Does setting or resetting one of the files thereby set or reset the other?

The answers to these questions follow from the basic premises on which ALGOL 68 is founded. One has merely to look at the coercions, etc. involved and the declarations in the standard environment of the modes **file, channel,** etc. to determine the required answers.

To recap the relevant parts of the definition of the mode **file** (remember that the various fields cannot be accessed in the usual way – they are hidden):

> **mode file** = **struct** (**ref book** *book*, . . .
>   **channel** *chan*, . . .
>   **ref bool** *read mood, write mood, char mood,*
>   *bin mood, opened,*
>   **ref pos** *cpos*, # current position #
>   **string** *term*, # terminators #
>   **conv** *conv*, # character conversion key #
>   **proc** (**ref file**) **bool** *logical file mended*, . . .
>   **proc** (**ref file**, **ref char**) **bool** *char error*
>   *mended*
>   )

The fields with mode **ref bool** indicate the state of the file and the fields of mode **proc** . . . are just the event routines one normally associates with a file.

Consider now

> **file** *in 1, in 2*: *open* (*in 2*,*"initial data"*, *chan 3*);
> *in 1* := *in 2*;

Both *in 1* and *in 2* are of mode **ref file** and their declarations involve invoking generators and the subsequent creation of space. The call of the routine *open* links the book and the file via *chan 3* thus initialising the file referred to by *in 2* in the usual way. The assignation

> *in 1* := *in 2*

is perfectly legal. *in 2* is dereferenced and the resulting object of mode **file** is then assigned to the variable *in 1*. Thus the variable *in 1* is effectively initialised in the same way as *in 2* is initialised. In particular since the file referred to by *in 2* has been opened, the file referred to by *in 1* is also opened. If one file allows setting, resetting, reading, etc. the other file will also possess these same properties.

If a file is linked to a book by any other method – i.e. by use of *create* or *establish* – then a similar situation arises as a result of assignation. Closing, locking or scratching a file also gives a similar result.

Returning now to the original piece of program involving *in 1* and *in 2*, consider what happens to the fields of one of the files if the corresponding fields of the other are altered. Consider first the possibility of altering the character conversion key, the terminator string or any of its event routines. If, say, the character conversion key of the file referred to by *in 1* is altered to *new code* then effectively an assignation of the form

> *conv* **of** *in 1* := *new code*

takes place although, of course, the programmer must do this by calling a standard procedure, in this case *make conv*. From the modes of the objects involved and from the fact that different space was generated for *in 1* and *in 2* it follows that altering the character conversion key of *in 1* does not alter the character conversion key of *in 2*. Similarly, altering the terminator string or any of the event routines of one file does not alter the corresponding fields of the other.

Consider now any routine which alters the current position field or any of the fields of mode **ref book** or **ref bool**. Any attempt to alter any of these fields in *in1* results essentially in an assignation of the form

> *cpos* **of** *in1* := ... or *opened* **of** *in1* := ...

and so on. (Note that such changes may be brought about by using routines such as *newline*, *newpage*, *space*, *backspace*, *set* and *reset*.) The modes of the destinations begin **ref ref**. Consequently assignations are made to pointers. Since both *in 1* and *in 2* are initialised in such a way that these point to the same value it follows that altering one file results in altering the other. Thus altering the current position, the book or the state of the file referred to by *in1* will result in a change of the corresponding item in the file referred to by *in 2*. The two files cannot then get out of step and so the contents of the book, the current position and the state of both files are always the same.

This section can now be summarised as follows. Assume that the assignation

$$in1 := in2$$

has taken place, *in 1* and *in 2* being of mode **ref file**. Regarding a file as a structure then

(i) if the field of a file has an associated mode beginning with **ref** then altering one file will also alter the other;

(ii) if the associated mode does not begin with **ref** then altering one file will not alter the other file.

Note that the above is essentially a discussion about what happens to copies of a file when the original file is altered.

Note finally that the assignation

$$standin := standout$$

is perfectly legal since *standin* and *standout* are, like *in 1* and *in 2*, of mode **ref file**. Such an assignation should, of course, be discouraged.

9.4. Formatted transput

Formatted transput allows the programmer to have a very high degree of control over the way in which character transput is performed by a program.

Consider a file, from which information can be read in character form, containing the six digits 241174. By means of formatted transput these could be read as a single six-digit integer, as three two-digit integers, as a five-digit integer followed by a single-digit integer, and so on. If instead the data had appeared as 241 ⌞ 174 (⌞ denoting a space) it could be arranged that even this is read as a single integer. If it had appeared as 24-11-74 this could be read as three separate integers or even a single six-digit integer.

On output the single integer 241174 could be printed in many forms, e.g.

241174
24-11-74
$2411.74
24.11.74
24 11 74
2411 *m* 74 *cm*

and so on. Note that just a single integer is printed; the programmer need not perform any calculations to find the first two digits, for example.

The full range of facilities and the ways of using these will be investigated in this section. The standard procedures *read* and *print* or even *get* and *put* are inadequate for this purpose and other standard procedures have to be introduced. The extra facility required for achieving greater flexibility and control is the idea of a format – hence the term 'formatted transput'.

In formatted transput the transfer of a value from a program to the book of the appropriate file (and vice versa) is controlled by a *picture*. In the case of printing, the picture describes precisely how the item is to appear in the book. In the case of reading, the picture describes the layout expected from the item to be input. Pictures will vary depending on the mode of the item to be transferred. But, to illustrate, the programmer can specify by means of pictures such details as the number of digits, the exact position of the decimal point, whether or not leading zeros are to appear (i.e. whether fifteen appears as 0015, 015 or 15, etc.), the presence or absence of a sign, or the insertion of strings of characters (in the examples given above the dashes, periods, dollar sign, "*m*" and spaces are all examples of insertions of character strings).

To recap, a single item is transferred under the control of a single picture. A set of values is transferred under the control of as many pictures as there are items in the (straightened) data list. A grouping of pictures is called a *format*. Format texts, which correspond to denotations, are enclosed by $ and $ and have an associated (standard) mode **format**. Like **channel** and **file**, **format** can be expressed as a structure whose selectors are hidden.

When information is being transferred in formatted transput, as usual communication takes place between a program and a book opened on a file via a particular channel, but now there is an added complexity in that a format becomes associated with the file. When formatted transput takes place the format currently associated with the file will control the transput. If the mode **file** were expressed as a structure as in section 9.3.5 it would be seen that there are two new fields, **ref format** *format* and **ref int** *forp*. The first is for the format associated with the file, and the second is a kind of pointer indicating how many pictures of the format have so far been used for the transfer of information. There is also a new event routine which is invoked when all the pictures of the format have been used. This routine, like other similar event routines, can be altered by *on format end* (see section 9.4.6).

The standard routines to be used for formatted transput are similar to those for unformatted transput. Thus for input from *standin readf* is used; for output to *standout printf* or *writef* is used; and for transput to or from more general files *getf* and *putf* are used.

These procedures take the expected parameters apart from two important differences. First of all none of the items in a data list can be an object of mode **proc (ref file) void**. Thus the standard procedures *space, backspace, newline, newpage,* etc. cannot be used, but their effects can be obtained in a different way.

Secondly, formats themselves can be inserted into a data list: the formats then become associated with the file. In this way the format associated with a file can be changed. Indeed several formats can at different times become associated with the same file.

When the event routines associated with a file were changed using on routines it was often necessary to take a local copy of a file to overcome scope problems. Similar situations can arise in associating different formats with a file. If a format contains, for instance, occurrences of variables with limited scope (see section 9.4.1) then one must be aware of the scope problem arising from an attempt to associate such a format with a more global file.

9.4.1. Format texts
Format texts are a kind of format denotation. They are more general than mere denotations since there can be a dynamic element in their formation. A format text represents a sequence of pictures and so its general appearance is

$picture, picture, ... $

Each picture represents an individual item to be transferred. Some pictures might imply that only text is transferred or new lines, new pages, etc. taken. But if this is not the case then the first item is transferred under the control of the first picture in the format, the second item is transferred under the control of the second picture, and so on.

If a large (or unknown) number of items have to be transferred it would be most inconvenient to have to write as many pictures as there are items. To overcome this difficulty each picture can be

292

replaced by a collection, which takes the form

>replicator (picture)

or

>replicator (picture, picture, ...)

In their most general form these collections can include at the start and the end of the collection information indicating the taking of new lines, etc. or the insertion of text. Moreover the pictures in any collection may themselves be replaced by collections. Thus collections can be nested to an arbitrary depth.

The replicators return an integer indicating the number of times the picture or set of pictures has to be repeated. The replicator usually takes the form of an integer denotation but it can involve the elaboration of an arbitrary enclosed clause returning an integer, in which case the replicator is said to be *dynamic*. Dynamic replicators are elaborated as and when they are encountered and take the form

>n followed by an enclosed clause delivering an integer

The syntactic position of the enclosed clause is meek. Scopes of objects used in the enclosed clause affect the scope of the format.

Example 9.4.1a. Replicators.
Each of the following is a replicator:

> (i) 80.
> (ii) n (**int** m; *read* (m); m).
> (iii) n (*length* $- 1$) where *length* is of mode **int**.

Replicators are normally expected to return non-negative values; negative values are treated as if they were zero.

9.4.2. Pictures
Each picture consists of two parts. The first – the *pattern* – contains information to control the precise layout of the items to be transferred. The type of the pattern is closely related to the mode of the object being transferred. (In special cases the pattern of a picture may be absent.)

The second part of a picture – the *insertion* – contains information regarding the insertion of text or the taking of new lines, spaces, etc. Insertions need not be present in pictures; in their absence the various items to be transferred are merely laid end to end in the book of the file. Insertions will appear later in other positions but note that they can also appear at the start and end of collections.

9.4.3. Insertions

It is convenient to begin by separating the two functions of insertions. An insertion which implies the supplying of strings of characters only, i.e. contains no new lines, new pages, spaces, etc. is called a *literal*. An insertion involving the taking of new lines, etc. is called an *alignment*. The form of literals and alignments will be considered separately before showing how the two can be used to form more general insertions.

A literal is a sequence of replicators and string denotations. The syntactic position of the character string is strong and so a character denotation can also appear since it would be rowed to the required mode. The replicator, if absent, is assumed to have the value 1. Thus $5"x"$ is a literal and implies that on output five copies of the character $"x"$ would appear side by side. Also $5"x""y"4"z"$ is a literal and would produce on output

$$x"yx"yx"yx"yx"yzzzz$$

As in string and character denotations the single quote appears as a double quote. Note that any replicator after the first must be stated explicitly (otherwise ambiguity would result). On input this sequence of characters would be expected.

An alignment contains an alignment code (summarised below) possibly preceded by replicators and possibly followed by a literal. The replicator – if it is absent a replicator of 1 is implied – qualifies the alignment code it precedes. The alignment codes are:

x indicating that *space* is to be called;
y indicating that *backspace* is to be called;
l indicating that *newline* is to be called;
p indicating that *newpage* is to be called;
q causing blanks to be taken;
k indicating the exact position on the current line.

Note that the use of *blank* and *space* are different (see example 2.11.2c). The use of k is explained by illustration. An alignment of $5k$ causes the current position to become the fifth character position on the current line. $40k$ causes the current position to be the fortieth character position on the current line. The alignment sequence $5l6x$ causes five new lines to be taken and six spaces to be left on the then current line. Also $p40q$ causes a new page to be started and forty blanks to be printed on output or expected on input.

An insertion can now be described in its full generality in terms of literals and alignments. An insertion is a (possibly empty) sequence of alignments possibly preceded by a literal. On output each alignment is

294

performed and each character string printed. On input the corresponding items are expected.

Example 9.4.3a. Insertions.

$$l\,60k''!''n(60 - \mathbf{round}\,(40 \times sin(x)))k''.''$$

is an insertion that might be used in a program to draw a graph of the *sin* function. There is no initial literal and the insertion is composed of the alignments l, $60k''!''$, and $n\,(60 - \mathbf{round}\,(40 \times sin\,(x)))\,k''.''$.

9.4.4. Patterns, moulds and frames
Several types of pattern exist and to some extent these have to be considered individually. But there is a common structure associated with many of them and an understanding of this may be gained by first looking at some examples.

Consider the integer 241174. Suppose that this integer is required to be printed as

24–11–74

The pattern producing an integer must take care of the layout and position of the sign and also of the various digits to be transferred. The sign is controlled by a sign mould and the various digits by an integral mould. In the case mentioned above the integral mould has somehow to produce 24–11–74. This is done by splitting moulds into a number of frames. In general a frame is an insertion followed by a (possibly replicated) marker. The markers for a digit are either z or d, the z implying that a zero has to be replaced by a space. Thus the (integral) pattern controlling the above output might be $2d\,''-''$ $2d''-''\,2d$. The frames here are $2d,''-''\,2d,''-''\,2d$ and these control the printing of 24, $-$ 11, $-$ 74. Other patterns would achieve the same effect, e.g. $zd\,''-''\,zd\,''-''\,zd$. But with this pattern 10175 would appear as

$\_1 - \_1 - 75$

Using the earlier pattern $2d\,''-''\,2d''-''\,2d$ this would appear as

$01 - 01 - 75$

The frames in $zd\,''-''\,zd\,''-''\,zd$ are $z,d,''-''\,z,d,''-''\,z$ and d.

Patterns for other kinds of numbers are similar to integral patterns. They are composed of sign moulds and integral moulds together with special frames for decimal points, times-ten-to-the-power symbols, etc. The details will be discussed later.

Unlike the patterns for numbers the patterns for character strings and booleans must be composed of frames of only one kind. String patterns are built from character frames (denoted by *a*) and boolean patterns from boolean frames (denoted by *b*).

9.4.5. Use of the formatted transput routines

In the illustrations above no sign mould was present. This is quite acceptable provided that the value to be transferred is not negative; if it had been, the event routine corresponding to *on value error* would have resulted.

The format text could have been used in the following way, assuming that *date* is of mode **int**:

$$printf(($zd" - " zd" - " dd\,\$, date))$$

Since the data list contains more than one item, in this case a format text and *date*, it must be supplied to *printf* as a display; hence the double brackets. The effect of this call to *printf* is as follows. The format text, being an item of the data list, becomes the current format associated with the file being used, here the standard output file. The integer *date* is then transferred under control of the current format.

We could have written

$$writef(($zd" - " zd" - " dd\,\$, date\,1, date\,2, date\,3))$$

where *date 1*, *date 2* and *date 3* are all of mode **int**. The format again becomes the current format associated with the standard output file and *date1* is transferred under its control. Then the format becomes exhausted assuming that the transfer has taken place as planned. Assuming that the event routine corresponding to *on format end* returns **false** – this will happen in the default case – the format is repeated. In this way *date 2* and *date 3* can be printed.

Example 9.4.5a. Formatted output.

(i) If *x* is declared as in

[1000] **int** *x*

then consider

$$writef(($\,l\,8\,(5zd\,"metres\,")\,\$, x))$$

l is an insertion and is used to indicate that a new line is to be taken. The effect of this is that a new line is taken and then the first eight integers are printed each in a field of width 6 and each followed by *metres* and a space. After these first eight numbers, etc. are printed a

296

new line is taken and the next eight are printed. This is repeated until all 1000 numbers are transferred.

    (ii) *printf* (($ *zd* " − " *zd* " − " 2*d* $, *date*, $ "£" 3*zd* $, *cost*))
is acceptable if *date* and *cost* deliver integers. *date* is printed under control of the first format text which at that stage is the current format associated with the standard output file. After this is completed the second format becomes the format associated with the file and *cost* is transmitted under control of this second format.

Until now the examples on formatted transput have dealt exclusively with output. Consider now the effect of

$$readf \; (($ \; zd \; " − " \; zd \; " − " \; dd \; $, \; date))$$

where again since the data list has several items the list is presented to *readf* as a display. *date* is now assumed to have mode **ref int**. As before the integer is transferred under the control of the current format in this case from the standard input file. The current format at this stage is $ *zd* " − " *zd* " − " *dd* $. The *z*'s indicate that a digit or a space is expected. A space is treated as zero. The *d*'s indicate that digits are expected. The " − " means that a dash should appear in the data at this point. Thus using the above format the input would be expected to contain a digit or space followed by a digit, a dash, a digit or space, a digit, a dash and finally two digits. Thus ⌐ 1 − ⌐ 1 − 75 is acceptable and *date* takes the value 10174, and 24 − 11 − 74 is acceptable and *date* becomes 241174. But 1.01.74 would result in a call to the event routine corresponding to *on char error*.

9.4.6. The event routines revisited

The event routine corresponding to *on char error* is called when a character which was not expected is read. The possibility of this happening is increased with the introduction of formatted transput since now every character position is significant. When the event occurs the appropriate routine is called with some character supplied as suggestion. A list of the frames and corresponding suggestions is given in Table 9.1.

Example 9.4.6a. Using *on char error*.
Consider again *readf* (($ *zd* " − " *zd* " − " 2*d* $, *date*)) and suppose that the standard input file contains 24.11.74. Then the situation could be remedied by the following.

      on char error (*standin*,
          (**ref file** *f*, **ref char** *sugg*) **bool**:
          if *sugg* = " − "

TABLE 9.1.

Frame marker	Expected characters	Suggestions
z	space or digit (see note 1 below)	0
d	digit	0
a	any character	space
.	point symbol	point symbol
e	$\setminus_{10}e$	$_{10}$
i	$i \perp$	$\perp$
b	characters representing **true** or **false** i.e. *flip* or *flop*	*flop*

Notes

1. Zeros controlled by z frames are replaced by spaces only in certain positions. These are:
   (i) between the start of a string and the first non-zero digit;
   (ii) between each d, e, or i frame and the next non-zero digit.
2. If a certain character, such as $" - "$ in the example involving dates, is expected and does not appear the suggestion supplied to the event routine corresponding to *on char error* is just the expected character itself.

> **then char** c; *backspace* (f); *get* (f, c);
> $\quad c = "."$
> **else false**
> **fi**)

The event routine returns **true** only if the character $"."$ appeared in place of $" - "$. Thus either a period or a dash can separate different parts of the date.

It was pointed out earlier that a call to the event routine corresponding to *on value error* occurs whenever, for instance, an attempt is made to read an integer which is, say, larger than *max int*. This routine is also called under circumstances arising from the use of formatted transput, for example, when an attempt is made to transfer a value whose picture is unsuitable (i.e. the picture is of an incompatible type (section 9.4.9) or contains too few frames). If the event routine returns **true**, the picture and current value are skipped and transput proceeds, but if **false** is returned then if output is in progress the current value is transferred by a call to *put* and then the appropriate system action is initiated.

Example 9.4.6b. Using *on value error*.
If *char1* is of mode **ref char** and *int1* of mode **ref int** then a call to the event routine associated with *on value error* results from

$\quad$ *readf* $(($4d2x$, char1, int1))$

298

since $4d$ indicates an integral picture and, as will be seen shortly, this is incompatible with that expected by a character variable.

Note the distinction between *on value error* and *on char error*.

on value error is used when there is
    (i) a picture of an incompatible type,
    (ii) an insufficient number of frames, or
    (iii) during input a string which cannot be converted to a value of a given mode as would happen, for example, on attempting to read an integer which is too large for a particular machine.

on char error is used when either
    (i) a character conversion has not been successful, or
    (ii) during input a character was read and it was not expected.

Now consider the event routine associated with the ending of a format. The corresponding on routine is *on format end*. Suppose that certain items still remain to be transferred and yet the current format, i.e. the format associated with the file being used, becomes exhausted. The appropriate event routine is called. If this returns **true**, and if the current format has been replaced, e.g. by the event routine, then the new format is used; but if the current format has not been replaced, the default system action occurs. If the event routine returns **false**, then the current format is repeated and used again.

Like other similar routines the event routine corresponding to *on format end* is initialised to

      (ref file f**) bool: false**

In formatted transput the default actions of the other event routines are, with one exception, similar to the corresponding default actions in formatless transput. The event corresponding to *on line end* no longer results in a default call of *newline*.

9.4.7. Sign moulds
Sign moulds, like integral moulds, are built from a sequence of frames. The last frame must be a sign frame. Other frames, and there might be none of these, must be zero frames. The sign frames contain an insertion, which may be null, followed by a $+$ or a $-$. Zero frames have as their marker z which can be replicated; these have the significance described earlier when considering integral moulds.

Example 9.4.7a. Sign moulds.
    (i) $4z+$ (ii) $2z\,"---"\,2z\,"---"\,-$

In the sign frame the $+$ or $-$ determines the sign, if any, appearing in output or expected on input. A $+$ indicates that a sign will always be present. A $-$ indicates that for a negative value the sign appears but for a non-negative value the $+$ is replaced by a space.

The z marker in a sign mould indicates that on output zeros are replaced by spaces and on input spaces are, in effect, replaced by zeros. Moreover whenever this occurs the sign, if present, is moved across all the leading zeros in the section controlled by this sign mould. Thus in the sign mould $4z +$ the sign will be present and is moved at most four spaces to the right.

Example 9.4.7b. Effect of sign moulds.

(i) Using the pattern $4z + d$ the integer 999 would appear as $⊥ ⊥ + 999$ and using $z + 4d$ it would appear as $⊥ + 0999$.

(ii) Using $4z - d$ the integer $- 999$ would appear as $⊥ ⊥ - 999$ and 999 would appear as $⊥ ⊥ ⊥ 999$.

(iii) The pattern $z'' \ ''3z'' \ ''2z - d$ has as its sign mould $z'' \ ''3z'' \ ''2z -$ and will produce output such as

$$-6⊥774⊥331$$
$$⊥6⊥774⊥331$$
$$⊥⊥⊥⊥-1⊥000$$

At this stage there may appear to be a contradiction. It has been shown that the pattern $z'' \ ''3z'' \ ''2z - d$ causes $⊥ ⊥ ⊥ ⊥ - 1 ⊥ 000$ to be printed and the pattern $zd'' - '' \ zd'' - '' \ zd$ causes $⊥ 1 - ⊥ 1 - 75$ to be printed. In the first case some non-leading zeros have not been replaced by spaces and in the second case they have. But see note 1 of table 9.1.

9.4.8. Special frames

As previously described a picture used for the transfer of integers is a sequence of replicators and markers separated and surrounded by (possibly null) insertions. A picture may contain no pattern, i.e. a void pattern (see section 9.4.11). A similar structure controls the transfer of real numbers, complex numbers and other kinds of item. But some special kinds of frame do arise.

Take, for example, the point marker used for indicating the decimal point in transferring real and complex numbers, the exponent marker e, and the complex marker i; these must always have a replicator of 1. A sign frame as used in sign moulds also has this property. Thus in the construction of real and complex patterns the point marker, etc. appear as frames rather than as moulds.

With these restrictions in mind real patterns and complex patterns

300

are built from sign moulds, integral moulds, point frames, exponent frames, complex frames and insertions. Their precise structure is considered in section 9.4.9 when individual patterns are discussed in more detail.

To take another special case consider 241174. Suppose one wishes to read these six digits into a real variable in such a way that the value referred to by the variable is 241.174. This is possible using *suppressible frames*.

Consider the statement

$$readf\,((\$\,3d.\,3d\$,\,length))$$

where *length* is of mode **ref real**. The format text contains a single real pattern. The appearance of the point implies that a point symbol is expected after the first three digits. Thus 241.174 appearing on the standard input file would satisfy the requirements of the format text.

Consider instead

$$readf\,((\$\,3ds.\,3d\$,\,length))$$

Note the frame *s.* which now replaces the point marker. The *s* implies that the point symbol has been suppressed and is not expected to appear on the standard input file. But the first six digits will be read as if a point did appear between the third and the fourth digit. Thus 241174 appearing on *standin* would make *length* refer to the value 241.174.

On output the use of *s.* would mean that the point would not appear. Thus *printf* $((\$z + s.3d\$, pi))$ would produce $+ 3142$ on the standard output file.

Further examples of the use of suppressible frames are given below. These illustrate the use of replicators and insertions with suppressed frames.

Example 9.4.8a. Suppressed frames.

(i) Assuming *length* is of mode **ref real** the statement

$$putf\,(measures,\,(\$\,3z - d''\,m\,''s.zd''\,cm''\,\$,\,length))$$

would produce output such as

$$1000\ m\ 0\ cm$$

or

$$9\ m\ 49\ cm$$

on the file referred to by *measures*.

(ii) Assuming *thou1* to be of mode **ref int** the statement

$$readf\,((\$2d3sd\$,\,thou1))$$

reads two digits, say 45, and treats these as thousands. After this has been elaborated *thou1* might refer to 45000. The frame 3*sd* implies three digits have been suppressed: it is understood that zeros replace the suppressed digits.

Note that some frames cannot be suppressed – for example, the items appearing in sign moulds. The suppressible frames are:

the point frame used for the transput of real, and therefore also complex, numbers; on input when the point is suppressed it is automatically supplied in the desired position

the complex frame used in the transput of complex numbers; when suppressed it is automatically supplied on input in the desired position

the exponent frame as used in the transput of real (and therefore also complex) numbers; again it is automatically supplied where desired

a digit or zero frame as used in integral moulds; this therefore includes among others (see section 9.4.9) the transput of integers, bits values and also real and complex numbers; when suppressed on input a zero is automatically supplied

a character frame as used in the transput of strings; when suppressed on input a space is automatically supplied

9.4.9. Patterns
The modes compatible with each type of pattern are of importance. For example, integers, short integers, long integers, etc. can all be output under the control of integral patterns. Consequently the modes **int**, **short int**, **long int**, **long long int**, etc. are said to be output compatible with integral patterns, whereas the modes **ref int**, **ref short int**, etc. are said to be input compatible with integral patterns. In the following paragraphs the input compatible and output compatible modes for each type of pattern are discussed, together with the allowable structure of the patterns.

Integral patterns
Integral patterns consist of either a sign mould followed by an integral mould or an integral mould itself. On output the modes compatible with integral patterns are **short int**, **int**, **long int**, *etc.* If there is no sign mould and the value that is transferred is negative the event routine corresponding to *on value error* is called.

On input the compatible modes include **ref short int, ref int, ref long**

int, etc. If no sign mould is present and a sign appears on the input stream then the event routine corresponding to *on char error* is called with "0" as suggestion. If the integer supplied happens to be larger than the maximum number to which a particular variable may refer then the event routine corresponding to *on value error* is called (see also section 9.4.6.)

Example 9.4.9a. Integral patterns.
Each of the following is an acceptable integral pattern.
- (i) $3z''$ $''3z''$ $''2zd$; note that no sign mould is present here.
- (ii) $3z - ''$ $''3d$
- (iii) $''height''$ $4z - d$
- (iv) $- d$

Real patterns
Real patterns have two basic forms, both of which may or may not contain a sign mould. The first of the two forms is, ignoring the possibility of an initial sign mould, a point frame with an integral mould before it, after it or both before and after it. The second is, again ignoring possible sign moulds, either a pattern of the first form described above or an integral mould, followed by an exponent frame which is followed in turn by an integral pattern.

For the significance of sign moulds, see the description of integral patterns.

Example 9.4.9b. Real patterns.
The following are real patterns.
- (i) $4z + d.d3z$

This is of the first kind described above and a sign mould is present.
- (ii) $2d.d6z$

is again of the first kind and there is no sign mould.
- (iii) $4z + dez - d$

is a real pattern of the second kind; the pattern $z - d$ is an integral pattern with a sign mould.
- (iv) $7z + d.ed$

is again a real pattern of the second kind.

The modes which are output compatible with real patterns include **short real**, **real**, **long real**, **short int**, **int**, **long int**, etc. When an integer (**short int**, **int**, **long int**, etc.) has to be output under the control of a real pattern it is first widened and then transferred. The modes input compatible with real patterns are **ref short real**, **ref real**, **ref long real**, etc.

Whenever an e frame is present in a real pattern the exponent part of the number printed (i.e. the integer following the $_{10}$) is adjusted in such a way that the rest of the number will be as large in magnitude as possible subject of course to the constraints of the rest of the real pattern.

The event routines corresponding to *on value error* and *on char error* are called under the usual circumstances.

Complex patterns

Complex patterns consist of two real patterns separated by a complex frame. The output compatible modes include **short int**, **int**, **long int**, **short real**, **real**, **long real**, **short compl**, **compl**, **long compl**, etc. When an integer is output under the control of a complex pattern then it is widened twice and hence changed to an item of mode **compl**. In the same kind of way objects of mode **real** are also widened. The input compatible modes are just **ref short compl**, **ref compl**, **ref long compl**, etc.

The event routines corresponding to *on value error* and *on char error* are called in circumstances similar to those arising with real and integer patterns.

Example 9.4.9c. Complex patterns.
The following are complex patterns.
   (i) $6z + d. i\,3zdez + d$ (ii) $4z.i4z$.

Boolean patterns
A boolean pattern consists simply of a boolean frame. The appropriate marker is b. The only output compatible mode is **bool** and the only input compatible mode is **ref bool**.

Example 9.4.9d. Boolean patterns.
The following contains acceptable boolean patterns.
   (i) *"the value of the boolean is"* b
   (ii) *"the truth table follows"* $2l\,n(2{\uparrow}\,m)\,(n(m+1)\,b\,l)$
Here it is assumed that m is of a posteriori mode **int**.

String patterns
A string pattern consists of one or more character frames. The marker for a character frame is the letter a.

Example 9.4.9e. String patterns.
The following all contain acceptable string patterns.
   (i) *"name" a".."* $20a\,l$

304

a name being supplied as a single initial followed by a period and a 20-character surname.

(ii) *"address " 5ax20ax20a l*

an address being supplied as a string composed of a number containing five digits followed by a two-word street name, each word being 20 letters long; note that the digits are here treated as characters.

The output compatible modes are **char** and [ ] **char**, objects of mode **char** being rowed. The length of the string of characters being output must coincide with the length of string expected by the pattern. Otherwise the event routine corresponding to *on value error* is invoked.

The input compatible modes are **ref char**, **ref [ ] char** and **ref string**. If the variable receiving the input is of mode **ref char** then the string pattern should indicate a single character which is supplied. Otherwise the event routine corresponding to *on value error* is invoked. If the variable is of mode **ref [ ] char** the size of the multiple value referred to by the variable should equal the number of characters read under control of the string pattern. Again failure in this respect causes the invoking of the event routine corresponding to *on value error*. However, if the mode of the variable receiving the input is **ref string** then the string pattern controls the input and this string is supplied to the variable. The bounds of the multiple value referred to by the variable will in general be altered as a result.

In using string patterns there is a difficulty which does not occur in transmitting objects other than characters. It has been stated that a single picture controls each item involved in transput. A character multiple value is regarded as a single item (see section 9.2.1). Note that 5 (12*a*) is a collection of five pictures. Therefore

> **begin** [60] **char** *ch*; *read* (*ch*); *printf* (($5 (12*a*) $, *ch*)) **end**

would result in a call of the event routine corresponding to *on value error*.

Bits patterns

A bits pattern consists of a radix frame followed by an integral mould. Note that there is no possibility of a sign mould being present. A radix frame will consist of a (possibly null) insertion followed by 2*r*, 4*r*, 8*r*, or 16*r*. If the value of the radix happens to be 4 then the digits involved must of course be only 0, 1, 2 or 3. Similarly for the other radices, with, if necessary, *a*, *b*, *c*, *d*, *e* and *f* being used for 10, 11, 12, 13, 14 and 15 respectively.

On input an integer is read and this is converted to an appropriate bits value using the operator **bin**. On output the bits value is converted to an integer using **abs** and this is then printed using the appropriate radix.

Example 9.4.9f. Bits patterns.
The following are acceptable bits patterns.

(i) *2r zzzd*
(ii) *"register 0" 2r 16d*

The output compatible modes are **short bits**, **bits**, **long bits**, etc. and the input compatible modes are **ref short bits**, **ref bits**, **ref long bits**, etc. On output conversion may be unsuccessful due to the fact that the value will not fit the supplied pattern. Then the usual event routine, i.e. that corresponding to *on value error*, is invoked. On input a similar situation occurs if for some reason conversion to a bits value with the required properties is unsuccessful.

Choice patterns
Choice patterns are used for the printing or reading of one of several possible strings of characters. Choosing one of several posibilities can be done in ALGOL 68 in at least two ways. First there is the case clause where the choice is made by an integer and, secondly, there is the conditional clause where the choice is made by a boolean. There are choice patterns corresponding to both of these constructions.

Consider first the choice pattern corresponding to the case clause. This takes the form of a (possibly null) insertion followed by a construction looking like

$$c\,(\text{literal}\,1, \text{literal}\,2, \ldots, \text{literal}\,n)$$

Remember that literals are special kinds of insertions – they contain no alignments. The item in a data list corresponding to such a pattern is an integer or integer variable.

On output the integer (of mode **int**), call it i, selects the ith literal which is then output assuming that i lies between 1 and the number of literals present. If i happens to be out of range the event routine corresponding to *on value error* is invoked.

On input one would expect to find at the current position of the relevant file one of the literals listed in the pattern; failure to do so results in a call to the event routine corresponding to *on value error*. If literal i is found then i is the integer received by the integer variable (of mode **ref int**).

Choice patterns which make use of booleans are similar in design and effect to choice patterns using integers. They have the form

b(literal 1, literal 2)

On output a boolean is transferred. If it is **true** then literal 1 appears in the output file and if it is **false** literal 2 appears. On input if literal 1 is present then the boolean variable receives the value **true**, if literal 2 is present the boolean variable receives the value **false**. As before the *on value error* event routine is invoked if neither literal 1 nor literal 2 is present on input.

Example 9.4.9g. Choice patterns.
The following all contain legal choice patterns.
   (i) *c("first", "second", "third")*
  (ii) *printf (($"integer" 4zd, "is" b("","not") "prime" $,n,pr))*
 (iii) *printf (($c("spring", "summer", "autumn", "winter") $, season)).*

In dealing with input under the control of choice patterns there is a pitfall. Consider a program reading, for instance, assembly code instructions. One instruction might be *MOV* and another *MOVB*, the first indicating that the contents of a word should be moved to some location and the other indicating that the contents of a byte should be moved. If *instr* is of mode **ref int** then

readf (($c("MOV","MOVB") $, instr))

may lead to trouble. Suppose the string appearing at the current position in the standard input file is *MOVB*. The *readf* statement operates as follows: it will first check if the first three characters are *M*, *O* and *V*. They are and so *instr* receives the value 1. This is presumably not what is intended. The problem can be overcome by instead writing the instruction as

readf(($c ("MOVB","MOV") $, instr))

In general, if two literals start with the same sequence of characters the longer should appear first.

This in turn raises another possibility. If, using the above example *MOV* happened to be the last three characters in the book a search for *MOVB* would result in a violation of the logical end of file. However, special precautions are taken and the event routine is not called.

Format patterns
Format patterns allow the programmer to choose dynamically which format he wishes to employ in transferring a particular item.

Format patterns consist of a (possibly null) insertion followed by f, the marker for format patterns, and then an enclosed clause yielding a format, i.e. a result of a posteriori mode **format**. The syntactic position of the clause is meek.

Example 9.4.9h. Format patterns.
 (i) If *irc* is of mode **union** (**int**, **real**, [ ] **char**) then

$$f(irc|(\textbf{int}): \$\, 4zd\,\$, (\textbf{real}): \$\, 2z.2d\,\$, ([\,]\,\textbf{char}): \$\, 5a\,\$)$$

is a format pattern in which the clause is a case clause, the choice being by mode.
 (ii) If *text* is of mode **bool** then

$$f(text|\$\, l\, 20\, (80a\, l)\, \$|\$\, l\, (20\,(10\,(5z + 2d)\, l))\, \$)$$

is a format pattern where the clause is an **if-then-else-fi** conditional.

Strictly speaking the effect of a format pattern is that the result delivered by the clause then temporarily becomes the current format associated with the file in question. This is then used in the transfer of items between the program and that file. When the format becomes exhausted control resorts to the original format without any call to the *on format end* event routine.

General patterns
General patterns allow the facilities offered by the formatless transput routines *get*, *put*, *read*, *print* etc. possibly with the extra help of the standard routines *whole*, *fixed* and *float* to be used in formatted transput.

A general pattern takes the form of a (possibly null) insertion followed by a *g*, the marker for general patterns. The *g* can be further followed by up to three parameters, the set being surrounded by the brackets (and). If parameters are present they will take the form of arbitrary units delivering integers and will act as parameters for either *whole*, *fixed* or *float*. This will be further discussed below but for the moment the important point to note is that if parameters are present then only integers or reals can be involved in the transfer controlled by that pattern. Parameters are elaborated collaterally.

The fact that up to three parameters can follow the *g* gives rise to a total of four possibilities.
 (i) If *g* is present alone, i.e. without parameters, the item is transferred as if by the formatless transput routines *get* and *put*.
 (ii) If *g* has a single parameter, e.g. $g(0)$, the integer or real is transferred using *get* or *put*. If output is taking place *whole* is invoked

and receives the single parameter as its width specification. On input the parameter has no significance.

(iii) If g has two parameters these act as the parameters of *fixed* assuming output is taking place. If input is occurring the parameters are not significant.

(iv) If g has three parameters these are passed on to *float* which is invoked assuming output is taking place. Again, on input they are not significant.

If parameters are present and the items being transferred are not integers or reals of arbitrary size, the *on value error* event routine is invoked.

Example 9.4.9i. General patterns.
The elements of a multiple value referred to by a where a is declared as in

$\quad$ [10, 10] **int** a

might be output under control of the format text

$\quad$ $ 10 (10 (g (5) 3x) l) $

The parameter 5 acts as the parameter which is effectively supplied to *whole*.

9.4.10. Pragmatic remarks and comments in format texts
Any number of pragmatic remarks and/or comments can appear within format texts provided they do not separate two digits or two letters or a letter and a digit. They may come immediately after a dynamic replicator, before a string denotation, e.g. in an insertion or choice pattern, before a formatter symbol $, before the insertions which can surround a collection or after a choice, format or general pattern.

9.4.11. Controlling transput using formats
If a format appears in a data list the format becomes associated with the file being used and is then the current format associated with that file. The current format can be replaced in several ways: by a format appearing in the data list, by a format pattern, or by an event routine.

When transput takes place each value is transferred under the control of a picture. First the appropriate picture must be found. Usually this will be the next picture in the current format. But if, as may happen, a possibly dynamically replicated collection appears then the dynamic replicator and all the replicators in any preceding insertion (which may be absent) are elaborated collaterally. This then indicates the number of times the various items in the collection are expected on input or produced on output. Note that negative answers are treated as zero. An insertion occurring at the end of a collection is added to the final picture. Now that the values of replicators are known the next picture can be obtained (perhaps after having to repeat the above process several times due to the possibility of nested collections).

The picture itself may contain dynamic replicators. Assuming that the pattern is neither an integral choice nor a boolean choice – these cases are ignored for the moment – all replicators including those in insertions are elaborated collaterally. The picture that results by replacing its dynamic parts by the fixed values is called a *staticized* picture and it is this which now controls the transfer of the value. The type of the picture is then compared with the mode of the object being transferred and if it is compatible the transfer takes place. Incompatibility can result from errors in modes or types, erroneous bounds of multiple values, etc. but causes the event corresponding to *on value error*.

A special case can arise as a result of obtaining the next picture. Suppose the next pattern is of type *void*, i.e. the picture consists of only an insertion (which may itself be null). In this case the insertion is read on input or printed on output and the next picture is sought. Suppose a format contains a single picture with a *void* pattern. The format becomes the current format associated with the file. An attempt to locate the next picture will result in the format being repeated unless the programmer has taken special precautions by using *on format end*. Assuming no such precautions have been taken a loop results. In most cases this is terminated eventually by, on input, reading a character which does not match the insertion or, on output, reaching the end of file; in both cases event routines are called. The one situation in which this will not happen is when the format text contains both a *void* pattern and a null insertion. The format text is then $ $ and an infinite loop results.

Consider now the special case of choice patterns of either type, i.e. an integral choice or a boolean choice. In this situation the various dynamic replicators are not elaborated collaterally. Instead the following happens. The initial insertion of the choice pattern is staticized and performed, i.e. it is expected on input or produced on output. On output the appropriate literal is chosen, staticized and printed. Then the insertion part of the picture containing the choice pattern is staticized and printed. If the value selecting the appropriate literal is out of range then the routine corresponding to *on value error* is called.

310

On input the first of the alternative literals is selected and staticized. This is then expected from the input file. If there is no match the second alternative literal is selected, staticized and expected. This process is repeated until a match is found. Then the insertion part of the picture containing the choice pattern is staticized and expected. If no match is found the event routine corresponding to *on value error* is again called.

Consider now another special case, the case of a format pattern. A format pattern like any other pattern is part of a picture and as such can be followed by an insertion. The format pattern itself consists of an initial insertion and a clause delivering a format. This insertion is staticized and the clause elaborated collaterally. The insertion is then performed. The next picture is the first picture from the new format obtained by elaborating the clause. The insertion that is part of the picture containing the format pattern is added to the last picture of the new format. Successive pictures are taken from the new format until it becomes exhausted. The insertion part of the format pattern is added to the first picture of the new format and the insertion part of the picture containing the format pattern is added to the last picture of the new format. When this new format becomes exhausted control of transput is passed back to the original format without there being any intervening call to the event routine corresponding to *on format end*.

If on selecting the next picture it is found that the format has become exhausted the event format ended occurs and the appropriate event routine is called. The default action will be that the current format is started again from the beginning (see also section 9.4.6).

This then describes how transput actually occurs. When the next item is to be transferred, if there is a next item, the next picture is obtained and staticized. This is then used to transmit the required value. This process is repeated as often as necessary. The various pictures are staticized only when the appropriate item is about to be transmitted. Staticizing of pictures is therefore serial rather than collateral.

Note finally that it is quite possible to have *readf*, *putf*, etc. statements that do not have any format texts or units delivering formats in their data list. Once a format becomes associated with a file it remains so associated until it is replaced. Thus a data list not containing any formats will just make use of the current format. Note that on opening a file the format associated with that file is undefined.

9.4.12. Manipulating formats
Since **format** is a standard mode, the full power of orthogonality

can be employed to allow the manipulation of formats. However, ALGOL 68 provides no standard procedures or standard operators for their manipulation and there is relatively little one can do with formats except perform assignations or use them to control transput. Two formats cannot even be tested for equality.

When the mode **file** is expressed as a structure there is, as was mentioned earlier, a field containing an object of mode **ref format**. It follows that if a copy is taken of a file both files will have the same current format and since the format pointer is of mode **ref int** the formats are always in step.

There is a dynamic aspect associated with formats and this merits some discussion. Replicators can be dynamic in nature in that they are elaborated only when encountered and the value they deliver may depend on the values of certain variables. This dynamic aspect can occur also in format patterns and in general patterns where the parameters can be units delivering integers.

This dynamic feature necessitates some care since one must not associate with a file a format of lesser scope.

Example 9.4.12a. The scope problem and formats.
The statement

$$writef (($ n(length) x 4d $, size))$$

where *length* is of mode **ref int** would produce a scoping error. The scope of the format is equal to the scope of *length*, at most the whole of the user's program. The standard output file has a larger scope.

9.5. Binary transput

Binary transput was described briefly in the introduction to this chapter. This form of transput is used when information has to be sent out to a book only to be read in again by the same or a different program. It is assumed that the information has not to be read by a programmer and hence there is no need to put the information in an intelligible form.

Binary transput can only be performed using files for which the standard routine *bin possible* returns **true**. Moreover, binary output can be sent to a book only if the file on which the book is opened admits writing and binary transput. Similarly binary input can be taken from a book only if the file on which the book is opened admits reading and binary transput.

Using binary transput is an efficiency measure since there is a

312

saving in converting to character form on output and from character form on input. But though this saving exists there is a subsequent danger: all the protection afforded by modes is thrown to the wind. To illustrate this last point consider what happens on reading an integer such as 123 using *read*, i.e. assuming the data is in character form. The reading takes place quite satisfactorily if the data is in the required form. But if 123 appears as, say, *A* then an event would have occurred and presumably a message given as part of the default action indicating that *A* is illegal and a sign or digit was expected. But if the *A* were in binary form rather than in character form no such error would be flagged. An appropriate bit pattern would be absorbed by the appropriate input routine and this would be used as an integer. In fact, in general the programmer can assume only that if his information was written to a given position in a file then it can be read back by first positioning the file as before and then reading.

The procedures used to transfer information to the standard file referred to by *standback* are *writebin* for output and *readbin* for input. Note that this file can be used for both output and input. These procedures are denoted by identifiers reminiscent of their counterparts for character transput. They have as their parameter a single item or a list of items similar in all respects but one to the parameter of a *read* or *print* statement: the only difference is that procedures cannot appear as parameters. In particular, *space*, *newline*, *newpage*, *backspace*, etc. cannot now be used.

One consequence of the use of binary transput is that the terminator string associated with a file is not used to end input of a dynamic number of items. If this is attempted, e.g. by reading into a flexible array, the effect is to take the current size of the array and to read that number of elements. However, it may still be sensible to have the terminator associated with a file, for many files which accept binary information can under the appropriate circumstances also accept character transput.

With binary transput the event routines are still meaningful and will be called at the appropriate time. Thus when the end of a line is reached the line end event routine is called, similarly for page end, etc.

The routines *writebin* and *readbin* transput information to and from *standback*. The routines provided for transput of binary information to and from other files which accept binary are *putbin* and *getbin*. These have two parameters, the first of which is a reference to the relevant file and the second of which is a data list similar in form to the data list allowed by *readbin* and *writebin*.

Example 9.5a. Using binary transput.

Consider the problem of creating a temporary file to hold the various elements of a multiple value q of size 10000. Thus the elements of q have to be written to the temporary file and later read back. It is assumed that the information to be placed in the file has not to be read by the programmer. Hence binary transput is used.

The pieces of program below indicate a possible solution to this problem. The first piece of program indicates the creating of a file and the writing of information to it. *chan5* is assumed to be a channel with the necessary properties, i.e. it allows the reading and writing of binary information and it can be reset.

> **file** *temp*; *create* (*temp*, *chan5*);
> **begin** [10000] **int** q;
>   # there follow calculations to evaluate the elements of
>   the multiple value referred to by q #
>   . . .
>   *putbin* (*temp*, *q*)
> **end**

The next piece of program indicates the retrieving of the information and the closing of the temporary file.

> **begin** [10000] **int** q;
>   *reset* (*temp*); *getbin* (*temp*, *q*); *scratch* (*temp*);
>   # remaining calculations involving q follow #
>   . . .
> **end**

Certain kinds of files will allow both binary and character transput. It would be highly undesirable for these kinds of information to be freely mixed.

For suitable sequential access files the programmer can decide, once the file has been opened, to transmit information in either binary or character form. Once he so decides he must not change the form of the information until he resets the file (assuming this is possible). At that stage he can again decide on what form of information to transmit. The earlier restrictions (see section 9.3.4) regarding the reading and writing of information to sequential files still apply.

For suitable random access files the programmer can mix binary and character transput as he so wishes. However what has been printed in character form must be read back in character form, and similarly for binary information. Thus the programmer himself has the responsibility of remembering where various kinds of information have been placed. Again the restrictions of section 9.3.4 apply.

This completes the chapter on ALGOL 68 transput and indeed the book (the word being used here in the non-technical sense!). No attempt has been made to cover every single detail of the programming language ALGOL 68. Ultimately the interested reader will have to refer to the (Revised) ALGOL 68 Report. This is the document that defines the language and it is the ultimate authoritative guide.

Exercises on chapter 9

1. What is the effect of both $printf(-1000)$ and $printf(1000)$ when the format associated with *standout* is
   (i) $\$4zd\$$ (ii) $\$3z+d\$$
   (iii) $\$4z-d\$$ (iv) $\$d3z\$$
   (v) $\$-d3z\$$?

2. What is the effect of each of $printf(1.234e4)$, $printf(-1.234e4)$ and $printf(-1.234e-4)$ when the format associated with *standout* is
   (i) $\$+.4d\$$ (ii) $\$+s.4d\$$
   (iii) $\$-s.4d\$$ (iv) $\$d.3dezd\$$
   (v) $\$-d.3de+d\$$ (vi) $\$+zzd.dde-d\$$?

3. Suppose that in reading an item of mode **bits** only the
   (i) leftmost 4 bits are supplied
   (ii) rightmost 4 bits are supplied.
   The remaining bits are suppressed. Design *readf* statements to cope with these two situations.

4. How is the string terminator of a file, opened by means of the standard procedure *open*, initialised?

5. In unformatted transput *print* (123) would cause an integer to be printed. Could it conceivably happen that, without resorting to the use of choice patterns, $printf(123)$ would result in the printing of a real number with an exponent part?

6. Given

   $[10, 10]$ **int** aa

   would the following be acceptable?
   (i) $printf((\$6z+d\$, aa))$
   (ii) $printf((\$10(6z+d) \, l\$, aa))$
   (iii) $printf((\$10(6z+d)\$, aa, newline))$

7. Given

   $[10, 10]$ **char** a, $[100]$ **char** b

which of the following would be correct?

   (i) *printf*((a, a, b))   (ii) *printf*(($10al$, a))
  (iii) *printf*(($10al$, b))   (iv) *printf*(($100a$, a))
   (v) *printf*(($100a$, b))

8. It is required to have procedures for performing the following three separate tasks:

    (i) replace the first occurrence of a substring s in a string u by a string t;

    (ii) insert the string t before the first occurrence of the substring s in the string u;

    (iii) insert the string t after the first occurrence of the substring s in the string u.

Design one single procedure which when suitably called will achieve the effect of (i), (ii) or (iii) as appropriate.

9. The letters r, a and b are used to denote the 'replace', 'after' and 'before' commands corresponding to (i), (ii) and (iii) of the previous question. If c denotes any of these commands then

$$c/string1/string2/$$

will indicate that, using the notation of the previous example, s is replaced by *string 1* and t by *string 2*. The string u is assumed to be some line in a file. Using the procedure obtained as a result of the previous example show how this command can be implemented. Note that the character following r, a or b (not necessarily "/") should act as delimiter.

10. Write procedures which will (assuming suitable sequential files)

    (i) append the contents of one file to the end of another file;

    (ii) insert the contents of one file after line n of another file; produce an error message if n is inappropriate.

11. A user wishes to print page numbers at the foot of each page of his output file. Can he do this by adjusting the page size so that the *on page end* routine can be programmed to take the necessary action? If not how can he achieve the desired effect?

12. Design a procedure which will produce a copy of another file. Note that the contents, format, terminator string, etc., have all to be copied. The two files should differ in only one respect: their identification strings should be different.

13. Can the event routine corresponding to *on char error* ever be called as a result of output and, if so, under what circumstances?

14. In printing information it is required to always start printing at column n, say. Indicate how this can be achieved automatically by suitable adjustment of the event routines.

15. How might you arrange that integers can be read with
    (i) spaces
    (ii) either spaces or commas
used for indicating thousands? Thus 1024 could appear as 1,024.

16. The call *printf*(n) where n is an integer can result in n being widened. How do you reconcile this with the fact that the parameter of *printf* has mode

    [ ] **union** (**int, real, compl**, . . .)?

17. It is required to read a polynomial of the form

    $$4x \uparrow 6 + 7x \uparrow 2 + x + 4$$

    by writing

    do *readf* (($g''x\uparrow''$, $g\$, coeff, power$));
        poly := **loc term** := (*coeff, power, poly*)
    od

    where the various identifiers and modes have their obviously intended meanings. Design appropriate on routines to take care of terms such as x and 4.

18. In the programming language FORTRAN the notation F10.3 when used for input in a format means that the reading routine would expect to find a real number (F denotes a floating-point number without any exponent part) occupying 10 character positions including any sign, the decimal point and all the digits. The 3 indicates that, in the absence of a decimal point, it will be assumed that 3 digits follow the point (spaces act as zeros). However if the decimal point is present then its presence will over-ride that expected by the format. Could this effect be achieved in ALGOL 68
    (i) when the decimal point is absent
    (ii) when the decimal point is present?

19. Design a call of *readf* which has the effect of transferring an external real number with at least two digits after the decimal point and no exponent part to an internal value but in the process multiplying it by

    (i) 10   (ii) 10^2

Can you generalise this to perform multiplication by 10^r where $r \geq 1$?

20. It is required to read and process a sequence of records all of the same format. But unfortunately the exact format is unknown at the time of writing the program. However it is known that the records will consist of sequences of digits and characters separated by spaces. It is proposed that an extra record should be added at the start of the data and this would indicate the format of all subsequent records. The form of this preliminary record might typically be *ddddxxxaaaaaxxaaxd* where *d* denotes digit, *x* denotes space and *a* denotes character. If this preliminary record alone occupies the first line of input write appropriate instructions which will allow subsequent records to be read in the required format.

21. In defining the requirements for a job to be submitted to a computer it is decided to allow the specification of non-default requirements by means of an HLS (high-level scheduler) parameter in the job card, e.g. JOB ADMCG, :CADU10, HLS (JT = 120, MT = 2)
The parameters that can appear as part of the HLS parameter, their meaning and default values are given below:

MT number of magnetic tapes		0
JT job time in seconds		10
SIZE store requirements		10
OUT number of lines of output		500

Write a piece of program to process a job card and print out the job requirements.

Programming problems for chapter 9

1. Write a program to list an arbitrary file complete with line numbers and page numbers.

2. A set of data consists of a sequence of records each containing a person's name, a comma, the character "M" or "F" indicating the sex of the person, another comma and finally the person's age as a three-digit number (initial zeros can be replaced by blanks). Write a program to print at the left hand side of the page the names of those people who have retired and at the right hand side the names of those who have not retired. It is assumed that men retire at 65 and women retire at 60.

   The loop clause of your program should contain just one call of *readf* and one call of *printf*.

318

3. Implement a simple editor. Include commands to

(i) move forward to a particular line indicated by line number or by the first few (significant?) characters;

(ii) insert several lines of text;

(iii) delete lines of text;

(iv) include the contents of another file;

(v) insert information before or after a particular point in the current line;

(vi) replace in the current line the first occurrence of a string by another string.

4. A simple system to use a computer as a teaching aid can be designed as follows. (This is basically a very simple version of IBM's Coursewriter III.)

A file is prepared and each line is preceded by an operation code.

qu	indicates that the contents of this line is part of a question.
ca	indicates that the line contains the correct answer to the previous question.
ty	indicates that the information on this line has to be typed.
wa	indicates wrong answer is on the line (it has been anticipated)
un	indicates unanticipated answer; there will be a request to try again.

A typical lesson might look like

qu	Simple Arithmetic
qu	Lesson I
qu	Add 2 and 3
ca	5
ty	Very good
wa	23
ty	You seem to have made a mistake. The numbers
ty	have to be added.
un	Wrong. Try again
qu	Next question
qu	. . .

Implement such a system.

5. Devise a program which takes a piece of text and attempts to output that text in such a manner that the right hand edges are not ragged. Each full-stop should be separated from the start of the next sentence by at least two spaces and each word should be separated from its neighbour by at least one space.

Extra spaces should be added from the left side of a line and the right side of a line alternatively. Moreover the distinguishing

319

feature of the end of a sentence should be maintained.

6. Design a simple system to facilitate document preparation. Each line of input is either text – and therefore part of the document – or a control line which passes information to the program. Assume that control lines start with the character " ?".

It will be necessary to devise codes for the control lines but

S5   might indicate skip 5 lines

N   might mean take new page

K4   might imply that the next 4 lines should be on the same page, etc.

It might also be necessary to have page numbers appearing at the top left of left hand pages and the top right of right hand pages, different headings at the top of alternate pages, etc.

(Note that the above and the program from the previous example could be conveniently combined.)

7. Write a program to produce a sensible layout of ALGOL 68 programs. Document clearly any limiting assumptions you make.

Chapter 2

1. Only (i) and (iii) are legal.
2. Two numbers 6 and 324 are printed. Otherwise there would be ambiguity about whether two numbers or the one integer 6324 should be printed.
3. Only (ii), (vi) and (vii) are legal. See definition of real denotation.
4. No.
5. *ab* might mean multiplication of *a* and *b* or it might mean the variable *ab*.
6. (i) Each of *x, y, z* is of mode **ref real**.
   (ii) **char**. (iii) **real**. (iv) **ref real**.
   (v) *x, y* of mode **ref real**, *z* of mode **int** and *t* of mode **ref bool**.
7. (ii) and (iv) are already identity declarations.
   (i) **ref real** $x = $ **loc real** $:= 2.7$
   (iii) **ref char** $a = $ **loc char** $:= "A"$, **ref char** $b = $ **loc char**
8. (i) Legal. (ii) Illegal; *e* declared twice. (iii) Illegal; *e* must be a variable since it is used in *read(e)*.
9. (i) $(a \times b)/c$ (ii) $a + (b \uparrow n)$
   (iii) $(((a \times b) \times c) + ((a \uparrow b) \uparrow c)) + ((a/b)/c)$
   (iv) $(((-a) \uparrow b) \uparrow c) + d$ (v) $(-c) \times ((-d) \uparrow e)$
   (vi) $(a - (-(+b))) - (-(-c))$
10. (i) **real**, 1. (ii) **real**, 16. (iii) **int**, 81.
    (iv) **int**, 0. (v) **int**, 0. (vi) **int**, 2.
11. (i) $2, 7, 3$. (ii) $-26, 7, 3$. (iii) $-10, 1, 3$.
12. (i) Apply **abs** and then widen.
    (ii) Apply **abs** and widen.
    (iii) Apply **round** or **entier** and then **repr**.
    (iv) Widen. (v) Apply **abs** and **repr**.
13. (i), (iii) Result is undefined.

(ii) Legal and $n = 20$.　(iv) Illegal.

14. (i) n is dereferenced.　(ii) x is dereferenced.　(iii) Illegal.
(iv) Illegal.　(v) x dereferenced and **entier** x widened.
(vi) Illegal.　(vii) x dereferenced.　(viii) Illegal.
(ix) Legal.　(x) Result of $n + := 2$ is dereferenced.

15. $(((x + 4) < (y + z)) = ((a/b) < 2))$ **or** $((a < b)$ **and** $(x < y))$

16. (i), (iv), (vi) are illegal. In case (vi) the result of $y := 2$ cannot be assigned to n.　(ii) is legal, dereferencing of n and m takes place. In (iii) n and m are dereferenced and the result of $n + m \uparrow 2$ is widened. In (v) the result produced by $n := 2$ is dereferenced and widened. The result produced by $y := n := 2$ is dereferenced.

17. n **mod** $m = 0$.

18. A priori mode of n is always **ref int** and of x is **ref real**.
(i) A posteriori modes are **int** and **real**, syntactic position of n and x is firm.
(ii) A posteriori mode is **real**, and position is strong.
(iii) A posteriori modes are **int** and **ref real**; positions are firm and soft.
(iv) A posteriori mode of first occurrence of x is **ref real**, of second occurrence is **real**; a posteriori mode of n is **int**; corresponding syntactic positions are soft, strong and firm.

19. (i) and (iii) undefined since x is used and altered.

20. Yes.

21. Multiplies by 10.

22. No.

23. No.

Chapter 3

1. (i) *real width + exp width + 4*
(ii) *real width + exp width + 5*.

2. (i) **ref int**　(ii) **bool**　(iii) **char**　(iv) **ref int**.

3. The result of the serial clause, n, is dereferenced; in $y := n + 10$, n is dereferenced; the result of $n + 10$ is widened, $y := n + 10$ is voided. The source of $x := \ldots$ is widened.

4. No, numbers to be printed are elaborated collaterally.

5. No, since the conditional does not produce a balanced mode.

6. (i) (**int** $m := 0$; **while** $m\uparrow2 < n$ **do** $m + := 1$ **od**; $m\uparrow2 = n$)
   (ii) (**int** $m := n$; **while** m **mod** $2 = 0$ **do** $m \div := 2$ **od**; $m = 1$)
   (iii) $(n = 0)$.
   (iv) See 'prime numbers', section 3.10.4.

7. No, since space is relinquished at end of closed clause.

8. 4.7   7   4.7.

9. **begin to** (**int** n; $read\ (n)$; n) **do** $sum + := $ (**real** x; $read(x)$; x) **od**;
          $print\ (sum)$
   end.

10. 7   11.

11. 5   10   10   10   10   10   10.

12. (i) $n + := 1$ is never elaborated.
    (ii) $n + := 1$ is never elaborated.
    (iii) loops indefinitely.

13. $ch/ = "+"$ **or** $ch/ = "-"$ always produces **true**.

14. (i) 5 times.   (ii) 6 times.

15. Yes.

16. (i) The result produced by source is widened.
    (ii) y is dereferenced, and 0 widened.
    (iii) n and m are both dereferenced and widened.

17. **exit** must be followed by a label; nor can **exit** start a serial clause.

18. Yes.

Chapter 4

1. (i) **ref** [ ] **int** $nn = $ **loc** [10] **int**.
   (ii) **ref** [, ,] **int** $nnn = $ **loc** [10, 4, 6] **int**.
   (iii) The declaration is already an identity declaration.

2. (i) $n\ [0, j]$ $1 \le j \le 5$,   bounds being 1 and 5.
   (ii) $n\ [i, 1]$ $0 \le i \le 10$,   bounds being 1 and 11.
   (iii) $n\ [i, 0]$ $-7 \le i \le 100$,   bounds being 1 and 108.
   (iv) $n\ [1, j]$ $0 \le j \le 10$,   bounds being 2 and 12.
   (v) $n\ [i, 1]$ $-7 \le i \le 5$,   bounds being 1 and 13.

3. Arrays are not needed at all.

4. Assume set of $n+1$ integers is in *standin* $(n \geqq 0)$.
   (i) $max := (\textbf{int } d; read(d); d)$;
        for i **to** n **do** $(\textbf{int } d; read(d); d > max \mid max := d)$ **od**
   (iii) $max := (\textbf{int } d; read(d); d)$; $posn := 0$;
        for i **to** n **do** $(\textbf{int } d; read(d); d > max \mid (max := d,$
        $posn := i))$ **od**.

5. **int** *value* $:= 0$;
   for i **to** 32 **do** $value := 2 \times value + \textbf{abs } array[i]$ **od**;
   print (*value*).

6. No. Ambiguity could arise – trimming or labelled subscript?

7. $a[n-r+1:n] := a[1:r]$; **for** i **to** $n-r$ **do** $a[i] := 0$ **od**.

8. (i) $(max := mark[1,1]$;
         for i **from** 2 **to** 100
         do if $mark[1,i] > max$ **then** $max := mark[1,i]$ **fi**
         od; max)
    (ii) $(max := mark[1,1]$;
         for i **to** 10
         do for j **to** 100
             do if $max > mark[i,j]$ **then** $max := mark[i,j]$ **fi od**
         od; max)
    (iii) $mark[7,]$
    (iv) $([10] \textbf{ real } average$;
         for i **to** 10
         do $average[i] := (\textbf{int } sum := 0$;
                         for j **to** 100 **do** $sum +:= mark[i,j]$ **od**;
                         $sum/100)$
         od; $average$)

9. $(\textbf{bool } equal := \textbf{lwb } a = \textbf{lwb } b \textbf{ and upb } a = \textbf{upb } b$;
    for i **from** **lwb** a **to** **upb** a **while** $equal$
    do $equal := a[i] = b[i]$ **od**;
    $equal$)

10. **int** $t = r \textbf{ mod } n$;
    $[\,] \textbf{ int } p = q[n-t+1:n]$; $q[t+1:n] := q[1:n-t]$; $q[1:t] := p$
    For rotation to left, the last line would be replaced by
    $[\,] \textbf{ int } p = q[1:t]$; $q[1:n-t] := q[t+1:n]$; $q[n-t+1:n] := p$

11. Calculate x^2. From this, one multiplication produces x^4, etc.

12. Multiplication would be programmed as follows, assuming $n \times n$
    matrices a and b.

324

```
        for i to n
        do for j to n
           do c[i,j] := (int sum := 0;
                         for k to n do sum +:= a[i,k] × b[k,j] od;
                         sum)
           od
        od
```

The efficiency of the above could be improved by reducing the number of subscripts (see example 4.1.10d(ii)). Addition and subtraction are simpler and involve double loops containing

$$c[i,j] := a[i,j] + b[i,j] \text{ and } c[i,j] := a[i,j] - b[i,j].$$

13. When the required fields are known at compile time.

14.   (i)   **ref struct (int** a, b**)** $x =$ **loc struct (int** a, b**)** $:= (2, 3)$
   (ii) **ref struct ([ ] char** x**, int** a**)** $y =$ **loc struct (**[5] **char** x**, int** a**)**
  (iii) **ref struct ([,] real** x**, [ ] bool** t**)** $z =$ **loc struct**
        (**[4, 7] real** x**, [7] bool** t**)**

15. All are illegal due to mode considerations; conditionals require balanced mode.

16.   (i)   **mode ratn = struct (int** num, den**)**
   (ii) **mode point = struct (real** x $coord$, y $coord$**)**
  (iii) **mode poly =** [1 $:n$] **point**
  (iv) **mode circle = struct (point** $centre$, **real** $radius$**)**
   (v) **mode line = struct (real** m, c**)**
In case (v) the line is assumed to be of the form $y = mx + c$. Other representations may be better depending on circumstances.

Chapter 5

1. (i) **real.**   (ii) **proc (real) real.**   (iii) Depends on position of serial clause.

2. Parameter must be unit. Serial clause is not a unit.

3. (i) **op** $\uparrow$ **= (int** x, n**) real**: **(real** $y = x$; $y \uparrow n$**)**
Result of $2 \uparrow 3$ is real.
(ii) **op** $\uparrow$ **= (real** x, y**) real**: $(x \leqq 0 | error | exp$ $(y \times ln(x)))$

4. **op** $? =$ **(ref real** x, **real** y**) real**: **(real** $z = x$; $x := y$; z**)**
The values referred to by p and q are interchanged.

5. **op** $+ / =$ **(ref real** x, **real** y**) real**: **(real** $z = x$; $x := x + y$; z**)**
  op $- / =$ **(ref real** x, **real** y**) real**: **(real** $z = x$; $x := x - y$; z**)**

6. Monadic symbols: (i), (v), (vii). Dyadic symbols: (i), (iii), (v), (vii).

7. **proc** *two* = (**int** *n*) **int**:
    if *n* = 0 **then** − 1 **else int** *m* := *n*, *count* := 0;
        while *m* **mod** 2 = 0 **do** (*count* + := 1, *m* ÷ := 2)
            od;
        count
   fi

8. Yes. 　　　　　　9. No.

10. A jump to one of the three labels occurs.

11. *sin* (1) + *sin* (2) + ... + *sin* (100) is calculated.

12. No.

13. Elements of *a* are adjusted and then used in a subsequent calculation of a different element of *a*. To rectify, copy *a*.

14. *count* calculates the number of subsets of *st* with the property described by *pred*.

15. In all cases, yes, but it is not possible to access the outer operator.

16. (i)　**op straighten** = ([,] **int** *a*)[ ] **int**:
        begin int *l1* = 1 **lwb** *a*, *l2* = 2 **lwb** *a*,
            u1 = 1 **upb** *a*, *u2* = 2 **upb** *a*;
        int *length* = *u2* − *l2* + 1;
        [(*u1* − *l1* + 1) × *length*] **int** *result*;
        for *i* **to** *u1* − *l1* + 1
        do *result* [1 + (*i* − 1) × *length*: *i* × *length*]
                                := *a*[*i* + *l1* − 1, @1] **od**;
        result
      end
   (ii) is similar.

Chapter 7

1. Only (i) is legal since displays cannot occupy weak positions.

2. (i) No, since **ref string** is the mode of a name.
   (ii) Yes.　(iii) No.

3. (i) *x* [1]
   (ii) [4] **real** *z*; **for** *i* **to** 4 **do** *z* [*i*] := *x* [*i*] [1] **od**; *z*
   (iii) No, since coercions are not suitable.

4. Both are acceptable; dereferencing is only coercion.

5. No; coercions and deflexing not applicable.

6. (iii) and (iv) are legal.

7. All are legal.

8. (i) and (ii) are correct. (iii) would be illegal since = is not defined between united modes. (iv) is illegal since the required coercion cannot be performed.

9. Only (iv) and (vi) are illegal.

10. Mode is acceptable but declaration is illegal. Coercions applied to (1, 2, 3) move inside the brackets and cannot therefore give the required mode.

11. A syntax error. See previous answer.

12. (i) and (ii) are legitimate, the coercions being uniting and rowing. (iii) is not legitimate.

13. Acceptable. $t[1]$ is of a priori mode transient-reference-to-flexible-row-of-character. The deflexed mode required as source is therefore [ ] **char**.

14. (i) Illegal since $x[1]$ must be assigned a fixed length string.
    (ii) Illegal, for same reason as in (i).
    (iii) Legal, $"A"$ being rowed.
    (iv) Legal.
    (v) and (vi) are correct assuming bounds of sources are correct.

15. (i) transient-reference-to-flexible-row-of-string.
    (ii) transient-reference-to-string.
    (iii) transient-reference-to-character.
    (iv) transient-reference-to-row-of-string.
    (v) transient-reference-to-flexible-row-of-string.

16. No, result is 0.

17. Mode of a is **ref** [ ] **ref int** and this cannot be coerced to the required mode.

18. (i) is legal, (ii) is not.

19. Within the routine text would be a conformity to determine the original modes of a and b. The meaning of equality between two integers must be defined but this cannot be done using = since the operands would be united thereby producing a recursive call. Another operator symbol such as **eq** would have to be used.

20. All are legal. (i) 1 :2 and 1 :0. In cases (ii), (iii) and (iv) 1 :0 and 1 :0.

21. Not in cases (iii) or (iv).

22. Yes. Checks can be made by the compiler on the handling of transient names.

23. **b** and **ref a** are equivalent modes.

24. No. See calling mechanism and scope of routines.

Chapter 9

1. (i)   event takes place ⊥ 1000
    (ii) − 1000   + 1000
    (iii) ⊥ − 1000   ⊥ ⊥ 1000
    (iv) event takes place 1 ⊥ ⊥ ⊥
    (v)   − 1 ⊥ ⊥ ⊥   ⊥ 1 ⊥ ⊥ ⊥

2. (i)   event   event   − .0001
    (ii) event   event   − 0001
    (iii) event   event   − 0001
    (iv) 1.234_{10} ⊥ 4   event   event
    (v)   ⊥ 1.234_{10} + 4   − 1.234_{10} + 4   − 1.234_{10} − 4
    (vi) + 123.40_{10} ⊥ 2   − 123.40_{10} ⊥ 2   − 123.40_{10} − 6

3. (i) *readf* (($2r4d28sd$, *item*))
    (ii) *readf* (($2r28sd4d$, *item*))
    assuming in both cases that *bitswidth* is 32.

4. Initialised to the null string.

5. Yes.

6. (iii) is illegal since *newline* cannot be used.

7. (ii), (v) are correct.

8. Design a procedure to locate the start of string *s*. Then apply trimming, etc.

9. Use *make term* to obtain the strings.

10. (i) Use *on logical file end* to change to the other file.
    (ii) Create a new file and use *on logical file end* for error messages, etc.

11. No. Effect achieved using *on line end* and checking line number.

12. Use *create* and perform the copying.

13. Yes, if conversion is unsuccessful.

14. Use *on line end* to adjust current character number.

15. If expected character is 0, check for spaces (and perhaps commas). Use *on char error* to pick up the next character.

16. Within the alternative of the conformity clause dealing with real patterns, the integer is widened.

17. Use *on char error* to produce a routine to perform the necessary backspacing and supply the default characters.

18.   (i) Yes, use $\$ - 6zs.3z\ \$$ and make suitable adjustment to event routines to take care of possible initial $+$.

       (ii) Possible, but awkward, e.g. read next 10 characters, find position of point using *char in string*, then use dynamic replicators.

19. Suitable format texts would be $\$4d".''ds.d\ \$, \$4d".''dds.\ \$,$ $\$4d".''n(r)ds.\ \$$

20. Use dynamic replicators.

21. Use choice patterns to look for JT, MT, etc.

This appendix summarises the information contained in the ALGOL 68 standard environment, i.e. the standard modes, environment enquiries, mathematical constants and functions, the standard operations and transput declarations. Only a brief note is included on the meaning of each identifier, indication, etc.

To save needless repetition **l int** will be used to denote integers of any size (i.e. containing any number of **long**s or any number of **short**s). A similar notation is used in connection with **real, compl, bits** and **bytes**. Unless otherwise stated it will always happen that the operands of a dyadic operator are of the same size and the result will be of that size. Similarly the result of a monadic operator will, unless otherwise stated, be of the same size as the operand.

In certain cases a family of identifiers of different sizes must appear, e.g. *max int, long max int, short max int*, etc. For convenience these are typified by *l max int*, the corresponding mode being **l int**. The notation **long l int, short l int** is used to indicate that the size has been increased or decreased by 1.

A.1. Standard modes

The standard modes are

> **void, l int, l real, l compl, bool, char,**
> **l bits, l bytes, string, sema, channel, file, format.**

Other modes are constructed from these by using mode declarations together with **ref, struct, proc, flex, union,** [ ], [,], etc.

A.2. Environment enquiries

Identifiers	Mode	Meaning
int lengths	**int**	1 + number of **long**s that can be added to increase the number of distinguishable integers
int shorts	**int**	1 + number of **short**s that can be added to decrease the number of distinguishable integers

Identifiers	Mode	Meaning
l max int	l int	the largest l int value
real lengths	int	1 + number of **long**s that can be added to increase the number of distinguishable reals
real shorths	int	1 + number of **short**s that can be added to decrease the number of distinguishable reals
l max real	l real	largest l real value
l small real	l real	accuracy to which l real values are held
bits lengths	int	1 + number of **long**s that can be added to increase the number of distinguishable bits values
bits shorths	int	1 + number of **short**s that can be added to decrease the number of distinguishable bits values
l bits width	int	number of elements in an l **bits** value
bytes lengths	int	1 + number of **long**s that can be added to increase the number of distinguishable bytes values
bytes shorths	int	1 + number of **short**s that can be added to decrease the number of distinguishable bytes values
l bytes width	int	number of elements in an l **bytes** value
max abs char	int	largest character code
null character	char	some character
flip	char	representation of **true** during transput
flop	char	representation of **false** during transput
errorchar	char	used in transput for unconvertible arithmetic values
blank	char	**char** *blank* = " "

The environment enquiries properly include all those standard declarations which specify implementation dependent aspects of ALGOL 68 (ignoring transput). They therefore also include the operators **abs**, which converts from **char** to **int**, and **repr**, which converts from **int** to **char**.

A.3. Mathematical constants and functions

Identifier	Mode	Meaning
l pi	l real	3.14159...
l sqrt	proc (l real) l real	square root
l exp	proc (l real) l real	exponential
l ln	proc (l real) l real	logarithm
l cos	proc (l real) l real	cosine
l arccos	proc (l real) l real	inverse cosine
l sin	proc (l real) l real	sine

Identifier	Mode	Meaning
l arcsin	**proc (l real) l real**	inverse sine
l tan	**proc (l real) l real**	tan
l arctan	**proc (l real) l real**	inverse tan
l next random	**proc (ref l int) l real**	integer variable changes and corresponding real x where $0 \leq x < 1$ is produced
l last random	**ref l int**	integer variable whose values are random integers
l random	**proc l real**	produces random number x such that $0 \leq x < 1$

A.4. Standard operations

This section includes a summary of all the operators in the standard environment. Subsection A.4.1 contains a list of the symbols used for the standard operators. Included also is the standard priority of dyadic operators and a list of alternative representations. The other subsections summarise the effect of these and other monadic operators.

A.4.1. The operator symbols and standard priorities

Operator symbol	Alternative representations		Standard priority	Remarks
minusab	$-:=$		1	
plusab	$+:=$		1	
timesab	$\times :=$	$*:=$	1	
divab	$/:=$		1	
overab	$\div :=$	$\%:=$	1	
modab	$\div \times :=$	$\% \times :=$	1	
	$\div *:=$	$\% *:=$		
plusto	$+=:$		1	
or	$\vee$		2	
and	$\wedge$	&	3	
eq	$=$		4	
ne	$\neq$	$/=$	4	
lt	$<$		5	
le	$\leqq$	$<=$	5	
ge	$\geqq$	$>=$	5	
gt	$>$		5	
$-$			6	
$+$			6	
$\times$	$*$		7	
$/$			7	
$\div$	$\%$	**over**	7	
mod	$\div \times$	$\div *$	7	
	$\% \times$	$\% *$		
elem	$\square$		7	
$\uparrow$	$**$	**up**	8	exponential

Operator symbol	Alternative representations		Standard priority	Remarks
↑	**up**	**shl**	8	shift left
down	**shr**	↓	8	shift right
down				semaphores
up				semaphores
lwb	∟		8	
upb	⌐		8	
i	⊥ |	+× +*	9	

A.4.2. Operations on multiple values

1. When treated as dyadic operators (standard priority 8) i **lwb** a and i **upb** a give the lower and upper bounds respectively of the ith dimension of a.

2. When treated as monadic operators **lwb** a and **upb** a are equivalent to, respectively, 1 **lwb** a and 1 **upb** a.

A.4.3. The arithmetic operators

For convenience these operators are divided into three sets, the dyadic, monadic and comparison operators.

The dyadic operators

1. The operators $+$, $-$ and $\times$ are defined between operands of mode **l int**, **l real** and **l compl** of the same size in any combination. If a complex operand is involved the result is of mode **l compl**; otherwise, if a real operand is involved the result is of mode **l real**; otherwise the result is of mode **l int**.

2. The operator / is defined between operands of mode **l int**, **l real** and **l compl** of the same size in any combination. If a complex operand is involved the result is of mode **l compl**; otherwise it is of mode **l real**.

3. ÷ and **mod** are defined only for operands of mode **l int**. The result is also of this mode.

4. The exponential operator ↑ is defined for left hand operands of mode **l int**, **l real** or **l compl** and right hand operands of mode **int**. The mode of the result is always that of the left hand operand.

5. The operator **i** operates between objects of mode **l int** and **l real** in any combination and gives a result of mode **l compl**.

The monadic operators

Operator	Mode of operand	Mode of result	Remarks
+	l int	l int	
	l real	l real	
	l compl	l compl	

The monadic operators (*Contd.*)

Operator	Mode of operand	Mode of result	Remarks
−	l int	l int	negation
	l real	l real	
	l compl	l compl	
abs	l int	l int	absolute value
	l real	l real	
	l compl	l real	
sign	l int	int	sign of operand
	l real	int	
odd	l int	bool	parity
leng	l int	long l int	increases size
	l real	long l real	
	l compl	long l compl	
shorten	l int	short l int	decreases size
	l real	short l real	
	l compl	short l compl	
round	l real	l int	
entier	l real	l int	alternatively, L
re	l compl	l real	real part
im	l compl	l real	imaginary part
conj	l compl	l compl	complex conjugate
arg	l compl	l real	argument

The comparison operators

1. The comparison operators $<, \leq, =, \neq, \geq, >$ are defined between integers and reals of the same size in all combinations. The result is always of mode **bool**.

2. The operators $=$ and $\neq$ are defined between all combinations of integers, reals and complexes of the same size, the result being of mode **bool**.

A.4.4. Boolean and bit manipulation

The operators for manipulating boolean and bits values are summarised below. However the first remark concerns a family of procedures for converting booleans to bits values.

1. The procedures *l bits pack* convert a boolean multiple value to an object of mode **l bits**.

2. The boolean operators **and, or, not** ($\sim$, $\rightarrow$), **eq, ne** are defined for boolean operands; they are also defined on operands of mode **l bits**.

3. The comparison operators $\leq$ and $\geq$ are defined between operands of mode **l bits**. The result is of mode **bool**.

4. **abs** converts booleans to integers and **l bits** values to corresponding **l int** values; **bin** converts **l int** values to **l bits** values.

5. *lb* **shl** *i* and *lb* **shr** *i* shift the **l bits** value by an amount *i* (*i* is integral).

6. **leng** increases by 1 the size of a bits value; **shorten** corresponding-

ly decreases it by 1.

7. *i* **elem** *lb* selects the ith element of the **l bits** value *lb* (*i* is integral).

A.4.5. Character and string manipulation

A summary of the standard operators for manipulating characters, strings and all sizes of bytes is given below. However the first remark concerns a family of procedures.

1. The procedures *l bytes pack* convert a string to an object of mode **l bytes**.

2. The comparison operators ($<, \leq, =, \neq, >, \geq$) are defined to operate between all combinations of characters and strings; they are also defined between objects of mode **l bytes**.

3. The dyadic operator + is defined to operate between characters and strings in arbitrary combinations and it performs concatenation. The result is always of mode **string**.

4. The dyadic operator × with standard priority 7 allows concatenation of copies of a string or character. The result is of mode **string**. One operand is of mode **int**, the other of mode **char** or **string**.

5. **leng** lengthens the size of a bytes value by 1; **shorten** reduces the size of a bytes value by 1.

6. **elem** is a dyadic operator with standard priority 7. *i* **elem** *lb* will select the ith character from *lb* which is of mode **l bytes**.

A.4.6. Operators involving assignation

Operator	Mode of left operand *a*	Mode of right operand *b*	Mode of result	Effect
plusab	**ref l int**	**l int**	**ref l int**	a := a + b
	ref l real	**l int** **l real**	**ref l real**	
	ref l compl	**l int** **l real** **l compl**	**ref l compl**	
minusab		same as **plusab**		a := a − b
timesab		same as **plusab**		a := a × b
divab	**ref l real**	**l int** **l real**	**ref l real**	a := a/b
	ref l compl	**l int** **l real** **l compl**	**ref l compl**	
overab	**ref l int**	**l int**	**ref l int**	a := a **over** b
modab	**ref l int**	**l int**	**ref l int**	a := a **mod** b
plusto	**string** **char**	**ref string**	**ref string**	b := a + b
plusab	**ref string**	**string** **char**	**ref string**	a := a + b
timesab	**ref string**	**int**	**ref string**	a := a × b

A.4.7. Synchronisation operators

All the synchronisation operators are monadic.

Operator	Mode of operand	Mode of result	Effect
level	**int**	**sema**	initialises the semaphore to the integer operand
level	**sema**	**int**	gives the integer value of the semaphore
down	**sema**	**void**	either blocks the process or decreases the value referred to by the semaphore
up	**sema**	**void**	increases by one the value referred to by the semaphore

A.5. Transput declarations

In the lists of identifiers given below **conv** appears as a mode. This is the mode of character conversion keys, a mode inaccessible to the programmer.

A.5.1. Channels and files

Identifier	Mode	Meaning
stand in channel	**channel**	standard channel for input
standout channel	**channel**	standard channel for output
standback channel	**channel**	standard channel for binary transput
estab possible	**proc (channel) bool**	yields **true** if another file can be established on this channel
stand conv	**proc (channel) conv**	yields standard conversion key for that channel
standin	**ref file**	standard input file
standout	**ref file**	standard output file
standback	**ref file**	standard binary file

A.5.2. Routines for interrogating and altering files

Identifier	Mode	Effect
get possible	**proc (ref file) bool**	indicates if reading allowed
put possible	**proc (ref file) bool**	indicates if writing allowed
bin possible	**proc (ref file) bool**	indicates if binary transput allowed
compressible	**proc (ref file) bool**	indicates if book is compressible

336

Identifier	Mode	Effect
reset possible	**proc (ref file) bool**	indicates if file can be reset
set possible	**proc (ref file) bool**	indicates if file can be set
reidf possible	**proc (ref file) bool**	indicates if identification of book can be altered
chan	**proc (ref file) channel**	returns channel on which file is opened
make conv	**proc (ref file, conv) void**	for altering conversion key
make term	**proc (ref file, string) void**	for altering terminator string
on logical file end	**proc (ref file, proc (ref file) bool) void**	for taking special action on reaching logical end of file
on physical file end	**proc (ref file, proc (ref file) bool) void**	for taking special action on reaching physical end of file
on page end	**proc (ref file, proc (ref file) bool) void**	for taking special action on reaching end of page
on line end	**proc (ref file, proc (ref file) bool) void**	for taking special action on reaching end of line
on format end	**proc (ref file, proc (ref file) bool) void**	for taking special action on reaching end of format
on value error	**proc (ref file, proc (ref file) bool) void**	for taking special kinds of action during formatted transput or during input
on char error	**proc (ref file, proc (ref file, ref char) bool) void**	for taking special action when conversion unsuccessful
reidf	**proc (ref file, string) void**	for altering identification of book
char number	**proc (ref file) int**	gives character position on current line
line number	**proc (ref file) int**	gives line number on current page
page number	**proc (ref file) int**	gives page number of book connected to file

A.5.3. Opening and closing files

Routine	Mode	Effect
establish	**proc (ref file, string, channel, int, int, int) int**	generates a book of given identification and size and connects this to file
create	**proc (ref file, channel) int**	establishes a file on the channel, the book is of default size
open	**proc (ref file, string, channel) int**	connects a book with given identification to the file
associate	**proc (ref file, ref [ ] [ ] [ ] char) void**	associates a file with an object of mode **ref [ ] [ ] [ ] char**
close	**proc (ref file) void**	closes the file
lock	**proc (ref file) void**	locks the file
scratch	**proc (ref file) void**	scratches a file

A.5.4. Identifiers associated with the layout and conversion routines

In the table below the mode **number** appears. This should be taken to include integers and reals of any size (i.e. of mode **int, long int, short int**, etc.).

Identifier	Mode	Effect
space	**proc (ref file) void**	advance to next character
backspace	**proc (ref file) void**	reduces current character position by one
newline	**proc (ref file) void**	advance to next line
newpage	**proc (ref file) void**	advance to next page
set	**proc (ref file, int, int, int) void**	sets file to stated position
reset	**proc (ref file) void**	resets file
set char number	**proc (ref file, int) void**	alter current character position
whole	**proc (number, int) string**	for printing numbers as integers
fixed	**proc (number, int, int) string**	for printing numbers as fixed point numerals
float	**proc (number, int, int, int) string**	for printing numbers as floating point numerals
char in string	**proc (char, ref int, string) bool**	tests if a character is in a string
l int width	**int**	number of digits in *l max int*
l real width	**int**	1 + number of significant digits after the point in printing a real
l exp width	**int**	number of digits in exponent part of *l max real*

A.5.5. Transput routines

Routine	Use
read	unformatted input from *stand in*
print	unformatted output to *stand out*
write	unformatted output to *standout*
get	unformatted input
put	unformatted output
readf	formatted input from *stand in*
printf	formatted output to *stand out*
writef	formatted output to *standout*
getf	formatted input
putf	formatted output
read bin	binary input from *standback*
write bin	binary output to *standback*
get bin	binary input
put bin	binary output

APPENDIX B–THE SYNTAX CHART

The chart on the following pages is due originally to J. M. Watt, J. E. L. Peck and M. Sintzoff. It summarises in a convenient form the various rules about the syntax of ALGOL 68 programs. The following notes supplement the chart which had to be modified for the purposes of printing.

1. The distinction between capital and small letters can be ignored.
2. Certain items are not defined in the chart:
   (i) LETTER-symbol: includes all the letters $a, b, c, \ldots, z$
   (ii) DIGIT-symbol: includes $0, 1, \ldots, 9$
   (iii) RADIX-symbol: for a radix of 8 this would include $0, 1, \ldots, 7$; similarly for other radices
   (iv) character-glyph: includes letters and digits together with the symbols for open and closing round brackets, a point, comma, space, plus or minus
   (v) other-string-item: includes characters other than the quotes symbol ″ or characters contained in (iv) above
   (vi) bold-TAG-symbol: identifiers in bold type
   (vii) format-texts.
3. (i) Throughout a declarer or slice, [,] may be replaced by (,)
   (ii) Throughout an ENCLOSED-clause, **begin**, **end** may be replaced by (,)
   (iii) Throughout a conditional clause, **if, then, elif, else, fi** may be replaced by (,|,|:,|,)
   (iv) Throughout a conditional clause, **case, in, ouse, out, esac** may be replaced by (,|,|:,|,)
4. A comment or pragmat, i.e. a sequence of symbols enclosed by #, ¢, **co, comment, pr** or **pragmat** can occur anywhere except within symbols or denotations.
5. For 'paranotion' read 'technical term'.

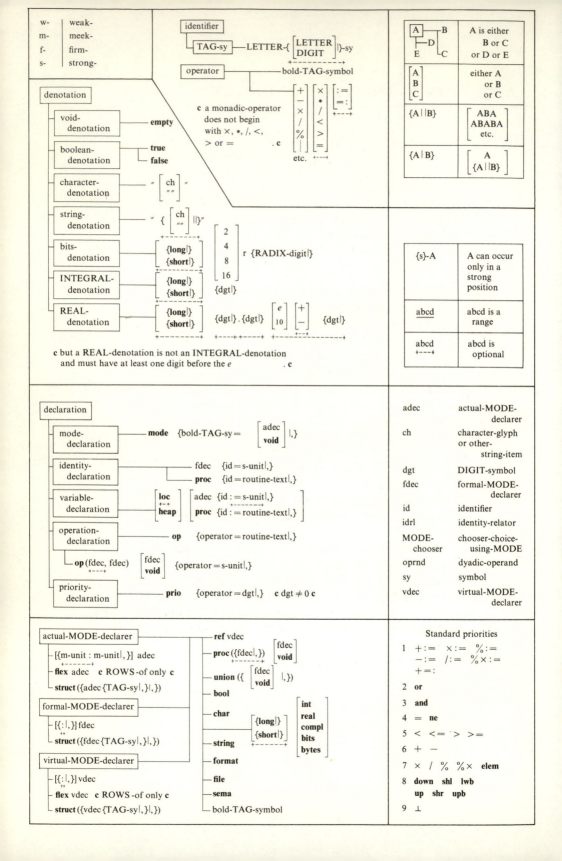

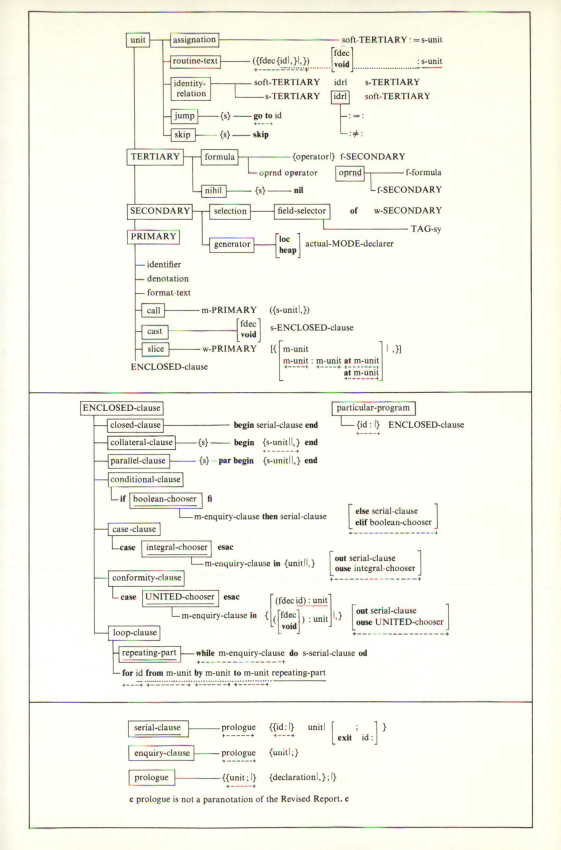

INDEX

Items in the index are ordered letter-by-letter. After the entries for the letter L there appear other entries which begin with *l* or **l**. This is the notation of page 330 for multiple length items.